"An exceptionally well-written, thorough, and competent book for an author who is a non-attorney. Bobby's book is extremely valuable for anyone trying to understand the music business."
—PETER PATERNO, the law offices of King, Holmes, Paterno & Berliner, representing Metallica, Dr. Dre, and Pearl Jam

"The music business is full of minefields. *The Musician's Handbook* helps steer you through them in a way that allows you to enjoy the journey. It's packed with valuable information that you'll use time and time again."
—DON GORDER, chairman of the music business/ management department, Berklee College of Music

"The cliché is sex, drugs, and rock 'n' roll, but it takes knowledge, information, wisdom, and a genuine love for music to truly survive and thrive in the music industry. *The Musician's Handbook* resonates that and so much more."
—CARMINE ROJAS, music director/bassist for Rod Stewart and David Bowie

"Trust is good, but control is better. Good information is key to taking control of your career, and that's what *The Musician's Handbook* offers. It's a necessity for any recording artist serious about advancing his or her music career."
—TESS TAYLOR, president of the National Association of Record Industry Professionals

"Bobby Borg knows about rock 'n' roll because he's been in the trenches. He doesn't theorize—he's lived it . . . It's a refreshing change to learn about the music business without feeling like you're reading a textbook."
—GERRY GITTELSON, music critic for the *Los Angeles Daily News*

" . . . loaded with real-life, honest, and candid anecdotes and interviews with top industry professionals. Musicians need to get this book. A must-read!"
—BILL ZILDJIAN, vice president and head of research development and artist relations, Sabian Cymbal Company

"Knowledge is power. Without it, even the best music by the most talented musicians will fall on deaf ears, which is why *The Musician's Handbook* is so valuable. The wisdom to be gained by reading this comprehensive, easy-to-understand book will help musicians position themselves to have a successful career in the
—GERRY BRYANT, secretary of the board of directors of (

"If you can read this sentence, you are already more than qualified
to be an international rock superstar. If you can read this book, you might even
get your music into the record stores and make some money off of it."
—MIKE INEZ, bassist for Ozzy Osbourne and Alice in Chains

" . . . reminds aspiring musicians and veterans alike that 'music business'
is actually two separate words—'music' and 'business.'"
—MARK L. HEATER, American Federation of Musicians, Division of Touring,
Theaters, Booking Agent Agreements, and Immigration Matters

"Thoughtful, sobering, and, above all, useful insights and advice for anyone
in need of a roadmap through the tangled jungle that is the music industry."
—MARK NARDONE, senior editor of *Music Connection*

"There's only so much information about the music business
that you can absorb at one time. *The Musician's Handbook* does a great
job of summing it up clearly and concisely."
—IAN COPELAND, talent agent for the Police, Sting, and No Doubt

"I'm not saying you'll fail miserably and die penniless and alone if you
don't read this book, but why take a chance?"
—DAVID DARLING, producer for Brian Setzer and Meredith Brooks

" . . . An invaluable layman's guide to the music industry."
—RANDY CASTILLO, drummer for Ozzy Osbourne and Mötley Crüe

(Note: Randy Castillo tragically died shortly after reading
an early draft of this book and offering his endorsement.)

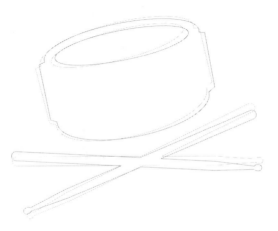

The
MUSICIAN'S
HANDBOOK

A Practical Guide
to Understanding
the Music Business

BOBBY BORG

BILLBOARD BOOKS
AN IMPRINT OF WATSON-GUPTILL PUBLICATIONS/NEW YORK

Executive Editor: Bob Nirkind
Editor: Elizabeth Wright
Cover designed by Cooley Design Lab
Interior designed by Leah Lococo

Copyright © 2003 Bobby Borg
First published in 2003 by Billboard Books, an imprint of Watson-Guptill Publications,
a division of VNU Business Media, Inc.
770 Broadway New York, NY 10003
www.watsonguptill.com

Library of Congress Cataloging-in-Publication Data
The CIP data for this title is on file with the Library of Congress.
Library of Congress Control Number: 2003103457
ISBN-13: 978-0-8230-8357-2
ISBN: 0-8230-8357-8

Manufactured in the U.S.A.

3 4 5 6 7 8 9 / 10 09 08 07 06

ACKNOWLEDGMENTS

Thanks to everyone at Billboard Books: Executive Editor Bob Nirkind for his genius, foresight, and belief in this project; Editor Elizabeth Wright for her patience; Publicity and Promotions Manager Lee Wiggins for her wonderful work; designer Leah Lococo; and everyone in the sales department.

Thanks to my family: Dad, Mom, Peter, Chris, Joe Jr., Wendy, Michael, and Jonathan Borg for their loving support.

Thanks to my friends: Francine Uyetake, Gail Hickman, Pam Moseberry, Jeanne Schantz, Crystal Bowers, Nard Berrings, Karyn Bryant, Sheri Thomas, James Marcey, Marty Rock, Girl Named Jaen, Dave Millette, and Marshmellow for being there when I needed you.

Thanks to my friends/advisors: Neil Gillis (vice president of creative services & advertising, Warner/Chappell Music), Mark Goldstein (senior vice president of business affairs, Warner Bros. Records), Chris Arnstein (Arnstein Organization), Jeff Hinkle (Gudvi, Sussman, & Oppenheim), Michael Eames (president, Penn Music Group), Ed Pierson (vice president of legal affairs, Warner/Chappell Music), Peter Paterno (Law Offices of King, Holmes, Paterno & Berliner), Jeff Cohen (Millen, White, Zelano, and Branigan), Kenwood Dennard, Henry Rollins, Carmine Rojas, Randy Castillo, Jonathan Urdan (vice president of legal affairs, Maverick Records), Shawna Hilleary (Artist Law Group), Stan Findelle (attorney at law), Fred Croshal (GM Maverick Recording Company), Jeffrey Jampol (Jampoll/Attensio Management), Richard Schullenberg (attorney at law), Sindee Levin (attorney at law; president, American Mechanical Rights Society), Todd Brabec (Senior V.P., Pres., Dir. of Membership), Kevin McManus (writer/publisher relations, SESAC), James Leech (writer/public relations, SESAC), Joseph J. DiMona (vice president, Legal Affairs, BMI), Sharon Chambers (Down To Earth Business Management), Ian Copeland (Frontier Booking International), Rob Light (CAA), Mikal Reid (producer), David Darling (producer), Bob Fierro (president, Zebra Marketing), J.D. Hailprin (strategic advisor, MTV), Jed Simon (Dream Works), Gerry Bryant (California Lawyers for the Arts), Dina LaPolt (LaPolt Law, P.C.), Don Gorder (chairman of music business dept., Berklee College of Music), Bill Zildjian (vice president, research development & artist relations, Sabian Cymbal Company), Brian Tichy, Ray Luzier, Al Rubealcava (AFM), Mark Heter (AFM), Pat Varriale (AFM), Matt Allen (AFM), Ennex Steale (AFM), Pam Fair (AFTRA), George Fernandez (certified public accountant), Glen Kennedy (certified public accountant), Ned Brown (Virgin Records), Mike Inez, Steve Vai, Owen Yost, Michael Mallow (Kirkpatrick & Lockhart, LLP), Kenny Kener (*Music Biz* Magazine), Gerry Gittelson (*Los Angeles Daily News*), Jen Frisvold (managing editor, *Performing Songwriter*), Mark Nardone (senior editor, *Music Connection*), SeaGoddess (SeaGoddess Entertainment), Dayle Deanna Schwartz, Dan Kimpell, Steven Rosen, Shawn Fields (founder, Getsigned.com), Kimmie & Kristie (*Score* magazine), Graham Sale, Bobby (Kinkos), David Wimble (editor, *Indie Bible*), Roy Elkins (Broadjam.com), Glenn Tutwiler (*Singer* magazine), Doug Minnick (Taxi), Tess Taylor (president, NARIP), Jimi Yamagishi (Songwriter's Network), Gilli Moon (Songsalive), Kimberly Stallworth (California Lawyers For The Arts), Pascale Helm (UCLA extension), and everyone else who graciously assisted in making this book the success that it is. I also thank all those whose names wouldn't fit on this page—you know who you are.

Table of
Contents

Preface

Why should you read this book? Most musicians spend years developing their musical talent only to learn about the music business the hard way—one mistake at a time. Focused on their creative passions and the dream of an exciting career, musicians often leave business matters entirely in the hands of others. As a result, they are frequently taken advantage of, or they develop unrealistic expectations, which inevitably are not met. If you want music to be your livelihood, you must treat it as a business or the business will take advantage of you. You must understand the basics of the music business and learn how to manage the professional relationships you will encounter. This will give you a tremendous advantage. You will also thereby earn the respect of your employers, your fellow band members, and others within the music industry. Most importantly, you will be able to make informed, intelligent, and realistic career decisions, greatly reducing the risk of making serious mistakes.

What inspired me to write this book? Though musicians must understand the music business in order to succeed, many books on this subject are not readily comprehensible to them. When I began my career in music as a member of a band signed to a major label, I bought a book about the industry because I wanted to understand contracts, record royalties, music publishing, and everything else that the music business entailed. I got about eighteen pages into the book and stopped. The text was too complex; it seemed that the author was writing for attorneys rather than for a guy who was about to jump on a tour bus. At the time, I was more interested in playing music than studying law. I needed a book that spoke to me in plain English. I soon found that many other musicians shared my sentiments.

Several years later, after experiencing the highs of success as well as the frustrations of being repeatedly mistreated, I realized more than ever that there had to be a simpler way for musicians to understand the music business without spending a fortune in legal fees. I concluded that a layman's guide to understanding the music business was necessary—one written by a musician for musicians; a book written by someone who had actually been in the trenches himself, from recording studios to tour buses to concert stages. The language of business is very different from the language of art, and who better than a discerning and sympathetic musician to serve as an instructor for other artists? *The Musician's Handbook* is the result of several years of painstaking research, which involved consulting with literally hundreds of musicians to uncover what they wanted and needed to know, analyzing nearly every book about the music industry, and interviewing numerous music business professionals who were willing to speak candidly.

How is this book different? *The Musician's Handbook* is the first book of its kind. It contains invaluable tips for pursuing a career in music that could only be revealed by someone who's learned them through real experience. *The Musician's Handbook's* one-on-one interviews, real-life anecdotes, and invaluable wisdom from a variety of industry professionals give it a broad perspective and a universal appeal. This book was not written by someone affiliated with a corporate entity, so there's no question of bias—I offer honest information on every aspect of the music business. Thus, the book is not only for musicians: Fledgling attorneys, personal managers, and producers will gain an invaluable perspective on the artists they represent and a solid understanding of the industry. *The Musician's Handbook* is a solid, concise, easy-to-read introduction to the business of music that cuts to the chase; it arms musicians with practical tools that will allow them to get back to doing what they love best: playing music!

The organization of this book. *The Musician's Handbook* is divided into four parts, each of which covers an important aspect of the music business:

+ **Part One:** "Pursuing a Career in the Music Business" discusses "important tips to consider on your path to success." Although the greatest lessons often come from experience itself, you can learn a great deal from those who have been down a path before you. Topics include creating your own destiny by being proactive, climbing through back windows when front doors aren't opening, building career awareness by expanding your Internet presence, increasing your odds of getting signed by understanding more about A&R, developing a realistic attitude by ignoring the media hype, and being practical about money by keeping it and making it grow.

+ **Part Two:** "Types Of Business Relationships" covers the primary business situations in which you may find yourself: as a band member, as a contract employee or a self-employed musician, as a contract employee with profit shares, or as a solo artist and employer. Not only is it important to understand the differences between these relationships, it is equally important to understand the various business issues associated with each one. From union minimum scale wages to group revenue streams to protective measures, the discussions in these chapters help you to digest valuable information slowly, giving you the basic facts specifically related to your career status.

+ **Part Three:** "Key Players In Your Career" focuses on the many business professionals whose expertise you may need to help you make the right career decisions. Individual chapters cover the vital roles played by attorneys, personal managers, business managers, talent agents, and record producers. It is important to understand what role each of these important team members plays, as well as at what point in the development of your career their assistance is necessary.

+ **Part Four:** "Sources Of Revenue" provides an analysis of the different means by which income may be derived from your musical efforts, including record royalties and advances, music publishing, live performances and touring, and merchandising. Chapters in this section include discussions of how record royalties are computed, the dangers of recoupable expenses, the pros and cons of giving up your publishing rights, the misconceptions about touring, and the types of merchandising that may be considered. *The Musician's Handbook* simplifies complex topics so that you can make your way safely through the legal minefield of the music business.

NOTE: *The Musician's Handbook* investigates the "realities" behind the glamorous fantasy world of the music business that is often portrayed in the media. The book is designed to help you to understand the ins and outs of the music industry. At times it will seem harsh. But the more aware you are of the potential obstacles in your path, the better prepared you will be to overcome them. Whether you're out on the road, or just getting ready to cut your first record, it pays to be armed with as much ammunition as possible. Perhaps these quotes from *The Art of War,* a classic work of military strategy and Eastern philosophy popular among music industry executives, will help illustrate my point:

"Know yourself and know your enemy and you will fight
a hundred battles without disaster."

"Know the ground, know the weather; your victory will then be total."
—Sun Tzu, *The Art of War*

How to Use This Book. The best way to read this book is from cover to cover so that you don't miss a single beat. However, *The Musician's Handbook* is designed so that each section stands alone, allowing you to refer to individual chapters as they relate to your personal career status. That way, you can get exactly what you want, when you need it. And for those of you who are really on the fast track, *The Musician's Handbook* is full of boxed anecdotes and sidebars that relate to important aspects of the text, making it easy to flip through these pages and read interesting stories and facts. Every attempt has been made to keep the information as current as possible, but understand that the music business is fast and ever changing—especially in the face of emerging technologies and the World Wide Web—so be sure to keep up with the weekly trades. *The Musician's Handbook* is also designed to provide you with a strong foundation in the music business, but every business situation you encounter will be unique; therefore I strongly recommend that you always consider the advice of the appropriate business professional.

Keep in mind that the music business is not always easy to understand, and it will require some patience and work to do so. But remember that a journey of a thousand miles begins with a single step. The information presented here is only as good as your desire to comprehend and use it.

With talent, preparation, and a lot of luck, you can have an extremely rewarding career (creatively and financially) in music. I hope this book will be a valuable tool that helps you achieve your professional goals. Let's get to it!

1

Pursuing a
CAREER
in the
MUSIC
BUSINESS

> "The music business is a cruel and shallow
> money trench; a long plastic hallway where thieves
> and pimps run free, and good men die like dogs.
> There's also a negative side."
> **—HUNTER S. THOMPSON**

Let there be no mistake—pursuing a career in the music industry is not easy, nor is it for the thin-skinned. The truth is that all the successful bands you see on television or in newspapers and magazine articles represent only a minuscule percentage of all the bands in or trying to break into the music business today. Even after getting signed to a recording agreement, there are still no guarantees for success. As estimated by the Recording Industry Association of America (R.I.A.A.), the average number of records sold by a new band signed to a major label is about 12,000 copies (as of the year 2001). That's not even close to what the record companies need to sell in order to turn a profit. Most new bands are usually dropped from their record contracts and are never heard from again.

Knowing these odds, why would anyone in their right mind continue to pursue a career in the music business? The love of playing music and the success stories of renowned artists inspire plenty of people to try. Hey, why can't you be one of the lucky ones who achieves tremendous success or at least makes a comfortable living? You're talented, you're smart, and you're reading this book to better understand the inner workings of the music industry. That's more than the majority of musicians out there can say. You've already got a lot going in your favor!

Chapter One highlights some important issues and tips you should consider as you pursue your path to success. Although you may already be familiar with many of the topics covered here, it'll be worth your while to give them a quick review. For those of you on the fast track, skim through the various headlines and decide which tips are the most useful to you.

Important Tips
to Consider on Your
Path to Success

I once heard someone say that pursuing a career in the music business is no different than learning to cook. You can follow a specific recipe to the very last ingredient and still end up with unpredictable results.

Although there are no rules or guidelines that can guarantee a prosperous and long-lasting career in the music business, there are a number of tried-and-true tips earned through experience by seasoned professionals that will at least point you in the right direction. Whether you're a musician or songwriter trying to make connections and get gigs or a member of a band trying to get signed to a record contract, these tips apply to you!

ANALYZE YOUR CAREER MOTIVATIONS AND GOALS

Understand what truly motivates you. Do you want to be rich? Do you want to be famous? Do you want to be both rich and famous (the two do not necessarily go hand in hand)? Are you pursuing a career in music to attract members of the opposite sex? Or because you want to party? Are you pursuing music for spiritual reasons or artistic reasons? Are you motivated by a love of creating, and a desire to make a valid contribution to the world of music?

Ultimately, your answers to these questions are going to affect the career decisions you make. For that reason, you need to be totally honest with yourself about your goals. Having said that, it's also extremely important to interpret the goals of the other people with whom you may become professionally involved. What motivates them? Do you really want to do business with these people? Do you truly respect and like them, and do they in return truly respect and like you? Tour manager/agent/promoter Chris Arnstein calls this approach to self-awareness the "decision-making tree." Your decisions (or branches) should be based on the core (or root) of who you truly are as a person. If you haven't thought about your real motivation for pursuing music professionally, now is a good time to do so.

DEVELOP A REALISTIC OUTLOOK BY IGNORING THE MEDIA HYPE

Don't be blinded by media hype or glamour. It's no secret that the expensive houses, the cars, the yachts, the beautiful women and handsome men, and the large screaming audiences that you see in the videos for most new bands are actually rented or hired for the video. When you're signed to a record company, these expenses (which can cost as much as $500,000, sometimes more) are all charged against your future earnings. The majority of artists is never able to pay these back; these artists are then eventually dropped by their labels. Singer Johnny Rzeznik of the band the Goo Goo Dolls says, "Record companies sell the dream. They never talk about the struggle." It's important for you to completely understand the realities of the music business. Are you willing to give it your all—sleep on floors if needed, work odd jobs just to survive, perform for free, and take rejection after rejection for a crack at the big time? Even then, your break may never come. Most successful artists have lived and breathed music with no thoughts of ever turning back. Is this the path for you?

MAKE REALISTIC CAREER DECISIONS BY EDUCATING YOURSELF FIRST

Understand how the music industry works behind the scenes. Learn the business inside and out so that you can make realistic and educated business decisions, rather than decisions based on dreams. Read music trade magazines such as *Billboard* and *Hits*. Read music books such as Don Passman's *All You Need To Know About the Music Business* and M. William Krasilovsky and Sidney Schemel's *This Business of Music,* as well as books on the life stories of popular artists; Mötley Crüe's book *The Dirt* chronicles the band's rise and fall and makes for very interesting reading. Check out the VH1 video series *Behind the Music* for a dose of reality television. Take a music industry course offered at a nearby college; New York University (NYU), Berklee College of Music in Boston, and The University of California at Los Angeles (UCLA) offer excellent classes. Speak to others in the business who have more experience than you and who have been in the trenches themselves. Make sure you're willing to make the major sacrifices and take the risks necessary to pursue your goals. The life of a musician is not an easy one. As Billy Mitchell says in his book *The Gigging Musician,* "The music business is a living thing, a beautiful yet vicious animal that sometimes eats its young. It is important that you know what it [the business] is . . . and who you are."

COME TO TERMS WITH THE ECONOMIC REALITIES OF THE MUSIC BUSINESS

Understand that there are far easier ways to make money than being in the music business. The truth is that most musicians get involved in the business for love of music—not for love of money. In fact, for most of them, music is akin to a fever that never goes away. It's an addiction—a need to express oneself. Those musicians who are in the business only to become wealthy are fooling themselves. Sure, there are exceptions to every rule, but the majority of bands never reach financial security, even after being signed. Make sure you're playing music because there's nothing else that you'd rather do. *You've got to love it.* If you can make a lot of money doing it, then that's icing on the cake.

SET REALISTIC GOALS FOR YOURSELF

Though age can be a sensitive subject for most musicians, you should know that there's a general prejudice against age in the commercial music industry: the industry views music as a youth-oriented business. The feeling is that a musician's life expectancy in the pop, rock, R&B, and rap genres parallels that of an athlete's life span in the sports world. As you approach the age of 35, your chances of succeeding have significantly diminished. That fact is somewhat paradoxical, since musicians' skills tend only to improve with age and experience, but record companies rely heav-

> When a Los Angeles DJ at KROQ asked Coldplay to what they attributed their success in the music business, the British band quickly responded, "Not caring about fame and fortune. Whatever comes our way is only gravy."

ily on youth, vitality, and sex appeal to sell albums. Record labels also prefer signing younger acts that, if successful, can bring them a return on their initial investment for several years to come. A record company is a business just like any other, and the bottom line of that business comes first and foremost.

So, does all this mean that unsigned artists nearing their mid-thirties should throw in the towel and abandoned their life dreams if they still haven't found success with the MTV generation? Of course not! The professional artist who takes care of his health and image can get away with looking, acting, and seeming much younger than he actually is. And, of course, there's always the rare exception to the rule whereby an older, more "adult" artist breaks all barriers and is signed strictly on the virtue of his musical talent and songwriting abilities—bravo! But even if you're one of the lucky artists who gets that big break, only the most creative and business-minded artist can still appeal to younger audiences musically and physically as he/she approaches the age of 50 or 60. Do I agree with this type of thinking? NO! But, the music business has consistently maintained this age-bias.

So, what's the whole point of this discussion? Though age is not something you think about in the entertainment business when you're in your teens or twenties, *age and image in the commercial marketplace are very real issues for musicians in their later years.* Therefore, unless you want to go on a personal crusade to change the status quo (and some artists do—hats off to them), it's advisable to look at your career reasonably and have the foresight to set realistic goals for yourself. For instance, if you are older, when considering your career status, your age, and your image, it might be prudent to focus on a genre of music whose audience has a more sophisticated demographic profile, or to seek a recording deal with a smaller, less commercial, independent record label, or to simply resort to a do it yourself (DIY) approach—a situation in which you can make all of your own business decisions and *not let the record companies dictate what you can and cannot do and how old you have to be to do it!* Taking this one step further, some musicians find more purpose in doing "behind the scenes" work—composing for other artists, for film and television, and even for video games; there's big money there! To be sure, doing such work is not about abandoning your original dreams or succumbing to this age-prejudice, it's about looking at age and image in the music business realistically and learning how to continually reinvent and brand yourself over time to find your appropriate audience.

REALIZE YOUR DREAMS BY VISUALIZING THEM FIRST

In the early 1990s, in a small club called the Button South in Fort Lauderdale, Florida, Marilyn Manson gazed out into the audience and said, "One day I'm going to be a pop star who shocks the world." He truly believed this. Over ten years later, with one successful album and tour after another, Manson was 100 percent right.

Visualize your dreams. As the old saying goes, "A picture is worth a thousand words." If you can hold a picture of success in your mind and keep it focused by having faith in yourself, your subconscious can bring it to pass. In his bestselling book *The Power Of Your Subconscious Mind,* author Joseph Murphy calls this the "mental-movie method." In his words, "[If I] act as though I am . . . I will be."

PREPARE FOR THE LONG HAUL BY BECOMING FINANCIALLY SOUND

There are countless stories about people who move to the "big city" and give themselves six months to "make it." Needless to say, that is a completely unrealistic plan. Most of these people end up either returning home broke or living on a friend's couch feeling helpless. Be prepared (both financially and mentally) to spend years pursuing your goals. Find ways to live comfortably while working towards your dream. If you do, you'll be in a better position to make connections with important people without appearing desperate. Success won't happen overnight. Billy Mitchell sums things up once again: "Too many of us think that the world of music is a magic-carpet ride, from the garage to superstardom. It ain't. It's blood, sweat, and tears—and then you still might not get the gig." Learn to be simultaneously persistent and patient.

EXPECT THE WORST TO HAPPEN SO THAT
THE WORST WON'T SEEM SO BAD

David Geffen once said jokingly, "There's your plan, and there's God's plan—and yours doesn't matter." Realize you can't control everything that happens in your life. Focus on the positive, but remember the old saying, "Shit happens!" Bands get dropped from their labels, tours get cancelled, names get misspelled on venue marquees and in magazines, bands break up, and people will try to rip you off. Such events are an inevitable part of pursuing a career in music and an aspect that's certainly not for the thin-skinned. Expect to be knocked down, but learn how to get up quickly and see the lesson in every negative experience. In order to survive in the music business, you must be resilient. As Jon Kabat-Zinn says in his book *Wherever You Go, There You Are,* "You can't stop the waves, but you can surely learn to surf."

LEARNING HOW TO OVERCOME REJECTION
BY NOT TAKING IT PERSONALLY

Don't take the music business too personally. Don't abandon your dreams every time you receive a rejection letter or a door shuts in your face.. Most successful artists knocked on doors and created their own opportunities for years before finally getting their big break. Even then, if a record company fails to promote your band and suddenly drops you, keep the fact that it's strictly business in mind. Companies are interested in one thing: an immediate return on their investments. No matter how talented you think you are, the music business is about profit and the bottom line. After all, this is show business: if there's no business, there's no show.

ENJOY THE JOURNEY BY LEARNING TO LIGHTEN UP

I once heard a great expression: "Be happy now, for you're a long time dead." Working hard towards achieving your goals is extremely important, but it's equally important to learn not to take yourself too seriously. Have a little fun in your endeavors. Lighten up! You'll project a much more confident and positive attitude. You'll be less stressed-out and more approachable. This is the entertainment industry—how can you expect to entertain others if you can't entertain yourself? Don't waste valuable energy being hateful, envious, or jealous of others' success! Believe that one day you, too, will get your big break. Just keep in mind that a record contract is not the key to happiness, it's the beginning of a long journey—and for many artists, it's the beginning of a long nightmare. There are no guarantees in the music business, no matter how hard you work, so learn to enjoy the ride each and every day. You'll be healthier mentally and much happier.

LET GO OF YOUR FEARS AND LEARN HOW TO GO FOR IT

According to Danny Sugerman's book *No One Gets Out Alive,* Jim Morrison once asked, "If your life was a movie, would anyone want to watch it?" The answer is up to you. Many artists claim they want exciting and extremely successful careers, yet they never take the serious steps and make the real commitment necessary to realize their goals. Unfortunately, a half-assed approach just doesn't cut it in the music business. If you have what it takes—if you're realistic, smart, and talented—then what's holding you back from giving your career your best shot? Perhaps it's the fear of moving to the big city, the fear of rejection, or the fear of going broke. Regardless of your reasons, understand that your fears are just that—fears. They can be overcome.

> According to boxer Mike Tyson, "Fear is like fire. It can either cook for you or it can burn you." Make it cook for you.

By learning to replace your negative thoughts with more positive ones, you will have won half the battle already. You'll be armed with the determination that's necessary to forge ahead in this competitive business. You'll have the mental clarity to devise a logical plan of attack. What's the worst that can happen, anyway? You might fall short of getting what you want. But you'll at least know you gave your career your best shot. As the saying goes, "When you reach for the stars, you may not quite get one, but you won't come up with a handful of mud either." Singer/songwriter Jewel suffered through one full-time job after another before she finally decided to move into her van and devote 100 percent of her time to her musical career. She supposedly ate fruit off trees at times just to survive. She began playing local coffeehouses and was eventually signed to Atlantic Records. Her record *Pieces Of You* was released in 1995 and took 14 months to break, but became a bestseller with the hit song "Who Will Save Your Soul."

KNOW YOUR LIMITATIONS AND EXPLOIT YOUR STRENGTHS

The three most significant benefits of knowing your limitations and exploiting your strengths are as follows. First, you will be able to concentrate on improving your weaknesses (for example, instead of pretending to know everything about the music business, you'll read this book and others like it and acquire some useful knowledge). Second, you'll learn to surround yourself with people who can help minimize your limitations (e.g., you'll choose your band members wisely and know when to step back and let them shine). And finally, knowing your limitations and exploiting your strengths allows you to focus, capitalize on, and build upon your best attributes (you'll exploit your best physical characteristics when defining your visual image, write songs to show off your strongest vocal range, or use your sense of humor or ability to dance to produce stage routines that get the audience engaged and excited every time). Drummer Kenwood Dennard, who has performed with Sting and Dizzy Gillespie, says, "Find your forte and excel. No one is going to judge you for what they don't see, they're going to judge you for what is presented before them." This brings to mind the old expression, "It's not how much you have, it's how you use what you've got." Or, in the unforgettable words of James Brown, "You gotta use whatcha got ta get jus what ya want."

AC/DC knew that they were not musical geniuses, but they capitalized on their abilities to use the same three chords to write one successful record after another. Charlie Watts and Bill Wyman knew that they weren't the focus or stars of the Rolling Stones, but they became integral to the band's signature sound by supporting Mick Jagger and Keith Richards with tasty and simple rhythms. By knowing your limitations and exploiting your strengths, you'll not only put your best foot forward 100 percent of the time, but also know when to step back and allow others to shine in areas in which you're lacking.

LOCATE YOURSELF IN THE MOST OPPORTUNE CITY TO SUCCEED

Where is the best place to live and pursue your musical career anyway? Is it Los Angeles? New York? Nashville? Your very own hometown? Living in one of the larger cities in the country will

SHOULD I STAY OR SHOULD I GO? Guitarist Jimi Hendrix played in a number of successful R&B bands in Seattle, but it wasn't until he went to New York and later to London that he put together his sensational group the Jimi Hendrix Experience. The group's debut record *Are You Experienced?* scored three number one hits in the U.K. in 1967, and quickly became a smash in the U.S. Although singer/songwriter Alanis Morissette enjoyed modest success in her native Toronto, it took a move to Los Angeles to bring her to the attention of producer Glen Ballard, ultimately resulting in her hit record *Jagged Little Pill* in 1994. Singer/songwriter Sheryl Crow packed her bags and moved across the country from Missouri to California before landing a gig with Michael Jackson and Don Henley and being discovered and signed by A&M. What do all these artists have in common? They went hunting for success in the big cities and eventually found it! On the other hand, bands like Mudhoney, Soundgarden, Mother Love Bone, and Nirvana all stayed in Seattle and helped create a sound of their own, which was dubbed "the Seattle sound." These bands, along with many others, gave birth to a musical revolution by releasing independent recordings, performing relentlessly, and creating such a strong buzz in the press that the record companies went scurrying to sign them. The saying soon became, "Go Northwest young man."

NOTE: Though Seattle became a hot spot for fledgling rock or "grunge" artists in the early '90s, freelance singer Paul Lawrence Washington says, "It was definitely not the right city for R&B artists." It's important to do your research before moving to any city. Find out which bands are being featured in local magazines, which bands are getting booked into clubs, and which bands are getting signed to record deals. Most importantly, find out whether the city has a new and thriving scene, or whether it's already dying out. Make sure that wherever it is you decide to move, it's the right location for what you're trying to accomplish.

present you with more opportunities to meet other musicians and make you more accessible to record company executives who may be interested in signing your band. On the other hand, there's more competition in larger cities and you may get lost in the sauce. You may be able to create a big enough wave in your small town to entice the record companies to come to you. Record company representatives and scouts check local music papers, surf the web for MP3 files, and review college radio play lists. If your band is really good and has something to offer, the record companies will find you regardless of where you are.

PROTECT YOURSELF FROM THE START BY GETTING EVERYTHING IN WRITING

Always get the terms and conditions of all business agreements in writing and keep a signed and dated copy of them in your files. This will clarify the expectations of each party and provide protection in case there's a dispute; people often forget what they promise. Even between friends, a written agreement is an essential tool for establishing a professional relationship. Though you may initially question this point, you'll see its importance illustrated in several real-life examples throughout this book.

> As the old adage says, "An oral agreement isn't worth the paper it's written on." Believe it!

By law, an agreement should consist of three basic requirements: offer, consideration, and acceptance. When an offer is made with mutual consideration (i.e., when there's a benefit for both parties, such as a service in return for a fee), and said offer is accepted, then a contract is formed.

> The more involved a business transaction, such as the signing of a recording agreement, the more necessary it is to retain an experienced entertainment attorney to make sure your rights and interests are protected. Attorneys are covered in detail in Chapter 6.

An agreement doesn't necessarily have to be in writing, but if a dispute occurs, clear and convincing written evidence produces a firm account of the truth.

Sometimes the people with whom you're doing business (employers, bands, managers, etc.) may respond unfavorably to your requests for a written agreement. Or, they'll present you with an agreement and then be unwilling to negotiate the terms. This type of behavior will offer insight into what you can ultimately expect from the relationship. In these predicaments, it's especially important that you have a clear understanding of your objectives and goals, and what you will and will not give up.

PAY YOUR DUES BUT USE YOUR HEAD

Paying your dues means paying the price for your lack of professional experience. That price is your time and hard work. Sometimes it can involve a lot of time and work with little or no compensation. But keep in mind that the more experience you gain, the more valuable a commodity you become. Whether you're in a band that's playing local clubs for free or a musician who's performing on demo recordings for pennies, the day will come when you're justly compensated. It's not always what you earn, but what you learn that matters.

> The music business is very complex and confusing, but learn to trust your gut instincts. If a situation doesn't feel right from the beginning, it probably isn't.

Warning: There are many people in the business who will attempt to take advantage of your inexperience. Welcome to the

RIGHT VERSUS MIGHT: A popular rock singer employed a talented young bass player who co-wrote what turned out to be one of the singer's greatest hits. Realizing the potential in the song, the singer tried to convince the bass player to sign over his rights to the composition in return for a small payment. Wisely, the bass player sought advice from his attorney and didn't give up his rights. Although the bass player was fired from the group, he receives a substantial amount of money in royalty payments from the song every year (for the last 13 years, as of this writing). Needless to say, he made the right choice.

"school of hard knocks," or as some call it, "the new kid" treatment. Stay focused! Use the relationships you develop as stepping stones towards your professional goals. But draw the line if you feel that the outcome may have a negative impact on your career, or if you generally feel that you're being ripped off!

DELIVER THE GOODS BY KNOWING YOUR CRAFT, AND THEN SOME

Know your craft and be prepared to deliver the goods. Whether you play an instrument, write songs, or sing in a band, take the time to become as proficient as possible. At first glance, the music business appears to be glamorous and all about fun, but most successful artists have sweat blood and tears honing their professional skills. Work at developing your communication and networking skills as well. Become a better writer and speaker, develop your telephone and computer skills, and learn to have a sense of humor. Your physical presentation is also very important; make your health and diet a priority. Become a well-rounded and well-balanced person. As Dan Kimpel says in his book *Networking In The Music Business,* "Once you've opened up some doors, you need something amazing to shove inside." In other words, be prepared to deliver the goods.

> Develop your craft to the best of your ability, but don't become obsessed with perfection. Learn to appreciate what Dennis Hopper refers to as "the perfection of imperfection."

GET AHEAD BY ADOPTING A SALES APPROACH

Many musicians over-use the excuse that they're all about the music and not about the sale. Wrong! Nobody is going to invest their time or energy in your career if you're not willing to invest a little time and energy into it yourself. Read books such as *Zig Zigler's Secrets Of Closing The Sale* by Zig Ziglar and *How To Master The Art Of Selling* by Tom Hawkins. Selling doesn't have to be sleazy or deceptive. As long as you're honest and your intentions are pure, it's simply a way of letting people know what you have to offer. Even after you're signed, most artists don't realize that they still have to continue selling themselves. Your success is not left entirely in the record company's hands! It's a team effort. You'll have to meet with radio station personnel and participate in interviews so that they'll play your single. Schmooze with retail buyers at record stores so that they'll stock your record. Try to get gigs opening for more well-known bands with enthusiastic fans to develop a strong following of your own. Let your live audience know where it can purchase your record. (Many musicians actually feel they're "selling out" by doing this. Wrong!) Meet with fans after your live performances to sign autographs, and participate in internet chat rooms to collect fan names for your promotional street teams. The list goes on . . . In the words of Andy Gould, who has managed Linkin Park and Rob Zombie, "A band's idea of working can't be smoking pot and doing groupies." Simply put, if you expect to get ahead, you must be willing to work hard at selling yourself.

GET THINGS DONE BY DOING WHAT YOU SAY

The best musicians in the world aren't worth a damn if they're unreliable. It's amazing how many musicians are passive when it comes to business. Many find it difficult to follow through in a timely manner with simple business matters such as returning a phone call or showing up to a rehearsal on time. This may be due to the general artistic nature of musicians or simply a lack of motivation. They tend to talk about what they're going to do, but never do it. In what may seem to be a simple concept, music publicist Laurie Gorman with HK Management says, "The key to success is simply doing what you say you're going to do." Or, to put it another way, as hockey legend Wayne Gretsky once said, "One hundred percent of all the shots you don't take are guaranteed not to go in." It may appear that most musicians lead a carefree and laid-back life, but those who are the most successful had a clear vision of their goals and worked extremely hard to achieve them.

DEFINE YOUR TARGET AUDIENCE AND INCREASE YOUR ODDS

Author Jeffrey P. Fisher, in his book *Ruthless Self-Promotion in the Music Industry,* says, "Research your market and know who your fans are. The world is not your market." This is an extremely important point. Many artists lose their focus by trying to reach everyone at once. How often have you heard a band describe their music as something like, "R&B funk rock with an alternative jazz flair"? All the while, they look like a group of high school teachers disguised in biker's clothing. This, of course, is an exaggerated example, but you get the point. It's admirable for artists to try to appease audiences of all genres, but record companies are looking for bands with a clear and well-defined vision of their target demographic market. What specific radio format does your music fit into? What age group is your music the most attractive to? What category does your album fit into on the record store shelves?

Defining your market is not an issue of "selling out" or of lacking originality. Artists such as Elvis Presley, Prince, Madonna, Michael Jackson, David Bowie, and Lenny Kravitz are all unique in their own way, but they still knew exactly who their target audiences were. From album covers and logos to merchandising and videos to photographs and interviews, they had a consistent package or "brand." Branding is vital to the overall success of any artist. It gives consumers something to latch onto. In the words of Jeffrey Jampol (personal manager for Tal Bachman), "No one really cares about just the soap in a box, but the brand name Tide is worth millions."

Rather than grumbling about why your music has to be labeled and why it has to fit into specific categories, take a course on marketing at your local college and research the answers. Your outlook will be forever changed. Check out books like *This Business of Music Marketing and Promotion* by Tad Lathrop and Jim Pettigrew, Jr., and *Ogilvy on Marketing,* written by advertising mogul David Ogilvy. Understand that it's simply not economically practical for record companies to market your music to the world. It costs millions of dollars just trying to break an artist in a very specific market. And, it's simply not how the business is run. By attempting to cover too many things, nothing is ever achieved.

Keep in mind that creating music is an art, but getting it heard is a very strategic and serious business. It may take some time to figure out what your identity or niche market is, but you should at least start giving it some serious thought today.

PREPARE THE PROPER PROMOTIONAL MATERIALS AND KNOW WHEN TO USE THEM

Promotional materials, such as demo tapes, photographs, biographies, and press clippings help people to get to know you. When these materials are assembled in one package or folder, they are most commonly known as a press kit.

Press kits are most useful when you are trying to get exposure in newspapers, magazines, and websites. They are also helpful when trying to get booked in clubs and in other live performance venues. A press kit may even entice an attorney or personal manager into representing you.

On the other hand, they are not very helpful in getting your band signed to a recording contract. The reality is that out of thousands of tapes record companies receive in the mail per year, maybe one group gets discovered, if even that. There are tremendous odds against getting a contract that way. In fact, your package will likely end up in the wastebasket without ever having anyone review it. This is the harsh reality! Though there are unusual cases, record companies typically do not accept unsolicited mail.

Another misconception is that a press kit will lead you to a great audition and gig. Many musicians waste their time, energy, and money sending packages in the mail; just getting out there, being heard, and making friends is more effective. Keep in mind that the majority of all the work you get will be based on personal relationships that you form and nurture over the years. If anything, building a website and then personally handing out cards that include your uniform resource locator (URL) is by far a more useful way to promote yourself than is a press kit. Websites are still relatively new and exciting, and people will want to take a look at what you've got online. Files of your music that people can download, photos, and biographical material can be reviewed in one click. It may cost you some money to get a site up and running, but you won't have to deal with the copying charges, packaging costs, and mailing expenses that a press kit entails.

We've discussed some misconceptions about press kits—let's focus on what one should include. Your press kit should contain a demo that highlights three of your best songs, with your best song first. If you include too many songs, or if you include songs that are too diverse in style, you may send the message that you're not sure what it is you do.

A RARE INSTANCE: When singer/songwriter Jackson Browne was first starting out in the music business, he sent Asylum Records his photo and tape. They were immediately tossed into the garbage. Fortunately for Browne, a secretary for the label saw Jackson's picture and thought he was attractive. She insisted that David Geffen (founder of Asylum Records and later Geffen Records) listen to the tape, and he liked it. Geffen flew out to Colorado and signed Browne, as well as Browne's neighbors, a young rock group which later named themselves the Eagles. Needless to say, stories of this kind are unbelievably rare.

TECHNOLOGY AND PROMOTION AT ITS BEST: Bassist Mel Brown, who has worked with Brian McKnight and Marc Anthony, takes networking to new heights. Rather than sending packages in the mail or handing out business cards, Mel personally hands out his own CD-ROMs. The information on these discs includes his biography (which he narrates himself), video files with footage from live performances, MP3 files containing his most recent recordings, press articles, pictures, and contact information. This "electronic press kit" makes for a very clean and effective presentation and shows that Mel takes his business seriously. (We'll discuss Internet promotion in more detail later in this chapter.)

The production of your demo should also be as high in quality as you can afford. The key is not to leave anything to the imagination of your intended audience. Fortunately, digital equipment has enabled musicians to cut quality demos right in their own homes. If you don't own your own recording gear, chances are that you have a friend who has home equipment and will be willing to help. Make sure your demo is clearly marked with both song titles and contact information. You can send either a CD or cassette tape, although sending a CD is more common. If you send a cassette, just make sure it's rewound to the beginning.

Also included in the press kit should be your photograph. People will not only want to hear what you sound like, but also see what you look like. It ties your whole package together. Keep in mind that photographs are also used for reprinting in newspapers and magazines, so make sure your prints aren't too dark or dingy. Give your image and style some serious consideration as well. Your picture must be consistent with your music—if you're in a hard rock band, then you must look hard rock. If you're not sure what image you want to portray, review magazines like *Rolling Stone* and *Details* to see what other bands are doing. The print size of your photo should be 8 x 10" and should include your band name and contact information at the bottom (phone number, mailing address, e-mail address, and website URL). Because you only have one chance to make a good first impression, I highly recommend hiring a professional photographer who has experience working with musicians.

A biography (or bio) should be as short as possible (typically 500 words) and written without a lot of flowery adjectives and big words. If there's a unique story about how your band formed or about the various members in your group, include it. This gives writers at newspapers and magazines a special twist or hook when writing about your band. If you have any flattering quotes or reviews, include them here as well—but don't overdo it. Including 15 quotes from people no one knows is pointless. Check out other bands' bios on the Web and see what their approaches are. If you're not an experienced writer, finding someone skilled to write your bio is a good idea. If you can find someone with influence, such as a local radio personality or journalist, all the better.

A press kit should also include clippings, known as tear sheets, from newspapers and magazines you've collected over the months. Clippings help prove that you're established and not just another fly-by-night operation. Again, don't over-use them. Use the best reviews and articles, and highlight the most interesting paragraphs or quotes.

Lastly, when mailing out your press kit, include a cover letter that clearly addresses who you are, what you do, and what you want. Be sure to include all of your contact information here as well.

To ensure your package arrives intact, put all of your materials in a padded envelope. If you have any special items that may help make a lasting impression, such as promotional stickers, send them along in your kit. It also helps to call the person you're soliciting to inform them that your package is on the way. Follow up in a few weeks with another call to see if they liked what you sent. Be realistic, though. Keep in mind that editors at magazines, just like people at record companies, receive hundreds of packages per week. Chances are that if they haven't asked you to mail a press kit or they haven't heard of your band, your package will be left unopened in a pile or tossed in the garbage can. Just don't give up. If you work hard enough at getting your name out there, you'll eventually succeed.

APPRECIATE THE VALUE OF MAKING CONNECTIONS

Networking is an important part of establishing a career in the music industry. A lot really does depend on who you know! Put yourself in situations in which you can meet others who are already doing what you want to do, are working towards similar goals, or are in positions that can further your career. Some of the people around you right now who are pursuing a career in music will one day be successful. Learn to recognize those who are talented, intelligent, and ambitious and create your own "clique of the future." Rather than consuming all your energy trying to break into established and seemingly impenetrable cliques, get in on the ground floor and work at creating your own. The majority of the work you do will be based on word-of-mouth recommendations and the personal relationships that you form over the years. Surround yourself with positive people who have goals similar to yours. Jam sessions, adult education classes, college courses, music conventions, songwriting workshops, and networking groups are great places to make new connections. Again, get to know as many people in the music business as you possibly can. It really does matter who you know—and who knows you.

> ASCAP (www.ascap.com), BMI (www.bmi.com), and SESAC (www.sesac.com) are performing rights organizations that frequently hold songwriter's workshops. NARIP (www.narip.com) is a networking group founded in Los Angeles worth exploring. Check out the Web for an event near you.

> Here's a brief rundown of some of the more popular music conventions: Association for Independent Music (www.afim.com), CMJ New Music Convention (www.cmj.com), Eat'm (www.eat-m.com), National Association of Music Merchants (www.namm.com), National Association of recording merchandisers (www.narm.com), and South by Southwest (www.sxsw.com).

HELP YOURSELF BY HELPING OTHERS

Surround yourself with as many people as possible who may be able to help you; surround yourself with people whom you may be able to help as well. As the old proverb goes, one hand washes the other. If you're able to find opportunities to offer something to others, there's a good chance they'll return the favor in the future. In *Zig Zigler's Secrets of Closing The Sale,* Zig Zigler suggests that learning how to give people what they want is important in the business world. Whether it's putting together a band for a well-paying gig that you booked, hooking someone up with a gig on a recording session, turning someone on to a band that's looking for musicians, or reviewing a band's live performance for a music paper or website, helping others is a good way to nurture relationships and open up doors for yourself.

NURTURE NEW CAREER OPPORTUNITIES
WHILE YOU'RE ALREADY ON THE JOB

The best time to find work is when you're already working. It's only natural for younger musicians to believe that their current musical relationships will exist indefinitely—and they very well might. However, many of the most successful groups are composed of musicians who were originally with other established bands. Gary Cherone (who had a short stint with Van Halen) was originally the vocalist for the once successful rock group Extreme, who opened for Van Halen. Mike Inez (Alice In Chains) originally played bass with the legendary singer Ozzy Osbourne when Alice In Chains was his opening act. Dave Navarro of Jane's Addiction eventually worked with the Red Hot Chili Peppers. Matt Sorum worked with the Cult before joining Guns N' Roses. Kirk Hammett and Jason Newsted played with Exodus and Flotsam & Jetsam (respectively) before joining forces with Metallica. And the list goes on . . . If you're currently an employee of a group or even a member of a band, use your situation to make as many new connections as you possibly can. People will have the opportunity to see you perform in situations where you feel confident and comfortable. Remember, networking does not have to feel deceptive or dishonest. Putting all your eggs in one basket can often backfire—a mixed metaphor never made more sense. The music business is very fickle. Tours are canceled, record releases are postponed, and bands are suddenly dumped. That's the reality! In the words of Miyamoto Musashi in *The Book of Five Rings:* "The best time to prepare for adversity is when all appears calm."

A BIRD IN HAND IS WORTH TWO IN THE BUSH. One musician, who was working with a very successful singer/songwriter, was growing tired of his life on the road. When he heard of an audition to be part of the house band for a television talk show, he jumped at the opportunity. But in order to make the audition, the musician had to back out of a prior obligation to the singer/songwriter. As it turns out, the musician not only failed to get the television gig, but he was also fired from the singer/songwriter's band for being unreliable. The moral of the story: It's important to take advantage of every opportunity to make connections and find work, but not at the expense of your current situation. If you make a commitment to an employer or band, you must honor it first or suffer the consequences. While networking is important, maintaining the highest professional standard should be your top priority.

CLIMB THROUGH BACK WINDOWS WHEN FRONT DOORS AREN'T OPENING

If doors aren't opening, then climb through back windows. As the old saying goes, the definition of insanity is doing the same thing over and over and expecting different results. For instance, instead of trying to put your tape directly in the hands of higher-ups who are unapproachable and stand-offish, get to know them personally in more casual settings. Jeff "Skunk" Baxter of the Doobie Brothers and Steely Dan says, "It doesn't matter whether you're driving an equipment truck or sweeping studio floors, get yourself into the music business any way you can." You may find that working as an intern for a management or publishing company, working at a recording studio, or writing for a local music magazine provides great opportunities to make connections. You'll have the opportunity to get to know people more naturally than you will in situations that make you appear desperate and needy. Whatever it is you're trying to accomplish, consider a variety of approaches to achieving your goals. It's important to be tenacious and not abandon your initial plan of attack, but banging your head against the same stone wall is pointless. (For listings of available jobs in the music business, try logging onto www.EntertainmentJobs.com or the www.velvetrope.com.)

KNOW WHO'S WHO IN THE MUSIC BUSINESS BY KEEPING UP TO DATE WITH THE TRADES

Stay up to date on who the power brokers in the business are. How are you supposed to network and meet people in the business if you don't know who's running the business in the first place?

Billboard magazine regularly provides information about the movers and shakers in the industry. Read the liner notes of CD booklets and find out who's producing and managing the most successful artists. You'll be more knowledgeable and you'll appear informed and on top of your game when networking and conversing with other people in the business. It also helps to stay on top of which records are at the top ten of the record charts and to have a basic understanding of why. When you walk into retail stores, what type of promotion do you see for the artist? Did you hear the artist on college radio stations before hearing him or her on commercial stations? Did the band tour before its record came out? How well did the tour do? All of this information will make you more knowledgeable about how the music business is run and who's running it.

Check out these magazines: *Hits* (www.hitsmagazine.com), *CMJ New Music Report* (www.cmj.com), *Radio and Records* (www.rronline.com), *The Gavin Report* (www.gavin.report.com), *Album Network* (www.albumnetwork.com), and *Pollstar* (www.pollstar.com).

KEEP YOUR OPTIONS OPEN BY DROPPING YOUR ATTITUDE

Though most of us hate to admit it, musicians can have a tendency to be somewhat aloof and rude, even to those in the business. Let's face it, it takes a lot of attitude to get on stage and be a performer, and some people just don't know how to turn themselves off. Realize that you never know who may be in a position to help you one day. An unknown musician at a jam session may become the hottest and most well-connected session player. An intern at a recording studio may be the next big producer or engineer. An opening act could go on to sell millions of records. A stage tech might someday become a successful manager. A writer from a local fanzine may one day write for *Rolling Stone*. These people can all serve as valuable connections to you one day. Understand that the music community represents only a small percentage of the entire working world. If you stay in the business long enough, you'll start to see the same people over and over again. Learn to treat others in all facets of the business as your comrades rather than your subordinates, your competition, or your adversaries. Look at the big picture. You'll open doors down the road that you never imagined entering.

If you're fortunate enough to have a successful career in the music business, have some understanding that your success is not single-handed. Whether you're the hottest local band around, or a group that just signed a recording agreement, remember that there are a number of people behind the scenes who are just as responsible for your success as you are. Make a conscious effort to be pleasant with everyone because no one in this business owes you anything. Don't learn this lesson

THERE WILL BE ROTTENNESS. When the Sex Pistols were signed by EMI in 1976, they were soon dropped after a series of outrageous events. First, according to a 1977 *Rolling Stone* article, vocalist Johnny Rotten declared himself an anti-Christ who "wanted to destroy everything." The BBC radio network didn't find this funny and refused to play the Pistols' single. Then, the band publicly insulted an interviewer on the British *Today* show, calling him a "dirty fucker" and a "fuckin' rotter." The Pistols were asked to apologize, but they refused. Next, the band was involved in an incident at Heathrow Airport in which they allegedly vomited on a number of female passengers. After public pressure mounted, the Pistols were dropped from EMI. On March 10th, 1977, the band was picked up by A&M records, only to be dropped one week later. Apparently, the Pistols vandalized several offices at the A&M headquarters and were involved in a bar fight with the head of programming for the BBC. A&M was also under a great deal of pressure from distributors, disc jockeys, and A&M's own employees to drop the band. So A&M let the group go. The Pistols received yet another shot when Virgin signed the band a few months later. Not many bands today would get as many chances as they did. Johnny Rotten sums up the Pistols' attitude in his typically arrogant, simple style, "We were right thick cunts, we were."

the hard way! If you develop an attitude with a club booker, you may never be asked to play his or her club again. If you fail to appreciate your fans, they may stop buying tickets to your shows. If you're unpleasant with a music journalist during an interview, you may get years of bad press or no press at all. If you piss off the music director at a radio station, you may not get your records played. If you're rude to someone at your record company, they may spend their time and energy on someone who appreciates their hard work. Being an artist may make you feel special, but don't fool yourself into believing that the world revolves around you. This brings to mind the old adage, "the people you see on the way up are the same people you see on the way down." Very few artists stay on top forever. Get the point?

KEEP BRIDGES INTACT BY KNOWING WHEN TO WALK AWAY GRACEFULLY

Don't burn bridges. Whether you're in a band you're unhappy with, or working a gig that's getting you nowhere, if a relationship doesn't feel right from the start, know how to walk away before it gets worse. Tom Collins, the former manager for Aerosmith, says, "Always take the high road." The music business consists of a very small community of people, and you cannot afford to have negative energy circulating. This is important! Only fight the battles that are really worth fighting.

LOOK TO FORM RELATIONSHIPS AND NOT JUST BUSINESS DEALS

Deals come and go. Once any deal is signed, you want to be assured that you're going to have a productive and ongoing relationship with the parties involved. Will your phone calls be returned promptly or will you feel like you're being avoided? Will the other party communicate openly with you or lie and string you along? When the going gets tough, will the other party stand by you and see things through? Legendary R&B singer Barry White suggests, "Regardless of the business deals offered, don't jump at the first one just because it's available. Make sure it also feels right. Listen to your gut."

CREATE YOUR OWN DESTINY BY BEING PROACTIVE

In his book *Wild Thing: The Backstage, on the Road, in the Studio, Off the Charts Memoirs of Ian Copeland,* Ian Copeland, founder of Frontier Booking International (FBI) and talent agent to the Police, Sting, and No Doubt, says, "Doors were usually closed to newcomers in the industry. We decided to stop beating on them and create new ones."

It's not enough to simply give someone a business card or demo tape and then sit back and expect to gain employment or procure a record or publishing deal. No one's going to hand you success on a silver platter. You need to take more control of your career and create your own destiny. Whether you're an individual musician, a songwriter, a solo artist or a member of a band, *attract the attention of those who can help you by first helping yourself!*

If you're a musician who wants to be known as a great player rather than simply a member of a band, and you want to perform with successful artists and play on lots of recordings, then get out there and be heard! Don't wait for the phone to ring. Try starting your own band first. You'll have the opportunity to showcase your individual style, letting people know what you do best and most comfortably. Attend local jam sessions to find other musicians whose personalities and abilities you admire and then perform together everywhere you can. Eventually, more successful musicians and bands will begin to notice you, and they may even ask you to play on their records or tours. Get to know the producers and managers of these acts. Your reputation and opportunities can grow from there. For instance, when Guns N' Roses was looking for a replacement drummer, GNR's guitarist Slash happened to attend a concert at which drummer Matt Sorum was performing. Slash liked Sorum's heavy, solid style, and without auditioning thousands of candidates, Slash offered Sorum the gig. Sorum worked hard at putting himself in situations in which he could shine. As a result, he got a great job with Guns N' Roses, one of the greatest rock bands in the world at that time.

If you're a songwriter (not an artist/performer) who wants to get a publishing deal and get your music placed with successful artists and in television commercials and films, you can start off by contacting some of the more popular bands in your area yourself and see if they'd be interested in performing one of your songs or co-writing one with you. If the group ends up getting a record deal, bingo, you're in business! Some writers even go so far as to develop their own artists, writing songs for them to perform, and then producing them and helping them get signed to a recording contract. It's a long-term approach, but you have to start somewhere. You can also try contacting the film departments at local colleges to make your music available for student films. The film may go on to win an award, or that student may even go on to become a successful director one day, and you'll be one of the first people he or she calls. Try contacting some of your local radio stations to see if they're interested in using your material for their advertising spots. Start with the smaller radio stations and work your way up from there. Also try contacting a few of the many "music libraries" that exist (organizations who help place songs in video games, corporate video presentations, phone music on-hold, elevators, etc.) such as www.mastersource.com, and see if they'd be interested in using your material. Another viable option to further your career can be to try services such as Taxi (www.taxi.com) and Tonos (www.tonos.com), which generally serve as screeners for industry professionals who are looking for material. Also, keep your eyes open for the number of songwriter's workshops and competitions offered by the performing rights societies (ASCAP, BMI, or SESAC) as a way to gain exposure, earn a few bucks, and also improve your songwriting skills. Check out www.ascap.com, www.bmi.com, and www.sesac.com. Other organizations to check out include the Songwriter's Guild of America at www.songwriter's.org, Association of Independent Music Publishers (AIMP) at www.aimp.org, and Society of Composers & Lyricists at www.filmscore.org. The opportunities to take charge of your career are endless. For over 8,000 more places to promote your music, try checking out the Indie Bible, now in its fourth edition, at www.indiebible.com.

If you're a solo artist or part of a band that wants to get a record deal, cut your own record first! Digital technology has greatly reduced studio costs and has made home recording equipment more practical to own. CD manufacturing has also become more affordable. You can sell your CDs at live performances or over the Internet (the Internet provides a number of marketing opportunities through online stores and MP3 sites). Create a buzz! Build a following. You'll be surprised at how many people in the industry you'll attract once you set the wheels in motion. Everybody likes a winner and will want to be part of your success by associating themselves with you. Singer/songwriter Ani DiFranco was actually able to bypass the record companies altogether by starting her own label out of her parent's garage. She was only twenty years old when Righteous Babe Records began. At the time of this writing, sales of her albums are known to reach up to 30,000 copies per month. This brings the old saying to mind, "You ever notice how fast firewood burns when you cut and then chop it yourself?" Though DiFranco's is a rare example, it shows what you can accomplish when you take the initiative. In yet another example, both Guns N' Roses and Mötley Crüe were selling out Los Angeles clubs before Geffen Records A&R man Tom Zutaut "discovered" and then signed the bands. There were literally lines around the block to see the band's performances. As Zutaut says, "You don't need ears to be a talent scout; you need eyes."

BUILD CAREER AWARENESS BY EXPANDING YOUR INTERNET PRESENCE

Most of you are already up to speed on the vast opportunities the Internet provides, but in case you've missed out on something, let's take a quick look at some of the ways you can be more proactive about your career by promoting yourself over the World Wide Web. Below is a brief discussion covering online stores, digital downloads, Web radio, live webcasting, chat rooms, Web rings, newsgroups, mailing lists, webzines, and personal websites.

Digital recording equipment and home studio gear has made it far easier for artists to record their musical compositions. The cost of CD duplication and packaging is also more affordable. But if the thought of selling 1,000 or more CDs seems like a daunting undertaking, then you should know that there are a number of "online stores" who can provide you with some help. Highly traveled websites such as Amazon.com, Mp3.com, and CD Baby will advertise your CD on their sites and process orders. You'll receive a percentage of sales, and in some cases, you'll even receive detail tracking information about the fans who purchased your music. Surely you can also sell your music on your own website, but keep in mind that you'll not only have to design an interesting website that people frequent, but you'll have to set up a system that accepts credit card payments, and/or you'll have to deal with the lengthy process of accepting personal checks in the mail. Visit Amazon.com at www.amazon.com, MP3.com at www.mp3.com, and CD Baby at www.cdbaby.com.

Taking your music online via websites such as MP3.com allows you to upload MP3 music files, as well as biographical information and photographs. People surfing the Web can both listen to your music and download files for a small fee for which you'll be compensated! This is a great way to get both your name and music out over the World Wide Web, make new fans, and essentially get immediate feedback from the "net community"—you'll be happy to know that A&R scouts at record labels also keep their eyes glued to the Internet for new talent. MP3.com also provides a number of special services such as the "payback for playback" program in which you can earn money every time someone visits your home page and listens to your music. There's also a music "licensing program" in which your music is made available to producers and directors who may be interested in using your music in television commercials and movies. As if that weren't enough, MP3.com also has an "on demand" CD manufacturing program in which they'll manufacture CDs as people request them and send them out for a reasonable price—of course, you'll be compensated for every CD sold. Some of MP3.com's services are free, while others require a small monthly fee. Visit MP3.com's Web site at www.MP3.com. Other Web sites worth checking out are Ampcast.com at www.ampcast.com, and Vitaminic at www.vitaminic.com.

Another interesting way to get your music exposed on the Internet is to get it played on Internet radio stations. Net radio stations are just that; radio stations that broadcast over the Internet. With nothing more than your computer, a modem, and speakers, you can tune into radio shows around the world. Sites such as Bwbk.com (www.bwbk.com), Virtual Radio (www.virtualradio.com), Knac.com (www.knac.com), and Launch.com (www.launch.com) are just a few of the many net radio stations that exist. By sending out your music to net radio stations like these, you may even find that you get some exposure. However, to take even a more proactive approach, you can actually create your own net radio station and broadcast your own music. That's right! It's not entirely difficult to do, and in fact, SHOUTcast radio (www.shoutcast.com) is one site that can help make it possible. From what I'm told, SHOUTcast allows anyone—you, me, and our moms—to broadcast our MP3 collections. Be sure to check this site out.

Live "Web casting" is a great way to take your live concerts to those people who live in another part of the world. Web casts are essentially live performances over the Internet. Sites such as L.A. Live (www.lalive.com) introduce the Web community to the underground world of L.A.'s music culture. Companies such as L.A. Live actually show up at live performances, wire up the club, and broadcast performances over the net. In fact, more and more clubs are becoming "wired" clubs themselves. The House of Blues (www.hob.com) brings concerts online to its own site. The Knitting Factory, in New York and L.A. is also wired. There are many others. Check out Live Online (www.live-online.com), Hotconcerts (www.hotconcerts.com), Much Music (www.muchmusic.com), and Live Web Casts (www.livewebcasts.com) for a larger view of online concerts.

Getting on the Web and just hanging out with the online music community is another good way to spread the word about your music. By getting on a site such as iMusic (www.imusic.com), you can find over 1.5 million fans of all shapes and sizes and begin spreading the word 24/7 via message boards and live "chat rooms" (chat rooms are places where you can talk with other people over the Web in real time). The Internet also allows you to join and/or create what's known as "Web rings." Web rings are groups of websites all linked together by people who share similar interests. For instance, there's a U2 Web ring. For a directory of existing Web rings, log on to webring (www.webring.com). "Newsgroups" are also a great way to make new contacts and increase your fan base. Web newsgroups allow you to post messages and converse with other readers about specific topics. For a list of all types of newsgroups, log on to Deja.com (www.deja.com). Also try logging on to CD Baby's newsgroup at www.musicthoughts.com. Another great way to connect with particular interest groups is to become part of email based discussion groups called "mailing lists." Mailing lists are similar to newsgroups, but more private. Messages on niche topics are sent directly to your computer from other people who have chosen to subscribe. You can find a variety of existing mailing lists by connecting to Liszt (www.liszt.com/channels/music). And finally, there are a number of online magazines known as "fanzines" or "webzines" in which you can get your music reviewed, post pictures, and list your concert events. Needless to say, the Internet provides endless opportunities to spread the word about your music. The key to becoming part of the net community is to get involved a little bit at a time. You'll be surprised at how fast you get the hang of it.

The Indie Link Exchange is a list of over 500 musicians who wish to exchange links with other music-related sites. For free exposure, go to www.indielink exchange.com.

Even if you make your presence known on a variety of other Web sites, creating your own Web site is still a good idea—it's your place to shine! Your personal Web site becomes your headquarters, in which you can provide links to other places on the Web where your information and music can be found. You can get listed in search engines and directories such as Excite, Lycos, and Alta Vista to help people find you. But once someone logs on to your site, the key is to a give them a reason to want to keep coming back. Keep your Web design simple and easy to navigate. Keep your site fresh and up to date so that visitors can always expect something new. Create your own newsletter. Provide message boards where people can post messages for other fans visiting your sites. Give people an opportunity to converse with other fans in chat rooms. Provide your email address so that fans can contact you personally and so that you can respond to as many people as possible. You can also include MP3 files of your music for people to download, and give people an opportunity to purchase your CD. You can include streaming video clips of concert footage, live interviews, or even your own homemade music video. Try posting pictures and posters that fans can download. You can provide concert and tour information. You can also create opportunities for people to join and form "street teams" to help you promote your music in their own home. The opportunities are limitless. Be sure to surf the Web and see what your favorite bands are including on their websites. You will be sure to find some really impressive sites. Check out Radiohead's site at www.radiohead.com, and Dream Theater's site at www.dreamtheater.net as a start.

Okay, that's about all on Internet promotion for now. For more ideas, or to brush up on some terms you may be unfamiliar with, check out Peter Spellman's book *The Musician's Internet* (Berklee Press), or David Kushner's *Music Online for Dummies* (IDG Books Worldwide, Inc.).

INCREASE YOUR ODDS OF GETTING SIGNED
BY UNDERSTANDING MORE ABOUT A&R

Most artists dream about getting signed to a recording agreement, yet few know anything about the record company personnel responsible for discovering new talent, what these people look for in an artist, and where and when they look to find it. A discussion on A&R can easily take up hundreds of pages, but here's a brief overview.

A&R representatives (an acronym for Artists and Repertoire) are record company personnel whose job it is to discover new talent and help develop careers. The further A&R reps can climb up the corporate ladder and the bigger their salaries, the more stressful their jobs become, and also the more fearful the reps become of losing them. They have a great responsibility to make money for their companies and to justify their career positions. For this reason, A&R reps often follow trends, look for "sure things," or wait to see what A&R reps at other labels are pursuing. Contrary to popular belief, most A&R personnel do not have "signing power." Once an A&R representative finds a potential artist, they have the difficult task of getting the approval of their record company presidents—and getting approval is often the hardest part of the job! The average life span of an A&R rep at a label is three years.

A&R reps look for artists who have potential hit songs, a signature sound, a marketable image, long-term career potential (i.e., youthfulness, and adaptability), and a great live show.

A&R reps prefer business-minded bands that first help themselves. Artists who press and sell their own recordings, perform live, build a strong fan base, design their own Web sites, establish a strong Web presence, and have a very clear vision of their goals are far more attractive to record company representatives than artists who don't. Musicians who know everything from what sort of image they want to how they want their album cover artwork and videos to appear make an A&R rep's job that much easier.

A&R reps also look for artists who have a strong work ethic. Will the members of the band continue to work hard at creating their own breaks once they get signed, or will they rely entirely on their label to do everything? Will they have the endurance to tour relentlessly or will they burn out quickly? Do they have spouses, kids, substantial bills, and other domestic responsibilities that may inhibit the pursuit of their goals? Simply put, record labels look for the path of least resistance to ensure that they'll make a profit from their investments.

A&R representatives discover new bands through independent record labels, listening to college radio stations, searching the bins of mom-and-pop record stores, attending local club performances, reading reviews in local and national trade magazines, attending annual music conventions and conferences, surfing the Internet for MP3 music files, and keeping a watchful eye on *Sound Scan* reports (a magazine that reports album sales figures by tracking registered bar codes). They also rely on referrals made from established bands, record label scouts, friends and relatives of industry executives, reputable producers, managers, attorneys, and publishing companies.

Pinpointing the exact time of year that A&R representatives are most likely to sign new talent is difficult; however one thing is certain: there are usually not many signings during the fourth quarter of the year (October through December). During this period, most companies' financial budgets for new projects have likely been accounted for or depleted. Additionally, being that it's the holiday season, most companies are focusing on pushing their major artists whose new albums are usually timed for release right before the holiday shopping season. Of course, there are exceptions to the aforementioned; it's possible for a really hot band in the middle of a bidding war to get signed in the fourth quarter, but generally October through December is not a good time for new bands.

In general, A&R representatives don't like to be approached directly by fledging artists. In fact, most record companies don't even accept unsolicited materials through the mail. Though, as I've said, there are exceptions to every rule, the rep's philosophy is that when you're truly ready to get to a recording agreement, the rep will find you! So be realistic about the music biz and your career goals, learn to be more proactive about your career, and just get out there and be heard doing what you love best—*playing music!*

BE PRACTICAL ABOUT MONEY BY KEEPING IT AND MAKING IT GROW

When you make money in the music business, learn how to keep it and make it grow. There are far too many musicians who sell millions of records yet end up penniless. In 1991, *Forbes* magazine estimated rapper M.C. Hammer's worth at $33 million. Today, as a result of living an extravagant lifestyle (he toured with 60 performers, employed an entourage of 100 friends, drove 17 exotic cars, and owned a mansion worth $14 million), he's now penniless and doing commercials for a credit repair company. Invest your money wisely! It doesn't take much to get started, so even if you have very few funds, contact a successful financial planner. The money you invest today could be the money you depend on tomorrow.

ADAPT TO CHANGE BY DIVERSIFYING YOURSELF NOW

Broaden your career opportunities to increase your earning potential and "staying power" in the business. It was Charles Darwin who once said, "It is not the strongest of species that tend to survive, it is those that are most adaptable to change." Work on song/lyric writing, singing, playing multiple instruments, production, and engineering. Dave Grohl, the drummer for the grunge-rock sensation Nirvana, was able to transform his career after Kurt Cobain (Nirvana's lead singer/songwriter) took his own life in 1994. Grohl formed a new band, The Foo Fighters, and assumed the role of vocalist, guitarist, and songwriter. The Foo Fighters entered the *Billboard* charts at No. 24 with their first album and have enjoyed a successful career ever since. If Dave hadn't been prepared, he could easily have been at the end of his musical career. Way back in the 16th century, Niccolo Machiavelli said it this way in his famous book *The Prince:* "One who adapts his policy to times prospers."

Develop a back-up plan through related music business opportunities such as artist relations, management, Internet-related careers, video production, record production, building your own studio, music publicity, musical equipment design and manufacturing, instruction, or starting your own label (to name a few). You may not think that you'll need something to fall back on, but you never know. Very few musicians and bands are able to sustain long-term careers as performers. Session guitarist Steve Lukathur puts it best, "You can only be the number one session cat for so long." Lukathur has now moved on to producing records. Even the group Korn, with two platinum records to their credit and no sign of their careers slowing down, took precautionary steps by starting their own record label, called Elementree Records, distributed by Reprise/Warner, in 1997. The majority of the group's members had families to support and could not risk relying solely on the success of their next CD. They also didn't want to spend as much time out on the road and away from their families as they had in the past. People grow up and their lives change—and so do dreams. The band Orgy, Elementree's first signing, sold over 500,000 copies with their release *Candyass*. Needless to say, Korn made a smart move!

STAY ON TRACK WITHOUT BURNING OUT MENTALLY OR PHYSICALLY

Take precautions against both physical and mental burnout. Fast food, lack of sleep, and stress can all contribute to physical burnout. It's important to make every effort to stay as healthy as possible, especially while out on the road. You'd be surprised at the number of artists' tours that have been cut short while they were hospitalized for exhaustion. Manager Tom Atensio warns, "When your record is in the top ten you're like an athlete. You get up in the morning, do morning shows, spend the afternoon doing press, you go to sound checks, do phoners, go to dinner with the record company, perform your show, and then hang out with retail buyers. If you're feeble and weak, eventually you'll crack."

You must also be careful to avoid mental burnout, which is far more serious and permanent than physical burnout, often resulting from suffering one rejection and disappointment after the other. The best way to combat mental burnout is to remember why you got in the music business in the first place—for the love of playing music. As musician/author/poet Henry Rollins says, "Music is the master, and we are only there to serve it. It's going to be fun, but it's also going to be a lot of work. Stick to the reason you got into it in the first place. You wanted to play music, right? So you won't mind playing in front of a few people as long as you get to play, right? Good. Also, know that all the greats played through all kinds of highs and lows and ebbs and tides. If you're a player, then play!"

MAINTAIN CONTROL IN THE FACE OF DRUGS AND ALCOHOL

Drugs and alcohol are a big part of music culture and have led to the downfall of many successful artists and bands. What might begin as casual partying can end up spiraling out of control. Keep yourself in check! Mike McCready of Pearl Jam was nearly fired at the apex of the group's career due to his drinking. Steven Adler of Guns N' Roses was booted out of his band for his drug abuse. Scott Weiland of Stone Temple Pilots jeopardized the continued existence of his band after being jailed on drug possession charges. And in a far more tragic example, Layne Staley of Alice in Chains thrust his band into a permanent hiatus because of his addiction to heroin; the band hasn't recorded a new record since the height of their career in 1996. Even worse, Layne Staley finally died in 2002 of an overdose. Blind Melon's career also ended when singer Shannon Hoon died of an overdose.

Finding solutions to these problems is clearly beyond the

If you think that you're developing a serious problem with drugs or alcohol, both Alcoholics Anonymous (AA) and Narcotics Anonymous (NA) offer free meetings in a city near you. Check your local yellow pages. On a lighter note, would you believe that some people use AA meetings as a way to make new contacts; especially in bigger cities such as Los Angeles? People who have never had a problem with drugs or alcohol are actually known to frequent meetings. It shows you what some people are willing to do to get ahead.

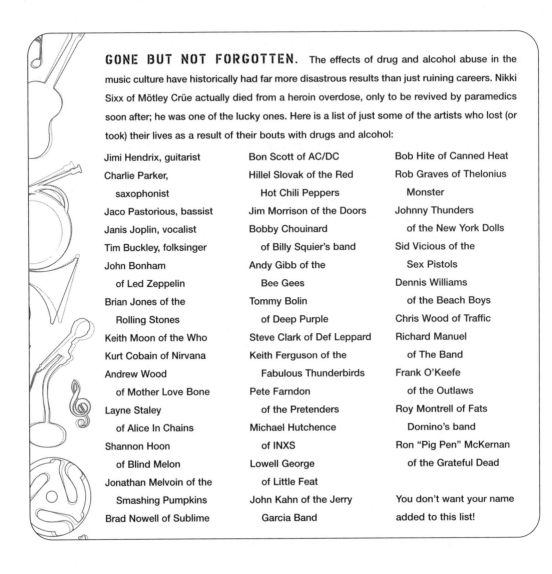

GONE BUT NOT FORGOTTEN. The effects of drug and alcohol abuse in the music culture have historically had far more disastrous results than just ruining careers. Nikki Sixx of Mötley Crüe actually died from a heroin overdose, only to be revived by paramedics soon after; he was one of the lucky ones. Here is a list of just some of the artists who lost (or took) their lives as a result of their bouts with drugs and alcohol:

Jimi Hendrix, guitarist

Charlie Parker,
   saxophonist

Jaco Pastorious, bassist

Janis Joplin, vocalist

Tim Buckley, folksinger

John Bonham
   of Led Zeppelin

Brian Jones of the
   Rolling Stones

Keith Moon of the Who

Kurt Cobain of Nirvana

Andrew Wood
   of Mother Love Bone

Layne Staley
   of Alice In Chains

Shannon Hoon
   of Blind Melon

Jonathan Melvoin of the
   Smashing Pumpkins

Brad Nowell of Sublime

Bon Scott of AC/DC

Hillel Slovak of the Red
   Hot Chili Peppers

Jim Morrison of the Doors

Bobby Chouinard
   of Billy Squier's band

Andy Gibb of the
   Bee Gees

Tommy Bolin
   of Deep Purple

Steve Clark of Def Leppard

Keith Ferguson of the
   Fabulous Thunderbirds

Pete Farndon
   of the Pretenders

Michael Hutchence
   of INXS

Lowell George
   of Little Feat

John Kahn of the Jerry
   Garcia Band

Bob Hite of Canned Heat

Rob Graves of Thelonius
   Monster

Johnny Thunders
   of the New York Dolls

Sid Vicious of the
   Sex Pistols

Dennis Williams
   of the Beach Boys

Chris Wood of Traffic

Richard Manuel
   of The Band

Frank O'Keefe
   of the Outlaws

Roy Montrell of Fats
   Domino's band

Ron "Pig Pen" McKernan
   of the Grateful Dead

You don't want your name
added to this list!

scope of this book, but one thing's for sure—you're not going to find answers to your problems with excessive behavior. As illustrated above, the problems only worsen. If this advice means nothing to you, at least consider your professional responsibilities to the other members of your band, as well your professional responsibilities to the people who have invested hundreds of thousands of dollars in your career. Keep in mind that record labels are less tolerant today of artists who have drug and alcohol problems than they were in the past. With other talent waiting in line to take your place, record companies simply don't have the time to waste on your personal issues. Don't throw your career and hard work away.

CLOSING REMARKS: THE FAT LADY SINGS

Pursuing a career in music isn't easy and there are no surefire ways to ensure success. But by reviewing the tips in this chapter passed down by seasoned professionals, you'll at least set yourself on the right track. By learning from others who have been down the path before you, you can save yourself a great deal of time. Take the tips that work for you and throw away the rest. Don't be afraid to forge new ground.

One extremely important tip to take away here is to be proactive. Don't wait for anyone to wave a wand over your head and magically make you a star. Work towards becoming a success on your own by getting out there and making yourself heard. It's natural to be attracted to those who help themselves. You'll be surprised at what you accomplish by setting the wheels in motion.

It's also important to remember the reason why you became a musician in the first place. Don't let the challenges of the music business get you down. If you started playing because you truly love it, then you shouldn't mind working through both the ups and downs.

Creating music is an art—but getting it out to the masses and making money from it is a business that, just like any other, requires a lot of work and planning. It's a hard road that's definitely not for the thin skinned, but as long as your dreams are well thought out and realistic, it is possible to make them a reality.

2

Types of

BUSINESS
RELATIONSHIPS

> "It's only rock 'n' roll. Is it really?"
>
> —BILL WYMAN OF THE ROLLING STONES
>
> (from his book *Stone Alone*)

Until now, you have probably spent most of your time honing your skills as a musician with little or no concern about the particulars of business or band politics. But as you begin to get more seriously involved in a music career, you need to understand the dynamics of the various business relationships you may encounter. Are you a band member, self-employed, a contract employee, a contract employee with profit shares, or a solo artist and employer? Aside from being able to differentiate among these job classifications, it's important that you have an understanding of some of the key business issues associated with each one. In Part Two, I will explain each of these classifications. (Note: For those of you on the fast track, refer to the chart below to determine your employment status.)

AT A GLANCE

- ✦ **Band Membership:** If you're part of a band in which each member collectively plays a role in the musical direction or marketed persona of the group, and every member shares in sacrifices on "the road to success," the band will most likely have some form of membership agreement that deals with divisions of record advances, record royalties, music publishing royalties, concert money, and merchandising.
- ✦ **Contract Employment or Self-Employment:** If you're employed by and working under the direction of one artist, or if you're self-employed and freelancing with a variety of artists, your agreement with your employer(s) may simply consist of

a weekly salary or set wage as well as special perks such as a retainer, per diem, and something called a buy out.

✦ **Contract Employee with Profit Shares:** If you're an employee of an established band that desires your contributions to the writing and recording of an album, as well as touring in support of an album, your agreement may provide for more than the standard employee/employer relationship salary. Such arrangements are called salary/percentage involvements.

✦ **Solo Artist and Employer:** If you're an exceptional writer or instrumentalist, a skilled vocalist, or a highly motivated individual who possesses the desire to lead, then chances are you have what it takes to be a solo artist. Though your name and likeness may be displayed individually on album cover artwork and venue marquees, you'll rarely work alone. You'll employ a group of studio and touring musicians and may even collaborate with skilled composers and producers.

CHAPTER 2

Band Membership

Being a member of a band is no different than being a member of a professional sports team; you're among a group of individuals united in the pursuit of a common goal, each person playing a unique and integral part in achieving a dream. The motto—at least in theory—is, "All for one and one for all."

But unlike the sports world, where professional teams expect young athletes to meet extremely high standards before drafting them, young bands often form simply because the members are friends who share musical tastes. As I'll discuss in the next section, this common denominator is unfortunately not enough to create a successful band. Personality differences, as well as opposing views of how business matters should be handled, eventually rear their ugly heads. The results: the band calls it quits, or a member is unfairly kicked out, or the group suffers setbacks due to its revolving lineup, or its members get entangled in an ongoing legal battle with one another. It happens all the time! This fate can be avoided, however, if a band maps out a simple business plan from its inception, ensuring that every member has similar expectations and goals. Although playing music is supposed to be fun, a serious band is a business just like any other, and it should never be regarded as anything less.

CRITERIA FOR CHOOSING BAND MEMBERS

Before getting down to the legalities of running your band, it's extremely important to consider the personalities and goals of the people with whom you're about to get involved. At first, when everyone is excited and eager to get things rolling, character flaws and differences of opinion are often overlooked, but if you ignore problems with the intention of dealing with them later, they always come back to bite you in the you-know-what. By asking each of its members a few honest questions up front such as the ones that follow, a band will immediately know whether or not it's even worthwhile to proceed in business:

- ✦ Are you ready to devote three or four years of your life to the group and stick with them through thick and thin?
- ✦ Are you ready to work your ass off and treat the band as a serious business?
- ✦ Could you relocate to another city and commit to staying there for a few years?
- ✦ Are you able to hit the road for extended periods of time for little or no pay?
- ✦ Can you tolerate sleeping in one hotel room with three or four other band members?
- ✦ Can you deal with traveling across the country in a small passenger van in the dead of winter?
- ✦ If you are in a relationship with someone, how serious are you about getting married and starting a family?
- ✦ Are you committed to rehearsing and being the best musician you can be?
- ✦ Are you open to experimenting with your visual image however the band may evolve in the following years?

Although the questions may seem personal and numerous, don't look at this as an interrogation! Think of this as a screening process to ensure that your proposed business venture is fruitful and long lasting. No matter how well you get along or how similar your musical tastes may be, if there are too many opposing opinions regarding how the group's business should be run, problems will eventually occur. The last thing you want to deal with is having to fire someone, having someone quit, or having the band break up after spending several months or years building it from the ground up.

To illustrate my point, according to the book *"What'd I Say": The Atlantic Story, 50 Years of Music,* one of the inspirational slogans written on the walls of the band Rush's studio read, "Individually, we are an ass, but together we are a genius."

FOUR CAPTAINS ON A SINKING SHIP. A band that formed in California consisted of two members from New York and two members from Florida. After investing a full year of time in the group, one of its members decided the band should move to New York because that was where he needed to live. Another member wanted to stick to what he believed was the original plan of staying in California. The other two members suggested the band should move to their homeland of Florida simply because they hated California. As it turns out, the entire band moved to Florida, but shortly thereafter they broke up after one member reneged on his agreement and moved to New York anyway. What a headache! If everyone had expressed their expectations and goals at the group's inception, the members might have realized they had no business being a band in the first place. This is hardly an isolated incident. Though it might sound as though everyone should have known better, you'd be surprised at the number of similar tragedies that exist because band members fail to communicate with each other.

EXCUSES, EXCUSES. A common excuse bands give for not putting together a preliminary band membership agreement is that they simply don't have the money for the attorney's fees in the early stages of their career. Although it's best to have an attorney draft such an agreement, there are a number of other resources that provide adequate form agreements. Check out the book *Music Law* by attorney Richard Stim, or contact Nolo Press at www.nolo.com. Another excuse bands have for not putting together a preliminary membership agreement is that it's not necessary at the beginning stages of their career when they're not making money. The rationale is, "Any percentage of zero is still zero." But if the band has any aspirations toward procuring a record deal down the line, their short-sightedness may end up causing serious partnership problems later. Some members may have different ideas about how their business should be handled, leaving other members feeling as though they're getting the short end of the stick.

BAND MEMBERSHIP AGREEMENTS

Once all of your members are in place, and everyone seems to share similar goals and their attitudes are in check, you need a written agreement defining the terms of your business relationship. This document, a "band membership agreement," compels a band to deal with important business issues before they become problems. The terms of the agreement should include language stipulating:

- ✦ How the band will make decisions (for example, by unanimous or majority vote)
- ✦ How income, such as that earned from record royalties, music publishing, concert money, and merchandising will be divided
- ✦ When members will be required to put money back into the band for expenses or investments
- ✦ What happens to a member's share of assets acquired by the group (such as equipment) when he or she quits or is voted out of the band
- ✦ What services will be expected of each member in the band
- ✦ What the guidelines are for hiring and firing band members
- ✦ How disputes will be resolved (in a court of law or outside the courts)
- ✦ Who owns or controls the rights to the band name and its continued use

Whether you're in a band that's just forming, or you're in a band on the verge of signing a new record deal, if you don't have a band membership agreement, then schedule a meeting and come up with one today. While an agreement won't stop a band from breaking up or running into conflicts, it will help define the individual beliefs, desires, and perspectives of the members from the start. I highly recommend hiring an experienced entertainment attorney to help you draft the terms of such an agreement. (See the interview with attorney Jeff Cohen at the end of this chapter.)

Key Members and Minority Partners

All members of a band do not necessarily have to share an equal level of control over the business or an equal share of the profits. Sometimes one member may feel he or she deserves more compensation than the others because he or she does the bulk of the work. Sometimes the founder, the lead singer, or the main songwriter are the only members who own the rights to the band name or who control the vote and have the final word in making business decisions. In any case, the record company may consider these individuals to be the group's "key members," those most important to the functioning of the band. In some instances, a non-key member or "minority partner" may not even be signed to the initial recording agreement. If you're not a signatory, the benefit is that you can walk away without any financial or recording obligation to the record company. As a minority partner you have the freedom to leave and start your own group. Keep in mind, though, that this doesn't negate any internal agreement you may have with the band itself. For example, there may be a clause in your band membership agreement that says you have the right to quit the band if you're unhappy, but not in the middle of a tour where the band can incur a loss as a result.

> Your individual interests and the band's interests may not always coincide. Therefore, unless the group is dividing the profits and control over business matters equally, seeking the advice of your own entertainment attorney is worth a small investment to ensure that your interests are protected. You can get inexpensive legal advice by contacting your local office of the Volunteer Lawyers For The Arts.

Potential Revenue Sources and Group Percentage Shares

Every band and its members should understand the various sources of revenue that may become available to them, and, more importantly, include a description of the way that money will be divided among the members in their band membership agreement. Why is this so important? In the words of Mick Jagger, "There is nothing like money to break up the band." Ain't that the truth! We've all heard stories about one band member driving a Mercedes and others driving beat-up station wagons. Needless to say, you don't want this to happen to you.

> Although many bands may adopt an all-for-one-and-one-for-all philosophy (at least at first), it's simply not enough to say, "we're going to split everything equally" without first understanding what "everything" really means.

At the beginning of a band's career, there may be very little money to split. Once a group has been signed to a record label, revenue sources may include record advances, recording fees, special payment funds, record royalties, video royalties, live performance monies, merchandising revenues (e.g., income from the sale of T-shirts and hats), and music publishing royalties. A brief discussion of each topic follows. Pay attention! There's a lot of information here, but educating your-

A BIT OF HISTORY. When Jimmy Page moved on from the Yardbirds to form Led Zeppelin, Columbia Records claimed it owned the rights to the new band. However, Jimmy Page had never signed the Yardbirds contract. Free and clear of any ties to Columbia, manager Peter Grant was able to negotiate an unprecedented deal on the Atlantic Records label (at the time, one of the most lucrative deals ever given to an unknown band) for the band that Page renamed Led Zeppelin.

self about it now will help you understand how you'll be compensated down the line for all your hard work and effort—and teach you how to avoid getting screwed! (Revenue sources are covered in more detail in Chapters 11–14 of this book.)

Record Advances. In recording contracts, most record advances are structured as "recording funds." The recording fund covers all recording expenses and any monies that are paid to the band in the form of an "artist advance." For instance, if you are a new rock or pop band signed to a major label such as Sony, BMG, WEA, UMG, or EMI, the recording fund is negotiable, though it's usually about $250,000. From this fund, $200,000 may be budgeted towards the "recording cost budget" of an album and submitted by the producer to the record company for approval. Recording costs can include the producer's advance, equipment rentals and accessories, techs, transportation, hotels, and per diems. The remaining $50,000 from the recording fund may be budgeted as an artist advance. That the manager is first entitled to a commission, and that there are also fees due to your attorney for negotiating the record deal. After taxes are deducted, there is very little money left over from the advance to be split among the members of the band. Nevertheless, these monies are what the group typically will depend upon for survival while preparing to record. (Chapter 11 covers recording advances in detail).

> Many of the examples in this book relate to contracts with major labels, but agreements with independent and production companies also exist (see Chapter 11 for more information). Although the royalty rates and the advances differ between these companies, the general concepts discussed are the same.

Recording Fees. Usually factored into a band's recording budget are the union minimum scale wages to which each musician is entitled for recording an album. Most record companies are affiliated with the American Federation of Musicians (AFM) and the American Federation of Television and Radio Artists (AFTRA) and must report all recording sessions to their local branch under an agreement called the "collective bargaining agreement." The record company is required to pay the band a wage at union minimum scale and to make additional contributions to pension and welfare funds. Though it's your option, the record company will ask each band member to affiliate with the union before recording an album; consequently, dues should also be factored into the recording budget. (For more information on unions, see Chapter 3.)

Special Payment Funds. One of the benefits born of the collective bargaining agreements between recording companies and the AFM is something called a "sound recording special payment fund" (SPF). The SPF pays out monies to all instrumentalists who work on AFM covered recording sessions. ("Covered" refers to all sessions that are reported to the union; each musician's name must be included on union form B4 and turned in to the record company by the producer.) The monies paid to you from the special payment fund are based on a percentage (ranging from 20 to 60 percent) of your total earnings in sessions the prior year; sessions for which you will continue to be paid for the next five years. For instance, if you participate in only one recording session in the year 2003 and receive scale rate of approximately $300 for three hours or less of work, from the year 2004 to 2009 you will receive monies from the special payment fund that are 20 percent of these earnings. The more AFM sessions in which you participate and the more money you make, the bigger percentage you will receive in SPF payments. Some musicians receive as much as six-figure paychecks each year from the SPF. Note that both the AFM and AFTRA collect and pay out monies for "new use" every time a recording is used in a new medium such as film or television. (Again, unions will be discussed in Chapter 3).

Record Royalties. Record royalties are percentages (also called "points") that the record company pays to you for the sale of your record. A common royalty rate for a band is anywhere from 11 to 16 percent of the suggested retail price (SRP) per unit sold. After deducting up to 4 percent for the record producer, the band may divide the remaining points equally. For example, 16 percent (the royalty rate) minus 4 percent (the producer's share) equals the band's "net royalty rate" of 12 percent per unit sold. If the group consists of four members, each member receives three points. To determine precisely how much each point is worth and what you make per CD, there are a number of advanced calculations and deductions that I will explain in Chapter 11 of this book. Just keep in mind that before receiving even one dime in record royalties, *the band must sell enough albums to "recoup" (earn back) all the record company's recording and advanced expenses.* Ninety-five percent of all bands fail to do this!

Video Royalties. Home videos may be collections of individual video clips, documentaries of "the making of" videos, or live concert videos. A common royalty rate for a band is anywhere from 11 to 21 percent of the wholesale price (as opposed to the retail price, which applies to record royalties). If someone other than the record company does the manufacturing, the band usually gets 50 percent of the net sales receipts (i.e., 50 percent after the designated company deducts duplication and distribution fees). The band members may divide any profits that remain equally.

> Are promotional music videos really necessary? Many classic albums, such as Fleetwood Mac's *Rumors*, were successfully marketed long before the advent of videos. Sales of *Rumors* reached 28 million copies. Korn had two platinum records long before MTV showed full-court support in 1998. Since only a small percentage of videos are ever aired, a new group may benefit more from monies and effort spent on touring and radio promotion.

In general, there isn't much money to be made directly from videos. Most videos are primarily shot for promotional purposes on MTV and VH1, and production isn't cheap! The costs for a single promotional video can range from $75,000 to $350,000 and up into the millions. (For instance, the rock group Limp Bizkit spent $3 million for one of their videos). These expenses are all paid back to the record company before you ever see dime one from sales. To make matters worse, once all video expenses are recouped, video royalties are then used to repay all record expenses that have not been recouped, and vice versa for the record royalties (i.e., once record expenses are recouped from record royalties, record royalties are then used to repaying unrecouped video expenses). Note: Typically, only 50 percent of video expenses are charged against record royalties.

Live Performance Monies. Because of the minimal payment a new band may receive for a live performance, there's usually little, if any, money left to split between the band members. The overhead incurred from "hitting the road" is tremendous. Most bands usually return home from a tour *owing* money! This debt may initially be paid by the record company in the form of "tour support" (additional funds up to $50,000), but every penny must be paid back by the band; tour support is 100 per-

REALITY BITES! It's not uncommon for a new group to make a $250,000 promotional video that never makes rotation (frequent play) on MTV or VH1; an estimated 94 percent of all videos produced are never aired. Video play, radio play, and how well your record is stocked in stores all depend on the amount of money, time, and effort the record company spends on promotion. And all of that depends on how important you are to the label. Most major record companies only have enough money to effectively market six bands per year, although they sign an average of 30. This means that someone gets screwed! Most bands do not realize that when they get signed to a record company they are competing with other groups on their label for marketing money. It all comes down to a question of how excited the label is about a band's finished "product." The record company may lose money by signing several bands a year, but it makes up for its loss with the few bands that are successful. The hits pay for the stiffs. CBS Records made $60 million from one band alone: the Australian rock group Men At Work, whose debut album sold 38.5 million copies worldwide. [For more on the history of the music business and record promotion, check out Fredric Dannen's book *Hit Men: Power Brokers and Fast Money Inside the Music Business*. Money (payola), cocaine (drugola), and prostitutes were commonly offered to radio program directors in the '70s and '80s in exchange for record spins. Today, there are more subtle forms of "bribery," such as concert tickets and contest giveaways.

cent recoupable from record sales.

As part of the total expenses and budget for a tour, the band may pay each member a daily allowance for food called a per diem and a weekly salary. However, since this money is usually available by way of tour support only, it, too, has to be paid back to the record company and is usually deducted from your future record royalties. Keep in mind that the main purpose of touring for most new bands is not to make a direct profit, but to build a fan base and sell records. Detailed information on touring will be provided in Chapter 13.

Merchandising Revenue. Selling merchandise such as T-shirts, hats, and posters can generate a substantial amount of money during a tour. However, newer bands usually use these monies to subsidize their touring expenses. Merchandising, particularly the manufacturing and shipping of products, also costs money. Finally, a percentage of the revenue from the sale of the merchandise must be paid to the performance venue. That can mean that as much as 40 percent of the money earned from the sale of merchandise stays with the concert hall. After all is said and done, the members of the band may split whatever money is left equally.

In many cases, a band will sign a "merchandising deal" with a merchandising company to manufacture products and oversee their sale. In return, the band receives a royalty ranging from 25 to 35 percent of the gross sales generated, less taxes. The company may pay a merchandising advance against royalties to the band

> Artists make more money per item sold when they have product manufactured by a printer and sell it themselves. However, the burdens of manufacturing, shipping, etc., are not practical once an artist has progressed to playing larger venues—hence the need for a merchandising company.

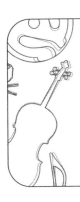

BANKRUPT! In merchandising contracts, "performance guarantees" stipulate that unless the merchandiser recoups the advance it paid to the band, the band must repay the outstanding balance—even if the group breaks up. One successful group that received a substantial advance for merchandising on its forthcoming tour was sued when the lead singer quit and the band subsequently fell apart. Thus, no tour, no merchandising sales, no return on the merchandiser's investment. Each band member had to file for bankruptcy because none of them had the funds to pay back the advance.

throughout the course of the tour of up to $100,000 for newer bands; extremely successful bands can get millions. The advance is usually used by the band to cover expenses while it's out on the road. (Merchandising is covered in detail in Chapter 14.)

Music Publishing Royalties. The way music publishing royalties from a song are divided among band members is different from the way the group percentage shares of other monies I explained previously are dispersed. This is because the songwriting process can be an individual effort, or it can be a collaborative effort involving any combination of the band members. A successful song can earn hundreds of thousands of dollars long after the band has parted ways. If you haven't been paying attention before, you had better start now.

Under copyright law, when two or more people collaborate on writing a song, and each writer contributes either musically, lyrically, or in both ways, the ownership split is "pro rata" (equal), unless there is an agreement between the writers that stipulates otherwise. A "musical contribution" is the song's melody or any original riff or groove that becomes an integral hook to the song, for example, the bass line by John Deacon in Queen's "Another One Bites the Dust," or John Bonham's drum intro to Led Zeppelin's "Rock and Roll."

When groups spend hours together in rehearsal, experimenting with song arrangements, tempos, and instrumentation, a certain percentage of the credits may initially be divided among all members, allotting a larger share of the copyright ownership to the actual author(s) of the song. For instance, one group composed of four members allotted 12.5 percent of every song to each member in the band. The remaining 50 percent per song went to the member(s) who contributed to the music and/or lyrics.

Often, when it is each member's unique performance that shapes the band's signature sound, the band simply divides all of the composition credits equally. For example, guitarist Stone Gossard and vocalist Eddie Vedder wrote most of Pearl Jam's songs, yet the band originally split the ownership in its compositions equally—each member (five in total) received 20 percent of the copyright. However, as the group became more successful and vocalist Eddie Vedder was recognized as "the star," essentially becoming the only irreplaceable member of the group, the band wanted to keep him happy. The group allotted 36 percent of each song to Vedder, and 16 percent to each of the other three members of the band. In any case, division shares in your songs must be communicated to the record company before the release of your record. As you'll see, this is very important!

When you share in a percentage of the rights to songs, you are entitled to special monies from the record company for every record that is sold. These monies are called "mechanical royalties." Mechanical royalties, which are licensing fees the record company pays to you for using your songs on a record, are different from record royalties and are most typically not used by the record company for recouping recording costs. As of the year 2002, the statutory mechanical license rate is 8 cents per composition per CD made and distributed. (The rate increases to 8.5 cents in 2004.)

However, the record company typically negotiates a lower rate for new bands at 75 percent of statutory per each record actually sold. Mechanical royalties are one of the more immediate sources of income related to record sales. Statements are sent out to you either four times yearly or semi-annually, depending on the record company and the terms of your contract. (Mechanical royalties are covered in detail in Chapter 12.)

> There are also licensing fees for the use of your compositions in promotional and home videos; these are called "synchronization" fees. However, since videos are shot mostly for promotional purposes, the record company typically negotiates for the "free use" (free of licensing fees) of your songs in videos.

In addition to mechanical royalties, you'll also receive royalties from public performances of your compositions on radio (assuming that these compositions are played regularly) and television, including MTV and VH1. These are called "performance royalties." Performance royalties are paid out after joining one of the major performing rights organizations and registering your songs and percentage shares with them. The three U.S. societies include the American Society of Composers, Authors and Publishers (ASCAP), Broadcast Music Incorporated (BMI), and what was formerly known as the Society of European Stage Authors And Composers, today known as (SESAC). (For more on member information, see Chapter 12.)

In cases in which a publishing agreement has been signed with a music publishing company, an organization that specializes in collecting royalties and exploiting musical compositions in film, television, print, and other uses, a specified percentage of the income is designated between the "publisher" and "the writer." The publisher offers an advance, recoupable from future earnings, that should be divided between the writers in proportion to their individual shares in a song. Music publishing companies are discussed in Chapter 12.

Who Else Gets A Piece of The Pie? Keep in mind that there are other members of your team who will also earn a percentage of your earnings. These include your attorney, personal manager, business manager, talent agent, and record producer. Your attorney, who provides legal advice and who may act as your litigator and also provide shopping services (shopping your band to record labels),

ONE WAY TICKET. For a crack at the big time, many rap artists relinquished their song rights to their producer or record company. The rappers figured that if they made a fuss over "paperwork," their careers wouldn't receive top priority. In return for the rights to his song that later, in 1990, became a huge hit, one rapper received no more than a watch and chain. (Check out Ronin Ro's book *Have Gun Will Travel—The Spectacular Rise and Violent Fall of Death Row Records* about one of the most successful music labels ever.)

generally receives a flat fee or a percentage of the deals he or she negotiates (typically 5 percent). Your personal manager, who handles tour activities, artist development, public relations, recording contracts, and much more, may get as much as 15 to 25 percent of the gross monies earned. Your business manager, who oversees all your financial issues, such as taxes, investments, and tour budgets, and who also makes sure that all of the bills are paid, typically charges 5 percent of the gross, but may also agree to work for an hourly or flat fee. Your talent agent, who secures work in the form of live performances, television appearances, motion pictures, and other avenues, may charge 10 percent of the gross, but can charge as much as 20 percent in some cases. And finally, your record producer, who guides you through the entire recording process, may charge up to $50,000 (which is deducted from the recording fund), and up to 4 percent of your record royalties (and that's only for a mid-level producer).

DRAFT THAT AGREEMENT NOW!

When a group of individuals joins forces as a band, it's each member's responsibility to define the terms of their relationship from the start. This will avert any potential misunderstandings or confusion regarding compensation and control. It could very well turn out that the founders, main songwriters, or key members of the band have other ideas about how business is handled. Schedule a group meeting now and discuss the terms of your agreement! It's much easier to discuss business while a relationship is new and everyone is friendly. Music is supposed to be about having fun and being carefree, but it's also a business.

> Someone once said that a band membership agreement is like a prenuptial agreement: the best time to write one is when you're the best of friends; the problem, however, is that you don't realize how true that is until you're already in the middle of a bitter divorce.

Another group that let success and greed prevail is the shock metal band Marilyn Manson. At the apex of the group's career, Daisy Berkowitz (the original guitarist) was voted out of the band over a dispute concerning money he was owed from his participation in writing songs with the band. Apparently, he trusted Marilyn, who allegedly chose to hang on to the money himself to handle business matters. Whether or not Berkowitz was able to successfully sue Manson and get his money back is not the point. The point is that it's necessary to identify the individual feelings of each member in a band membership agreement. That way you'll have a better chance of preventing misunderstandings that can lead to expensive lawsuits down the road.

FRIEND OR FOE? It's all too typical that after years of sacrifice, when a band is finally on the verge of being signed, the egos of some of the key band members take over. One now very successful rock group encountered problems when its record company showed more interest in the lead singer and main songwriter than in the rest of the band. Those two then began making decisions and calling the shots without consulting the other members. Eventually they made a power play, signing with the label and leaving the other members out altogether. This was after ten long years of friendship and sacrifice. A lawsuit is pending.

As a final illustration of what can happen when you don't have everyone's understandings in writing, in 1962, keyboardist Ian Stewart ("Stu") joined forces with guitarist Brian Jones as founding members of what was soon to become one of the greatest rock bands in the world. A year later, after being joined by Mick Jagger, Keith Richards, Bill Wyman, and Charlie Watts and having played the London club circuit night after night practically for free, the band was finally on the verge of signing its first management agreement with Andrew Oldham. But Jones, who was determined to be a star at any price, suddenly fired Stu from the band's front lineup. Apparently Oldham felt that Stu's physical appearance did not fit with the band's "sexy" image on stage. Because he felt sympathetic toward him, Jones promised Stu one-sixth of the band's profits and the position of studio keyboardist and road manager. Stu reluctantly accepted. As it turns out, Stu was relegated to the status of a regular employee and paid a salary. Needless to say, he did not earn an equal share as promised. The group, of course, was the Rolling Stones.

Q & A WITH ATTORNEY JEFF COHEN

Jeff Cohen is the publisher of *Music Biz* magazine, an educational publication for both musicians and industry executives. He is also a partner in the law firm Millen, White, Zelano, and Branigan, where he heads up the firm's trademark, copyright, and entertainment practice. In this interview, Jeff discusses some important aspects of band membership agreements such as band names and trademarks, the common misconceptions regarding band agreements and disputes, and the basics of business entities such as partnerships and corporations.

Upon a group's signing of a recording agreement, the record company usually insists that the group draft a band member agreement addressing internal issues such as ownership of the band name. Even with a written band agreement, disputes will arise. Nevertheless, an agreement makes resolving group problems much easier and can potentially save the band hundreds of thousands of dollars in court and legal fees. As part of a preliminary agreement, a group may concede to resolve all disputes outside the courts.

Q: How important is it for a newly formed band to have a written band membership agreement that stipulates the terms of their relationship?

J.C.: A written agreement is obviously important for any band. It helps to explain, sadly enough, what would transpire should a problem between them occur. The reality is, though, that most younger bands will not have a written agreement. They simply don't want to spend the time or the effort to do so. What usually happens is [that] at the time someone in the industry (such as a record label) expresses an interest in the band, the group will hire an attorney to define the specific terms of their relationship, either through a written partnership, corporation, or an LLC agreement, which will all be touched on later.

Q: Some bands are already considered a partnership without even knowing it. Can you briefly discuss partnerships?

J.C.: Under partnership law, as long as two or more people (such as a band) come together and are willing to share in the profits and losses of their business, they already are a partnership. Without a written agreement, though, they would have to rely on the partnership laws of their particular state should a problem or dispute occur. State partnership laws vary, but most states have adapted a baseline that makes certain presumptions under law. For example, if a group does not have a written agreement that stipulates otherwise, all members may be presumed to have an equal right to the profits and financial losses of the band, an equal say in making decisions, the rights to use the band name should they decide to leave the group, and liability for the other member's negligence while conducting business. Though most groups are usually mature in wanting to share in the profits and losses equally, some people may want to break up the relationship based on their individual feelings. The earlier these issues can be addressed in a written agreement, the better off they will be in the long run.

> The most important time to file a DBA, also called an FBN (fictional business name), is when you're receiving payment under a fictitious name. In other words, if a club owner is writing checks out to your band's name rather than to the name of an individual in the band, you need to file a DBA. A DBA shows proof that you're an authorized representative of the band. Without proof, you cannot walk into a bank and cash the check.

Q: Are there any required state or local filings when setting up a new partnership? Does a band need to file a DBA (doing business as)?

J.C.: Every state is really unique when it comes to partnerships. I suggest that you either find someone to assist you or research the matters yourself so that you are perfectly sure that you're abiding by the laws of the state in which the band is located.

As far as filing a DBA, some states do require a mandatory "fictitious business name" statement; but again, it's state dependent and I'd hate to drive your readers crazy. The truth is that 99 percent of all young bands never file a DBA. I've never seen a band arrested or fined for it. It's an issue, but it's really a non-issue in my opinion.

Q: Besides deciding on how the percentage shares of a group's revenue will be divided, ownership and control of a band's name is one of the most important aspects of a band membership agreement, especially when considering departing members. What is the normal policy for leaving members' rights (or non-rights) to a group's name?

J.C.: There should be a clause in every band's agreement explaining where the ownership rights and control in a name reside. For many of the agreements that are drafted, the band's name is held by the group itself so that none of the departing members have permission to utilize it. Should the entire group fall apart, any member requesting the name would be able to use it as long as all of the departed members gave permission and signed off on it. It's entirely contract dependent, though. If you have no agreement, the partnership laws of the state may allow each member, even departed members, the right to use it. It's possible that each departed member of a band simultaneously use the

> Pink Floyd, Deep Purple, the Byrds, and Buffalo Springfield are all popular groups who have had disputes with former members over the use of their band name. For instance, when Buffalo Springfield's drummer left the band, he reorganized the group under the same name. The original members all ruled him a "phony" in the press. He was able to successfully use the band name for some time, but eventually a judge ruled that the name was held as an asset of the original partnership, and should only be used to identify the original group. Needless to say, this cost everyone a lot of money. In a more recent case, Stephen Pearcy (former vocalist of the group Ratt) was ordered by a Los Angeles court that he could no longer tour under the name "Ratt featuring Stephen Pearcy." Pearcy was also ordered to turn over all profits earned during his unauthorized tour.

band name on their own. The issue, however, may come down to a messy and expensive lawsuit as to which member is defrauding the public, the argument being that one or two key members are the identity of the group, and anyone else using it is defrauding the public. Needless to say, this can still cost thousands of dollars to prove in a court of law.

Q: Just because an individual band member thinks up a group's name, it does not necessarily give him or her jurisdiction to ownership. Can you elaborate?

J.C.: The issue is not who thought up a band name, but rather who is commercially exploiting the name. Trademarks are based on usage in commerce. Therefore, if a member comes into a band with a name that he intends to keep, it behooves him to make sure that the band agreement represents that it's really his asset—that he's only loaning the band the name and at no time is the band entitled to assert any rights of ownership.

Q: Most bands don't realize that their name is automatically trademarked as soon as they publicly perform their music live, sell their CDs, or commercially exploit their name by some other means. The rights, however, are limited to the geographical area in which the name is being used. At what time should a band apply for federal trademark registration, and how can a band conduct a search to make sure their band name is not already being used?

J.C.: The purpose of registering with the federal government is to provide a band with nationwide protection. Is registration priority one for a young band? I would suggest spending their money on other things until they get to the level where they are sure the name is going to be exploited at the national level and the band may break, such as when they are preparing to sign a record deal. At that time, the band could conduct a thorough name search by either hiring a professional trademark searching company, or an attorney who is well versed in the area of trademarks.

Another good time to apply for federal trademark protection is when using the Internet to contact fans or to sell merchandise outside your state. Registration provides nationwide protection. As of the writing of this book, the fee for federal trademark registration is $245. Foreign registration is recommended only when your band is having success on the international scale. Registration laws and fees differ from country to country and are beyond the scope of this book. When you're reaching international success, contact your attorney.

In the meantime, if you want to conduct a limited search yourself, you can utilize the United States Patent and Trademark office's website at www.uspto.gov. Here, you can search at the federal level, but not at the state level. The problem with this is that you cannot find the bands that have not yet registered. As previously mentioned, a trademark is automatically established by usage. Therefore, you may later find out that there are a number of bands that have already been using the same name, and have limited rights to the small geographical area where they've played or sold material.

Another way that you can conduct a limited search is by looking through the *Billboard International Touring Directory*. The Directory, which can be found in your local library or book store, has a listing of all touring bands. You might also try looking through local music publications that sometimes provide lists of unsigned groups, or search record store shelves to see if someone else is already using your band name. All you can do is conduct the best search possible before registering. Contact the US Patent and Trademark office for more information and for current registration charges and registration procedures.

Q: Getting back to band agreements, what legal recourse can a musician take if he or she is kicked out of a band that has no written agreement?

J.C.: It really depends whether that person has rights as a songwriter in the material. There may be some real valuable rights they can attach, too. For example, if the band is unsigned, and the departed member is the sole writer of a composition, then he or she holds the rights of first-use for commercial release on phonorecord. If the departed member is a co-writer of a song, then each of the writers must agree on the first commercial release and license their own shares distinctly. If the band is already signed and has a record out that includes compositions in which the departed member participated in writing, then he or she is naturally entitled to their share of generated income. Needless to say, the band would likely have a written band membership agreement at this time in their careers anyway.

The other big question is whether the departed member has any rights in the band name. They would have to look at the state partnership law to determine their rights.

If there are any assets purchased by the band, such as equipment, or otherwise any leftover debts incurred as a band, all matters may have to immediately be resolved.

In any case, I would certainly suggest that whatever it is the person has lost, they pursue getting it back. The norm for groups that are unsigned, though, is that the person that ends up getting kicked out simply moves on and does something new, because the band assets are very limited and are not worth pursuing. When a band is signed, however, the departed member typically continues to get his or her percentage from past activities (such as record royalties), but not on future activities.

Q: I've heard many stories where band leaders have pressured musicians into signing agreements against their will. Is it true that in a court of law, a contract can be considered void if one of the parties claims they did not understand what they were signing? Take the example of Steven Adler from Guns N' Roses. A court ruled that because he was strung out on drugs at the time of signing the terms of his termination, the agreement was invalid. Can you elaborate?

J.C.: As you pointed out, Steven was able to claim that drugs caused him not to think clearly and therefore the terms of his termination agreement were ruled invalid. The chances of something like this happening again, however, are so slight that invariably you are going to be held accountable. Nobody is putting a gun to your head and asking you to sign something, and nobody is suggesting that you don't have the opportunity to retain the services of an attorney. It's always your prerogative to walk away from a situation.

So the answer to this story is, if you feel pressured to sign an agreement and you feel uncomfortable with it, you better understand the terms first. The reality is that you're going to be held accountable for whatever you sign and agree on—unless, of course, you decide to take a lot of drugs!

Q: For most non-attorneys, writing a contract is like building an airplane in your basement. It might fly, but you won't know what important parts you left out until it crashes and burns. That said, does a band need to have an attorney present when putting together the basic terms of a band membership or partnership agreement?

J.C.: Obviously I'm uncomfortable with any non-professional putting together an agreement because they may have left out important aspects. I will cautiously say, however, that there are a number of adequate resources available in book stores that contain plenty of band membership agreements. As long as the parties are capable of understanding what a clause means, or contacting someone that can explain it to them, then I'm not as uncomfortable with it.

Q: An important part of a band membership agreement is how the band will make decisions (such as by unanimous or majority vote). Can a band agree to have a unanimous vote for some issues and a majority vote for others? Also, what usually happens in the case of a deadlock. Who is usually the tie-breaker?

J.C.: On significant issues, such as hiring a personal manager, a band may want to have an agreement where it's a unanimous decision. On the other issues, such as expenditures or making decisions about merchandise, things that might be considered less important but more peripheral, a band may want to decide on a majority vote. Majority votes work well when you have an odd number of people in a band, but when you have an even number, the question is, what do you do if there's a deadlock vote? You want to appoint an objective third party, such as a personal manager, to be the tie-breaker.

Q: In a band membership agreement, is it helpful to define the services that each member will be providing to the band? On the other hand, is it helpful to define the grounds on which a member can be fired, such as not fulfilling his or her obligations to the band?

J.C.: I do believe it's helpful to define the services that each member will provide to the band, but I'm not overwhelmed with it. I think it's simple enough to say that each member is going to provide their undivided attention to creating and performing music. On the other hand, though, I think that it is very important to define the parameters of when one can be fired from the band, and a procedure to allow the person being accused of misconduct to potentially cure it. You can't just willy nilly dump somebody. The well-developed contract will have a cure provision granting a person the chance to correct their mistakes within a 30 to 45 day period. For instance, 35 days after the drummer has not chosen to go into a detox center, and within three months thereafter if he is not cleaned up, then the band may terminate his agreement. Another instance may be if a member repeatedly fails to show up for rehearsals in connection with a tour. Notification goes out to the member in writing saying that given the contract itself, they have an obligation to make it to practices. If they fail over the next thirty-five days to make it to rehearsals, then that member can be terminated. Actually, your question dovetails nicely. Once the definitions of responsibilities are defined, and a member fails at fulfilling these obligations, then that person can be held accountable.

Q: What does it take to change the terms of a band membership agreement once it has actually been established?

J.C.: There should be an amendment clause in a band membership agreement that stipulates what type of vote it will take to change the terms. Once again, for more significant terms, aspects of unanimity might apply. For less significant terms, a majority vote might be sufficient. Without an amendment clause in your agreement though, state partnership law says it would take a unanimous vote to change all terms.

Q: A band can save thousands of dollars in legal and court fees by signing a preliminary band agreement stipulating all disputes will be resolved in mediation or arbitration. Can you please explain both methods?

J.C.: Mediation is when an appointed third party, such as an attorney, is brought in to help a band resolve its disputes. Arbitration is similar to mediation, only the appointed third party decides on the outcome of the dispute. I'm not a huge fan of arbitration or mediation because you don't allow yourself the opportunity to present your issues to a court. Having said that, if you think mediation or arbitration will work, then you can include this in your band membership agreement.

Q: Under state partnership law, each member is liable for the other members' negligence while conducting business. If one member gets into a fight with a bar owner and is sued, the partnerships' assets as well as the personal assets of each member in the band are at risk. Have you found that including an indemnification clause in a band membership agreement is important?

J.C.: You can include a clause in your band membership agreement saying that if certain behavior is considered to be damaging or negligent to the band, then that person stands independent and the band is not responsible for their actions. To be clear, though, all members of the band will still have to pay out if successfully sued, but then they can turn to the offending party and request [that] the money . . . be paid back. So is it really a solution? It is, but the problem is that the person you have to collect the money from will probably be bankrupt himself. Keep in mind that none of this would be an issue if a band [were] incorporated, because only the assets of the corporation could be grabbed, not the personal assets of each member.

Q: As you mentioned earlier, a partnership requires minimal set up and is also relatively easy to run. At what point does it make the most sense for a band to form their own corporation or LLC, and why?

J.C.: As I just pointed out, a partnership has unlimited personal liability. If sued, each partner's personal assets can be at risk. If the band is in the genre of music where there's a lot of energy and there's a high possibility for serious injuries in the mosh pit, then a partnership can be a potential disaster.

The benefit of forming a corporation is that it is treated as a separate legal entity. Your personal assets are not at risk. Corporations are also entitled to certain tax advantages that partnerships are not. Running a corporation, however, requires far more paperwork because you have to file a separate corporate tax return, among other things.

An LLC, or limited liability corporation, is rather a new concept in comparison to the other business entities we've discussed. Like a classic corporation, an LLC limits the liabilities that someone suing you can grab, but the problem is that you can't take advantage of the same tax breaks provided by a classic corporation. The profits and losses of an LLC flow through to the individual members and are filed on their personal tax returns. The good news though, is that an LLC provides for less tax paperwork than a corporation.

> Like an LLC, the profits and losses of a partnership flow through to the individual members. The band is responsible for filing an informational tax return on Federal Partnership Return of Income form 1065 provided by the Internal Revenue Service (IRS), and then each member may have to pay a pro-rated share of the taxes on their individual return.

There's also something called an S corporation that is very similar to an LLC. The entity is treated as a partnership for tax purposes and affords the shareholders a shield from personal liability. This means that at the end of the year, the profit or loss will be accounted for on the shareholder's tax return based on that shareholder's pro-rata share ownership percentage. An S does have certain restrictions that include the number of shareholders and the nature of who those shareholders can be. For the most part, this won't apply to those reading this book. There may also be certain tax benefits you may want to ask your accountant about. An S is a good corporate structure for those aspiring to have a career in the music business and [who] are contemplating opening a business.

So there's really no absolute answer as to which business entity works best for every band. I'd say for baby bands, the partnership works fine in the beginning. As the band begins to make money and wants to protect their assets, the LLC may be the next step. Later, to take advantage of certain tax breaks while continuing to limit their liabilities, a band may look into the classic C or S corporation. An attorney or accountant is always advised to help a band decide what's best for them.

Q: Though I am sure a group will have an attorney at this time, can you briefly discuss how you go about setting up a corporation? What steps should you take, what bureaus do you contact, and how much does it cost?

J.C.: First of all, the smart thing to do is to contact your accountant or attorney to advise you. You have to file articles of incorporation (also called articles of association). Then you have to file an SS4 form with the IRS in order to get a tax payer ID number. This is the number that allows you to open a bank account. Then you need to have an operating agreement, which is like your band membership agreement. This agreement defines who owns the band name, what happens if a member leaves, and what shares each individual has in the company.

Corporations are not terribly expensive to set up, but it really differs from state to state. In California, it costs approximately $100 for the initial paperwork with an annual payment of $800. Keep in mind, you also have fees for your attorney and/or accountant. There may also be fees for local business licenses and permits. That's why many people like partnerships at the beginning of their career. Partnerships require very little effort and money to set up.

Q: Unless there is a written agreement stipulating otherwise, as soon as a member leaves a band or is fired, a partnership immediately ends and all debts need to be resolved. The remaining members can choose to continue, but it's considered a new partnership. What is involved in dissolving a classic C corporation or LLC?

J.C.: As indicated, a partnership ends as soon as you snap your fingers and say you're no longer partners. The exception is if the group has an agreement that specifically dictates what will happen if a member leaves and/or if another member is added.

On the other hand, dissolving an LLC and a corporation involves so much more. For example, a corporation can exist forever unless the shareholders vote to end it or if it cannot exist financially. It's more than likely that you'll have a team of advisors at this stage of the game anyway. Again, the recommended course of action would be to contact your attorney or accountant.

Q: When each member of a band is signed to a recording agreement, what obligation does the leaving member have to the record company? Please discuss the "leaving member clause" in recording agreements and how it can affect the profits and losses of both the band and the departed member.

J.C.: Up until now, we've mostly been discussing internal issues between band members. A leaving member clause is actually between the record company and the departing member. The record label will want to latch on to the leaving members' new career, and in a sense, almost all of the contract provisions of the existing contract will apply. More importantly, that leaving member could get swamped with the fact that they still owe hundreds of thousands of dollars from their previous band, which will carry over to their new band. Even worse, if the existing band stays together when a member leaves, they will be responsible for any new debts the solo artist incurs to the record label. Usually what happens, though, is that the band is able to negotiate that only a pro-rated share of all debts apply. For instance, if there are four people in a band, and one person leaves to start a new group, that person is only responsible for one-fourth of the existing debt. Conversely, the existing band will only be responsible for one-forth of the solo artist's new debt.

Keep in mind that the record company may also exercise their right to drop a band when a member leaves. In theory, they feel the original group they signed has been altered, and therefore they have the right to drop the band. However, if a key member provision is in place identifying the persons most vital to the functioning of the band, then the record company can only terminate the contract when these members leave the band. Usually the key members are the main songwriter or lead singer of the band.

In some cases, a non key-member or minority partner may not even be signed to the record company. These members are essentially free to leave and start their own group without any obligation to the record label. In most cases, though, the record company will want the rights to all leaving members, key member or not.

Q: Is there anything else that you would like to add (e.g., additional resources, suggestions, etc.) that would further educate musicians on the subjects covered in this interview?

J.C.: Don Passman's book *All You Need to Know About the Music Business* is a good choice. Also Richard Schullenberg's book *Legal Aspects of the Music Industry*.

BAND MEMBERSHIP AGREEMENTS: KEY POINTS IN REVIEW

✦ *Voting*: How will the members vote on key issues—by unanimous or majority vote? Depending on the seriousness of the matter, such as the hiring and firing of members, different issues can require a different vote. In case of a deadlock, one person can be appointed as the tie-breaker.

✦ *Division of income:* How will the profits and losses be split between band members? Although most bands usually split income equally (at least in the beginning), sometimes the main songwriters or founders of the band are allotted a larger share.

✦ *Purchases*: What vote will permit the band to make equipment purchases? As an example, an investment under $250 may require a majority vote, while a purchase over $500 may require a unanimous vote.

✦ *Investments and debts:* What happens to the assets acquired as a group when one member departs or is terminated? Usually, all debts need to be resolved immediately. For equipment already owned, the band may buy out the departed member's share.

✦ *Band name:* In the event that a member is fired or quits, or in the event that the band breaks up, who has the right to use the band name? Usually a band will agree that any departing or terminated member has no right to use the name. In case the band breaks up, and one member wants to use the name, everyone must sign off on it.

✦ *Hiring and firing:* Hiring a manager may require a unanimous vote. Firing a band member may require a majority vote. A band may also want to stipulate the conditions under which a band member may be terminated—for instance, not fulfilling his or her obligations to the band.

✦ *Obligations*: A band may want to list what is expected of each member in the band, such as first priority over outside work, showing up to rehearsals, etc.

✦ *Quitting*: A member may be able to leave if he or she is unhappy, as long as it is not in the middle of a tour, or in other situations in which the band may incur a loss as a result.

✦ *Departed members' rights to profits*: A departed member will continue to earn their share of income on work in which they were involved, but not on new work by the band.

✦ *Amendment of agreement*: What kind of vote can change the terms of the agreement? Usually a band will choose a majority vote.

✦ *Arbitration or mediation*: How will disputes be settled? Rather than incurring excessive fees in the courts, a band may choose mediation or arbitration as a more practical alternative.

✦ *Term:* The term of the agreement may be for one to two years.

✦ *Signature and date*: All members must sign and date the agreement.

CHAPTER 3
Contract Employment or Self-Employment

W e've all heard the stories about young musicians who watched the Beatles perform on the *Ed Sullivan Show,* and from that point forward wanted to be in a band just like John, Paul, George, and Ringo. But what almost every aspiring musician comes to realize is that being in a band is not easy. It requires years of hard work and sacrifice, and even after that, there are no guarantees of a big pay-off! This is one of the reasons many musicians resort to hiring out their services in return for a sure and immediate paycheck. Musicians who choose to do such work are contract employees or self-employed performers.

Generally speaking, the term contract employee refers to anyone who agrees to work on a long-term, continuing basis under a set of conditions usually specified by a contract; such situations include working with a regularly touring and recording act, or with a house band for a national television show such as *Conan O'Brien* or *Saturday Night Live.* A self-employed performer, or independent contractor, is essentially anyone who makes his or her services available for hire for shorter-term relationships. For instance, after a musician finishes performing one gig for which he or she has been hired as an independent contractor, such as over-dubbing a solo on another musician's record or sitting in with a band for one night at a local club, he or she moves on to the next job. This requires a bit more hustling for work than being a contract employee, but as long as the phone keeps ringing, independent contractors do just fine.

Keep in mind that the distinction between contract employees and independent contractors is not always so black and white; the distinction is really only important when you are dealing with business issues such as taxes and workers' compensation insurance. But we'll get to those issues in more detail later in this chapter.

The most important thing to grasp is that, whether you're a contract employee or an independent contractor, *you're in the business of you!* You have no claim in the organizations for which you work, no share in the band's future profits (such as record royalties, publishing royalties, or merchandising monies), and for that matter, no real security in your job. You're simply hired to perform a service for a set fee. For this reason, it's your responsibility to understand your rights as a working musician, and to make sure you're compensated fairly for each and every job you perform. "What rights and fair treatment?" you might ask. "Aren't all musicians just happy to be working, regardless of what they're being paid and how they're being treated?" You may feel this way early in your career, while you're still paying your dues, but if you ever expect music to be your livelihood, then eventually you'll have to adopt a more professional outlook.

UNIONS PROTECTING ACTIVE MUSICIANS

Many aspiring artists don't know what music unions do, let alone even realize they exist. You should know that both the American Federation of Musicians (AFM) and The American Federation of Radio and Television Artists (AFTRA) were specifically established to secure and enforce fair wages and good working conditions for musicians. Additionally, the AFM and AFTRA provide a variety of benefits packages as well as health and retirement funds to their members. Though the music business may often seem like the Wild West, with no apparent guidelines, regulations, or support for musicians, these unions may offer some hope! Regardless of whether or not becoming a union member makes sense at this point in your career, you'll find the information provided here extremely useful.

The American Federation of Musicians

Founded in 1897, the American Federation of Musicians is one of the oldest entertainment labor organizations in existence today. Like any other labor union, the AFM is based on the idea that through "strength in numbers," or as they put it, "collective empowerment," musicians will have a stronger voice in the workplace. The AFM is 120,000 members strong and includes artists from every field of musical endeavor. Bruce Springsteen is an AFM member, so are the guys in Bon Jovi; Paul Shaffer and the whole CBS Orchestra, and Kevin Eubanks and *The Tonight Show* band. Metallica are members booked on AFM contracts, and so is Aerosmith. The list of famous AFM members could fill this book.

> Contact the AFM at (800) 762-3444 or at www.afm.org.

The AFM has 360 branch offices, called "locals," in cities throughout the United States and Canada. These include The Professional Musicians Union Local 47 of Los Angeles and The Associated Musicians Local 802 of Greater New York City. Since each local is run autonomously, the benefits they offer may fluctuate slightly from branch to branch, depending on its membership strength. The following information outlines the major benefits of joining the union, requirements for joining and receiving certain benefits, and considerations as to why joining the union may not be right for you. There's a lot of information to digest here, but keep in mind that a representative at your local is always available to answer any questions that you may have.

Major Union Benefits. Though the AFM provides a variety of benefits to its members, the most significant of them is the bargaining they do with thousands of employers—record companies, broadcasting and cable companies, motion pictures companies, theaters, symphony managements, circuses, and theme parks—to establish fair wages, good working conditions, and fringe benefits for their members. The union enforces these rules and regulations, and collects payment defaults by the employer when necessary. Some of the specific situations unions regulate include:

- ✦ Live performances, including performance rehearsals, cartage (the cost of transporting your equipment), travel expenses (such as air travel and hotels), travel time (the time it takes to go back and fourth from each gig), personal mileage on your vehicle (when using your own car or van to get back and forth to gigs), per diems (daily allowances for food), and holiday payment scales (for performing on New Year's Eve and other holidays)
- ✦ Recording sessions, including major label recording sessions and some smaller label sessions, as well as live concert recordings
- ✦ Television and radio performances, including all commercial advertisements
- ✦ Video taping, including live concert performances, promotional video shoots such as for MTV and VH1, and performances on live television such as *The Tonight Show, Conan O'Brien, Saturday Night Live,* and *Late Night with David Letterman*
- ✦ Motion picture performances, including on-camera appearances (for instance, the filming of a bar or concert scene in a movie), and off-camera appearances (for instance, a studio recording for a movie sound track)

UNION TO THE RESCUE. A group of ska musicians from Los Angeles who had only been in the union around three months played a New Year's Eve gig in Florida and drove there to do it. The group received a bad check for the show, and their van broke down in Texas on the way home. They got in touch with the AFM, who was able to pursue their claim, help them get their van fixed, and coordinate the whole mess through Local 23 in San Antonio, Texas. Though the band had to endure a lecture from the union about their poor business practices, they seemed to actually welcome it—after all, they were no longer stranded thousands of miles from home. The promoter subsequently settled up on the bad check, by the way. The AFM pursues claims less dramatic than this all over the country every day.

In another instance, an artist who performed with her band on *Late Night with David Letterman* believed that since her musicians were being paid by Letterman's television production company via the union, she wasn't responsible for paying them for the job as well. She was wrong; under the Collective Bargaining Agreement for Video Taping, the American Federation of Musicians stipulates that musicians shall receive payment when taped for television appearances. This fee is in addition to the standard wage musicians should receive from their employer for a live performance. As it turned out, all of the musicians in the artist's band were paid. Note: Musicians are also paid "re-use" payments for reruns of a taped performance. The AFM monitors, collects, and pays musicians for these uses.

The union also provides health care and retirement benefits for qualifying members. Through the union's health care programs, you will receive medical and hospital benefits (subject to availability at your local branch). If you've ever been sick or injured and incurred costly hospital bills, then you know how important insurance is. Your local may also provide dental plans and prescription drug benefits for qualifying members. And though retirement may seem like a long way off, it's comforting to know that money will be waiting for you—even if you're no longer working in the music business.

Other Union Benefits. Now that you have a good idea of some of the major benefits you get from joining the AFM, lets take a look at some of the other benefits you receive.

- ✦ The AFM will monitor the recordings on which you perform and collect residuals if they're used in film, television, and commercials. These payments are called "new use" payments.
- ✦ Your membership entitles you to the sound recording special fund payments— an additional payment issued to you based on the number of AFM covered recording sessions on which you perform in one year. The special payment fund is made available through annual contributions by record companies and paid out by the union. *Note:* Though the SPF is a benefit provided by the union, *you do not need to be a member to receive these monies.* For more information, call the SPF hotline at 1-866-711-Fund.
- ✦ Your name will be registered in the union's job referral database, offering you new employment opportunities.
- ✦ The AFM provides limited legal supervision and career development to its members.
- ✦ If you have problems on the road, or if you have questions about contracts or what you should be paid, the AFM provides 24-hour telephone assistance.
- ✦ AFM members have access to discounted recording and rehearsal studios.
- ✦ Insurance for theft and damage to your instruments is also provided through membership in the AFM.
- ✦ By joining the AFM, you'll receive travel discounts, health club discounts, credit card options, loan programs, mortgage programs, and more.
- ✦ The AFM also offers you a subscription to the their monthly newspaper, *International Musician,* which will keep you up to date on all industry happenings.

Requirements for Membership. In order to receive all of the AFM benefits we discussed above, now it's time to discuss some of the qualifications you'll need to meet. Note that the rates discussed below are subject to change and vary from one local to another.

- ✦ To become a member, you must pay a one-time registration charge of approximately $200, and about $180 per year in membership fees.
- ✦ Members are required to work "union gigs" only. A union gig means that the person or organization for which you work must be a signatory to the union. Your employer is required to pay you at least the minimum scale wages. Your employer must also report all of the gigs in which you work to the union, and make an additional contribution towards your pension and health care fund.

◆ To qualify for a pension, your employer's contributions (typically 10 percent of the union's suggested minimum scales) must total $1,500 each year for five years. You can begin collecting early retirement benefits at age 55, or you can wait and collect higher benefits at the full retirement age of 65.

Contact the AFM's nationwide pension department at 1-800-833-8065.

◆ To qualify for health care, your employer's contributions must reach a minimum dollar amount, usually within six-month periods (from April to September, and October to March). Since contributions and health benefits vary considerably depending on the job performed and on your local union, contact your local branch office for specific details.

◆ You are required to pay union dues of approximately 2.5 percent of the suggested minimum scale for live performances, and 4 percent of the suggested minimum wage for recording sessions. Contact your branch office for local rates.

◆ You are encouraged to attend monthly local meetings to discuss current union events, to meet other union members, and to offer input for future policy development.

Is Joining the Union Right for You? Now that you have a good idea of what the AFM provides, and what some of the member requirements are, you can decide if joining is right for you. Keep in mind that the union is most beneficial when you're working union gigs often. This is how you'll qualify for the major benefits, such as the health care and pension funds, and receive the union's assistance in collecting payment defaults. However, keep in mind that:

◆ Not all employers are union-affiliated, nor are they willing to comply with union requirements. Note that the union's strengths lie mostly in major venue performances, major label recordings, and television, theater, orchestral, and motion picture work.

◆ It is not considered "good standing" to accept any non-union gig. Though the union is known occasionally to turn a blind eye and allow you to perform non-union gigs, they may still require you to pay dues for the job performed. Unions are known to review performance listings in local magazines to police members who are not complying with this rule. Members that are not in good standing may be subject to expulsion.

◆ The musician's job referral database, made available through the union, has been appraised by many musicians as being not very effective. The competition among members to get the gigs that are offered is fierce, and unless you're calling your local union office 24/7, there aren't too many gigs that will come your way.

There you have it. Regardless of whether or not you feel that it's time to become a member of the AFM, be sure at least to talk to a representative at your local branch. Mark Heter, who heads the Division of Touring, Theatres, Booking Agent Agreements and Immigration Matters for The American Federation of Musicians in New York City, adds these final words:

"Membership is a participatory experience. AFM membership goes beyond paying dues and being taken care of by the union. By joining, you become a vital part of the union itself, and acquire the empowerment to make positive changes in your own life.

MEMBER OR NOT, HERE THEY COME. A contract musician touring with a pop/rock group and earning a weekly salary for his performances encountered a situation in which the group was scheduled to record a live performance for release on phonorecord. The group was not willing to negotiate an additional fee for this recording; the employer felt that the employee's salary covered an unlimited number of services to be determined at their discretion. However, union law provides that all location recordings shall be reported to the AFM prior to such recordings, and that each musician shall receive a rate for each day the recording takes place. Although neither the musician, the band, nor the independent record company (to which the group was signed) were union signatories, the major record label that handled the distribution of the recording was a union signatory. As a result, the independent record label was covered under the major label's agreement, and the musician eventually received compensation with a union representative's assistance. Needless to say, the musician thereafter became a union member.

Membership is a commitment, not only for the member's personal benefit, but towards the betterment of everyone else in the union, to make things better for musicians. There is spiritual and personal satisfaction to be found by becoming engaged in the labor movement. The union is here to serve you."

The American Federation of Radio and Television Artists

The 88,000 member American Federation of Radio and Television Artists (AFTRA) has been representing singers, actors, announcers, and news broadcasters in sound recordings, radio and television programs, and commercials since 1937. AFTRA's headquarters is located in New York City, with 36 branch offices located in major cities throughout the United States. Since some benefits may vary slightly from local to local, it's always wise to contact a local branch near you.

> Contact AFTRA at (212) 532-0800 or www.aftra.com.

Major Union Benefits. AFTRA negotiates with employers to provide fair wages, professional working conditions, and benefits for vocalists in sound recordings, radio and television programs, and commercials. AFTRA enforces recognition of these standards and collects payment defaults and original earnings on behalf of its members. AFTRA also works hard to promote legislation that benefits recording artists on the federal and state level.

> A major distinction between the AFM and AFTRA is that the AFM handles instrumentalists, and AFTRA represents vocalists. This means you could potentially end up being a member of both unions.

In addition, AFTRA offers one of the best health and retirement plans in the business, and depending on your eligibility, it will pay up to $1 million dollars in medical bills and hospital expenses. Through AFTRA's health plan, you may also be eligible for confidential mental health and substance abuse programs, a prescription drug program reimbursing out-of-pocket costs, a dental plan, life and accident insurance, a wellness plan, and discounted life insurance rates. Depending upon your eligibility, AFTRA's retirement fund may pay you an income when you reach retirement age as well.

Other Union Benefits. As if the advantages of joining AFTRA discussed above were not enough, there are more. Below are some of the other benefits you get by becoming an AFTRA member.

◆ AFTRA will track and monitor the recordings on which its members sing. When these recordings are used in new mediums like motion pictures, television, or commercials, AFTRA will collect and pay you residuals.

◆ Under something called AFTRA's "Sound Recording Code," AFTRA members who are also signed recording artists will receive additional health and retirement payments from their record company based on the number of royalties earned (this is whether your record company has recouped its expenses or not).

◆ Members of AFTRA will have access to a professional staff who can answer your questions about contracts and salary minimums. Additionally, there will always be a helpful staff available to assist you in payment disputes and other important issues.

◆ Joining AFTRA also entitles you to new employment opportunities. For instance, AFTRA's local branch offices cater to vocalists in their area by offering job listings, programs to increase your résumé writing skills and audition techniques, and seminars where you can meet potential employers.

◆ By becoming a member of AFTRA, you may be able to qualify for special scholarship programs through the George Heller Memorial Foundation.

◆ AFTRA provides its members with low-fee credit card options, high-yield savings accounts, low-interest loans, and other services offered though The AFTRA/SAG Federal Credit Union.

◆ When joining AFTRA, you will receive a subscription to *AFTRA Magazine*, which will help keep you up to date on various developments in the music industry.

Requirements For Membership. In order to receive the many benefits offered by AFTRA, you'll have to meet a number of qualifications discussed below. Note that some of the rates discussed are subject to change. Be sure to contact a local AFTRA branch office for updated information.

◆ To join AFTRA, you are required to complete an application for membership, fill out an enrollment card, and attach a check for the initiation fees, which are $1200 at the time of this writing. Minimum dues for the first period are $58. Dues are payable every six months (May and November), and are usually based on gross earnings combined from all AFTRA work done in the previous year.

◆ As an AFTRA member, you must be sure that the employer (i.e., the record company, producer, etc.) for whom you are working is a signatory to AFTRA before accepting work. Members who accept non-union gigs are subject to disciplinary action and expulsion. Employers are required to pay minimum scale wages and make contributions to the AFTRA Health & Retirement Fund on the member's behalf.

◆ In order to be covered by AFTRA's major medical and hospitalization, your gross earnings must be at least $7500 within 12 months of beginning work under AFTRA's jurisdiction. For gross earnings over $15,000, you are entitled to dependant medical coverage for family members.

Contact AFTRA's Health and Retirement office at (800) 562-4690.

◆ To qualify for retirement benefits, you must have five years of AFTRA-covered earnings. You must earn $5000 each year, for five years.

Is Joining the Union Right for You? Major benefits of joining AFTRA are eligibility for minimum scale wages and fair treatment from employers. Unfortunately, however, not all employers are union signatories who comply with union requirements. When you accept work from non-union employers, you not only undermine the strength of the union, but also forfeit the benefits of the health care and retirement funds. Even if you only work AFTRA-covered gigs, you must still work a minimum number of gigs to meet the health and retirement requirements listed above.

By speaking with your local AFTRA office, you'll have a better sense of whether joining the union at this time in your career is right for you. One thing is certain—whether you join or not, there are thousands of singers who swear by AFTRA's membership. Jon Joyce, a well-known session singer on recordings, television, jingles, and motion pictures, says: "If there were no such thing as AFTRA today, we would be meeting together to form such a union. It is run for members by members, and AFTRA membership is the best bargain in the business."

Kevin Dorsey, backup singer for top recording artists, adds: "I have been a member of AFTRA for 13 years and currently serve on both the Los Angeles Local and National Board. Whether representing me in the workplace or making me feel at ease knowing that my health and retirement benefits are there, AFTRA has always been with me throughout my career."

Finally, Jevetta Steel, Columbia recording artist, sums things up: "AFTRA is a union united for the good of all artists. AFTRA is the prototype of the future."

NEGOTIATING YOUR EMPLOYMENT AGREEMENT

Regardless of what the AFM and AFTRA have to say about fair treatment and minimum scale wages for musicians, the truth is that there's nothing "fair" in the music business...unless you're referring to the county "fairs" at which aging rock stars end up playing during the course of nostalgia tours in order to pay their rent. All jokes aside, it's no secret that gigs in the music business don't simply grow on trees, and musicians often have to accept whatever gig ever is presented them—bad or good—just to survive. In either case, you should look out for the following things.

Working For Employers With Limited Budgets

As either a contract employee or a self-employed musician, especially early in your career, frequently you'll be offered work that pays substandard wages far below minimum scale. This may be due to your inexperience, or to an employer's greed, or to a group's financial restrictions (i.e., a limited budget). When you accept employment from an employer who has a limited budget, there are really no fairness guidelines, but you should at least establish that your pay will increase when the group starts to make more money. This is especially important if you're a contract employee working with one employer on a regular basis. Otherwise, you may continue to be paid the same low fee

SINGING THE BLUES! A group of musicians agreed to work with an up-and-coming blues guitarist for a minimal fee of $275 per week, due to the guitarist's limited budget. As the tour progressed, the guitarist's new record began to do extremely well. In no time, the group was performing in larger venues with the Rolling Stones, Aerosmith, and appearing on national television shows such as *The Tonight Show.* The guitarist was now earning substantially more and could afford to pay his musicians comparable union scale. When the group requested a raise (which was only fair), they were replaced on the following tour with musicians who were "hungry" and looking for a break. This "burn and turn" philosophy is unfortunately used by a lot of employers in the music business in order to avoid paying their musicians higher fees. Taking this type of shrewd thinking one step further, Chuck Berry has never hired permanent musicians to go out on the road with him. Instead, he uses pick-up musicians (willing to work for cheap) in every city of his scheduled tour, who rehearse his material prior to his arrival.

in spite of the group's newfound success and subsequent profits. It's common sense to establish that safeguard.

Working for Employers With Larger Budgets

The day will eventually come when you're asked to work with successful and reputable employers who are willing to pay fairly and offer special perks—even greater than the minimum scales and treatment suggested by the union. But after adapting an "anything goes" approach to business for so long in your formative years, you may end up undercutting yourself in these new and potentially advantageous situations. To avoid that, you need to understand what you may be entitled to. The following discussion sheds light on your wages, per diems, retainers, equipment, equipment techs, buy outs, and much more. Keep in mind that the agreement you're able to negotiate here as either a contract employee or as an independent contractor is substantially influenced by your reputation and experience, and/or how badly a potential employer may want to work with you.

Wages. The wages you can expect from employers that have larger budgets will naturally be much greater than the compensation offered from employers with limited budgets. For instance, in 2001 the Backstreet Boys paid a relatively unknown horn player a weekly salary of $4000 to tour (which is a far cry from the $250 salary our blues artist friend was paid in the previous text box). Session musicians sometimes get paid double or triple the union minimum scale (known as "double scale" or "triple scale") to record an album or to overdub a solo. When negotiating your fee, take notice of the strength of the record company for whom you're recording, the capacity of the venue in which you are playing, the time of year in which you're working (such as on a national holiday), and the length of the tour on which you may be embarking. Consider other factors as well: How much work will you be giving up to take on a new job? What are your personal monthly bills? How much will you net after your basic expenses? How long will you be able to survive financially after the completion of a tour? Sometimes an employer may be willing to guarantee you a flat salary to cover your services for an entire year. For instance, in 1999 one drummer earned an annual salary of $100,000 while working with one of the greatest rock groups in the world—sorry, their identity must be left anonymous. Though these situations may be rare, it pays to be sure that all of your obligations (e.g., rehearsals, recording, and touring) are clearly outlined in your agreement with the band.

Rehearsals. You've probably been participating in rehearsals with little or no pay for years, but employers with larger budgets will typically compensate you for rehearsals in preparation for "phonograph" recording sessions, single live performances, and extended tours. The amount will vary between employers, but minimum compensation of $90 for a two-and-a-half hour rehearsal is not uncommon.

Per Diems. Per diems (PDs) are standard in the industry, and negotiating a reasonable PD is usually not too difficult. A per diem is a daily allowance for food. The amount varies greatly, but can range anywhere from $50 to $200 per day. Keep in mind that if you're performing a gig out of the country, your per diem should be adjusted to reasonably accommodate the exchange rate.

Buy Outs. In addition to receiving a "per diem," employers with larger budgets may offer you money in something called a "buy out." A buy out occurs when the concert promoter does not fulfill his or her contractual obligation to provide food and drink back stage. This obligation is stipulated in a band "rider," a contractual addendum in live performance contracts which also includes lighting and sound requirements for the group, dressing room accommodations, and security needs. For one reason or another, a promoter may not be able to provide the requested food, so he "buys" the band "out." A buy out is based on the number of people traveling with the band; a group may provide you with additional funds ranging from $15 to $50 per buy out (and more). There are cases where musicians receive hundreds of dollars in buy outs over the course of a tour. The amount is subject to the individual situation.

Equipment. Musical equipment is another important factor to consider when arranging your deal with an employer. Instruments and protective travel cases may be provided via your employer's

ISN'T THERE AN EASIER WAY? Rather than be hired as an employee, isn't it possible to become a *member* of a band that's already established and successful, earn an equal share of the future profits, and live happily ever after? Though anything is possible, it's not very likely! You may hear of auditions for slots in successful acts, but what usually happens when established bands make personnel changes is that they simply hire you as an employee and pay out a flat salary. For instance, Paul Stanley and Gene Simmons of KISS employed guitarist Bruce Kulick and drummer Eric Singer to be in their band for a modest annual salary. After a few years of working with KISS, both Kulick and Singer were simply dismissed when the original members Ace Frehley and Peter Criss were asked to rejoin the band. By the way, both Frehley and Criss are now treated as employees of the band.

recording and/or tour budgets. For instance, a musician hired to play drums on a band's record negotiated to have the group pay for the rental of high-quality drums for the session. In another situation, a drummer needed heavy duty travel cases for an upcoming European tour, so the group paid over $3000 to have the cases custom built. When he parted ways with the band, they offered him the option of purchasing the gear.

Equipment Endorsements. Your employer may cover minor equipment expenses for maintenance or usage of items such as guitar picks, guitar strings, amplifier tubes, drumsticks, and drum skins. If your employer doesn't cover the cost of these expenses, you may try to obtain sponsorship from a variety of equipment manufacturers if your group is already successful or gaining additional exposure from radio play and record sales. Most companies will begin your relationship by offering you a reduced price on equipment (usually 60 to 70 percent off the retail price). If you're currently working regularly for a very large and successful organization, some companies may offer you free equipment and advertise your name and likeness with their product.

> Endorsements are not limited to just musical equipment. In 1998, Korn signed a deal with Puma athletic gear for a reported "six figures." But note that these types of corporate sponsorship are not common and are usually reserved for artists who sell millions of records.

Develop as many relationships with manufacturers as possible, but focus on companies whose products you truly desire; a company will want to know that you're not just looking for free equipment. Introduce yourself in a telephone call or at trade shows such as the annual National Association of Music Merchants (NAMM conventions). Send manufacturers your recent record releases, updated tour "itineraries" (i.e., performance dates and locations), performance reviews, and magazine articles.

Bill Zildjian, vice president of the Sabian cymbal company, offers this advice: "Show manufacturers that you are attracting attention from the community,

> Contact NAMM at (760) 438-8001 or at www.namm. com.

especially from the demographic of fans between the ages of 18 to 24. This age group is more likely to buy manufacturer's products, and that makes manufacturers happy!"

Equipment Techs. The care and maintenance of your musical equipment is critical, both in the recording studio and out on the road. When you're working for employers with larger budgets, they may hire studio techs to tune and maintain your equipment when recording. On a tour, road techs are usually hired to handle the setup of your musical equipment and to ensure its proper functioning before a concert performance. Techs also help during a performance when a guitar string or drum head breaks, a vocal mike needs to be replaced, or a cord is accidentally pulled out of an amplifier. At the end of the night, techs are responsible for breaking down musical equipment and making sure that it's loaded in the vans, trucks, or buses. A tech adds to the professionalism of a tour by allowing musicians to concentrate on their principle job at hand—performing. Should an employer fail to provide you with a tech, negotiate your fee accordingly so that you can afford to hire one yourself. (Note: Whomever ends up providing an equipment tech, know that if your musical equipment is lost or damaged on the road (e.g., if an amplifier is dropped from a truck or a guitar is left at the last gig), the group's organization or, in some cases, the venue in which you are performing should cover the repair or replacement costs under their own insurance coverage.

Travel and Lodging. Although your employer will generally cover or reimburse you for air travel costs and lodging, the quality of service is usually uncertain. Employers with larger budgets may take more care in providing the best possible travel and hotel accommodations; you may be provided with first class airline tickets and/or single hotel room accommodations. Though this may seem unimportant, after being out on the road for several months, your comfort can mean the world to you. Whether you receive this type of special treatment or not depends on your employer, but keep in mind that it does exist. (Note: Hotel "incidentals" such as phone calls, room service fees, and movie rentals are your responsibility. So be careful! Incidentals can add up quickly—especially telephone and on-line costs.) Employers with larger budgets also pay for the costs for traveling to gigs in or around your hometown. Reimbursable expenses include mileage on your car, cartage (the costs of transporting heavy or multiple pieces of musical equipment), and parking expenses. Check with your local union to see what else you can have covered in your agreement with an employer.

Employers typically purchase airline tickets for you, but be sure to personally register with the frequent flyer programs offered by most major airlines. You'll be surprised at the mileage you can rack up and the number of free flights you can earn over the years. These tickets can come in handy for personal use, but more importantly, they can come in handy when you have an opportunity to audition for an act that may be 3,000 miles away. Make sure to register your name with every available airline and keep updated records of the mileage you earn.

Special Clothing. If specific clothing that is not "standard" or "ordinary" is required for a promotional video shoot, stage show, or tour, the group will usually reimburse you for the cost of that clothing. For instance, one musician was allotted $500 to buy clothes for a video shoot that only lasted a day. The artist and video director specifically wanted the band and dancers to dress in black, studded leather pants (in case you're wondering, the shoot was for a hardcore rap artist). Keep in mind that the amount of money you're offered depends on the specifics of each individual situation.

Retainers. In times of temporary unemployment, such as during a break in a tour schedule, employers with larger budgets may provide you with additional benefits such as a "retainer." A retainer enables you to maintain an income while your services are on hold. You are expected to be more-or-less on call and are thus limited or excluded from taking on other work. A retainer is usually 50 percent of your weekly salary. Retainers are most common when you're working regularly for one artist.

UNDERSTANDING YOUR TAXES: UNCLE SAM'S CUT

Contact the Internal Revenue Service at (800) 829-1040, (800) Tax Form, or at www.irs.gov.

Taxes may not be the most exciting topic, but they are something all of us have to deal with eventually. As I mentioned earlier, here's where the distinction between contract employees and those who are self-employed (i.e., working on a freelance basis) is especially important. Why? Because the Internal Revenue Service treats contract employees and self-employed individuals differently, and the difference in taxes can be substantial.

Contract Employment

If you're a contract employee in an ongoing working relationship, then your employer is responsible for deducting taxes from your paycheck. But if you're wondering why your pay (after taxes) ends up being significantly less by the time you receive your check, then here's some information you'd better know. Remember, this is your money were talking about here, so listen up!

Income Taxes. Income taxes make up the largest portion of your total annual tax bill, which can consist of federal, state, and/or local income taxes. You are required to pay these taxes on business income and on other compensation, such as wages, a portion of per diems, etc., for services rendered. Your employer is responsible for withholding these taxes—indicated on your paycheck as FITW, SITW and/or local tax withholdings—from your pay. Keep in mind that the amount withheld only represents an estimate of the taxes you owe, and is based in part on the information that you provide on federal tax form "W4" (and the state equivalent) as to whether you are single or married, have children, own a home, etc. You should complete and turn in a W4 form to your employer at the time your employment begins. If you have any questions about completing this form, your employer should provide you with assistance, or you can contact the Internal Revenue Service (see p. 75).

Social Security and Medicare. Employers are also required to withhold social security and medicare taxes—indicated on your paycheck as FICA-OASDI and FICA-HI withholding, respectively—from your pay. In general, these taxes provide retirement and health insurance for people over 65. The social security tax you pay is 6.2 percent of your income, up to a maximum of $80,400 (for the 2001 tax year). The medicare tax you pay is 1.45 percent with no limit on your income.

Contact the Social Security Administration at (800) 772-1213 or at www.ssa.gov.

State Unemployment Taxes/Insurance. In addition, state unemployment taxes/insurance, normally indicated on your paycheck as SUI, must be withheld from your pay by your employer, except for those employers who reside in Alaska, Florida, Nevada, Texas, South Dakota, Washington, and Wyoming. These taxes provide benefits to employees who are laid off or are between seasonal work (e.g., touring). Eligibility for state unemployment benefits is based on a specific minimum amount of dollars withheld by your employer for taxes during a specified period of time. Because laws vary from state to state, it's important to contact your State Disability Department to make sure you qualify for assistance. If you're unemployed, be sure to contact them immediately. A little extra cash can come in handy until you resume work.

State Disability Insurance. Employers who reside in California, Hawaii, New Jersey, New York, and Rhode Island must withhold state disability insurance—normally indicated as SDI—from your paycheck as well. State disability insurance provides benefits if you are injured on or off the job, or if you become sick or pregnant. If you're unable to work for several months due to an injury, disability insurance can be a lifesaver. Your employer is required to provide you with information about both state unemployment and disability insurance at the time of your employment.

Year End Reporting. At the end of the year, your employer will issue you tax form "W2," which indicates both your total income and the total amount of taxes withheld from your paycheck during the calendar year. This form must be issued by your employer no later than January 31st (following the tax year). After reporting your total taxable income and the applicable taxes withheld from it on your returns, you must then attach Form W2 to your returns and send both to the Internal Revenue Service and/or state tax authorities. In general, the last date to file your tax return is April 15th (after the end of the applicable tax year). Keep in mind that the amount withheld from your paychecks throughout the year only represents an estimate of the taxes you owe. Therefore, it makes sense to seek the advice of an experienced entertainment accountant or tax attorney to help you minimize your ultimate tax liability. This may be accomplished in part by "itemizing" (i.e., listing) and deducting the business expenses related to your employment that you incur throughout the year for which you have not been reimbursed.

Itemized deductions, also called "Schedule A" deductions (reported on tax form "Schedule A"), include miscellaneous expenses such as home office expenses, magazine subscriptions, union dues, stage clothing costs, dry cleaning costs, educational expenses, travel costs, legal fees, tax preparation charges, etc. You may be surprised at what you can write off, so hang on to all the business-related expense receipts for which you are not repaid, and be sure to hire an experienced entertainment accountant or tax attorney to review the expenses you can and cannot deduct. (See the box that follows for a comprehensive list of deductions to which you may be entitled.)

Self-Employment/Independent Contractor Status

For self-employed musicians working on a freelance basis, the tax laws differ from those governing contract employees. As you'll see below, you'll also have a lot more responsibilities.

Income Taxes. Similar to contract employees, self-employed musicians are also subject to income taxes, including federal, state, and/or local taxes. However, if you're self-employed and working as an independent contractor, taxes are not taken out of the payments made to you by the various organizations for whom you work.

You're responsible for estimating and paying your own taxes throughout the tax year. As a self-employed musician, you're required to make estimated payments on a quarterly basis: on April 15, June 15, September 15, and January 15. In addition, you may have to pay a "self-employment tax"—approximately 15.3 percent on net earnings—consisting of 12.4 percent for social security and 2.9 percent for Medicare. This tax is approximately double that of the social security and Medicare taxes that you pay as a contract employee.

Year End Reporting. At the end of the year, the bands or organizations for whom you have worked should provide you with tax form "1099," which indicates the total income that you received from them for the calendar year. You must then report the total income received as reflected on all 1099 forms (and related expenses) on your federal and state returns. You may be able to reduce the amount of money you owe in taxes throughout the year by deducting what the IRS considers "ordinary" and "necessary" expenses related to your trade/business. These expenses, called "Schedule C" deductions (filed on IRS tax form "Schedule C") are office supplies, business travel expenses, car expenses, legal expenses, union dues, etc. Just be sure to hang on to all of your business expense receipts throughout the year. The rules regarding tax deductions for independent contractors, as well as for contract employees, are tricky and subject to interpretation. Therefore, it's always a good idea to contact an experienced entertainment accountant or tax attorney for assistance.

Below are some examples of deductions that you may be able to claim on your tax returns—either miscellaneous itemized deductions if you're a contract employee (Schedule A deductions), or trade/business deductions if you're an independent contractor (Schedule C deductions).

◆ Union dues

◆ Mail and fax expenses: résumés, promotional kits, etc.

◆ Dry cleaning costs for stage clothes, etc.

◆ Conventions: music conferences such as the NAMM convention, etc.

◆ Business gifts: greeting cards, etc.

◆ Attorney fees

◆ Tax preparation costs

◆ Educational expenses: music lessons, seminars

◆ Telephone calls for business: if originating from your residence, it's a good idea to have a second line; otherwise, you must be able to determine what percentage of calls made from a single residence phone were business-related, and what calls were personal

◆ Entertainment and meal expenses for business: deductions may include show tickets, etc.

◆ Related work tools: recording gear, drumsticks, guitar strings, instrument fees, repairs, maintenance, and insurance may be deductible. The cost of CDs and cassettes may also be considered a deductable expense as long as the music was purchased in connection to your work, rather than for your leisure enjoyment

◆ Depreciation of work tools: you can deduct a portion of your equipment's cost over several years as it depreciates in value

◆ Subscriptions: magazines such as *Billboard, Guitar Player, Rolling Stone*

◆ Home office expenses (office space in your home or apartment used exclusively for business, such as home studios, rehearsal rooms, etc.): deductions may include a portion of your rent, utilities, cable, i.e., MTV, VH1. . .

◆ Travel expenses: airline tickets, lodging, taxis, limousines, food, personal grooming related to work (shampoos & conditioners, etc.), uniform clothing (stage clothes that are not used in everyday circumstances), tips (for meals, baggage handlers, etc.), travel costs for an associate (if for a bona fide business reason), passport photo & application fees

◆ Car expenses or standard mileage on vehicle: There are two ways to deduct auto expenses. You can deduct car expenses such as leasing fees, insurance, gas, tolls, parking, depreciation of vehicle, and fees for hauling a trailer, or you can deduct mileage. If you deduct mileage, you can do so only when your vehicle is used for commuting to a temporary, but not a regular place of business

WORKERS' COMPENSATION INSURANCE

Like taxes, insurance is not the most exciting subject, but your risk of injury is increased when traveling from city to city, night after night, and it should not be underestimated. Contract employees and independent contractors are treated differently when it comes to insurance, and it's important that you understand exactly what your employment status entitles you to.

Contract Employees

State laws provide that all employers must purchase insurance to cover their employees in case of an injury that occurs on the job. As a contract employee on your employers' payroll, you should be covered by this insurance. "Workers' compensation insurance" covers medical expenses and pays you an income while disabled. If you're permanently unable to return to work, "vocational rehabilitation" may also be provided. Don't confuse workers' compensation with state disability insurance, which is deducted from your paycheck. Workers' compensation insurance must be purchased by your employer from a licensed workers' compensation carrier or state disability insurance office. Note: the laws regarding workers' compensation vary from state to state. For instance, in some states an employer may not have to purchase workers' compensation insurance for two or fewer employees. Ask your employer about your rights to workers' compensation insurance at the time of your employment. This is important!

Self-Employment/Independent Contractor Status

Unlike contract employees, when you're working on a freelance basis as an independent contractor, the people for whom you work are *not* responsible for providing you with workers' compensation insurance. This means that you're responsible for providing your own disability insurance. Disability insurance is rather expensive, although health insurance may be obtained by joining the music unions. If you have a spouse who works, you may be covered by his or her policy. While on the general topic of insurance, you may also want to know that you're personally responsible for investing in insurance for theft and damage to your musical instruments. This is important and should not be underestimated. Instrument insurance can also be obtained through the music unions.

CONTRACT EMPLOYEE OR INDEPENDENT CONTRACTOR?

By now it should be apparent that there are major differences between contract employees and independent contractors when it comes to tax issues and workers' compensation insurance. But do you have a choice between one kind of employment status and the other?

An employee may prefer to be treated as an independent contractor so he or she will not have any taxes taken out of his or her paycheck, and therefore, in theory, have a bigger paycheck. As you know, an employer is required by law to withhold taxes from an employee's paycheck, reducing their before-tax salary or gross income significantly. If those taxes weren't withheld, the amount of money you'd be making would appear significantly larger. Remember, however, that you can run from Uncle Sam, but you can't hide, and eventually you'll need to report your income to the IRS, and you will owe taxes on what you earned. Also keep in mind that if you're treated as an independent contractor, you won't be eligible for state unemployment benefits.

An employer may prefer to treat you as an independent contractor rather than as a contract employee because it limits his or her responsibility to you. Remember, employers are required to

withhold 6.2 percent of your income for Social Security (up to a set limit) and 1.45 percent for Medicare (unlimited), for a combined total of 7.65 percent. Employers are also required to make a matching contribution for Social Security taxes on the income paid to you. By treating you as an independent contractor, however, employers can avoid making this payment, as well as payments towards workers' compensation insurance. This means that you either have to purchase your own disability insurance, or risk not being covered.

The IRS has very specific guidelines as to whether a musician should be considered a contract employee or an independent contractor. Employers may tend to bend these rules from time to time, however. To be sure you conduct your business lawfully, below are a few factors used by the IRS to help you determine your work status. (A more comprehensive list offered by the IRS can be found at the end of Chapter 5.)

The IRS considers you a contract employee if you fit the following criteria:

+ If you're given specific directions as to how your job should be performed
+ If you're given set hours as to when work must be performed
+ If you're paid in regular intervals, such as by the week or bi-monthly
+ If the work you perform with an employer is on an ongoing and continuing basis
+ If the person for whom you work pays for your travel expenses
+ If the work you do is on a full-time basis, or prevents you from taking on other work
+ If you can be terminated, or if you have the right to quit at any time

NOTE: Anyone who does not meet the above criteria may be classified as an independent contractor.

EMPLOYEE OR NOT, THAT IS THE QUESTION. Suppose you were hired by a band to go out on the road for three months, and were promised a weekly salary as compensation for your services. Before the tour starts, you're required to show up for rehearsals Monday through Friday from 8 PM to 12 midnight to learn the band's material at the direction of the group's musical director. The day before the first performance, you're flown out on a commercial airliner (at the band's expense) to the city where the first date of the tour is to begin. From that point forward, you travel on a tour bus under the direction of a tour manager, who makes sure that you get on stage on time, and that you're on the bus every morning when traveling to the next city. Additionally, all of your hotel accommodations are paid for. In this scenario, you would be considered an employee by the IRS.

NOTHING FOR MONEY

If music is your primary means of income, you must make sure that all of your business matters such as taxes and insurance are in order and that you are also compensated fairly for your services. Even when you decide to work for free, someone is either going to make money or benefit eventually. So why shouldn't you? If you choose to perform on an artist's demo for free because he or she doesn't have the money to pay you, arrange a written agreement on speculation (or spec). This agreement can stipulate that you'll be compensated for your services at the time the artist signs a record deal and subsequently receives an advance. Keep in mind, though, that if you have other sources of income, or if money is generally not a concern, your compensation may simply be the experience gained from participating, as well as the pleasures received by performing with and/or helping a friend. In return, your friend may help you when you're in need. Bartering, as it's called, is how many musicians gain exposure and experience in the early stages of their careers.

As an employee or self-employed performer, you are your own entity, providing a service for someone else's organization. Remember what I've emphasized before: YOU ARE IN THE BUSINESS OF YOU. Be professional, work hard to establish your reputation, and make connections that may lead to other work. Even when your current situation appears to present the potential for long-term employment, remember there are no guarantees.

PROMISES, PROMISES. One musician worked on an artist's demo for free in exchange for a promise that if the artist received a recording agreement, the musician would have the opportunity to play on the record and subsequently receive compensation. However, when the artist inked a record deal and received a large advance, the musician did not receive an offer to record on the artist's album, nor was he offered compensation for the many hours he spent participating in the demo recordings. You cannot control another person's business ethics, but you can certainly handle your own business matters prudently by covering your proverbial butt. Be passionate about playing music, but never forget that it's also a business.

Q & A WITH FREELANCE DRUMMER KENWOOD DENNARD

Kenwood Dennard is a freelance drummer in New York City who has worked with such notable artists as Sting, George Benson, Dizzy Gillespie, Maceo Parker, Wayne Shorter, Vanessa Williams, Jaco Pastorius, the Manhattan Transfer, Pat Martino, Brand X, John McLaughlin, the Gil Evans Orchestra, and Miles Davis. In addition, Mr. Dennard is employed as a professor of music at Berklee College of Music in Boston, Massachusettes.

Q: Employees are generally people working with one employer on a long-term basis, while independent contractors are people working with a variety of employers on a shorter-term basis. There are also business differences between the two, such as taxes and state unemployment benefits. Which professional status do you prefer: that of employee or that of independent contractor, and why?

K.D: Each situation has [its] strong points. Being an employee means steady money. I worked for three years with the group the Manhattan Transfer, and even when we weren't on the road, we were paid a retainer. The employee-oriented situations in my career were less of a hassle because taxes were taken out of my paychecks each week, along with unemployment, social security, etc. On the other hand, freelancing is fantastic, and a little less restricting schedule-wise than being an employee. I get to be called upon by a variety of artists for my own style and particular strengths. I'm in a position to arrange my own schedule, and nurture my own price. Independent contractors must have more self-determination than employees in order to stay on top of business issues such as finding gigs, doing paperwork, taxes, etc.

Q: According to state laws, employers are responsible for providing their employees with workers' compensation insurance for injuries that might occur on the road, while independent contractors are responsible for providing their own disability insurance. Are you covered?

K.D: Most of my jobs have been independent contractor gigs, but the real bonanza for me in terms of health insurance comes from being a full-time employee at Berklee College of Music. I have also been employed part time as an adjunct professor at NYU, Parsons School of Design, and Manhattan School of Music. These were also much appreciated modes of employment at the time.

Q: How about equipment insurance? Again, as an employee you're generally covered by your employer's policy, but as an independent contractor you're responsible for buying your own equipment insurance. Are you covered?

K.D: I've been covered by insurance on my own, though the musicians' union has tried to make instrument insurance fairly affordable for a lot of freelance musicians. Congratulations to New York Local 802.

Q: Are you a member of the American Federation of Musicians, the American Federation of Radio and Television Artists, or (if you play an instrument and sing), both organizations? Please explain.

K.D: I'm no longer an active member of the AFM. I requested to change my status and became an inactive member. This way I maintained a good relationship with the union without having to pay dues. I became an inactive member because I wasn't doing enough of the gigs the AFM specializes in (studio work, Broadway shows, jingles, etc.) to fully benefit. I was doing more live jazz and pop gigs.

Q: Solo artists and band members may benefit from percentages of publishing royalties, record royalties, and merchandising monies, while an employee or independent contractor usually works for a straight wage. What criteria do you use for establishing your employment agreement with an employer. For instance, how do you determine your wage?

K.D: You're right. In a band situation you typically write music as a unit, and receive composer's royalties that can last for many years. When freelancing, you simply play the music that other (albeit wonderful) musicians composed separately. You work for a wage. I negotiate my fee based on what the employer has in mind in terms of my obligations and what I feel I'm worth. As long as the resulting figure is not below my personal minimum standard, I take the gig. As far as your readers [go], I suggest that they refer to the union's minimum scale wages, and use their rates as a starting point for negotiating their wage. Whether you're a member of the union or not, you'll get a good idea about what's fair.

Q: Employees or independent contractors may find work as session players, live performers, musical instructors, copyists, arrangers, songwriters, engineers, and producers. What are some of the other ways that you've kept busy throughout your career?

K.D: All of the above, plus co-producing with Delmar Brown [keyboardist, producer], producing my solo albums, and other projects. Production is nice because, in the situations [in which] I've worked, I received a lump sum budget and then paid the others. If I was able to save time and money, I was able to pocket even more cash.

Q: Do you have any advice about getting your name out in the music community?

K.D: Older, more established musicians, sometimes benefit from associating themselves with current fresh up-and-coming musicians. By associating yourself with them, you can then parlay the exposure into creating your own "niche." Being in Jaco's [Pastorious] band was fantastic exposure. When the tours with Jaco finished, other musicians who had seen me on the road or at the Bottom Line or the Blue Note in NYC, etc., would call me for gigs.

Q: What are some of the methods or personal attributes that have helped you stay busy over the years as an employee or independent contractor?

K.D: As an employee, spending social time with your colleagues is important for the morale of the group as a whole. Simply put, people want to play with people they want to be around. As for independent contractor work, punctuality, professionalism, and your physical appearance are very important attributes. Reading music and stylistic versatility helps so that if one kind of gig dries up, the other can kick in.

Q: Have you relied on other business professionals throughout your career, such as accountants?

K.D: An accountant is necessary for taxes, of course. Attorneys have also offered valuable advice over the years, especially in negotiating contracts. Sometimes lawyers find gigs for artists as well.

Q: Employees and independent contractors don't benefit as "normal" corporate folk in that they don't have savings plans, vacation plans, or (in some cases) any business plans at all. What types of business techniques, investment tips, or general advice have you adopted over the years in order to secure your future?

K.D: As far as your comment about "not having any plans at all," I say failing to plan is like planning to fail. As an independent contractor, I was kind of "winging it by the seat of my pants." I didn't have health insurance and didn't worry about money for retirement. As I have grown older, that approach no longer seems wise to me. I found that the best strategy for the future has been to at least have one "employee" gig. This way I could get health benefits, and have federal, local, and social security taxes deducted from my paychecks, which I've found is like [having] a forced savings plan. [Some people like to take the lump sum or tax refund you may get back at the end of the calendar year and put it into a savings account. Speak to your accountant for advice.] So, my strategy is to maintain and nurture my professorship at Berklee College of Music over the long term. This puts my other touring, recording, and sideman activities in a stable perspective. Thankfully, Berklee has allowed me to do this since they have a flexible schedule.

Q: Is there any other advice about employees or independent contractors that you think is important for our readers to know?

K.D: Music is a business, but I hope your readers are able to maintain the reason why they started playing—to have fun! If every single gig is not fun, at least try to make each job lead to fun and fulfillment down the road. I feel that's up to each individual. Peace!

CHAPTER 4

Contract
Employment
with Profit Shares

In some situations, established artists employ musicians and offer more than the typical salary for such relationships. These are called "salary/percentage involvements," and they often occur when an established artist desires your contributions to the writing and recording of an album as well as your participation on a tour in support of that album. An employer may offer you percentages of profits from the following sources in order to secure your involvement: record royalties, music publishing royalties, and merchandising monies. The process by which percentages are determined depends on each individual situation, although the percentages you get should be equal to the level of your contribution to the project.

Of all the distinct business relationships covered in this book, salary/percentage involvements may be one of the most difficult to understand. You may feel as if you're occupying the gray area between being an employee and a band member. Yes, the opportunity to offer your creativity to a band and the inclusion of percentages in your agreement are two attractive aspects of the relationship, but don't be misled—you're still an employee. (Or as a high profile New York attorney once put it, you are a glorified sideman.) This means that all the employment issues we covered in Chapter 3 are applicable here.

In salary/percentage involvements, the group's management, attorneys, and accountants are hired to be responsible for, and to act in the best interest of, the band members and not you! As a result, it's highly recommended that you set up your own team of advisers to insure the proper handling of your business affairs. In this way, you can avoid a "conflict of interest," a situation that arises when one person—an attorney, for example—is asked to represent both sides of a deal. Since each side has its own best interests in mind, the attorney can't represent both sides fairly. The exception to this rule is the instance in which both parties consent to representation by the same attorney. The following discussion sheds light on a few issues you should look out for when arranging your deal with an employer.

SALARY EXCEPTIONS

As an employee, you should always be compensated fairly for your time and services, whether it be for rehearsals, touring, or recording. As discussed in Chapter 3, both the American Federation of Musicians (AFM) and the American Federation of Radio and Television Artists (AFTRA) can offer guidance in this area if you're not sure what you should be paid. If, however, you own a share in the record royalties, the music publishing royalties, and/or the merchandising monies that might be available, keep in mind that you may be expected to make some of the same sacrifices that the members of the band have to make, such as attending "promotional events." Promotional events include group photo shoots, video shoots, press interviews, radio interviews, live television performances, and record store promotions (in-stores). These events usually do not generate a direct source of income, and therefore you may not be compensated for your time by the group. Keep in mind, though, that if you're asked to work for free, it shouldn't cost you a dime to do so; you should always receive a per diem, and have all your expenses paid.

For some bands, your salary may create an issue. On the one hand, you're an employee, but on the other, you've negotiated percentages of record royalties, publishing royalties, and merchandising monies. Why shouldn't you have to make the same sacrifices the group makes? Whether or not this type of thinking is reasonable, to avoid conflict, make sure that all of your obligations and wages are defined in your agreement from the very beginning! Keep in mind that, as an employee in a salary/percentage situation, you're not a member of the band. You're an employee who's essentially serving at the will and needs of your employer. Once again, in the words of tour manager, agent, and promoter Chris Arnstien, "You are in the business of you." It's important to make sure that you're compensated fairly for your time and hard work, and that your best interests are always protected.

A DOUBLE STANDARD! The vocalist of a popular rock group was asked by the band to take a significant pay cut (approximately $70,000) in order to make up for the financial losses that the group incurred on tour. As an employee, he was not responsible for the band's debt, but to secure their friendship and his position in the band, he chose to comply. A few months after the tour, the vocalist was in dire need of money and began borrowing money from his family and selling off personal property just to survive. According to an interview in *Metal Edge* magazine, the vocalist made the band aware of his financial problems on several occasions, but allegedly was not able to get any money out of them. [When it was beneficial to the group, he was treated like a band member, and when it was not beneficial he was treated as an outsider.] To make matters worse, in spite of the many sacrifices the vocalist made, he was eventually fired when the original singer rejoined the band. The vocalist who lost out was John Carabi, and the band was Mötley Crüe.

RECORD ROYALTIES

Record royalties are percentages (also called points) that the record company pays you for the sale of your record. A common royalty rate for a new band can range anywhere from 11 to 16 percent of the suggested retail list price (SRLP) per unit sold. If the band offers you points on a record (1/2 to 2 points is typical in salary/percentage involvements), ask the group's organization to forward a "letter of direction" to the record company, announcing your share of royalties in the U.S. as well as in foreign territories. Make sure this is signed by both the band and the record company; the record company will then direct royalties payable to you or to your representatives separately. Thus, if you leave the group, if you're fired, or if the group splits up, you won't have to chase down the group's organization for your royalty statements. This is especially valuable if you and the band don't part on amicable terms.

The group's recording debt and all other recoupable expenses are paid back to the record company by both your and the band's share of points. Until the record company is paid back, you won't keep a dime from record sales. Approximately 95 percent of all bands fail to repay the record company for its investment. Therefore, you need to consider the actual value of your points. What are the chances that you'll earn any money from record royalties on this album? What are the projected record sales? How strong is the promotional support from the record company? Does the group have any prior unpaid balances?

It's not uncommon for a group to incur a debt of hundreds of thousands of dollars they haven't been able to recoup. This debt can consist of the artist advance, the album and video budget, tour support, and previously recorded albums (with which you were not even involved) whose expenses have compounded through "cross-collateralization". Cross-collateralization refers to arrangements wherein current earnings also pay for prior debts. For example, royalty earnings from record #2 help repay outstanding expenses from record #1 and record number #2 long before you see a profit from your points. Unless the record for which you're entitled to royalties turns out to be a smash hit and the record company recoups all its expenses, a point could mean zilch!

Your objective is to negotiate record royalties in your agreement with the band. But, don't be deceived by the apparent significance of these royalties when negotiating other aspects of your deal. For example, you may be offered a share in record royalties, but a low fee for recording the album. (Note: Whatever fee you negotiate for recording the album, keep in mind—assuming that you, the group, and/or the record company are union affiliated—you're at least entitled to minimum scale wages set by two music unions: American Federation of Musicians (AFM) for instrumentalists, and American Federation of Radio and Television Artists (AFTRA) for vocalists.

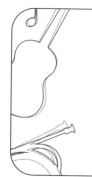

STAR TREATMENT. According to Attorney Jonathan Urdan of Maverick records, when Dave Navarro and Flea of The Red Hot Chili Peppers guest-starred on singer Alanis Morissette's third record *Jagged Little Pill,* they negotiated points on the album that were subject to the recoupment of the recording cost budget only—exclusive of all other recoupable expenses to the record company (such as tour support, video budgets, etc.). In other words, Dave and Flea were paid record royalties before Alanis. This is not uncommon for "guest stars."

Additionally, the AFM pays out monies through a sound recording special payment fund available to all instrumentalists who perform on AFM covered recording sessions (i.e., sessions that are reported to the union; the record producer must include your name on the union form B4 and turn it in to the record company). Note that both the AFM and AFTRA also collect and pay out monies for new use every time a recording is used in a new medium such as film and television. (Union benefits are discussed in more detail in Chapter 3. Record royalties are discussed in Chapter 11.)

MUSIC PUBLISHING ROYALTIES

If you're asked by the band to participate in the songwriting process, and it appears that you'll be contributing a great deal of your time, establish an agreement with the group that stipulates some form of guaranteed compensation. Since no one can foresee whether the songs to which you contribute will make the final cut on the album (everyone but you will have the final say), you could end up investing weeks or months of your time arranging and making demos for the group's song ideas without gaining much, if any, in music publishing royalties on the record. Therefore, ask the group for a guaranteed minimum share in the compositions. If the group reacts unfavorably to this request, ask for an hourly fee. Either way, a preliminary agreement insures that you're going to be compensated for your time and hard work.

When working on songs with the group, be sure to record your musical ideas (a small tape recorder will do), and keep an original copy of your lyrics or song titles; include dates and times as well. You'll benefit if there's a disagreement about whether or not you participated in creating and developing a composition.

CREDIT CHECK. Writing disuputes are common. In 1990, when Robert Van Winkle (a.k.a. Vanilla Ice) had the first rap song ("Ice Ice Baby") to top the *Billboard* charts, a Dallas, Texas disk jockey claimed he wrote the song for the artist and did not receive credit and compensation. According to Ronin Ro's book *Have Gun Will Travel: The Spectacular Rise and Fall of Death Row Records,* when "Ice" was dangled over the edge of a 15-floor hotel balcony by Suge Knight and his associates, he was persuaded to sign over a portion of the rights in the song (an estimated value of four million dollars)—not a very legal way of handling business, but definitely effective!

When you share in a percentage of the rights to songs, you need to take a series of steps to make sure you're protected and paid. First, to receive performance royalties from radio play and television, you must register your compositions in their proper percentage shares with one of the major U.S. performing rights societies: American Society of Composers, Authors, and Publishers (ASCAP), Broadcast Music Incorporated (BMI), or Society of European Stage Authors and Composers, today known only as SESAC. Second, all works must be registered with the Copyright office in Washington, D.C. on the required form "p.a." (an acronym for performing arts). Third, you're required to fill out something called a "first use mechanical license," indicating to the record company the song titles and percentages in which you share. A mechanical license grants the record company the legal right to use your songs on a record. The record company will then send you or

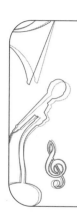

your personal representatives licensing fees called mechanical royalties, or you can have The Harry Fox Agency, a major mechanical rights collection society, collect for you. (Publishing issues will be covered in more detail in Chapter 12.)

As a non-signatory to the group's recording contract, you may not be subject to something called the "controlled composition clause." This clause sets a limit on how much the record company has to pay the artist, or an outside co-writer, in mechanical licensing fees. If you are the sole writer of a composition, you're legally entitled to mechanical royalties paid at the full statutory rate of $.08 (8 cents) per composition per CD made and distributed. In addition, you should be paid on a "floating scale with changing rates"; this means that the rate, by law, periodically increases. (In the year 2004, the statutory rate will increase to 8.5 cents per composition.) Although the group will want you to agree to taking a lower rate, at usually 75 percent of statutory per CD sold, it's your choice. Keep in mind that—assuming you keep a good relationship with the band—it is usually wise to make this concession. Otherwise, the band may choose not to use your song.

If the group already has an agreement with a publishing company to exploit their musical compositions in film, television, and print, and to collect generated incomes, the publisher will most likely be interested in representing your song shares as well. Be sure that your agreement as a collaborating songwriter is not subject to specific terms of the group's contract (for example, cross-collateralization). You may be better off finding your own publishing company to represent your shares. In addition, all royalty statements may be directed to the group at one address, such as the group's business management. The band's management is entitled to commission a portion of the group's royalties, but pay close attention—you're not a member, you're an employee. The management is not entitled to a percentage of your royalty earnings unless you've entered into some sort of agreement that permits it to do so. Keep a watchful eye on your finances, and get your attorney's opinion before signing anything.

MERCHANDISING

If your image is used on T-shirts and hats, or if merchandise generally reflects work in which you were involved (e.g., a T-shirt including the title from a song you helped to write), you may receive some percentage of the merchandising revenue. Your agreement with the band can be worked out in a number of ways. For example, if the group handles its own merchandising, your agreement may consist of a percentage of the net profit during the time that you're with the group. If the group is signed with a merchandising company, you might be able to negotiate for a portion of your royalties up front from the advance monies typically offered in merchandising deals. (Note: When negotiating your employment agreement with the band, ask for statements of merchandising sales, promotional give-aways, and expenses. This will help you to keep track of your share of merchandising revenue. Merchandising is covered in more detail in Chapter 14.)

CHAPTER 5

Solo Artist
and Employer

The solo artist is a rare and special breed of musician—an exceptional writer or instrumentalist who plays a melodic instrument, a skilled vocalist who's blessed with undeniable looks and image, or a highly motivated individual who possesses the desire to lead (or any combination of the above). Although your name and likeness may be individually displayed on album cover artwork and venue marquees, you'll rarely be working alone. You'll employ a group of studio and touring musicians, and you may even collaborate with skilled composers and producers. It's also likely that you'll have a team of advisors consisting of a personal manager, a business manager, a talent agent, and an attorney. The solo artist sits at the helm, steering this musical battleship into the turbulent waters of the music business.

THE ADVANTAGES OF GOING SOLO

In many instances, solo artists were once members of self-contained bands that eventually imploded due to creative, personal, or business differences. Although it's such polarity that has shaped some of the most unique music to date (the Who, the Beatles, and the Police were all bands that were known to have internal differences), most artists prefer the autonomy of pursuing a solo career over being in a band. In short, the decision-making process is far simpler. You don't have to worry about getting everyone on the same page.

"You have to listen to each other as a band, not only musically, but also verbally," said former Alice in Chains' guitarist Jerry Cantrell in a 2001 interview in *Guitar Player* magazine. "It's a human thing, full of errors and surprises, and all kinds of bullshit."

Commenting on The Police and his career as a solo artist in a 1983 interview in *Rolling Stone* magazine, Sting said, "I'll argue till the cows come home about something I believe in, and so will

SOLO ARTISTS WHO HAVE LEFT SUCCESSFUL GROUPS & SUCCEEDED

Bobby Brown of New Edition

Cher of Sonny and Cher

Eric Clapton of Cream

Phil Collins of Genesis

Ice Cube of NWA

Dr. Dre of NWA

Peter Gabriel of Genesis

Lauryn Hill of the Fugees

Michael Jackson of the Jackson Five

Chaka Khan of Rufus

John Lennon of the Beatles

Ricky Martin of Menudo

Paul McCartney of the Beatles

Michael McDonald of the Doobie Brothers

George Michael of Wham!

Morrissey of the Smiths

Stevie Nicks of Fleetwood Mac

Ozzy Osbourne of Black Sabbath

Robert Plant of Led Zeppelin

Lionel Ritchie of the Commodores

Robbie Robertson of the Band

Henry Rollins of Black Flag

Diana Ross of The Supremes

Sting of The Police

Tina Turner of Ike and Tina Turner

Neil Young of Buffalo Springfield

Andy [Summers] and Stewart [Copeland]. A band is not an easy relationship by any means. Though I can't think of two musicians I'd rather play with, I don't think history is made of mass movements or teams. History is made of individuals."

Finally, in a 1971 *Rolling Stone* interview, John Lennon replied to a question about what had happened to the four parts that were the Beatles: "They remembered they were four individuals. After Brian Epstein died, we collapsed. Paul [McCartney] took over and supposedly led us. But what is leading when we went around in circles. We broke up then. That was the disintegration."

> One must consider whether or not a solo artist could ever have the chance at being a successful solo artist without first starting off in a band. Keep in mind that however talented you may be, pursuing a solo career from the start is not an easy or inexpensive proposition.

BANDS BREAK UP, BUT SOLO ARTISTS BREAK DOWN

Though being a solo artist may liberate you from the democracies of being in a band, it also means that you're "solely" responsible for each and every move you make. From press reviews to concert performances, you sink or swim on your own. Simply put, there is no one you can hide behind. You accept the heat, the criticism, and the stress!

"It's my shit," Jerry Cantrell has commented. "My name's on the marquee, as well as on the paychecks, so it all comes down to me."

"No one cares about what you don't do, but what you do do can ruin your career," says an anonymous record company executive.

Being a solo artist also means that the brunt of the work falls on you. Unlike being in a band, where each member shares sacrifices on the road to success, you're working 24/7. Whether it be a 6:00 AM phone interview with a radio station, making appearances at retail stores, conducting interviews with the press, or responding to fan mail, you're on your own! If this all sounds like fun, most artists will tell you that it gets old really fast. It's constant but necessary work.

LONELY IS THE NIGHT. Rocker Billy Squier earned national success in 1981 with hits such as "Lonely is the Night" and "The Stroke." However, when taking a rather drastic turn in his musical career towards bump-and-grind rhythms and tongue-in-cheek lyrics, Squier's career took an inevitable hard fall. In his video shoot for the song "Rock the Night," Squier decided that he would go all out by rolling around in pink satin sheets while batting his eyes at the camera. It looked more like a coming out of the closet announcement than what the public was used to seeing in his earlier work. Squier, who may otherwise have enjoyed a much longer career, was never able to recover from this disastrous career move.

As Vince Neil of Mötley Crüe reveals in their book, *The Dirt,* "Now that I was solo, I had to do all the interviews, write all the songs, make up the set lists, figure out the marketing, approve all the artwork, and deal with everything."

Additionally, solo artists must endure the pressures of keeping their employees happy, and that's no easy task! First, if you want to surround yourself with talented and experienced musicians, you must offer them something substantial, such as good pay, good gigs, and career growth. Second, you need to always make your musicians feel appreciated, while at the same reminding them who's in control. This can be one of the more difficult aspects of your job. It's important to recognize the fine line between being your employees' friend and their leader. One day you may even have to experience the difficult task of letting someone go.

In the early stages of a solo artist's career, when there are minimal or no funds available, it may be difficult to find musicians who will work with you. For this reason, you may need to rely on the support system of a band, promising everyone a share of the future profits. If this is the case, just make sure your intentions are genuine and you plan to live up to your word.

Being a solo artist also means that long after your musicians are paid and have gone home, all financial burdens rest entirely on you. These include all investments, debts, and loans. However,

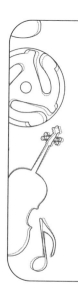

GET OFF THE BUS, GUS. Although many solo artists are known to be control freaks who pay their musicians little respect, they eventually realize that this attitude makes it difficult to keep talented musicians in their band. The exception, of course, is if you're a superstar and you choose to dangle the proverbial carrot of fame before your musicians' eyes. In this case, you can always find less experienced musicians who are willing to undercut seasoned pros just for a crack at the big time. Unfortunately, this perpetuates a major problem in the music business today, as it has for many years. Drummer Buddy Rich, who was famous for his big band sounds throughout the 1940s and into the '80s, was known to rule his band with an iron fist. In one story, while traveling to Vegas, he had the bus driver stop the bus in the middle of the Nevada desert and made his entire band get off and walk. All this because Rich was unhappy with the band's performance that evening! Despite his attitude, Rich never had a shortage of musicians.

one must consider that the pay-off from potential revenue streams, such as music publishing and record royalties and merchandise sales, may be far greater in the long run. (These topics are all discussed in more detail in Chapters 11-14.)

Last but not least, some solo artists may have to endure the added pressure of living up to the successes of their former bands. Critics in the press will never judge you purely on the strength of your music alone. Although many artists have gone on to succeed in their own right (and some have even become more successful), there are just as many solo artists who have failed miserably.

THE RECORD COMPANY'S RIGHTS TO SOLO ARTISTS

Upon signing a record agreement, the record company will usually want the rights to all members as a band, as well as the rights of any leaving member who becomes a solo artist or member of another band. In case you're not paying attention, this means that if you're an artist who was once a member of a signed group (successful or not), *their record company may own the rights to your new solo career!* This is called a "leaving member clause" and it may be found in your former band's recording agreement.

Leaving member clauses are especially useful to record companies when a band is unsuccessful. It basically gives the record label another shot at recouping their initial investment (you'll see how that works in a minute). At the same time, if your band ends up being a success, a leaving member clause benefits the record company by securing their right to continue making money from you if you have a successful solo career of your own. Their rationale is that if they're going to invest a lot of money into developing your career and making you a star, then it's their right to reap the long-term benefits as well.

Leaving member clauses can be good or bad for you. They can be good because you have a record company that's potentially interested in releasing your solo material. They can be bad because your royalty rate and advances are typically less favorable than your initial recording agreement with your band. Additionally, all debts incurred by your former band automatically carry over to you! That's right, just when you thought you were breaking away from the group of guys/girls that you grew to hate, you find you have continued financial responsibility to them. Here's how it works:

Let's say you decided to leave your group because their last record was a flop and they had an outstanding balance to the record company of $400,000. Before you even see a dime in record roy-

> Attorney Jeff Cohen points out that negotiating a leaving member clause for his clients is somewhat of a conflict of interest. On the one hand, you're trying to get the best deal for your band, while on the other, you're trying to get the best deal for each individual should the band break up.

PEARL JAMMED. Due to the "leaving member" clause, Pearl Jam already owed $500,000 to their label before ever recording an album. This debt carried over from Stone Gossard and Jeff Ament's first band, Mother Love Bone. Mother Love Bone's singer died of an overdose before their debut record *Apple* was ever released. Mother Love Bone broke up, but their label had the rights to Stone and Jeff as individual artists. When Stone and Jeff went on to form Pearl Jam, their debt followed, as per their contract.

ARTISTS THAT WERE NOT ABLE TO PARALLEL THE SUCCESSES OF THEIR FORMER BANDS:

Tony Banks of Genesis

Jerry Cantrell of Alice In Chains

Belinda Carlisle of the Go-Go's

Roger Daltrey of the Who

CC Deville of Poison

Ace Frehley of Kiss

Rob Halford of Judas Priest

Geri Halliwell of Spice Girls

Susanna Hoffs of the Bangles

Deborah Harry of Blondie

Steve Howe of Yes

George Lynch of Dokken

Dave Navarro of the Red Hot Chili Peppers

Vince Neil of Mötley Crüe

Stephen Pearcy of Ratt

Joe Perry of Aerosmith

Steve Perry of Journey

Slash of Guns N' Roses

Ringo Starr of the Beatles

David Lee Roth of Van Halen

Sonny Bono of Sonny and Cher (well, at least he succeeded in politics)

Donnie Wahlberg of New Kids on the Block

Bob Weir of the Grateful Dead

Rick Wakeman of Yes

alties from sales of your new record, all monies will go towards paying your former band's unrecouped balance as well as your new debt to the record company. If you spend another $250,000 recording your new record, you'll now be $650,000 in debt to the record company. But before you decide to throw the idea of your solo career away, consider the following.

In most instances, you can negotiate an agreement with the record company that stipulates that only your share of your band's unrecouped balance carries over to your new account as a solo artist. This means that if there were four members in your former band, only a quarter of the unrecouped balance can be charged against your royalty account. Therefore, staying with the previous example, only $100,000 can be carried over to your new account. Hey, it's better than $400,000! Conversely, keep in mind that if your former band stays together and goes on to record new records that are also flops, typically, no new debts to the record company will effect you. You had nothing to do with these records and are not responsible for any debt associated with them.

THE BUSINESS AND LEGAL RESPONSIBILITIES OF SOLO ARTISTS AS EMPLOYERS

As I have explained, it's very likely that as a solo artist, at some point, you'll employ musicians to rehearse, perform live, and record in the studio. As an employer, you'll be responsible for a variety of business and legal issues regarding your employees, such as paying them at least the minimum wage scales, deducting payroll taxes, and providing workers compensation insurance. Alhough it is very typical to "fly under radar" and ignore these issues in the early stages of your career, this can eventually lead to significant problems as your business becomes more and more successful. For this reason, it's especially important to work closely with an experienced entertainment accountant, business manager, or attorney who will provide advice and guidance on these often complex and tedious issues.

Wages and Commissions

Although most employers are known for trying to get the most out of their employees for the least possible compensation, take note that state and federal laws impose minimum wage obligations on employers. Information regarding wages, hours, and working conditions can be obtained by contacting your state Department of Labor. The American Federation of Musicians (AFM) and the American Federation of Television and Radio Artists (AFTRA) also provide information regarding "fairness" guidelines and recommended compensation. The various mediums these unions regulate include live performances, studio recordings, and television appearances. Both the AFM and AFTRA have local offices in nearly every major city in the United States and Canada. To better educate yourself about the fair treatment of employees and employee wages refer to Chapter 3, and be sure to contact both of these organizations.

> Contact the American Federation of Musicians at (800) 762-3444 or at www.afm.org.

> Contact the American Federation of Television and Radio Artists at (212) 532-0800 or at www.aftra.com.

The method by which employers choose to pay their employees is determined by the value they place on keeping them. Employers may choose to compensate their musicians by either paying them a flat salary or hourly wage, or a salary plus a percentage of the future profits. If you choose, you may pay employees wages that exceed the suggested minimum scales set by state laws or local unions. Special perks or percentages that you may offer can include royalties from record sales, royalties from music publishing, and royalties from the sale of merchandising such as T-shirts. Percentages are typically offered to those employees who are more involved in the writing and recording of an album, and who are generally considered irreplaceable and integral to the functioning of a band.

Keep in mind that an employer-employee relationship must be a win-win situation in order to be successful. If an employer resorts to a take-it-or-leave-it approach regarding compensation, it'll eventually lead to the "revolving-door-of-musicians" syndrome. For instance, you'll find yourself replacing bass players on every tour you do. Note that this typically diminishes your credibility in the eyes of your fans. Although you may feel like the "star" of the show, it's important to realize that your audience is there to see the other musicians in your band as well. It's not only about you and the extra dollar you can squeeze into your pocket. The happier your musicians are, the better they're going to make you look and sound. And remember the old adage, "If all you pay is peanuts, then all you get are monkeys."

If you're fortunate to find musicians with whom you're comfortable working, it's advisable to keep them hanging around by paying them well. Regardless of what you pay, take responsibility for at least understanding what's considered appropriate compensation for your employees, and try to abide by the minimum rules and regulations set by state law and the musicians unions.

Income, Social Security, and Payroll Taxes

As an employer, you're also responsible for deducting taxes from your employees' paychecks, including federal, state, and/or local income taxes, as well as Social Security taxes. Keep in mind that the IRS has severe penalties for employers who don't comply with federal and state withholding and other payroll tax requirements. Although it's likely you'll have an experienced accountant or business manager assisting you in these matters, it's important to have a basic understanding of the mechanics of taxation, no matter how dry and boring tax laws may seem. After all, it's your business we're talking about.

Income Taxes. As an employer, you're responsible for withholding federal, state, and/or local income taxes from salary, wages, commissions, and per diems (if applicable) paid to your employees. The amount of tax to be withheld is determined in part by the information your employees provide on tax form W4 as to whether they're single or married, have children, own a home, etc. Tax charts and tables can be obtained from the IRS to help you determine whether you are withholding the proper amount of taxes from your employees' checks.

Social Security and Medicare. Employers are also required to withhold Social Security and Medicare taxes from their employees' paychecks. In general, these taxes provide retirement and health insurance for people over 65. As an employer, you're also required to make matching Social Security and Medicare contributions (i.e., tax payments). It's a good idea to contact the Social Security Administration to ensure that you're complying with all Social Security tax requirements.

> Contact the Social Security Administration at (800) 772-1213 or at www.ssa.gov.

State Unemployment Tax. State unemployment tax is a payroll tax that's required to be withheld by employers from their employees' pay, except for those who reside in Alaska, Florida, Nevada, Texas, South Dakota, Washington, and Wyoming. Employees who pay this tax are entitled to state unemployment benefits, which provide funds to those who are laid off or whose work is seasonal (e.g., touring).

State Disability Tax/Insurance. State disability tax/insurance is also required to be withheld from an employee's pay by employers who reside in California, Hawaii, New Jersey, New York, and Rhode Island. State disability insurance pays an income to employees who are injured on or off the job, or who become sick or pregnant.

Finally, all taxes withheld from the employee's pay must be deposited in a commercial bank with the appropriate federal and state payroll tax forms. Deposits are normally made on a quarterly basis: on April 15, June 15, September 15, and January 15. Employers are then responsible for issuing tax form W2 at the end of the year, which indicates the total taxable wages paid to employees and the total amount of taxes withheld from their paycheck for the calendar year. This form must be issued no later than January 31st.

NOTE: Employers are not responsible for deducting income, Social Security, and payroll taxes from the earnings of individuals working on a freelance basis (also called "independent contractors status"). You must, however, issue tax form 1099 to such employees, which indicates the total gross income you paid to them during the year. If you paid each musician wages totaling less than $600, however, issuing a 1099 form is not necessary.

> For more information on taxes, contact the Internal Revenue Service at (800) 829-1040, (800) tax form, or at www.irs.gov.

Workers' Compensation Insurance

As an employer, you may also be required by state law to purchase workers' compensation insurance—don't confuse workers' compensation with state disability insurance, which is deducted from your employees' paychecks. Workers' compensation covers injuries that occur on the job and pays your employees' medical expenses and income while they are disabled.

Should an employee be permanently unable to return to work, vocational rehabilitation may also be provided to them through this insurance. Don't underestimate the importance of workers' compensation insurance; accidents, especially while musicians are touring out on the road, are not uncommon. The last thing you need is to be hit with a lawsuit, let alone have an employee suffer through the agony of an unfortunate incident without proper insurance.

Workers' compensation insurance can be purchased by contacting a licensed workers' compensation carrier or by contacting your State Disability Insurance office. In the event of an injury, you must inform your employees of their rights to this insurance. Note that workers' compensation laws vary from state to state. For instance, in some states an employer may not have to purchase workers' compensation insurance if he or she employs two or fewer employees. Contact your State Department of Labor to make sure that you're complying with the rules of your state.

NOTE: You're not responsible for providing workers' compensation insurance for musicians working on a freelance basis or with independent contractor status. Independent contractors are responsible for obtaining their own disability insurance and health coverage.

Contract Employee versus Independent Contractor Status: Who is an Employee?

Solo artists acting as employers may avoid Social Security and Medicare payments, the hassles of deducting payroll taxes, and the costs of purchasing workers' compensation insurance by treating the musicians they hire as independent contractors. Sometimes they do this innocently because they lack information or knowledge. In any case, if an employer is examined by the IRS and found accountable for mishandling his or her business, they can be charged with extremely steep fines. For this reason, it's extremely important that you have a clear understanding of the factors that the IRS uses to determine who is an employee. For instance, if a musician is expected to comply with certain instructions as to when, where, and how he or she should work, that may indicate an employee-employer relationship. If a musician provides his or her services in an ongoing relationship, that may also be a factor in determining an employer-employee relationship. The IRS outlines several factors that help you to determine whether a musician working for you is considered an employee or independent contractor (from the IRS guidelines for employee or independent contractor status, available in Publication 1779, Form 15, or Form SS8):

+ *Instructions:* A worker who is required to comply with another person's instructions about when, where, and how he or she is to work is ordinarily an employee. This control factor is present if the person or persons for whom the services are performed have the right to require compliance with instructions.
+ *Continuing Relationship:* A continuing relationship between the worker and the person or persons for whom the services are performed indicates that, where work is performed at frequently recurring although irregular intervals, an employer-employee relationship may exist.
+ *Set Hours of the Week:* The establishment of set hours of work by the person or persons for whom the services are performed is a factor indicating control and an employee-employer relationship.

- *Payment by Hour, Week, Month:* Payment by the hour, week, or month of regular amounts at stated intervals to a worker strongly indicates an employer-employee relationship.
- *Full Time Required:* If the worker must devote substantially full time to the business of the person or persons for whom the services are performed, such person or persons have control over the amount of time the worker spends working and impliedly restricts the worker from doing other gainful work. This suggests an employee-employer relationship.
- *Training:* Training a worker by requiring an experienced employee to oversee the worker, by corresponding with the worker, by requiring attendance at meetings, or by using other methods, indicates that one person or persons for whom the services are performed want(s) the services performed in a particular method or manner and suggests and employee-employer relationship.
- *Payment of Business and/or Traveling Expenses:* If the person or persons for whom the services are performed ordinarily pay the workers business and/or traveling expenses, the worker is ordinarily an employee. An employer, to be able to control expenses, generally retains the right to regulate and direct the worker's business activities.
- *Right To Discharge:* The right to discharge a worker is a factor indicating that the worker is an employee and the person possessing the right is an employer. An employer exercises control through the threat of dismissal, which causes the worker to obey the employer's instructions.

> Making the distinction between an employee and independent can get tricky, but it's necessary for both tax and workers compensation purposes. Be sure to contact an experienced entertainment accountant or tax attorney and the IRS to make sure that you're complying with the law.

IT'S YOUR THING

To be a solo artist, you must have a special creative, visual, and/or technical quality that makes you stand out and the ability to lead. With leadership comes responsibility. You'll depend on a group of musicians to perform live and record in the studio, but as their employer, you'll have professional obligations to them (such as appropriate compensation and perhaps tax and insurance issues). You'll also bear the brunt of the work and take the losses, but your pay-off in the long run will be worth it. Your revenue streams will consist of live performance monies, songwriting credits, record royalties, and T-shirt sales. As a solo artist, group leader, and employer, you ultimately call the shots.

"It's easier to look after number one," says Australian artist Gilli Moon. "Dealing with being a band goes beyond the enjoyment of jamming with music. It's about hierarchy, power, control, and finally, sabotage! I've heard so many bands break up just when they hit the big time. I, on the other hand, just stick to being a solo artist. Though it's more work, I have no regrets. I've learned to respect my band members with money, love, good gigs, and referrals to other projects that feed their personal careers. As a solo artist, it's my thing, and I like it that way."

Q & A WITH BAND LEADER HENRY ROLLINS

Henry Rollins started playing music live in 1980. Since then, he has averaged about 104 shows a year worldwide and has recorded and released a wealth of records, first with the pioneering punk band

Black Flag, and then on his own with Rollins Band. He's relentlessly busy writing books and a column for *Details* magazine, making cameo appearances in films, doing occasional stints as a VJ on MTV, and traveling the country performing his spoken word tours. In this interview, Rollins touches on his philosophy on being a bandleader, as well as on what has kept him alive as a voice in music for over 30 years.

Q: Describe some of the major differences between your role as a band member with Black Flag and your role as a solo artist and the leader of Rollins Band.

H.R: Black Flag was Greg Ginn's band. He wrote most of the songs and called the shots. My current status as bandleader has me making most of the decisions and deciding the band's schedule for touring and recording. The main difference is when you are in charge, you have many factors to take into account. The needs of others, what's best for all in the long run and what the objectives are. This is all entry-level stuff. There's just a lot more to deal with day-to-day than being a paid and working musician.

Q: In standard recording agreements, the record company will want the rights to all leaving members as either a solo artist or as a member of a self-contained band. When you parted ways with Black Flag, did you have any contractual obligations to the record company? How did you handle your exit?

H.R: Greg Ginn owned SST Records, which was the label Black Flag was on. There were no obligations to the label for any of the members when the band parted ways.

Q: As a bandleader, you are obviously responsible for putting together a group of musicians to perform live and in the studio. What are some of the attributes you look for in your musicians?

H.R: What I look for is a love of music by the people in the band. An open mindedness. Knowledge that the music is the master and we are only there to serve it. Understanding that it's going to be fun, but it's also going to be a lot of work. Hard work and a will to perform with much excellence in a live situation is a must. A good band is always good live. No exceptions.

Q: How do you find your musicians? Do you prefer to work with people whom you already know, or who are referred to you by people you know? Do you look for musicians who are experienced and have played with other successful acts?

H.R: I do not look to put together bands very often. I have not played with many lineups. I have been in three bands in 21 years. I first got together with the current members years ago, when I was producing a record for their band, Mother Superior. I was lucky to hook up with good people of such high-caliber musicianship, work-ethic, and desire to tour.

Q: Describe your professional relationship and interactions with your musicians. Although it's your name that is displayed on concert hall marquees and album cover artwork, how much do you rely on your band for feedback when making decisions (e.g., when writing songs)?

H.R: We are a band. We all get the same salary and all have an equal voice in the making of the music. We don't have a "he's the boss thing." I treat all with respect and get the same.

Q: What are the various responsibilities that bandleaders have to their musicians (e.g., from a creative, business, and/or legal perspective)? Please feel free to elaborate.

H.R: I think the leader of the band should be very careful of the welfare of all the other members from the financial to the emotional. The leader is to protect their interests and not do anything to limit their potential. I am very protective of the people I work with, from the band to the crew.

Q: I have noticed that for years you have been quite the entrepreneur. From the written and spoken word, to acting and recording and touring with the Rollins Band, you move from one endeavor to the next as if you were "part machine" [a slogan from Rollins' T-shirts]. How do you keep a balance between all of these activities?

H.R: I work steadily, not frenzied, so I get a lot done. Also, I do what I do to the exclusion of many other things, like friends and family. I just work, for the most part. I spend my down time, for the most part, alone.

Q: One of your T-shirt merchandising designs bears the slogan, "40 years of service." To what do you attribute your success and longevity as a solo artist?

H.R: Commitment, tenacity, and a love of what I do.

Q: It seems that most of your musicians have been pretty committed to Rollins Band over the past years. Has it ever been difficult keeping everyone on board during periods when you're focusing on your other talents? Are you in contact with your band during periods of inactivity?

H.R: When we are not together, the boys have their own band, Mother Superior, which is a full-on writing, touring, and recording unit. They rarely take any time off at all.

Q: You have CDs that are only available for purchase at your live performances and over the Internet. Why did you decide to handle some of your distribution this way? Would you comment on the current state of the record industry, and your predictions of how the Internet and the digital revolution may affect the business in the near future?

H.R: I put out CDs that are sold at the gigs and from our website so people who want to hear more, can. I don't want to clog up our already low priority bin space at retail. I think the music industry is a cesspool of corny bands, and luckily for me, I didn't get any on me. I have no idea as to what the Internet and the digital revolution will do to the recording industry.

Q: Do you have any advice for musicians who are just entering the business, or conversely, who are burned out or are frustrated due to their trials and tribulations in the industry?

H.R: Same advice to both parties: stick to the reason you got into it in the first place. You wanted to play music, right? So you won't mind playing in front of a few people as long as you get to play, right? Good. Also, know that all the greats played through all kinds of highs and lows and ebbs and tides. If you're a player, then play!

3 KEY PLAYERS in Your CAREER

> "If we do not hang together,
> we will surely hang separately."
> —NATHAN HALE

An important element in the development of your career as a musician is ensuring that you're surrounded by professionals who can help you in making critical business decisions. These key professionals are your attorney, personal manager, business manager, talent agent, and record producer. Not only is it important to understand what role each of these key team members play, but also at what point in the development of your career their assistance is necessary. In Part Three we will cover the responsibilities of these music business professionals and offer other helpful advice on developing your career. Note: For those of you on the fast track, refer to the chart below to determine which team player specifically relates to each career need.

AT A GLANCE

An attorney may be needed when:

✦ You're establishing an employment agreement to work with a successful artist.

✦ You're establishing an agreement between band members.

✦ You're ready to be shopped to record labels to get a record deal.

✦ You're preparing to sign a recording contract.

✦ You have serious legal disputes that need to be resolved.

A personal manager may be needed when:

✦ You've exhausted all personal efforts to advance your career.

✦ You need financial backing.

✦ You're ready to be shopped to record labels to get a record deal.

✦ You're preparing to sign a recording contract (or already have).

A business manager may be needed when:

+ You're working with an experienced personal manager.
+ You have a significant amount of money passing through your hands.
+ You've accumulated some assets.

A talent agent may be needed when:

+ You've successfully booked your own gigs and need help getting to the next level (better gigs, more money, expanded territories, etc.).
+ You've been signed to a recording agreement and you're planning to tour nationally or internationally.

A record producer may be needed when:

+ You're ready to demo your songs.
+ You need someone to invest in studio time and shop your record to labels.
+ You're already a signed act and are preparing to record your album.

CHAPTER 6

Your **Attorney**

In his play *Henry VI,* William Shakespeare wrote, "The first thing we do, let's kill all the lawyers." The fact is that most people don't trust attorneys. Part of this mistrust comes from the media's frequent portrayal of lawyers as self-serving mercenaries, and part of it is simply based on myth. We often don't trust what we don't understand—and nothing is more confusing to most of us than the language of lawyers. I once heard a musician joke that he needed an attorney just to explain to him what his other attorney was talking about and a secretary willing to try all day to get either of them on the phone. Nonetheless, attorneys are necessary to the business of music—and to your career. If you're going to survive in the business of music, you're going to need a lawyer you can trust.

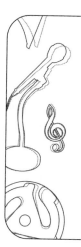

FOOL FOR A CLIENT. A familiar saying claims, "A man who is his own lawyer has a fool for a client." If you don't believe the foregoing, entertainment attorney Stan Findelle suggests you take note of the careers of such artists as Billy Joel, who lost a good portion of his earnings during his rise to stardom because he didn't have proper counsel at key junctures and thus made unwise decisions. One of the surviving members of the late 60's group Badfinger provides another example of the folly of not consulting an attorney. This man will attest he's a "surviving" member because two others in the group hung themselves when they fully realized that a nefarious manager absconded with all their recording contract funds. A half hour with the worst entertainment lawyer in town could've preserved their legal standing and their dough.

Just mentioning the word attorney is enough to send many musicians into a state of panic. After all, how can you pay an attorney's fees when you can barely afford to pay for your band's rehearsal space? Even if money isn't an issue, how do you go about finding a good attorney—one who's honest, responsible, and willing to devote the necessary time and attention to your affairs? Keep reading, and you'll discover the answers to all those questions and more.

THE ROLE OF AN ATTORNEY IN YOUR CAREER

An attorney may be part of a large law firm, an independent firm consisting of two or more lawyers, or work as a sole practitioner in a private practice. Although there's a general misconception that attorneys know "everything" about "anything," keep in mind that attorneys, like doctors, have their own areas of expertise. An attorney may be certified in family law, patent and trademark law, taxation, workers' compensation, or criminal law for instance. Did you notice that I didn't mention entertainment law? That's because no specific certification currently exists for entertainment law. So how can anyone claim to be an entertainment attorney?

Entertainment attorneys are lawyers who have acquired specialized knowledge in the music, film, and television business by representing clients in these industries. Since the entertainment industry is centered around New York, Nashville, and Los Angeles, the best entertainment attorneys can be found in these cities—although that doesn't mean you can't find great attorneys elsewhere.

Despite the number of bad attorney jokes that plague the music industry today (and I'm sure you've heard at least a few of them), an attorney can play a key role in your career and may very well be one of the most important members of your team. When you sign an agreement, an attorney's job is to make sure that your best interests are protected and that you understand exactly what you're signing. An attorney knows how to make sense out of all the complicated writing in contracts called "legalese" and knows what terms (such as royalty rates in record contracts) are considered "fair and standard." Some attorneys can represent you in lawsuits with other musicians and music companies and can also help attract the attention of record labels who might be interested in signing your band. In short, attorneys see the "big picture"; they handle all the business and legal matters involved in shaping your career. If there's a specialized area a particular attorney doesn't handle, such as litigation in a court of law, he or she will be able to refer you to an attorney who has expertise in that area.

An attorney may be one of the first professional people you hire. When you're in need of legal advise, be sure that you hire an attorney who has experience in the music business and who understands the ins and outs of a recording contract. Hiring a friend who is a real-estate attorney may initially save you a couple of bucks, but that isn't the most prudent approach to take with your career.

As a general rule, you should always speak with an attorney before signing anything—except, jokes author Mark Halloran in his book *The Musician's Business and Legal Guide,* your autograph! Not many people are crazy enough to sign a recording agreement without having a lawyer review its terms first. There are other scenarios, however, where the value of having a lawyer's assistance isn't so obvious.

For example, imagine that you're in a new band in which all the members get along really well and have committed to doing whatever it takes to make it to the top. You're really excited about the group, but after reading this book, you know you ought to have a preliminary band agreement that defines the terms of your business relationship (see Chapter 2). The last thing you want to do is rock the boat by, God forbid, talking about business, but on the other hand you don't want to get screwed down the road—something that you know happens all the time in bands. This, then, is a good time to consult with an experienced entertainment attorney who can serve as the middleman between the band members and keep the peace, and at the same time make sure the band gets started in business on the right foot. An attorney will explain the importance of having a band membership agreement and discuss the details of what an agreement should include. Other issues, such as how future profits will be divided between members, how the band will make decisions on business matters, and who has the right to the band name will also be determined. Remember, though, that a good attorney won't dictate the terms of the agreement, but, rather, assist the band members in drafting the terms they want.

Now let's imagine that your band has been rehearsing for several months; you've written some really great songs that your audiences seem to love, and you feel it's the perfect time to get your music recorded on tape. The only problem is that you don't own any home recording gear and you have limited funds to book a professional recording studio. Out of the blue, a studio owner offers to record and produce a ten-song CD for you on his downtime. He tells you not to worry about paying him at the moment and that you can work things out later. In the meantime, he suggests that you rewrite certain parts of your songs and that he's the guy to help you do it. He also tells you he's got tons of connections and that he can help get the project signed. You'd like to trust the guy, but something just doesn't feel right. What does this producer really have in mind? Who will end up owning the master tapes? Will you be able to sell your CDs at your shows if you haven't paid a dime for studio time? This may be an appropriate time for an experienced entertainment attorney to define the legal terms of your working relationship with the producer. It could very well be that your producer friend is trying to lock you into some kind of production deal that may not be your best option at the moment. On the other hand, it might be the big break for which you've been waiting. In either case, it's always best to protect yourself by being extremely clear about the terms of any working relationship from the start. Attorney Stan Findelle warns, "The so-called production deal scenario, as loosely described above, is one of the most potentially dangerous to a young artist or group's career. Here is the situation where your recording rights are sold for a pittance to a scoundrel with a label in his garage. The so-called producer can then wholesale you to a major label and keep most of the profit. Make sure to talk to an attorney before signing anything." (Chapter 10 discusses record producers in more detail.)

Now let's say that a year has passed since you formed your band, you've decided to blow off working with the local producer, and you've finally secured a loan to pay for your own CD. Your band is starting to get a lot of attention, and things are moving fast. Your songs are getting played on college radio stations, and you're receiving favorable reviews in a number of fan magazines. You're drawing good crowds to your shows and selling CDs and T-shirts over the Internet, too. You've got a great band name and everyone loves the logo. But you're beginning to worry that someone may rip off your band name or claim that they were using it first. Should you trademark the band's name at this stage of the game? If so, is it necessary to register your name in both domestic and foreign territories? How do you know if someone else is already using your band name? Books like this one you're reading can provide answers to these questions (see the interview with Jeff Cohen in Chapter 2), but you should always rely on an experienced entertainment attorney to address your individual concerns. Your attorney will help you decide if trademark registration is appropriate for your band and will advise you on how to go about doing it. Should you discover that another band is already using your name, an attorney can also help you determine whether it makes sense to take legal action or simply relinquish the name, and come up with another.

Finally, let's imagine that you're now the hottest local band in your area and are selling out medium-sized clubs. You're getting tons of press, and local colleges are playing your tunes. It's obvious your band is special, and you feel you have a really good chance at getting signed to a major label. The only problem is that no one is knocking on your door. You already know that record labels don't accept unsolicited materials in the mail, so how do you get them to recognize your band? A&R representatives are certainly not going to magically appear in the audience at one of your shows—you live in Idaho! This is another good time to contact an attorney who can help you by "shopping" your band to the record companies. Record companies know that a reputable attorney doesn't have time to represent a band he or she doesn't believe in, so when a lawyer they respect comes calling, they're likely to respond quickly. A good attorney is in constant touch with the movers and shakers of the entertainment industry and can be the person you need to help your band get a recording contract. Additionally, once a record deal is on the table and it's time to negotiate terms, you'll already have developed a working relationship and a level of trust with your attorney. (Note: Personal managers, as you'll learn in Chapter 7, are also known to shop tapes. But since a young band's first manager is likely to be someone just breaking into the music business, a well-connected attorney may be the best person to effectively shop the group.)

> Be wary of some of the tape "shopping services" advertised in magazines, as well as of lawyers who shop a number of bands at once. The record companies know that the screening process in these situations is minimal and will not give your music the attention it deserves if it's presented to them in such a way. Attorney Shawna Hilleary of Artist Law Group also notes that most of these tape shopping services charge you up-front fees. However, keep in mind that anyone truly interested in your career who thinks they can get you signed will be happy to work on commission.

HIRING YOUR ATTORNEY

The first step in hiring an attorney is to know what you're looking for. As the earlier part of this chapter explained, not all attorneys specialize in the same areas of law. Even within the category of entertainment law, not all attorneys shop tapes to record labels or have experience in trademark registration. So how do you find an attorney that specializes in your area of concern? And what specific qualities do you look for in an attorney once you've found some candidates to represent you?

Finding an Attorney

To find an attorney appropriate to your needs, begin by utilizing all available resources. These include personal referrals, lawyer referral services, music publications, music conferences, and college and adult education courses.

Personal Referrals. The best way to find a good attorney is by asking for referrals from other musicians and industry professionals. Just be sure to consider the source of the referral; just because a musician is successful doesn't mean his attorney is right for you. If you're still in the minors, a big-league lawyer may not be able to give you the personal attention you need. Consider the motive of the person making the referral as well. For instance, an individual who's an accountant may simply be returning a favor to an attorney who referred someone to him. If a record company or personal manager with whom you're doing business recommends a lawyer, you may need to consider a situation called a conflict of interest (discussed later in this chapter). In short, you not only need to use discretion when choosing your attorney, but also when asking for referrals.

Lawyer Referral Services Another way to find an attorney is through a referral service. Ask your state or local bar association whether there is a referral service available in your area. The California Lawyers for the Arts, located in San Francisco, refers callers to lawyers throughout California who deal exclusively with the arts. In Los Angeles, you can call the Lawyer Referral Service of the Los Angeles County Bar Association, and in Beverly Hills, there's the Beverly Hills Bar Association Lawyer Referral Service. In New York City, you can call the Association for the Bar of New York City, and in Nashville, there's the Lawyer Referral Service for the Nashville Bar Association. You get the point. Operators at referral services will listen to your legal concerns and direct you to one of the attorneys on their panel. These operators will not, however, guarantee the quality of an attorney's services or tell you which attorney you should choose. It's up to you to set up a phone consultation and assess the attorney for yourself. There will typically be a small fee for the initial consultation; fees for continued services are discussed between attorneys and clients on an individual basis. Since big league "heavy hitters" aren't part of referral services (you may not be ready for one of these guys anyway), it's unlikely you'll be referred to Mick Jagger's attorney. Nevertheless, it's well worth your time to call a service in your area to learn what it has to offer.

Attorney Stan Findelle adds, "So many prospective clients call law offices every week looking for an attorney to shop them that it's difficult for lawyers to discern who might be worth a second look. One question our office always asks is if the artist is presently appearing live. This indicates the act is a finished product as opposed to a half-baked studio creation that would be embarrassing to present to record labels. Before even thinking of calling an attorney, artists should just get out there and play. A band may even find that interested attorneys approach them. There are many young ambitious lawyers who actually troll the live club scene in search of upcoming talent."

Music Publications Music publications may also be helpful to you when searching for an attorney. Books such as *The Recording Industry Source Book* (published by Artistpro.com), *The Yellow Pages of Rock* (published by Album Network), and *Billboard International Talent and Touring Directory* (published by Billboard Books) list hundreds of attorneys, agents, and personal managers. These resources can all be found either in bookstores or online. Weekly trade magazines such as *Billboard* magazine are also good sources of information; they'll tell you which attorneys are signing the hottest bands. Finally, try checking to see whether your favorite band has listed its attorney's name and contact number on its CD artwork.

> Check out The Music Business Registry by Ritch Esra by contacting www.musicregistry.com.

Music Conferences Music conferences such as the National Association of Music Merchants (NAMM), South by Southwest (SXSW) Music and Media Conference, and National Association of Recording Merchandisers (NARM) are sure ways to meet people in the music business.

Attorneys and other industry professionals usually speak as panelists, which gives you a good opportunity to ask them a few questions, introduce yourself, and at the very least ask for a business card so that you're able to get in touch with them again later. Keep in mind, however, that music conferences usually draw the

For more information on music conferences, see www.sxsx.com, www.namm.com, and www.narm.com.

heavy hitters of the business, so don't despair if a panelist or speaker is unwilling to take the time to help you, they're just in high demand.

College and Adult Education Courses Another way to find and meet a good attorney is by taking college and adult education courses in music business, such as the ones offered in Los Angeles at

For information on college music programs and adult education classes, see www.uclaextension.org and www.musiciansatlas.com.

the UCLA Extension program (check a college near you for music-related classes). Entertainment courses at the Extension program are often taught by attorneys active in the business. Taking their class will not only teach you a great deal about the business, it will also provide you the opportunity to form new business relationships as well. Perhaps this may lead to a working relationship down the road.

Qualities to Look for in an Attorney

Once you've compiled a list of potential attorneys, you can begin the process of contacting them and setting up a first appointment. In most cases, an attorney will be willing to speak with you over the phone to discuss your needs and determine whether you even need legal assistance. If you're just starting out in the music business, or if your legal concerns are minor, it will be difficult for you to get a high-powered attorney on the phone at all. Be prepared to express your legal problems and concerns clearly, to ask questions about the services each attorney provides, and to discuss potential fees so that you can ultimately make an informed decision about your legal representation. If you're seeking an attorney to shop your band, you should also be ready to send him or her a press kit containing a sample of your music, a photograph of your band, and some biographical information. At worst, if an attorney doesn't have the time to get involved with you, he or she may be willing to refer you to someone who does.

Personality When you meet with attorneys, it's important to assess their personalities. You don't have to be the best of friends, but you want to at least feel comfortable when you're sitting in the same room or talking on the phone with him or her. Do they take time to explain things to you, or do they rush through the conversation or talk down to you? Do they have a genuine interest in your career and music, or do you feel that they're meeting you because you were referred by "so and so." Also of concern is your attorney's personality and his or her attitude towards other business professionals. You don't want a hothead for an attorney who can blow deals for you, or conversely a wimp who won't make any deals happen. These are all important concerns and ones that should be taken seriously before choosing your attorney.

Clout An attorney's clout can mean the difference between getting and losing a record deal. When you speak with lawyers, don't be afraid to ask them the names of the clients they represent and then check these references. If they shop tapes to record labels, ask them about the groups they've helped to get signed. Don't expect to get detailed information about the actual deals that they've negotiated, however. That is privileged information, and you should be wary of any attorney who violates such a confidence.

Keep in mind that powerful and well-connected attorneys get their calls returned more quickly than attorneys who are new in the business; however, if a star attorney is too busy handling star clients, you may very well get lost in the shuffle. Young, ambitious attorneys with great net-working skills may be even more valuable to you because they'll have more time to devote to your career. In any case, you should be aware of the fact that the attorney you choose to represent you will not always be the person who does most of the work. Many attorneys are gregarious types who work aggressively to bring in new business while their associates do the actual work of drafting the contracts. Be sure to ask attorneys who else will be involved in some of their day-to-day work, and how long they've been working with those people.

Last, but definitely not least, always remember that an attorney's clout can't do anything for your career if you don't have talent to deliver. If you don't have talent, an attorney's clout will at best only get you a more polite rejection.

ATTORNEY FEE STRUCTURES

Samuel Butler, the renowned 19th century English novelist, once said, "In the law, the only thing certain is the expense." People know attorneys aren't cheap, and that's why they avoid calling them in the first place. As a result, musicians often fly blindly and work without contracts or accept terms to agreements they barely understand. Inevitably, they run into legal problems.

Attorneys typically bill their clients according to either a flat fee, a percentage of the deal they negotiate for the client, or an hourly rate. At your initial meeting with an attorney, find out what billing method he or she uses.

Hourly Fees

The hourly fee an attorney charges can range anywhere from $100 for a young attorney to $500 or more for a high-powered attorney. But before you freak out completely, you should know that hourly billing is not as common as some of the other fee structures discussed here. Nonetheless, an attorney who charges by the hour will typically send you a monthly bill. Find out whether you can use a credit card to make payments and whether you'll be charged interest for late payments. You may also want to ask if your attorney can set a cap on his or her costs in the event of your case drag-ging out for an extended period of time. It's also important to ask exactly how you'll be billed. For instance, you may be billed at increments of an hour. This means that you may be charged a quar-ter of an hour's fee for a phone call that only takes three minutes to make. Finally, ask what expens-es you'll be charged for, such as faxes, photocopies, postage, messenger services, or even adminis-trative work. Your bill should be easy to understand—you should always be able to understand exactly what you're paying for.

Flat Fees

Most attorneys are willing to provide a flat estimate of what their services will cost; in actuality, this is their hourly rate multiplied by the number of hours they expect it will take to complete a job. To draft a short agreement, for instance, your fee may be $500 plus out-of-pocket expenses such as faxes and phone calls. Negotiating a recording agreement can cost anywhere from $2000 to $20,000, sometimes more. Of course, if you have a friend who's an attorney, you may be able to talk him or her into charging you much less.

Percentage of the Deal Most attorneys are also willing to work for a percentage of the advance from the deals they negotiate. For example, for negotiating a recording deal, an attorney may agree to work for 5 percent of the advance you receive (which, by the way, is the industry standard). Out-of-pocket expenses are again separate. When you first meet with an attorney, if he or she estimates that your bill will be more than $1000, regardless of how you're being charged, you have the right to ask for a "fee agreement" in writing. A good attorney will suggest that you price shop to make sure his or her fees are reasonable.

As I've pointed out, the fee most attorneys charge for what is known as a "label shopping agreement" is typically ten percent of the income derived from finding and negotiating the record deal. *This may apply for the full length of the deal.* For instance, for every album your band records—long after his job is done—your attorney may earn a ten percent fee for initially shopping your band. For this reason, a "cap" may be negotiated that determines the total amount the attorney's percentage will yield (e.g., $30,000 over the life of the recording deal). Otherwise, an attorney may be willing to drop the percentage he or she takes for subsequent recordings (i.e., 10 percent on the first recording, 7.5 percent on the second, 5 percent on the third, etc.).

Attorney Stan Findelle adds, "From my point of view, 'shopping' a deal is worth a hell of a lot more than being the service lawyer once a record label contract is propounded. If a lawyer hits the jackpot for an act by attaining a deal where there wasn't one previously—more than a minor miracle these days—that lawyer should be entitled to a hefty percentage of the take; as much as 20 per-

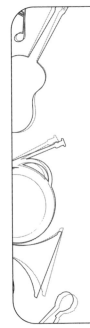

YOU GET WHAT YOU PAY FOR. In order to save money, or perhaps because they just don't have any, many musicians hire attorneys who are willing to represent them for a discounted fee. If you're lucky, you'll get all the attention you need and your issues will be resolved to your satisfaction. *This isn't always the way things work out, however!* For instance, one musician hired an attorney who was a friend of a friend to review a short eight page contract. As a favor, the attorney quoted the musician a flat fee of $250, but the job ultimately required much more time than the attorney had initially estimated. The attorney was obviously frustrated with the matter, and began rushing the musician through phone conversations, and taking forever before reviewing second drafts of the contract. It was clear the job wasn't a priority to him. Certain contractual terms that were important to the artist, such as creative control, were disregarded by the attorney as unimportant for negotiation. The attorney essentially reviewed the boilerplate terms of the contract to make sure the musician was protected, but didn't put much effort into reviewing the finer points. In the end, the musician was dissatisfied with the final contract, and this had a negative affect on his enthusiasm for the project.

cent is not unheard of. Why? Because this lawyer has turned water into wine: he or she got the artist plucked out of the unwashed mob and into the ballpark."

Retainers

Some attorneys may ask for a retainer up front against the cost of your legal bills. For example, if you pay a retainer of $500, and your attorney charges you $1000 in legal services, the $500 retainer will be deducted from your bill. At that time, you may be asked to pay the $500 balance as well as another retainer to be held in trust for further services rendered. In the event that your attorney never earns the amount of the initial retainer and you decide to discontinue your business relationship with him or her, the remaining retainer should be paid back; if you pay a retainer of $500 and your attorney's charges for the month are only $300, the attorney should return the extra $200.

GETTING THE MOST OUT OF YOUR ATTORNEY

Once you've hired an attorney, you want to make sure that the relationship runs as smoothly as possible. Attorneys are not inexpensive; nor do they have a lot of free time. Keeping that in mind, when you contact your attorney, make sure to get the most out of him. Consider the following tips.

> Do you really need to hire and pay an attorney just to answer one or two short legal questions you may have? Maybe not. Some musicians, under the pretense of becoming potential clients, are known to interview as many attorneys on the phone as possible and actually get their legal questions answered for free—this is, of course, really unfair to the attorneys. Instead of going through all that, check out the Nolo Self Help Legal Center on the web at www.nolo.com, and continue to read as many books about the music business as possible.

Be Prepared

Before contacting your attorney on any matter, be clear about what you want to accomplish. Make a list of all the points you'd like to discuss and write a list of questions for each. Though many attorneys will object, you might even ask if it's okay to tape record your conversation with him or her. That way, if something isn't immediately clear, you can replay the conversation later to figure it out. This is also helpful if you're in a band, and one of the members can't be present at a meeting with the band's lawyer.

> Many attorneys dislike having their consults taped. The last thing they want is to provide evidence of some misstatement they may make that fuels a frivolous malpractice action against them.

Be on Time

When a band meets with its lawyer as a group, your attorney won't be thrilled to have to repeat what has already been said for a member who walks in the door 15 minutes late. Make sure everyone shows up on time for important meetings.

Appoint a Band Representative

It's also best to appoint one band member to serve as your liaison between the attorney and the rest of the band to avoid having every member of the group call whenever they have a question or want an update on a particular matter. Attorney Stan Findelle says, "This is a must, especially if the artist is being charged by the hour. I've had four different guys call from a group constantly, where

I should've billed four times the amount." Appointing one member to make calls will also make life easier for your attorney, who won't have to re-explain issues to each band member, and will also prevent the awkward possibility of each member getting his or her own take on a matter. By having a liaison, your group can put together a list of questions, and then one individual can make the call or attend the meeting. As long as your liaison is effective in relaying information to the other members of the band, this system usually works adequately. Nevertheless, at times the other members may feel they're relinquishing control and are at the mercy of the appointed liaison. In these cases, your band can always make group phone calls via speaker phone so that everyone can participate in the conversation. A second solution is to have everyone attend meetings, but appoint one representative to do all the talking.

Keep Your Attorney Informed

It's important to keep your attorney up to date regarding business matters. For instance, if your attorney is shopping your band, and you're unexpectedly approached by an A&R representative from another label after one of your shows, your attorney should be the first person to hear about it.

Attorney Stan Findelle adds, "It's surprising how many acts may actually NOT inform their attorney that they've been approached directly by an A&R person—suddenly, they feel the worm has turned, and they can cut the deal themselves or look for a name lawyer. Thus, if a lawyer does take on an act for 'on the come' shopping, there should be a document involved that says the lawyer is in for a percentage of the record deal, regardless of the source of the offer."

Keep Good Records

Keep clear records of all business correspondence and be prepared to bring copies to business meetings or to fax copies to your attorney before a phone conversation. It can be difficult to explain to your attorney from memory what a producer is offering your band. You can ask the producer to put a proposal in writing so that your attorney has something tangible to review. Another effective way of keeping good records is to ask anyone you have an important phone conversation with to put a summary of your discussion into a letter. It's also helpful to save all email correspondence in a file in chronological order.

Tell The Truth

It's extremely important to be forthright with your attorney from day one. Your lawyer is there to help you, and if you're working at cross purposes, the only one you're hurting is yourself. An attorney needs to clearly understand the details of a situation in order to do his or her best to solve the problem. If someone is suing you, for instance, because you threw a bottle into the audience and cut a fan's face (this has actually happened), don't tell your attorney that you have no knowledge of the incident; later someone may turn up with the whole incident on videotape, and by that time, your attorney may be able to do little to defend you.

Pay Your Bills on Time

A surefire way to avoid putting a damper on your relationship with your lawyer is to pay your bills on time. Your attorney is running a business, just like you are.

Never Sign Anything without Your Attorney's Involvement

To avoid a lot of potential problems, never sign anything without having your attorney review it first. After all, that's why you retained legal counsel in the first place.

Keeping Your Attorney in Check

Once you've hired an attorney, monitor his or her progress on business dealings. Don't make the mistake of giving up too much responsibility to others. After all, no one should care more about your career than you.

Do you feel you're not receiving the attention you deserve? Is it difficult to get your attorney to return your calls? Is your attorney "out of town" and never available? If your lawyer isn't getting back to you in a timely fashion, there may be a problem. "I've been busy" is not an excuse.

Do you feel you're not being sufficiently informed about what's going on with regard to business or legal problems? There's an old joke: "How many lawyers does it take to screw in a lightbulb? None, they'd rather keep you in the dark." If you feel that you're being rushed through your meetings or phone conversations, or that your lawyer is always taking phone calls during your meetings, then perhaps those are clues that you're not being considered a priority. If your attorney intimidates you or makes you feel like a complete idiot during meetings, you may want to consider someone more sensitive to your needs. Remember, there's a fine line between a lawyer who's a tough go-getter attorney *for* you, and one who's a tough insensitive person *with* you.

Is resolution to your legal problems taking forever? Are you receiving no logical reason for the delays? You might want to take a second look at your attorney. In the music business, there's one expression you better memorize: "Hurry up and wait." Things usually take longer than you'd like. Recording contracts contain plenty of pages that must be carefully scrutinized by your attorney, and a deal can take time to negotiate. But nonetheless, there should always be a reasonable explanation. If your attorney doesn't have the enthusiasm, experience, or clout to get the job done in a timely manner, you may want to consider making a change to someone who can.

Are your legal bills twice as much as you were led to believe they would be? Are you being billed for services that don't seem compatible with the actual time your business relationship endured? You deserve

TIME KEEPS ON TICKING. A musician friend once told me he discovered that his legal problems were not being solved because the attorneys on the opposing side simply didn't respect his lawyer at all. They perceived him as a young, inexperienced guy from the sticks who was out of his league playing with top New York entertainment attorneys. They intentionally played contractual games with him by agreeing to strike one clause, and then reinserting it elsewhere in the agreement where it might be overlooked. The New York big-wigs never returned calls and claimed they never received faxes. They would conveniently leave town for weeks at a time (or so they said), dragging the case on for months. Not only did this cost my friend thousands of dollars in legal expenses, but he never got reasonable explanations from his attorney for the delays. Frustrated, confused, and feeling out of the loop, my friend finally decided to seek new legal counsel.

an explanation. If the method of your billing changes, or if the price you're being charged goes up in the middle of working with your attorney, you should demand an explanation.

Does your attorney appear to be unnecessarily aggressive in your business dealings? An aggressive attorney can break a deal just as fast as he or she can make one. Perhaps you're being advised to hold out for more money than a record company is willing to pay you. Consider one possible motive: If your attorney is working for a percentage of the deal that is being negotiated, then the bigger the deal, the bigger the commission. Don't blow your business opportunities because your attorney is being greedy.

And finally, do you feel your attorney is looking after your best interests at all times? Suppose you're on the verge of signing a record agreement and have hired the same attorney who is representing the record company. This is unlikely, but bear with me. You want the biggest advance and royalty rate you can get, while the record company wants to get away with giving you the smallest advance and royalty possible. How can an attorney look after the best interests of opposing sides in a business negotiation? This situation is called a "conflict of interest" because each party's best interests are at stake and the same lawyer cannot possibly represent both fairly.

Conflicts of interest are not always obvious. For example, a conflict may exist when an attorney is representing the members of a band who are putting together an internal band membership agreement. Does a conflict exist here? It does if the members decide not to divide the profits equally at the direct advice of their attorney. When a band hires its personal manager's lawyer to review their management agreement, a conflict of interest may exist there as well.

An ethical attorney should disclose when a conflict of interest exists and advise you to seek representation elsewhere. The exception to this rule is a situation in which both parties consent to the representation of the same attorney. The attorney must show that both parties can be represented fairly and then ask both parties to sign something called a "conflict waiver." A conflict waiver protects the attorney in case either party later claims it was represented unfairly.

When you are hiring an attorney, or even after hiring one, it's always advisable to keep your eyes open for potential conflicts of interest. If you think a conflict exists, it's probably fair to assume that neither side can be represented fairly, and you should therefore immediately seek representation elsewhere.

THE SNAKE AND THE HEADLESS HORSEMAN. In a classic example of a conflict of interest cited by Richard Stim in his book *Music Law,* singer Billy Joel claimed that his attorneys were giving his personal manager kickbacks and pay-offs for deals entered into on his behalf. The only evidence uncovered to support Joel's allegations was a loan made by his attorneys to his manager to buy a racehorse. The attorneys denied all of Joel's allegations and the case was eventually settled one year later, in 1993. The outcome of the case is confidential, but I'm told that Joel won a healthy settlement. As for the racehorse, it was allegedly killed to collect insurance money.

CHANGING YOUR LEGAL REPRESENTATION

If you're having problems with your attorney, if you don't feel you're receiving adequate legal representation, what can you do? The best way to resolve any problem is to bring it out in the open. Even when dealing with an attorney who's become your friend, it's important to remember that you're talking about business here, and immediate steps must be taken to amend any situation gone astray. If a situation can't be resolved, you should know that it's your legal right to change attorneys at any time.

Before you hire a new attorney, however, you must sever your relationship with your first attorney. At your request, your former attorney must allow your new attorney to review and photocopy all confidential records regarding your case, even if you have an outstanding bill. If there's unused money in your retainer, your former attorney must return it to you at the time you terminate your relationship.

Firing anyone is never an easy thing to do. But your career should be foremost in your mind. If you're not getting the kind of legal representation you need, don't be afraid to make a change.

CHAPTER 7

Your **Personal Manager**

The close-knit relationship that exists between an artist and a personal manager is not much different from that between a professional athlete and coach. The artist fully entrusts the manager to envision his or her goals and help put a strategic plan of attack into effect that will allow you to attain those goals. The artist relies on a manager to be a motivator, counselor, confidant, diplomat, and day-to-day business person. Having the right personal manager at your side can bring you success beyond your wildest imagination. Having the wrong personal manager, however, can be devastating to your career. Needless to say, choosing a personal manager may be one of the most important career decisions that you make.

THE ROLE OF A PERSONAL MANAGER IN YOUR CAREER

If you ask musicians to define what a personal manager does, their answers will vary from "They help you get better gigs" to "They help you get a record deal." Well, getting gigs is supposed to be a talent agent's job (see Chapter 9), and shopping your music to record labels may be better suited for an experienced entertainment attorney, as you'll see later in this chapter (and also in Chapter 6). So you might ask, "Why do you need a personal manager?"

Managers have been described by some in the business as the chief operating officers of an artist's company. I like to think of managers as air traffic controllers and of the artists, talent agents, A&R reps, business managers, publicists, stylists (and just about anyone else you can think of in the industry) as pilots. The air traffic controller has complete control of the runway, and guides the pilots flying in and out of the airport to safety. If the air traffic controller gives one wrong signal to any one pilot, complete disaster ensues.

By strict definition, a manager's role is to advise and counsel you in all aspects of the music business. The manager provides guidance and ensures that everyone involved in your career pulls together in the same direction to achieve success. Interestingly enough, in management, there are no surefire methods to achieve success. Every manager may take a different approach—whether it be conventional or unconventional. Therefore, the best way to understand what managers do is to take a look at the various ways they're involved in the different stages of your career—from before you secure a record deal onward, including artist development, securing contracts, dealing with record companies, and assisting with live engagements and touring.

Artist Development

Your manager helps you define your "target demographic audience," making sure that everything from your publicity photos to your public image to your stage presence to what you say to the press is consistent with your vibe and style of music. Your manager's role is to fully develop and package you as an artist, so that when the record labels get involved, they will be less inclined to attempt to remake you as something you're not. A good manager will help you find what feels the most comfortable and natural to you. In a lecture he delivered at UCLA in 2002[1], manager Andy Gould, whose clients include Rob Zombie, Linkin Park, and Static-X says, "The job of a manager is to let [his or her] artists breathe and develop into who they are."

Your manager may even find unique ways to associate you with certain "lifestyles" in order to create a specific image for you. This is called "lifestyle marketing." For instance, since heavy metal appeals to kids who skateboard and snowboard, if you were a member of a heavy metal band, your manager might try to find sponsorships for the group through skateboarding or snowboarding companies. Your manager might even look to certain clothing manufactures for endorsements. The options are limitless. Associating you with a particular lifestyle helps to define and make your image that much more believable and real.

Securing Contracts

Your manager helps get exposure for you by setting up industry showcases with potential record and publishing companies. Your manager must research what labels and A&R men are best suited to your talents and musical style, based not only on a company's past signings or successes, but also on a company's financial stability—whether they're in trouble and about to consolidate or go under. Your manager must also be able to distinguish between an A&R representative who understands your music and your vision and an A&R rep who's just blowing smoke up your rear end, so to speak.

Your manager may also help you to find an attorney who can shop your music to various record companies. Attorneys deal with hundreds of clients in the course of their careers, while managers may deal with just a few; therefore, many attorneys are very well connected in the industry and may provide the extra push you need to get a deal. In such an instance, your manager will work with the attorney on key contract points in your recording and publishing deals. For instance, your manager must understand essential points of negotiation in recording agreements such as the agreement term, the recording and video fund, tour support, publishing issues, and creative control. But in the words of Gary Borman, manager for artists such as Garbage, Faith Hill, and James Taylor, "The manager will also know when to shut up and let the attorney do his job."

[1] *Note: all the quotations from personal managers in this chapter are from a 2002 UCLA lecture series or from personal interviews.*

Dealing with Record Companies

Another of your manager's responsibilities is to meet with the various departments at the record label, from sales to radio to publicity, to make sure that everyone is acting in concert in preparation for an album release. Manager Andy Gould adds, "The manager must keep the entire record label talking. Believe it or not, the people at a label don't always talk to each other."

Your manager puts together a marketing plan and tries to sell the label and the A&R rep on making you a top priority. A marketing plan may include ideas for what the album artwork should look like, when the album should be shipped to stores, the number of records that should be shipped, how retail buyers at record stores can get excited about ordering the album, and whether or not the album should be released in foreign territories. Your manager must also persuade the label to agree with what he or she thinks the first radio single should be, as well as on how far in advance of the record hitting the stores the first single should be "serviced at radio" (promoted by any combination of sending your single to radio stations, having regional or independent radio promoters try to get your single added to play lists, and placing advertisements in trade magazines such as *Hits, Album Network,* and *Records and Radio*), and when you should begin filming your video. Additionally, the manager must try to sell the record company on what he or she thinks is the best time for you to begin touring in support of your album. Attorney Jeffrey Light suggests, "Get the band touring three or four months before [their] record comes out. Someone might see a poster or hear the band's name, and when they hear the single on the radio, they'll have something to connect to. If they go and buy their record—boom, there's a fire." It's also advisable that once it has been decided when a band is going to tour, the manager informs the record label of all the band's touring dates so that the sales departments can try to push the band's radio single in those key cities.

Personal managers and record companies often have different sets of priorities. While the personal manager wants to establish a long-term career for his or her artist, the record company worries about quarterly reports and turning a quick profit. However, it's important the manager does not view the record company as an adversary. Good management makes it possible for you to hold hands with your label and do your best to put your head on your pillow at the end of the day and know that you are a step further ahead than you were the day before.

Assisting with Live Engagements and Touring

Your manager will also help you to find a licensed talent agent who specifically works on procuring live performances. Your manager will work together with this agent to determine what tours are best for you, to make sure that you're getting the best offers from concert promoters, and even to help direct your performances from city to city.

Your manager will work with your business manager to put together a tour budget, and then arrange hotel accommodations and transportation, hire stage and lighting crews, and even help get equipment endorsements. Your manager may even travel with you or will hire a "tour manager" who is responsible for keeping a watchful eye on all activities on the road. Your manager makes sure that you are meeting and mingling with radio station personnel, retail sales people, magazine and newspaper journalists, and, of course, that you're shaking hands with fans all over the country. John Leshay, manager of pop sensation Mandy Moore, adds, "The idea is to get the fans to feel they own

TURNING BAD INTO GOOD. To illustrate yet another of a personal manager's roles, Bud Prager shares a classic road story concerning his band Foreigner. Tickets were not selling well for one of the band's performances, so Prager and the concert promoter put their heads together and decided to charge a "one car-one price" admission to the show. This meant that however many people could squeeze into a car, would only be charged for the price of one. To everyone's disbelief, the plan backfired when a tractor-trailer truck showed up with over 130 people crammed into the cargo space. Rather than turning the truck away, Prager quickly phoned up the local news media, and in minutes helicopters were buzzing above with cameras rolling. The exposure the band received on television that night was priceless. Prager took a potentially bad situation and made it good. In Prager's words, "That's the true essence of management."

a piece of the band from the start. That can be potentially worth millions in the long run." As you can see, a manager's touring responsibilities and concerns are endless, and he or she must be on top of them all. Touring is when you can build a grassroots following with your fans and an identity, or "brand," that can keep you earning money for years.

Manager Richard Bishop, who handles clients such as Henry Rollins, emphasizes that, "Just as important to touring, a manager must know when to take their artist off . . . the road. The last thing you want to do is oversaturate the artist. Too much time between an artist's first and second record is not always good." (Chapter 13 covers touring in detail.)

As you can see, personal managers are responsible for a great deal—and we've only touched the tip of the iceberg. Now let's take a quick look at your management options.

MANAGEMENT OPTIONS

Before seeking out and hiring a personal manager, it's important to understand the various types of management options that are available to you. The most common choices, depending on how far along you are in your career, are self-management, start-up management by an individual attempting to break into the music business, and established professional management.

Self-Management

In the early stages of your career, unless one of your relatives happens to be the president of Warner Bros. Records, *no one is going to help you until you first help yourself!* Remember that *good management must always begin with the artist.* Too often, musicians believe that the solution to their problems is finding some third party to magically whisk them up from rehearsal room to super-stardom. It's true that an experienced manager can make good things happen fast, but having a motivated manager does not make it okay for you to be lazy. First, you must seriously ask yourself if there's anything you can be doing yourself. For example:

✦ Have you written a large repertoire of songs and developed them
to the best of your ability?

- Have you demo'ed your songs and gone as far as selling your own CDs at live performances and over the Internet?
- Are you booking your own shows and doing everything you can to promote them?
- Are you building a strong fan base and getting fans excited about your music?
- Are you stimulating interest in the press and over the Internet?
- Have you given serious thought to your career vision or goals, and do you know exactly what you want to accomplish?
- Are all members of your band united in a common goal?

You must acquire a basic knowledge of the music business and devote some good old-fashioned hard work of your own to your career before ever thinking about a getting a personal manager. Even the members of Mötley Crüe, whose chaotic demeanor made them appear completely incapable of functioning at a professional business level, worked their butts off early on and generated career momentum, long before ever getting involved with their first manager (see "Banging Nails by Day, Banging Heads by Night," p. 123). Some artists have it so together that the first time a personal manager comes into play is after they've signed an agreement with a record company. A band may then be better positioned to pick a more powerful manager. But even then, the band must continue to monitor the progress of their business and work with their personal manager to build a successful career. After all, the personal manager ultimately works for the band!

Start-up Management

So, when is the right time to get a personal manager? Perhaps you've reached a point in your career when the time you spend running your business is inhibiting your creative development—or maybe you've done everything in your power to advance your career and can't go any further without a helping hand. If either of those things are true, perhaps finding a personal manager is the right solution. But the reality is that until you're a signed act or are close to being signed, most managers with any clout or power will not be interested in working with you. These managers are simply too busy handling artists that bring them an immediate return on their investment of time. Surely there are always exceptions to this rule, but it's likely that your first manager will be:

- A close friend who's willing to make phone calls and help promote shows without getting paid for the first few months or years. In fact, he may not even be called a "manager" at all, working with the understanding that as soon your career progresses, he will be replaced by an established professional manager and offered some other position in the band.
- An experienced musician who wants to "right all the wrongs" she's encountered in her professional career and has got all the passion and drive needed to set you on course. Or a businessperson who's always dreamed of being in a band and has the desire to live those dreams through you.
- A club owner in your hometown who sees hundreds of bands perform each year. This individual has a good idea of what works and what doesn't and is willing to offer you an objective point of view and career guidance.
- An intern or junior assistant of a professional manager by day who's looking to cut his teeth on managing his own band on his downtime at night. He's got

the advantage of having his boss's ear for guidance and observing how a professional office is run all day.

Regardless of the possibilities here, these people all have one thing in common—they are relative newcomers to the management business—or, as I once heard someone devotedly call them, "start-up managers." Start-up managers are usually young, aggressive, and ambitious individuals who are willing to work their tails off for you. They'll devote every minute of their day to helping you reach your goals. They're business savvy, good talkers, and eager to learn. These traits are exactly what you will need from a manager in the early developmental stages of your career.

Many start-up managers who find handling a band whose career is taking off often become overwhelmed because of their inexperience. In these circumstances, it is not uncommon for a less-experienced manager to partner up with a large, more experienced management firm.

But take note: The early stages of your career are when you have to be the most careful about picking your manager! A lot of wannabees will feel that they can adequately manage your career. Despite their good intentions, their inexperience and lack of connections may end up costing you time and money. They may promise you everything but deliver absolutely nothing. Keep in mind, becoming a personal manager does not require getting a license or state certification—anyone from a used car dealer to a snake oil salesman can be one—so proceed with caution when making your choice! There are managers in the business, and there are damagers. Watch out for the damagers.

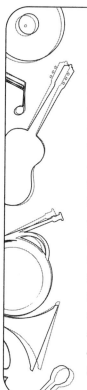

BANGING NAILS BY DAY, HEAD BANGING BY NIGHT. Alan Coffman, later described as having a brain the size of the television character Barney Fife's, was the first manager of the rock band Mötley Crüe. By day, Alan Coffman ran a successful construction company, but by night, he dreamed of getting into the glamorous music business. Coffman invested in the Crüe, buying them clothes and an apartment above Sunset Boulevard, but he was otherwise a complete nut case. Whenever he drank, he would have flashbacks of the Vietnam War and would search bushes and shrubs for Vietnamese soldiers. When Mötley was getting ready to sign their first deal with Elektra Records, Coffman flipped out during the business meeting, thinking that the enemy was in the restaurant's kitchen preparing for an attack. He dove under the table, and later that evening, he dove out of a moving car. Coffman eventually disappeared with a good portion of the band's advance money, never to be heard from again. (For more confessions from the world's most notorious rock band, check out Mötley Crüe's book *The Dirt: Confessions from the World's Most Notorious Rock Band.* Note: The band also recounts how they went on to be handled by the legendary managers Doug Thaler and Doc McGhee, who also managed Bon Jovi and The Scorpions. Although these two managers are responsible for helping Mötley Crüe sell millions of records, McGhee was reportedly busted for helping smuggle 40,000 pounds of pot from Columbia. *Welcome to the world of rock 'n' roll!* It should be noted, though, that Doc McGhee is still one of the most successful rock managers in the business today.

Established Professional Management

If you're ambitious and able to develop your career on your own to the point at which you're creating a buzz in your hometown clubs, in the press, and on college radio, and perhaps record companies are even beginning to ask about you, or if you've gone as far as signing a record deal, then your management options are going to open up considerably. At this point in your career, things are going to begin moving fast for you and you'll need an experienced pro to take the reins. Keep in mind that managers are in business to make money just like anyone else, and now that you're in a position to potentially make them money, they have a bigger incentive to work with you. You've come a long way on your own, and unless your ego starts to expand drastically or you decide to start shooting drugs (hey, it's been known to happen), you've already proved you have what it takes to go the long haul. The term "established professional management" covers a broad spectrum of types, but for the sake of clarity, we'll divide them into two distinct categories: "mid-level managers" and "big league managers."

Mid-level Managers. Mid-level managers are those who have a great deal of experience in the industry but have not quite broken a band into super-stardom. Maybe they have one client on their roster who was able to sell a respectable couple hundred thousand records, but still don't have a gold or platinum record hanging on the walls—and that's what they're shooting for! These are the guys who are typically very well liked in the industry for their enthusiasm and well-connected enough to open some doors for you. They may be exactly what you need to get the record companies from just being interested in you to actually closing a deal. Mid-level managers usually have a great understanding of the business and perhaps were even A&R representatives or marketing managers at a label before getting involved in the management business. They enjoy the entrepeneurial spirit and freedom provided by managing bands. The problem here is that they are not as powerful as someone like a big league manager and therefore it may take them longer to get things done.

Big-League Managers. Big-league managers are, needless to say, very well connected in the industry. The relationships they've formed, the respect they've earned, and the favors they can trade, give them the power to make things happen for you with just a few phone calls. These guys have been around for years and have lots of gold and platinum records hanging on their walls. They may even run a large firm and have a number of managers working under them. The clients these managers represent provide a number of touring opportunities for your band. In addition, these managers have established strong relationships with record companies over the years representing other clients, and the labels are happy to have them representing you. If a big-league manager is truly dedicated towards making you a huge success, then it's a pretty good bet that things are going to start moving fast for you. Everyone from your peers to people in the press are in awe that you've signed with such a powerful management company and you're already planning your getaway house in the Nevada desert. It's very possible that you're going to become a huge star!

There are a dozen or so experienced, professional, established managers out there of which any one of them are capable of doing the job. The important thing is picking the one that really WANTS to do it, not the one with the biggest star on the roster. Your manager must possess a genuine enthusiasm for your music, and a commitment to going the long haul through thick and thin.

It's become a trend recently for management companies to merge together under one management umbrella. Though it may appear that the bigger a firm is, the better it is, sometimes the priority of many of these larger firms changes from quality to quantity. In other words, the more bands they sign, the better their chances of one of those bands hitting it big. In fact, the firm may never have any intention of getting behind your band and giving you the full-court support you deserve over the long haul.

But take note: The danger with a major-league manager is that you may not always get the attention you deserve. Maybe you were taken on just so someone else couldn't sign you. Perhaps you were taken on as a favor to someone else in the industry? Maybe you're going to be turned over to a less experienced manager of the firm? Either way, when push comes to shove, you can bet that your manager is going to prioritize his or her more successful clients before you. After all, this is how the mortgage on that summer home in Hawaii is paid. One group, signed to Atlantic Records and managed by one of the most successful rock management firms in the world, was actually told that it should not even think about going on the road until it had three singles released to radio and three videos in rotation at MTV. (Most bands are lucky to have one single in rotation!) Needless to say, the band bit the dust. Were the managers unhappy with the record the band delivered and wanted to see if the album "had legs" on its own with minimal effort? Or was it just not worth their time to send the band out in a passenger van and slowly build a buzz over the next two years? Who knows really. But one thing is for sure—a manager who's been involved with a band from the very beginning has much more invested emotionally than someone who comes aboard later. These are typically the guys that will go down with the sinking ship before giving up. In the long run, this may be exactly what you may need.

HIRING YOUR PERSONAL MANAGER

Once you've reached a point in your career where you feel you need the assistance of a personal manager, there are a few things you must understand before beginning your search. When you find a manager who's willing to work with you, it's vital that you know the most important qualities a manager should possess.

Finding a Manager

The first thing to realize before looking for a personal manager is that the person you hire is going to be working closely with you for a potentially long period of time. Unlike dealings with your attorney, who, once a deal is negotiated, moves on to another client until the next time you need him, your relationship with a personal manager is, well, more personal. Are you going to look in a publication such as *The Yellow Pages of Rock* or *Billboard's International Talent and Touring Directory* and begin randomly calling managers? You can try, but the managers listed in these books probably won't have the time to work with you unless you're fairly advanced in your career. Are you going to call a manager referral service, where an operator refers you to a manager who's suited for your needs? I don't think a service like this exists, and even if it did, remember that *you need to think about your personal needs when looking for a personal manager!* The best way to find a manager is probably by asking people you trust for personal referrals. Just keep in mind that in the early stages of your career, your options are going to be limited, and once you've progressed to the point where you're about to sign, or have signed a recording agreement, your options will open up. If this seems like a paradox, it is. But hey, that's just the way the business works. This brings the old saying to mind, "The only time a bank will loan you money is when you can prove you don't need it."

In the early stages of your career, the best way to find a personal manager, besides looking to a friend or relative to manage you, may be to get out on your local music scene and begin asking other artists or club owners what bands are moving ahead most quickly with their careers. You might even try looking in your local music papers or keeping your ears glued to your local college radio stations to determine which bands are making headway. In either case, it's quite possible that behind the most promising bands on your local scene, you'll find a motivated individual who may be interested in giving your band some help. There will be plenty of people around town who can vouch for this manager's credibility, and you'll have the opportunity to meet with the manager yourself to determine whether or not there's a good working vibe between you. Sometimes you may be able to create enough career momentum around town yourself so that personal managers begin approaching you. In these cases, you must still ask for personal references to ensure that the person to whom you're about to entrust your career is someone reliable and able to help you to accomplish your goals.

Once you're close to signing a recording agreement, or if you have already inked a deal, you can look to your attorney or record company A&R representative for suggestions as to whom they think should manage you. Of course, the decision will ultimately be yours, but as I mentioned before, at this point your options will be considerable. It's also possible you may already have a good idea of whom you want managing your band based on stories you've read in the press or listings on the liner notes of your favorite band's CDs. You may have even had the opportunity to meet and speak with a manager at one of the many annual music conventions such as the Eat'm convention (www.eat-m.com), or you may have met a manager who was lecturing at a program held at a university or in an adult-education class such as UCLA's Entertainment Extension program (www.uclaextension.org). You may even know someone in a successful band who wants to introduce you to his or her manager. The possibilities are endless, making your search for a manager less difficult than ever before. However, now that your options have expanded greatly, how do you really know who the right person to manage your career is? Read on.

Qualities to Look for in a Manager

The classic concert film *The Song Remains The Same,* features a scene in which Led Zeppelin's manager Peter Grant, a 270-pound former wrestler from East London, is back stage screaming at one of the promoters at Madison Square Garden. Many artists may think that an intimidating personal manager is exactly what they need. But Jeffrey Jampol, who has managed artists such as Tal Bachman, says, "The days of the Peter Grants in this business are over." People in the music industry prefer to do business with nice guys. A manager must be able to nurture and maintain relationships while at the same time standing firm, being sensible, and demonstrating a strong knowledge of the business. (It's a balance between ticking people off and not being a push-over.) If a manager walks into the record label and starts pounding desks, insisting that things get done his way, *he's bound to get absolutely nowhere!*

So what are the most important things to look for in a manager? In addition to being ambitious, well-connected, a good negotiator, powerful, and accessible, a good manager should be someone who inspires your *trust and respect.*

Trust. Trustworthiness is an incredibly important attribute in a manager. Think about it, you've worked for many years learning how to play your instrument and write your songs, and your band has been rehearsing and promoting its shows for years—and now you're going to turn over a great deal of responsibility to someone you barely know! Sounds scary doesn't it? Trust must be earned over time, but if a manager doesn't show a genuine caring, enthusiasm, and understanding for your dreams and passions, you may not have the right person for the job. I remember one very famous manager firmly saying to a group that he didn't need to like their music in order to do business with them. Sounds rather insensitive, but because of his power and clout, the band decided to go ahead and work with him. Needless to say, the relationship ended in disaster. The band drove all the way across country in a van to perform a showcase, and the manager didn't even show up—nor did any industry people! True story. In fact, after that, the manager didn't even return the band's phone calls. Nice! In similar situations, many bands are promised that a record contract is waiting right around the corner and that the labels are ready to ink the deal. One or two years later, the band is still unsigned. A manager can't lie to his or her artists. Again, an initial feeling of genuine caring and trust is a major quality to look for in a manager. Without it, you may end up with a lot of broken promises down the road.

Respect. A manager must also be someone that you can respect. We're not just talking about the impressive number of successful bands this individual has managed or how many gold and platinum records he or she has on the wall, we're talking about morality and ethics. What does your manager really stand for? Does he or she have a spouse and kids? Is your manager well educated? Does he or she do anything to give back to the community? Or is your manager all about flash and making money—big houses, expensive cars, and arm-piece dates? Does she hang out with you and get twice as trashed as you do? Does he do drugs? Is she bitter about the business? Hey, I'm not making these examples up! It's not like you're an angel looking for a saint, but overall, a manager must maintain a level of authority and respect and perhaps even be somewhat of a parental figure to you. Many bands, not that they'll always admit it, want someone they know they can look up to and feel protected by—almost like a mother hen with her chicks. They want both someone who's going to take them under their wing and keep everything under control—a superhero who can do no wrong, and someone who knows how to admit that they don't have the answer to a particular situation. Of course you may initially be impressed with a complete madman who makes a lot of noise, blows a lot of smoke, and bullies everyone—but are you really going to trust your whole career to someone like this? A manager must be secure, grounded, firm, and fearless. If he or she shows any signs of weakness, it will be hard to both respect and trust him or her over the long haul.

MANAGEMENT AGREEMENTS

Trust is a crucial factor in the union between an artist and his personal manager, yet it's still extremely important to have a written contract between both parties defining the terms of their business relationship. In the event of a falling-out, a written contract leaves no doubt as to what each party initially agreed upon. Manager Gary Borman agrees: "I believe in agreements from the very beginning simply because people tend to forget."

But many managers, even those at larger firms, don't believe in detailed written contracts. They feel that the artist/manager relationship will either work or it won't, regardless of the words written on a piece of paper. If the artist is unhappy, they should always be free to go. However when you consider artists like Bruce Springsteen, who found himself trapped in a legal battle for over a year after firing manager Mike Appel in 1976, then perhaps you'll agree that there's a lot more to formulating a professional relationship than just a verbal or handshake agreement.

Key elements that all management contracts should include are exclusivity, a key person clause, the term of the agreement (period of time for which it's valid), the manager's commission, expenses, power of attorney, a talent agent disclaimer, and post term provisions.

Exclusivity

When entering into a relationship with a personal manager, keep in mind that you're taking on an "exclusive" manager. This means that, during the full term of your agreement, you cannot be managed by anyone else. Consequently, before entering into a relationship with a personal manager, be sure you're absolutely confident in that individual's ability to represent you. Remember, you're going to be working together for a long time.

Key Person Clause

When signing a management agreement, you're often not just signing with an individual, you're also signing with a management firm consisting of a few managers. But what happens in situations when your manager decides to leave the firm or is fired? The reality is that you could get stuck with the company and be assigned to another representative you don't like. This is why you want to make sure there's a clause in your agreement called a "key person" clause. A key person clause is exactly what it sounds like. The manager with whom you initially signed is your key person. If this individual leaves the firm, your agreement becomes void and you're free to follow.

A key person clause may also protect you from cases in which the sport who wined and dined you and inspired you to enter into a management agreement in the first place never seems to be doing much of the managing. Instead, he or she turns the bulk of the work over to a partner or office representative. Under the key person provision, you may be able to void your agreement if you insist that your key person clause expressly state this. But keep in mind, it's normal for a manager to delegate some of the less important responsibilities to other people on the team. A representative of the firm is just as capable of getting you equipment endorsements, and, as a result, provides your manager with more time to do something really important—like work with an agent to get you a national tour. Manager Gary Borman adds, "Artists begin to understand that it's a waste of time to be directing issues to the wrong person. Managers don't have to show up at every gig. As long as they're available at the more crucial times in your career, you don't have to feel uncomfortable in their absence."

The Term of the Agreement

The term of most management agreements ranges from one to five years, with three years being the norm. If this seems long, consider that it can take up to two years before an artist begins making money, and understandably, the manager will want a chance to make a return on his or her investment of time and hard work.

The artist, on the other hand, will want to commit to an agreement with the shortest term possible. Their fear is of being trapped in an agreement with a manager who's just not making things happen! As a result, the manager may be willing to stipulate certain "performance guarantees." For instance, the manager may guarantee you a recording deal within the first year. Or, once you're signed, the manager may guarantee that a licensed talent agent will be hired to work towards getting you an opening slot on a national tour. Or you'll be guaranteed a publishing deal. In any case, these performance guarantees must be fairly reasonable for your manager to achieve if you expect your manager to agree to them. It's not likely, for instance, that a young manager will be able to secure a recording agreement for a new band in a period of six months. On the other hand, it may be possible that you're not ready for a deal in the first place. Remember, managers aren't magicians. Even if you have a lot of talent, the best manager may not always be able to make things happen so quickly.

In addition, performance guarantees may apply to income. The artist may want a guaranteed specific income within a certain period of time. For example, a recording artist may expect to earn up to $200,000 over the first two years of his tenure with a manager. As your career becomes more established, you may ask for $300,000 in the third year, increasing to $400,000 in the fourth year. Keep in mind that these numbers are arbitrary and not necessarily based on reality. These figures will change according to the state of the economy, and there are many other factors that can affect an artist's earning ability. It's easy to see that a jazz group playing small clubs will produce less income than a young rock group playing larger venues.

The source from which money is earned should also be stipulated in a performance guarantee. For instance, the artist may stipulate that $200,000 in earnings be derived from live performances. Assuming you don't want to play circuses all year, you may need to clarify the types of live performances you have in mind. Thus, your agreement could state "live performances that can reasonably advance your career in the commercial marketplace, and that cater to your demographic audience."

Lastly, and in all fairness to the manager, your performance guarantee must not only be based on the monies you make, but also on the work you turn down. In other words, if your lead singer decides he'd rather hang out with his girlfriend for five months and turn down work, that should not be held against the personal manager and used as an excuse to break your contract with him.

The Manager's Commission

Personal managers risk a great deal when taking on new clients—they invest their time, reputation, and money with no guarantee of a big payoff. Therefore, managers can commission their artist's earnings anywhere from 15 to 30 percent, with the norm being 20 percent. Keep in mind that there are no regulations dictating the amount a personal manager can charge, it varies with each individual situation.

Gross Earnings and Deductions. A manager's commissions are almost always based on your gross earnings. But note: The word "gross," which typically means total earnings, must be defined here as *all monies other than those that pass through your hands for certain expenses.* Without a clear definition of what these expenses include, the manager may be taking a bigger commission than he or she deserves. Consider the following example.

Suppose you're advanced a recording fund of $300,000, and your manager earns a 20 percent commission off the top. The manager's take would be $60,000 ($300,000 x 20% = $60,000). This leaves you a new balance of $240,000 ($300,000—$60,000 = $240,000). If the costs for recording your album are $200,000, you're left with $40,000 to divide between the band members

($240,000—$200,000 = $40,000). If there are four members in the band, each member is advanced $10,000.

As you can clearly see, your manager's commission of $60,000 is far greater than each member's earnings of $10,000. How could this be? After all, you're the star! But before freaking out, remember that your manager's commission is based on monies *after* certain expenses are deducted. Recording costs, you'll be happy to know, are typically considered one of these deductions. Now let's take a look at the numbers.

Three hundred thousand dollars (your recording fund) minus $200,000 (your recording costs) equals a balance of $100,000. One hundred thousand dollars multiplied by your manager's commission of 20 percent equals $20,000—a far cry from the $60,000 in the above example. When dividing the remaining $80,000 ($100,000—$20,000 = $80,000), each band member is now advanced a grand total of $20,000—as opposed to the $10,000 in our first example.

It doesn't take a genius to see that the second situation works out much better for the artist. But don't assume that your manager is going to know what expenses to deduct. *It's vitally important that all monies that are not to be commissioned are detailed in the written agreement with your manager.*

Here are a few more examples of monies that are not to be commissioned by the manager:

In situations in which a band signs a recording agreement before hiring a personal manager, you may wonder whether a personal manager still receives a commission from the artist advance when this individual comes on board later. Major league managers may want their usual fee, mid-level managers may accept a reduced percentage of their standard fee, and some managers may take no commission at all. Nevertheless, if signing a recording agreement before hiring a manager, the band's attorney will typically advise them to put aside a portion of the fund for the manager, just in case. The initial advance can be the factor that decides whether or not a manager chooses to work with a band.

   ✦ Payments to record producers that are usually considered part of the recording costs
   ✦ Tour support, which is money advanced by the record company to help cover expenses on the road
   ✦ The costs for filming a promotional music video, which are advanced by the record company
   ✦ The fees paid to booking agents for scheduling live performances
   ✦ Payments made to opening acts once you get a headlining position

Escalating and De-escalating Commissions. Personal managers sometimes work on an escalating or de-escalating commission scale, depending on their artist's success. For instance, when you're first starting out and not making much money, a manager may agree to a 15 percent commission based on the premise that when you begin to earn more money, the commission escalate to 20 percent. Sounds fair enough, right? But what happens when the same concept is applied in reverse and your manager works on a de-escalating commission?

Suppose that in the beginning of your career, when there's not a whole lot of money, your manager asks for a commission of 20 percent. Later, if you're successful and earning more money, your manager's commission drops to 15 percent. At first, this may seem to make little or no sense. Why should a manager promote you if his or her commission continues to drop as you become more and more successful? If you do the math, it becomes clear how this type of arrangement works. $100,000 in earnings multiplied by a commission of 20 percent yields a payment of $20,000. However, $500,000 multiplied by a commission of 15 percent equals $75,000, and so on. The manager makes more money as the artist does, even though his or her commission is less.

Limitations and Exclusions Sometimes your personal manager may agree to charge you a lower commission, or even no commission at all, on money earned in areas in which you're already established. For instance, if you're a successful songwriter who writes for television and film, or if you're an accomplished musician who plays on a number of recording sessions, your manager may agree to only charge you a 10 percent commission on these incomes, as opposed to the 20 percent commission standard on everything else. It's also possible that, if the manager is not going to be involved in furthering your career in these areas (because of lack of time, expertise, or interest), he or she will usually agree not to charge you a commission at all.

You must also consider what the manager will be able to commission for work that becomes available after you become a successful artist. What if you get the opportunity to act in motion pictures, or write a book, or start your own clothing line? Will your manager be entitled to a commission? If these new opportunities are a direct result of your manager's years of hard work—*then yes!* But for the sake of clarity, it's extremely important to discuss these issues in advance.

Expenses

Besides the commissions I've outlined, your manager will also be entitled to be reimbursed for certain expenses. The expenses necessary to run the business, such as rent, office machines, and personnel, are typically your manager's responsibility, but what happens when he or she has to FedEx your tape to an interested A&R representative? Even better, what happens when your manager has to fly to New York to conduct business on your behalf? These costs are charged to you, and don't be mistaken, expenses can add up quickly.

To monitor the expenses that are reimbursed to your manager, a limit is usually set on what the manager can spend. For instance, a single expense above $200, or total monthly expenses that exceed $1000, should be approved by you first. In cases in which a manager handles more than one client, expenses may have to be pro-rated. I once knew a manager who flew out to an industry convention in Cannes, France, (Midem, www.midem.com), and charged the entire trip as an expense to one of his primary bands. He justified the expense by setting up a meeting or two, but also spent time shopping his other artists to record labels. The manager should have pro-rated his expenses and charged each band accordingly. If he was representing three bands, and each band was given equal attention, expenses should have been split three ways. However, a band that is not yet earning money should not have to take money out of its own pockets to pay its manager. Expenses are paid at a later time once the band has an income to do so.

So who actually monitors and pays the manager expenses and commissions? After all, if you wanted to handle your money, you probably would have become an accountant yourself. Though most managers may initially insist monies flow through them, they will accept an outside accountant or business manager (see Chapter 8). The business manager will collect and deposit money into an account on your behalf. Expenses and commissions are monitored and paid out as the manager submits them.

Power of Attorney

In almost all management agreements there is a clause called a "power of attorney," which basically gives your manager the legal right to act for you. This includes the right to make major career decisions, cash checks, and sign contracts. Needless to say, there are far too many nightmarish stories involving unscrupulous managers for you to agree to this clause without stipulating some limitations first. For instance, in the event that you're out of town, your manager can sign an agreement on your behalf only after you approve the deal verbally. The paperwork can then be faxed to you. Your manager may also be able to approve live performance engagements under a certain number of dates, and only after you've approved the time in which you want to tour. Realistically, offers of engagements by promoters don't stay open long, and your manager may have to make these decisions quickly.

Remember, there's a reason why you hired your manager in the first place. When you're on the road or in the studio trying to be creative, you don't want to be bothered with business issues. On the other hand, you don't want to get screwed either. It's not that you should distrust your manager—but putting limitations on how your manager can act on your behalf ensures that you'll always know what's going on.

Talent Agent Disclaimer

Some management agreements (depending on the state) will include a talent agency disclaimer clause which stipulates that your *manager will not act as your agent and procure employment or engagements.* If this sounds confusing, since that's exactly what most managers do in the early stages of a band's career, you should know a few basic facts here.

Under California state laws (as well other states, notably New York and Massachusetts), anyone who engages in the occupation of procuring employment for their artists *must be licensed as a talent agent.* The problem here is that most managers don't care to obtain this license for a number of reasons. For instance, in the state of California (which we all know is where a great deal of the music industry is centered) the personal manager must submit an agency contract form to the State Labor Commissioner for approval. Although there are some exceptions, the labor commissioner will not approve more than a 10 percent commission for an agent. As you know, managers typically earn 20 percent and simply don't want to work for any less.

Additionally, the agency contract will need to provide a clause stating that the artist is free to leave and their contract is void if they have not worked within a 90 day period. This could cause a lot of problems for the manager, since there must be some discretion in the gigs that their artist performs. It's possible that, in effort to meet the 90 day requirement, the manager may find himself or herself in approval to working certain gigs that may not be in the best interests of the artist. It's easy to see why a manager would not want to work under these circumstances. In fact, it's safe to say that very few managers ever become licensed agents.

So, does this mean that under California State law your manager is in violation when gigs are booked without a license? We all know this happens—managers book engagements for their young bands in order to help them develop into seasoned acts. In fact, Attorney Richard Schulenberg (author of the book *Legal Aspects of the Music Industry*) cautiously goes as far as saying, "In California, if a personal manager is not breaking the law, he's not doing his job." Well, it's not like someone is going to come and take your manager away in handcuffs, *but it could provide a way for you to get out of*

your contract with your manager if you are justly unhappy and your manager won't let you go any other way. In fact, in California your manager may even have to pay back all of the commissions that you've ever paid to him or her. Of course, it's not as easy as it sounds—you'd still have to go through legal proceedings and prove your manager booked gigs—but if you're ever in a position where you want to get out of your contract badly enough, it may be an option. This is not meant as advice; it's the law and you should always speak to your attorney first.

So, getting back to square one and the disclaimer clause, understandably, it's not a personal manager's general intention to book gigs for the artist, but, rather, to work together with a licensed talent agent who will be responsible for initiating engagements. But again, the problem here is that a young band usually can't attract the interest of a talent agent because young bands don't earn enough money to make them worth the talent agent's time. So, we're back to where we started once again. If this sounds like a catch-22 scenario for the manager, it actually is—and managers, especially in California, should know this. Nevertheless, it's important that managers look at their state laws to see whether a talent agency disclaimer clause is necessary in their agreements. At worst or best, depending on from whose perspective you're looking at the situation, the attorney who drafts the management agreement can't be sued for leaving the clause out.

Note: There are some exceptions to talent agency laws. For instance, in California anyone can procure a recording agreement on behalf of an artist without a license. In New York, anyone can book "incidental" performances, such as a showcase, to generate interest from record companies. Again, it's important that managers look at their individual state laws to make sure they understand their legal boundaries.

Post Term Provisions

When the term of your manager's agreement expires, he or she is still entitled to earn a commission on royalties from contracts entered into, or substantially negotiated during that contract term. For instance, suppose you sign a record deal a few months before the manager's term expires. If you've signed a five-record deal, then technically your manager is entitled to commission royalties from all five records—even without being involved with your career anymore. Is this fair? To make matters worse, if you hire a new manager, you'll be required to pay that manager a commission on your earnings as well. If both your former manager and your new manager are charging a 20 percent commission, you're now paying out 40 percent in commissions. Let me repeat this: 40 percent!

To limit the amount your manager can commission after the contract term expires, he or she may be willing to agree to something called a "sunset clause." A sunset clause gradually "ends the day" on the commissions to which the manager is entitled. For instance, in our previous example, the manager would continue to earn a commission after his or her term on all five records. However, with a sunset clause, your manager may be willing to accept the full commission on royalties for a limited period of five years after his or her term, and then no royalty. Or, the manager may agree to the full commission for the first three years after the lapse of the term, and then a reduced commission for the next two years, and then no royalty. Lastly, you may be able to exclude your manager altogether from earning a commission on the albums recorded after the term. A variety of interpretations can really exist here, depending on your personal manager and on your bargaining strength.

Obviously, not all managers are going to be happy with a sunset clause. In a UCLA lecture in 2002, manager Bud Prager revealed that he doesn't believe in sunset clauses. After all, it's the manager who helps take the artist from obscurity to popularity. If the artist continues to make money from recordings, then shouldn't the manager do likewise? Although this argument may be valid, your attorney will be able to advise you as to what is appropriate in your individual situation. An attorney who is skillful at negotiating should be able to reach terms that are acceptable to both sides.

CHAPTER 8

Your Business Manager

If you can make money in the music business playing the music you love, you're doing well. If you can make money, learn how to hang on to it, and make it grow, you're exceptional.

Unfortunately we've all heard stories of musicians who sell millions of records, yet end up penniless. Just think of rapper M.C. Hammer, who was once reported in *Forbes* magazine as being worth 40 million dollars, only to end up filing for bankruptcy. If you don't want this to happen to you, the assistance of a good business manager can be essential not only to your career, but also to the security of your future.

You know what they say, "Money isn't everything till you don't have any."

THE ROLE OF A BUSINESS MANAGER IN YOUR CAREER

The role of a business manager is not to be confused with that of a personal manager. A personal manager is more like the Chief Executive Officer (CEO) of your company, who helps *generate income* by setting up recording deals, publishing deals, and tours. A business manager, on the other hand, is more like the Chief Financial Officer (CFO) of your company, who helps *manage the income* from these deals once they're in place. A business manager handles all financial issues such as investments, financial planning, bookkeeping, tour account services, asset administration, tax services, insurance monitoring, royalty examination, and in some cases even publishing administration.

> You typically don't need a business manager until you have a substantial amount of money coming in. Learning about what a good business manager can do now, before you need one, can be worth millions later.

Investment Strategies and Financial Planning

One of the most important roles that a business manager can play in your career is to help you plan for your future. As a musician, there are many sacrifices you'll make while pursuing your dreams. You'll shell out money for press kits and demo recordings, pay for rehearsal rooms, and for rental of trucks to haul your gear from one gig to the next; all without ever making much money in return. To survive, you'll work odd jobs for little pay. If you're able go the distance and the gods are on your side, you'll reach the point where you're finally experiencing success and making money playing music. Almost immediately, you'll sense the natural urge to want to reward yourself. You can finally afford to eat in decent restaurants, drive nice cars, and buy a comfortable home. As long as your spending is in moderation, then fine, why shouldn't you enjoy the fruits of your labor? After all, your adoring fans would expect nothing less; public image is everything, right?

But what practically all musicians fail to recognize is that their days in the limelight are numbered. As you get older, the public's perception of you slowly but surely diminishes. In other words, you'll inevitably find yourself "yesterday's news" (see "Set Realistic Goals" in Chapter 1). If you've spent your money lavishly, you may also find that you've become used to a lifestyle that you can no longer afford. Even worse, with dwindling royalties and diminishing concert sales, you may find yourself faced with a very difficult decision about what to do next with your life.

This is where the assistance of a business manager is essential. As Samuel Butler once said, "The future is purchased by the present." A good business manager helps his or her clients plan ahead by first determining what investment strategy is best suited for their needs. For instance, is a high-risk, short-term strategy (such as stock investments in emerging technologies) a wise plan, or is a long-term, low-risk strategy (such as investing in pension plans, mutual funds, and municipal bonds) a more appropriate scheme? Jeff Hinkle of the Los Angeles-based business management firm Gudvi, Sussman & Oppenhiem, Inc. says, "We like to think in the long term for our clients. One of the first things that we would do, especially for our younger clients, is to set up a pension plan and start saving for their retirement. Depending on how much they can afford to put aside, we'll probably use the assistance of a professional money manager. The money manager opens the investment accounts and recommends appropriate investments such as stocks, mutual funds, treasury bills, and high quality bonds. Once the investment choices have been made, the money manager then oversees the portfolio on a day-to-day basis; he makes ongoing recommendations as to the mix of investments to maximize the client's return on their money and also minimize their downside risk. The business manager is always involved in these decisions, but the business manager is not a stock picker. That's the money manager's job."

The point of all this is not to get caught up on what all of these financial terms mean; that's a discussion beyond the scope of this book. The message to drive home here is that a business manager is a skilled money person who plays a key role in making sure that the money you're making today is invested in such a way that your future is a bright and well-secured one.

> Gudvi, Sussman & Oppenheim, Inc. in Sherman Oaks, CA, is one of the top entertainment business management firms (www.gsogroup.com). They can be reached by calling (818) 990-0550, or faxing (818) 990-5707.

Bookkeeping and Accounting

Business managers not only look out for your future by helping with investments and financial planning, they help manage your money on a daily basis by reviewing invoices, paying monthly bills, collecting royalty earnings, depositing money, and monitoring your bank accounts. All of these issues fall under a service known as bookkeeping and accounting.

Business managers have long established relationships with local banks that are familiar with the business management firm and its clients. Business managers open accounts with these banks usually consisting of a checking account (in order to pay all of your bills), and what's called a pocket account (for whatever personal expenses you may have, ATM withdrawals you may make, etc.). Your business manager then collects all of your income, which can range from touring and merchandising monies to publishing and record royalties, and deposits it into these accounts. He or she monitors your bank accounts to make sure there's enough money to meet your expenses, and then reviews and pays all of your bills, which can range from your car payments, credit card bills, and home mortgages, to the bill from your pool man, your gardener, and even your personal trainer. Your business manager ensures that all of the invoices and charges received on your behalf are justified, and in some cases may even forward certain bills to you so that you can authorize and sign off on them yourself—especially if he or she is uncertain whether that two-hour phone call to Italy ever really happened. But, Jeff Hinkle notes, "We encourage our clients to be involved in the bill paying process. Not paying your own bills can be a dangerous thing; it's the old 'out of sight, out of mind' problem. We prefer for clients to sign their own checks, although this isn't always possible due to their generally busy schedules. I've had clients who seemed to have a phobia when it came to bills and discussing their spending. Sometimes as long as they know they can meet all of their expenses, they would rather not deal with any of it at all."

Touring Services

Another important role played by your business manager is the handling of all financial matters pertaining to touring. Business managers are involved with a tour from its inception and planning to the very last show a band performs.

Pre-Touring Your business manager, along with your personal manager, is responsible for putting together tour budgets when you're planning to hit the road. He or she will review all of the performance deals offered by concert promoters around the country in order to determine the total gross earnings of the tour. A projection of expenses is then done to determine what the potential net profit or loss of the tour may be. Expenses may include:

+ Tour-bus expenses
+ Airfare
+ Hotels
+ Insurance (for personal injury, theft, etc.)
+ Rehearsal fees
+ Per diems (daily allowances paid to the band and crew for food)
+ Salaries for the band
+ Salaries for the crew
+ Production costs (for the sound and lighting equipment)
+ Trucking cost (to carry the sound and lights)

- Contingency [an additional percentage (usually 5 percent) calculated into the budget in case expenses are estimated low or there are unexpected emergencies]
- Your agent's fees
- Your manager's commission
- Your business manager's fees

The expenses listed above are an oversimplification of what is usually incurred by a band on the road; the list can easily be a page long. Nevertheless, after determining the total expenses of a tour and then deducting them for the projected gross income, the business manager then works at making any adjustments in areas in which he or she feels they may be able to save money. Careful planning is required. Any miscalculation of expenses can lead to serious problems at the end of a tour, and instead of making money, you can find yourself thousands of dollars in the red.

So what happens when your business manager projects a loss in profits for a tour? Do you stay home or go out on the road anyway? In the early stages of a band's career, a tour almost always shows a loss. But since a live performance is a valuable way for you to reach your audience and help sell albums, your record company may provide you monies in the form of something called "tour support" to subsidize a tour. However, this amount is always charged against any record royalties you may have earned. In other words, the money your record company may provide to make a tour economically feasible may feel like it's free, but it all comes out of your pocket in the end.

Once the Tour Starts Once you're on the road, your business manager's work does not end by any means. He or she collects all monies taken in from each performance, and makes sure that the concert promoter paid the appropriate sum. Your business manager then pays all bills owed to the tour bus companies and trucking companies, and pays salaries to the band and its crew. He or she also makes sure a tax return is filed in every state in which a tour is planned. By submitting a budget to the appropriate authorities in each state, your business manager can limit the band's tax obligations by making sure the band is taxed on the net profits of a performance rather than on the total gross earnings taken. Lastly, your business manager makes sure your band is properly insured while out on the road, especially with something called "non-appearance insurance." This means that if a concert is cancelled because your lead singer gets sick or your tour bus breaks down, the insurance company will pay the band the amount it was expecting to earn from that performance. As you can imagine, non-appearance insurance is extremely important. One or two live performance cancellations can cause a band to lose incredible sums of money.

Asset Administration

What happens once you have a little money rolling in and you decide you want to start making expensive purchases like a home or a car? This brings us to your business manager's next important role, known as asset administration.

Shopping for a Home When you're shopping for a home, your business manager will advise you as to what price range you can afford. Unless you're fortunate enough to be able to pay cash for a home, your business manager will rely on relationships with mortgage brokers to arrange loans. A good business manager understands all the various factors involved in buying a home, including

IN ONE EAR, OUT THE OTHER. A celebrated music industry journalist, who wishes to remain anonymous, shares a typical story of how fame and fortune can sometimes get the better of you. Vocalist Pat Benatar and guitarist/husband Neil Geraldo of the Pat Benatar band bought a huge house in Malibu, California during the prime of their career in the late '80s. Their business manager had forewarned them that they were overextending themselves by making the purchase, but they went ahead with it anyway. To make matters worse, Pat would regularly visit the business manager's office and ask for tens of thousands of dollars to put custom cabinets in the kitchen. Neil would ask for money to build a state-of-the-art recording studio. But before they could finish remodeling, their business manager had to tell them the inevitable—they were running out of money. Neil hit the roof, screaming as if the news were a surprise to him, but it was already too late! The couple ended up selling the house at a huge loss and had to move into a less affluent suburb in Los Angeles.

loan fees, points, title insurance, and credit reports. Depending on your income and the cost of the house you want to buy, your business manager may even be forced to inform you that buying a particular home may not be a wise choice to make.

Shopping for an Automobile After your business manager is informed as to what kind of car you want, the options you'd like included, and the color you'd like the car to be, he or she usually contacts an automobile broker. Jeff Hinkle remembers one instance where a client wanted a Mercedes CL 500, which was a particularly hard car to find. An automobile broker located the car down to the exact specifications, in Texas, and delivered the car to Jeff's client in California in a few short days; how's that for service!

Your business manager will also explain the advantages and disadvantages of either leasing or financing an automobile. When leasing, you can make low monthly payments and turn your car in for a new lease in two or three years, but with no money owed. When financing, you may have higher monthly payments, but you'll own a car with some equity after a few years. Your business manager will help you to weigh these pros and cons, and in some cases, may even have to advise you that purchasing that $130,000 car is not at all practical for you. But in the words of Jeff Hinkle, "All we can do is advise our clients as to what's best for them to do. The problem is that they don't always listen."

Financial Reporting

Every month, your business manager must send out a detailed statement to his or her clients which includes every deposit made, every transfer of funds made in and out of investment accounts, and every check written. Rather than these reports looking like something a bank would send out, your business manager may categorize items under certain headings, such as recording expenses, housing expenses, and business expenses. This makes it much easier for you to read and understand your statements. Your business managers will also meet periodically with you to review financial statements and to make projections as to where they see your finances in six months to a year. Jeff Hinkle adds that this is one of the most challenging parts of his job: "Communication with the client about their money is the key. Most artists would rather think about mixing their new album or an upcoming tour than their finances. That's why we make it a point to have regular financial meetings with all of our clients. Since most of our clients are touring artists, finding the time and place to meet can be difficult. So several times a year, we will get on an airplane and fly out to meet with a client who is on tour. I've had plenty of business meetings on tour buses and backstage in dressing rooms. Sometimes that's the only way to get in front of the client."

Tax Planning

Another important function undertaken by your business manager involves tax planning. This crucial responsibility can be divided into three categories: determination of an appropriate business entity, handling of payroll and income taxes, and estate planning.

Determining a Business Entity One of your business manager's major responsibilities is helping you determine what business entity best suits your needs. Should you be a partnership, a corporation, or an LLC (Limited Liability Company)? (See the interview with attorney Jeff Cohen in

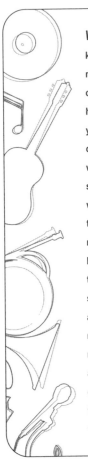

WATCH THE ONE YOU'RE WITH. Although business managers are hired to keep a watchful eye on your money, it's still your responsibility to understand how they're managing your funds every step of the way. In the 1970's, The Bay City Rollers were on top of the music world. They sold millions of records (estimates run in the range of 70 million), had a successful TV show in the U.K. called *Shang-A-Lang,* and everywhere you turned, young girls were wearing T-shirts with the band's image and logo sprawled across their chests. So, with all this wonderful success, you'd think that the five members of the band would all be living like kings these days, right? Wrong! When the band started to make some money, they were advised by their personal manager that their business dealings would be best handled by a particular business management firm. The band agreed, and the business management firm set up five individual holding companies (one for each member of the band). Through these holding companies, the funds earned by each member from royalties and merchandising were to be filtered to various limited partnerships and tax shelters. It was a very complex financial system, which neither the band nor the personal manager really understood, but the deal was signed by them anyway (no one knew any better). Then the unthinkable happened. When the members of the band tried to retrieve the money they had worked so hard to earn, they were informed by the business managers that "It's not that easy. You can't just cash in—it's going to take some time." In actuality, the money was gone, and the boys were never to see it. No one in the band's camp could ever really figure out what happened; the paper trail just seemed to end. Over twenty years and many costly legal battles later, the Bay City Rollers are still wondering just where their fortune ended up.

Chapter 2 for a detailed analysis.) Your business manager, together with expert lawyers, will help you set up the business entity best suited to your needs.

Payroll and Income Taxes Your business manager also handles payroll and income taxes. He or she writes checks and pays all personnel from the crew to the side musicians to the band itself, and deducts all applicable taxes. He or she also prepares all W2 and 1099 forms for the purpose of filing tax returns. Your business manager files tax returns on your behalf (in some cases, business managers hire an outside firm to do this), and also have a working knowledge of the special deductions that entertainers are allowed to take. In case you're audited by the Internal Revenue Service (IRS), your business manager will meet with the field agent assigned to the audit and show all proper documentation of receipts and deductions taken on your returns. If your business manager is doing his or her job correctly, this is usually not too difficult. But without a business manager working for you, an audit by the IRS can be a nightmare unless you have been extraordinarily organized and careful with your record keeping.

Estate Planning Lastly, your business manager helps you with estate planning. In plain English, this means that he or she will assist you in preparing for what will happen to your assets when you die. It may not be something you want to think about while you're young and healthy, but if you've worked hard all your life and are finally successful, you want to be sure your assets are left with the people you love. Estate planning includes such important issues as setting up wills, trust funds, life insurance, and gifting (the process of giving equitable gifts such as cash or property in order to reduce estate tax liability on inheritance). Your business manager will work with expert attorneys specializing in estate planning to make certain that you and your family are protected.

Monitoring Insurance

Your business manager also makes sure that you have all of the appropriate insurance coverage in place, including general liability, workers' compensation, auto insurance, home insurance, and non-appearance insurance.

When taking on a new client, a business manager typically contacts that client's current insurance broker to determine what insurance is already in place. If the broker is not experienced in entertainment, the business manager will recommend someone who is. Though business managers typically have established relationships with experienced entertainment brokers, they will not take their advice at face value. The business manager makes sure that his or her client is getting all of the best rates, premiums, and deductibles. Jeff Hinkle notes that insurance is a very important responsibility for business managers. If their clients are sued and don't have the adequate coverage, or the right kind of coverage, or have no coverage at all, it can lead to substantial losses and even bankruptcy.

Royalty Examination

Most business management firms have royalty examination departments that understand the detailed aspects of royalty earnings, such as when your record royalties should be paid, whether or not your royalties are being computed properly, and how many records you should be credited to date. In cases where your business manager finds discrepancies, he or she will contact your record

ROYALTIES OR NOT, HERE THEY COME. Most of the horror stories you hear in the music business pale in comparison to what took place in the early days of rock and roll. Take the Beatles, for example. If anyone should have been able to get a good deal, it's the "Fab Four" right? Wrong! In 1962, music attorneys didn't even exist. The Beatles' first recording contract with EMI called for a paltry one-cent-per-album royalty. Not one percent—*one cent!* And due to several one-year options contained in their contract, it wasn't until 1967 that personal manager Brian Epstein was able to renegotiate the band's record deal. To make this story even juicier, business manager Jeff Hinkle adds that in 1980, ten years after the Beatles broke up, an accounting firm was hired to audit EMI on the Beatles' behalf. *The audit resulted in a settlement in the Beatles favor of around $19 million.* (You can double that amount to get an idea of the money's value in today's dollars.) If you made a list of all the rock stars who signed one-sided contracts early on in their careers, your list would read like a "who's who" of the music world. So first and foremost, be extremely careful what you sign and what you agree to when you're nobody. If you later become somebody, I guarantee you that those early deals will come back to haunt you.

company with a series of detailed questions concerning the matter. If the problem at hand cannot be reasonably resolved, the business manager will contact a royalty-auditing service and conduct a field audit on your behalf. Jeff Hinkle says that these audits usually result in sizable settlements for the artist. (Disturbing, isn't it?)

Your business manager will also monitor royalties from publishing monies such as mechanical and performance royalties, and make sure you're paid appropriately for merchandising sales (T-shirts, hats, posters, etc.), should you have signed a deal with a merchandiser. Needless to say, your business manager must have a complete understanding of all contracts and deals you enter into in order to provide you with an efficient royalty examination service. (Royalties are covered in Chapters 11, 12, and 14).

Publishing Administration

Last but definitely not least, many of the larger business management firms have publishing administration departments that can function as administrators for the compositions you write. In other words, in addition to collecting royalties and making sure you're paid, the publishing administration department can negotiate licenses for the use of your songs in film and television, and also issue licenses for print uses (like the sheet music you see on the racks at your favorite music store). The publishing administration department may also handle the licensing of your songs in foreign territories and can arrange deals with publishers in foreign territories called foreign sub-publishers. However, due to the complex nature of publishing issues, you may choose to contract with an outside publishing company (independent of the business management firm) to handle these matters instead. (Chapter 12 covers music publishing.)

HIRING YOUR BUSINESS MANAGER

Now that you have a pretty good idea about the role a business manager plays in your career, you wonder when is the best time to employ their services. And once you determine that you're ready for a business manager, how do you go about finding him or her? More importantly, what are some of the qualities to look for in a business manager?

When to Hire a Business Manager

In the early stages of your career, before you've released an album or gone out on a major tour, you can usually rely on the services of a certified public accountant (CPA) to file your tax returns and provide general business advice. But once there's a substantial amount of money passing through your hands, the assistance of a business manager is necessary.

Jeff Hinkle warns, "Many artists wait until the last possible minute before hiring a business manager. Usually this is done to avoid paying the business manager a commission on their first round of advances. However, this can end up costing the artist more than they save in fees. The problem with waiting is that their money is often wasted or mismanaged, and more times than not, they forget to file their tax returns. By the time the artist decides to hire a business manager, they may have already blown through the advance but no taxes have been paid. Remember, advances are almost always taxable income in the year received. Once the delinquent tax returns are filed, the IRS adds penalties and interest to the tax bill, compounding the problem. As long as the artist hires a reputable CPA to handle tax issues in a timely manner, they can probably get away with waiting to hire a business manager until right before their record is released and they're planning to hit the road."

> CPAs usually charge by the hour. Rates vary depending on the experience and skill level of the individual and his or her staff. Sometimes a flat fee per return can be negotiated and is based on the complexity of your particular situation.

Finding a Business Manager

Finding the right business manager may be one of the most difficult processes you experience when putting together your professional team. Why? Because unlike your personal manager or attorney, the business manager is the one person to whom you're usually giving significant control of your money! And if that doesn't sound scary enough, did you know that a business manager needs no credentials, licensing, or educational requirements? You do need a license to give investment advice (such as the ones stock brokers have), but you'll find that most business managers don't have it— probably because they refer you to a stock broker anyway when investing in stocks. Taking all things into consideration, the best way to go about finding a business manager is usually through personal referrals from people you already know and trust.

Personal referrals from members of your professional team, such as your personal manager and attorney, are probably the most reliable source for finding a business manager. However, you may have to watch out for a potential conflict of interest here. Suppose your personal manager has three bands on his or her roster that all work with the same business manager. If you also take on the same business manager, and there's a dispute between you and your personal manager regarding money, who is your business manager going to side with? If your business manager sides with you, he or she may lose your personal manager's other artists. On the other hand, if the business manager sides with your personal manager, all he or she stands to lose is you as a client. Jeff Hinkle understands and is empathetic about how this can be a concern for the artist, but believes that when dealing with a reputable business management firm and personal manager, it's not likely this type of conflict issue will exist. Nevertheless, to give you some peace of mind, if your personal manager or attorney refers you to a specific business manager, ask for more than a single recommendation and then be sure to meet with all of them before making your final decision. A good alternative is to ask for recommendations from other artists who are more successful than you are.

Qualities to Look for in a Business Manager

Once you have some business managers in mind and have scheduled some appointments, there are a few things you need to consider before deciding whom to hire:

+ *Is the business manager a certified public accountant?* Being a CPA doesn't necessarily provide you with the skills to be a business manager (many great business managers aren't CPAs), but it does give you some assurance that your business manager is at least a college graduate, is board certified, and has some organizational and accounting skills. Remember, there are no qualifications needed to be a business manager, so essentially anyone can be one.

+ *Is the business manager part of a larger firm or a smaller firm?* Some smaller business management firms (ranging from a one- to 20-person staff) simply don't have the same resources larger firms do. For instance, they may not have the capabilities for royalty examination. You don't want to be with a firm that you're going to quickly outgrow. On the other hand, if you start out at a larger firm (ranging from a 50- to 100-person staff), they may have more resources, but you risk the possibility of being overshadowed by their larger, more successful clients.

+ *Who are some of the business manager's other clients?* If you haven't heard of any of the clients the business manager represents, it may not be a good idea to go with him or her.

+ *How long has the business manager been in business?* An established business management firm is one that has usually been in business for about ten years. That's not to imply that anyone who has been in business for less than ten years is not any good; it just means that they haven't handled as many clients and are not as experienced.

+ *Does the business manager specialize in music?* This is perhaps one of the most important questions to consider. If the business manager handles entertainment clients in only film and television, he or she may not be right for you. Your business manager must understand the complexities of touring and royalty issues.

+ *Is the business manager's office space well organized?* If the business manager can't manage his or her own work space, how do you expect him or her to manage your finances?

+ *Does the business manager handle new and developing artists?* This is important! You want to know that business manager has the patience and know-how to make your pennies grow into nickels and your nickels to grow into dollars.

+ *Is the business manager approachable and pleasant?* If you can't communicate with your business manager, or if you feel uncomfortable or stupid discussing money in his or her presence, then *no matter who he or she represents*, you should look for someone else to hire.

✦ *Does the business manager welcome your questions?* You want someone who's going to be helpful enough to take your calls on weekends or at home if you have an important question or concern.

✦ *Can you trust your business manager?* This is an obvious concern, but extremely important. You want a business manager who projects a genuine feeling of concern for the security of your future.

✦ *What investment strategies does the business manager have in mind for you?* As previously discussed, does the business manager have a long-term, low-risk plan, or a high-risk, short-term plan in mind for you? You probably want to look for someone who is thinking about the long term.

✦ *Is the business manager independent of the deals and investments they're putting your money into?* If the business manager owns a share in a shopping center and wants you to invest in it as well, you should be wary of his or her advice. Or if your business manager pushes you in the direction of investing in a particular stock, he or she may be getting a commission from the stock broker for making the referral.

✦ *What kind of financial reports will the business manager give you?* Will the financial reports be issued monthly? Will they be categorized in a way that is easy to read and that you can understand?

✦ *Will the business manager handle your tax returns?* Some business management firms hire outside CPAs to handle tax returns and as a result, they charge you extra. You want to know this in advance.

✦ *Is the business manager an expert in handling royalties?* Royalties from publishing and record sales can be a great source of income for you. A business manager needs to understand this very complex and detailed area to insure that no money is lost or uncollected.

✦ *Has the business manager ever been sued before?* If there were ever a heated question with which to end, this one tops them all. It's sure to narrow down your choices, don't you think? Sharon Chambers of Down To Earth Business Management in Sherman Oaks, California suggests, "Never be intimidated to ask this question to both the smaller and larger firms. It's often the smaller firms that get the bad rap for unscrupulous activity, but nine times out of ten it's the big firms that rip you off. The reason why you rarely hear about these cases is because they settle out of the courts. You should never prescribe to the 'the larger the firm the safer you are' way of thinking."

As you can see from this list of questions, there is a great deal to consider before hiring a business manager. Keep in mind that it may be impossible to ascertain which individual or firm is right for you in a brief one hour meeting. The most important thing is not to be afraid of trusting your good old gut instinct. If things don't feel right from the start, they're probably not!

IMPORTANT TERMS OF YOUR AGREEMENT

Usually no formal contract exists between a business manager and client. However, it's not a bad idea to get a few basic terms in writing. These include the payment structure, audit rights, power of attorney, and termination rights.

Payment Structure

There are three methods by which business managers are typically paid: a flat monthly retainer, an hourly fee, and a percentage of the deals negotiated.

Flat Retainer A retainer is a fixed monthly sum that is based on the success of the client. Obviously, the more successful a client is, the more attention he or she will need. A retainer gives the client a sense of predictability regarding what they can expect to pay each month. On average, a monthly retainer can range from $500 to $3,000 for new artists, and far more for successful clients.

Hourly Fees A straight hourly fee is just that: you're charged by the hour for your business manager's services. The hourly fee is based on the professional level of the person working with you. For instance, a file clerk can get around $30 per hour, while a partner of the firm can get up to $300 per hour or more. It's usually not possible to pay one hourly rate for everyone involved with your career, so your bill will reflect various rates and charges. For instance, during the tax season (January–April 15), you may see higher charges on your bill since the higher-level CPAs may be preparing your returns. The "by-the-hour" system of paying a business manager usually works best for artists making substantial sums of money. As you'll see in a minute, when you choose to pay your business manager a percentage of the deals you enter into, he or she can end up with substantially more money—especially if you're earning large sums from concert performances or publishing deals.

Percentage of the Deal The last method of payment is for your business manager to take a percentage of the gross income from deals you negotiate. This is typically 5 percent. *Note that this does not include a percentage of the monies earned through investments made by the business manager on your behalf.* Your business manager may sometimes agree to set a cap on the amount of income he or she can earn per year. For instance, a business manager may agree to take in no more than $100,000 in commissions, and no less than $30,000. "And make sure to ask your business manager if there is a minimum requirement they must earn in order for you to stay a client," says business manager Sharon Chambers. "Some firms dump you after the first year when there are no more advances coming in from which to take a commission."

Audit Rights

Another point that you may want to stipulate is your right to audit your business manager's book. Business managers will always allow their clients to review all financial records. That said, Jeff Hinkle adds, "It's extremely rare that an artist will feel the need to audit their business manager. Nevertheless, an audit can actually be a healthy exercise for the artist. If anything, they'll get a greater appreciation for what the business manager does by seeing that everything is in order. And in the worst case scenario, if the business manager is up to no good, an audit may help reveal whose

KEEPING OTHERS IN CHECK BY CHECKING UP ON THEM. In a perfect example of what can happen to a band when one person gets too much control of the finances without any checks and balances in place, the former keyboard player of a very successful band (sorry, can't give the details here) claims that his personal manager ripped off the band for hundreds of thousands of dollars. The keyboard player claims that the personal manager drove around in expensive cars (including a Rolls Royce) while the band barely had money for food. Apparently, the personal manager stole advances, record royalties, and everything else he could get his hands on. To make matters worse, it turns out the personal manager was giving more money to one member of the band in order to keep him happy—and keep him quiet. Needless to say, the group eventually disbanded. By the way, the band's record label also fell apart. As it turns out, the principals of the label were also doing shady things. What a mess!

pockets the artist's money has been going into. The stories you often hear of unscrupulous business managers, personal managers, attorneys, or whomever else ripping off unsuspecting artists occur when the artist allows one person to have too much control over their career and finances without having any checks and balances. *The artist must always pay attention to what's going on around him or her, and not get caught up in the whole fantasy of being a star* [my emphasis]."

Power of Attorney

Power of attorney simply grants another person "the right to act for you." For instance, if given power of attorney, your business manager can deposit cash and checks into your accounts, *but note that his or her rights are limited.* In other words, if you're buying a home, you must sign for the loan. If you're getting an automobile, you have to sign for the lease or finance agreement. When your business manager files your tax returns, you have to sign the forms. When opening a new bank account, you have to sign with the bank. You get the point! Remember, your business manager only has a limited power of attorney.

The Right to Terminate

Last but not least, in all relationships between a business manager and client, the client must have the right to terminate at will. But remember, it's your responsibility to be aware of your finances at all times! Stay involved with what your business manager is doing. Examine the monthly reports he or she sends you, ask questions, and listen to your business manager's advice. If you suddenly snap out of rock stardom and realize that you're running out of money due to excess spending or neglect of your finances, the only person to blame is yourself. No one should care more about your future than you!

CHAPTER 9

Your Talent Agent

Touring is the most direct way for artists to promote their music. Though retail and radio promotion are equally important, new or less established artists may find themselves competing with other bands on their own record label for a piece of that promotional pie. Therefore, establishing a strong touring base independent of the record company's support should become a major priority for artists over the long haul. And since the laws in most states including California (unquestionably the entertainment capital of the world), exclude anyone but a licensed agent from booking live performances, the role of an agent in your career becomes essential.

THE ROLE OF AN AGENT IN YOUR CAREER

Agents are not to be confused with personal managers. By definition, the role of an agent is to *procure employment,* whereas the personal manager's role is to *advise and counsel* the artist. Personal managers assist you in everything from defining your public image to targeting your demographic audience. Agents secure bookings for you in concert settings, as well as in television, motion pictures, and commercial work (for those of you who wish to be actors), and in literary work (for those of you who wish to write books and screenplays). Live performances and touring are the talent agent's primary realms in the music business.

Formulating Your Tour Strategy

After you've signed with an agency, the first thing that happens is that your personal manager and your agent come together and begin formulating your tour strategy. The issues they discuss may include whether you should tour by yourself or open for another artist, what band you should open for, how much you should charge for tickets, and when and where you should tour. However, Ian Copeland, founder of Frontier Booking Agency, whose roster includes artists such as Sting, the Police, R.E.M., No Doubt, and the Red Hot Chili Peppers, notes that a personal manager and agent can sit down and talk until they're blue in their faces, but a lot of what's discussed may never pan out. The reality is that your agent has to get on the phone with concert promoters around the country and test the waters. Your agent must first determine whether or not there's a real interest in your band. As Copeland puts it, "It's like an army discussing its plans for going into battle with an enemy they can't see yet. You have to survey the terrain and figure out from where they're going to be shooting at you. Once this is determined, you can begin matching your plans with actual reality. This is an important point for your readers to keep in mind while reading this chapter."

Packaging the Artist

Another important responsibility handled by your agent involves packaging. Packaging is the process of matching different bands with similar styles and demographic appeals for a concert tour. In other words, if you're in a metal band, it's probably not in your best interest to be touring with a country artist, and vice versa for the country artist. Careful consideration is required here, especially for a new group still trying to establish its "brand name" or identity in the marketplace. Although there may seem to be a basic logic that goes along with packaging, individual bands and agents are going to have significantly different ideas. Some agents have a very strict conservative approach, while others have a looser game plan. The truth is that no one really knows what will and won't work. For instance, what made Lollapalooza (a concert festival conceptualized by Perry Farrell of Jane's Addiction) so popular was that the lineup was incredibly varied. The 1997 lineup consisted of Snoop Doggy Dog, Tool, Korn, Prodigy, and Devo—everything from rap to alternative to metal to techno to new wave. It brought different audiences together and exposed fans to music to which they might not have listened otherwise. Ian Copeland says, "The Police, whose music was for the most part rock and roll, desired to tour with punk bands because they wanted to be a part of that movement. At the time, which was around 1978, most people in America really didn't even know what punk was. But it didn't matter! The tour went over great! Although there's a common sense rationale that goes along with packaging, sometimes you just have to push that envelope and try new things."

Determining Whether to Open or Headline

Sometimes your agent may determine that it's better for you not to open for anyone at all and go out as the headlining act. Opening slots aren't easy to get, but when the opportunity comes along, you definitely don't want to settle for opening for a group whose audience isn't right for your music. Most record companies are usually horrified, however, by the idea of a new band headlining their own club tour. They'd rather have you go out as the support act for a major group in larger venues no matter what band you're playing before. The theory is that if your band plays in front of a larger audience, *you'll sell more records.*

But there are major disadvantages to going out as a support act, notes Ian Copeland. To begin with, you're going to end up with a limited use of the stage because the headlining act won't strike their drum set. And because you're crammed all the way up to the front of the stage, you're also going to end up with a limited use of the lights. What's more, the headlining act is going to limit the amount of power you'll have over the PA system, so your volume is not going to be as strong as you'd like. If that's not enough, your set list will consist of about six or seven songs you'll have to play just as everyone is arriving to the venue. And the audience members who are already seated have probably never heard of your band anyway and are somewhat annoyed because you're keeping them from the band they really came out to see.

In Ian Copeland's experience, a band gets much better exposure and can make a better impression by headlining smaller clubs. Although you're playing in front of smaller audiences, the people who come out—from the fans to the publicists to the radio station personnel—are specifically coming out to see *you*. You own the show! This provides you with the opportunity to really connect with your audience and slowly but surely win over a grassroots following of loyal fans. From there, you can work your way up to playing two nights in the same club, to playing larger rooms, to performing in theatres, and eventually, stadiums. "But it's always a fight with the record companies to take this approach," says Copeland. "It's the same way they run their companies—they're worried about quarterly reports and quick results. If the artist fails to measure up, the label is on to the next act. They'd rather see a new group support a totally inappropriate band in stadiums than to see them headlining clubs in front of a few die-hard fans that really want to be at your show."

Routing the Tour

Routing a tour is exactly what it sounds like. Your agent helps route or map out the direction your tour will take, what venues you'll be playing, and when you'll be expected to perform. This information is then forwarded to you in what's called an itinerary.

When you're the support act for a major artist, you won't have much say in the routing of your tour—you're told when to show up, and you'd better be there. However, when you're going out as the headlining act, your personal manager needs to supply your talent agent with as much information as possible, including when your record is coming out, where your single is getting airplay, where your records are selling the most units, when you want to tour, where you want to tour, how many months you want to tour, and so on. Your agent then begins to mold the tour accordingly.

Agents must take many factors into consideration when routing a tour. For instance, your agent understands that the most strategic time to tour is in the spring and the summer months (when kids are on spring break or out of school), and that the worst time to tour is during the winter months (when snow is on the ground and traveling is more treacherous). But more importantly, your agent must make sure to route a tour with the least amount of distance between each performance. If possible, a tour should never be routed to backtrack and re-cross old ground. Even when you're successful and can afford to fly between performances, your agent must consider the road crew that hauls the equipment from one show to the next. If there's too much distance between venues, the road crew may be late setting up the production—and shows may be canceled. And canceled shows make for unhappy fans.

Ian Copeland notes that there really is no set method for the way a tour is routed: "I may get a call from a band in England that gives me no other information than that they want to tour the United States. I then make a few calls, put together 30 or 40 dates, arrange them in some sensible order, and then fax an itinerary back to the band. Either they'll think it's great, or they'll get back to me with a number of concerns. They may want fewer consecutive shows in the beginning of the tour, when the singer is still trying to get his voice in shape, or they may want fewer shows at the end of the tour, when the singer's voice is beginning to burn out. I then go back and begin to reformulate the tour from there. So as you can see, the process in which tours are routed and itineraries are established can vary considerably."

Pricing the Artist

When you're the headlining act of a tour, your agent is responsible for determining the ticket price for your show as well. Determining the ticket price for a live performance begins with your agent contacting concert promoters and getting a sense of the marketplace. Although it may seem that the main goal is to get the highest price possible, you don't want to set it so high that you turn people away. Your agent must therefore take on the role of investigator and learn what similarly popular bands are charging for a performance, and how well their tickets are selling. And if a similarly popular band had charged a different price for its performance, would its sales have been even better?

Ian Copeland says that pricing the artist has a great deal to do with the style of music they perform and the demographic audience they attract. If you're a classy band whose music caters primarily to an adult audience, you can get away with charging a higher ticket price. If you're a metal act that attracts a younger audience, you have to charge a much lower ticket price, or no one will be able afford to attend. As Ian Copeland puts it, "It's all about determining what the consumer is willing to pay and can afford to pay for a product. If you're selling beer, you might only charge $4.00 because that's what people expect to pay. But if you're selling cognac, you can get away with charging much more as long as it's high quality, because people won't care what it costs."

Determining When to Put Tickets on Sale

Agents are also responsible for determining the best time to put your concert tickets on sale. Although your agent's plan will vary from city to city, the key is not to put them on sale either too far in advance or too close to the day of the show. If you put the tickets on sale early, you have more time to monitor sales and add another show if you're selling out a specific market. The down side is that you have

---

TICKET PRICES TO THE STARS. From *Rolling Stone* magazine's summer tour special (July 4, 2002), here's what some of the stars were charging for their live performances. Note that the wide range in ticket costs has to do with the proximity of seat to the stage.

Dave Matthews: $32–$56	Korn: $23–$43	Tom Petty: $25–$60
Eminem: $15–$ 56	Nickelback: $15–$33	Weezer: $23–$28
Incubus: $24–$40	Sheryl Crow: $23–$53	Widespread Panic:
Jewel: $20–$204	The Eagles: $55–$500	$18–$35
John Mellencamp:	The Who: $30–$350	
$20–$83		

NOTE: Keep in mind that all of the above acts have opening acts to help boost ticket sales. And as you'll learn later in Chapter 13, "Touring," the headliner is then responsible for paying the openers from the money earned from gross ticket sales each night.

to commit to a consistent level of advertising over the long haul or the audience may simply forget about your show. On the other hand, if you put your tickets on sale too close to the day of performance, you obviously won't have as much time to devote to promotion. It's a fine balance and requires thoughtful planning and research on the part of your agent.

To avoid direct competition for the consumer's dollar, your agent must also be careful not to put your tickets on sale on or around the same day as another major act. The strategically-minded agent may even try to beat another group to the punch by purposely scheduling an earlier sales date. "Sometimes, it's a lot of butting heads with other agents," says Ian Copeland. "If two different agents representing different artists want [tickets for their shows] to go on sale on a particular date, and neither of them wants to let the other go first, the tickets will end up coming out on the same day. But this is rare. Usually things get worked out."

> Have you noticed how easy it is to purchase concert tickets online? For instance, Ticketmaster (www.ticketmaster.com) provides detailed maps of the seating arrangement for particular venues, will update you when your favorite band comes to town, and will allow you to print out an electronic ticket right on your own computer. Also check out sites like Sold Out (www.soldout.com), Ticket Web (www.ticketweb.com), and webtix (www.webtix.com).

Negotiating Live Performance Deals

In the early stages of your career, when you're the support act for other artists, your compensation may consist of whatever the headlining act wants to offer, which may not amount to very much. Even when going out on your own and headlining small clubs, there may still be little room for negotiation at first. In any case, what generally happens when you're determining your fee for a live performance is that your agent must first determine what's called the "gross potential" of the venue. To simplify, once your agent and the promoter determine the ticket price they can charge for the artist, the agent multiplies this price by the capacity of the venue. For instance, if the average price of a ticket is $20 and the venue holds 500 people, the gross potential for the show would be $10,000 ($20 x 500 = $10,000). The agent and the promoter then negotiate backward from this price until it makes sense for all parties involved to put on the show. (Note: The various methods by which you're paid for a live performance, as well as how these deals are negotiated, are covered in Chapter 13.)

Ian Copeland notes that the negotiation process is really where your agent's skill comes into play. He or she must try to get the promoter to pay more money than your band is actually worth, but not so much that the promoter never wants you back again. It's important to understand that although your agent ultimately works for you, in a sense he or she also works for the promoter. In other words, once your band plays a venue and moves on to the next city, your agent must continue to book other acts in that very same room and needs to deal with the very same promoter. This also works in reverse. The promoter knows that the reputable agent books a number of viable touring acts and will therefore work hard at preserving his or her relationship with the agent.

Collecting Deposits

Besides negotiating live performance deals with promoters, your agent is responsible for collecting a deposit to ensure that you're not screwed out of what the promoter promises you. Most typically, the agent collects 50 percent of the negotiated fee for a performance, usually 30 days in advance of the show. Ian Copeland points out that, although this is the standard protocol in the business, the amount of money the talent agent can collect depends on his or her negotiating power. When dealing with Sting, Ian collects 100 percent of the money in advance—no questions asked! In fact, this holds true for Copeland when booking any band in foreign territories. In any case, *the money collected by your talent agent on your behalf is held until after you perform the gig*. Before this, you must be clear that your deposit remains the property of the promoter until the contract for a performance is consummated. After the show, the agent then subtracts his commission and forwards the rest to your business manager.

Putting Together the Rider

A contract rider is an attachment to a live performance agreement that indicates the specific items or accommodations (or specs) a band will need to put on its show. For instance, a band may have specific lighting and sound requirements and security needs, and may desire particular dressing room accommodations and certain foods and drinks backstage after the show. Although putting the rider together is generally your personal manager's responsibility, your agent will usually assist the manager if it's necessary and may even go so far as to type it up. Your agent then sends out the contract rider to concert promoters when putting together a tour. The promoter may take a look at the rider and send it back to your agent with some changes, at which point your agent must work with you and your personal manager to achieve reasonable terms for all parties involved. But note that in the early stages of your career, when you're an opening act or headlining small clubs, you're not going to have much leverage in your rider requests. You'll probably end up munching on the food that was left over from the band that played the night before. (Note: Riders are covered in Chapter 13.)

Dealing with Radio Promotion

When a band is on tour and passing through various cities, radio stations often want the rights to "present" a show to its listening audience. In other words, you might hear a radio station DJ say, "KROQ is proud to present Ozzy Osbourne at the Blockbuster Pavilion." The station may hold contests and give away a number of free tickets as well. This not only gives a station a certain level of prestige and helps boost its ratings, it also helps promote a show and sell more tickets. But what happens when two competing stations in the same city want the rights to present a show? To complicate matters even more, what happens when both of these stations are playing your single and supporting your band? Which station gets the rights to present the show?

Sorting out the "present rights" with radio stations is ultimately left to the record companies; however, it's worth noting that your talent agent must be cognizant of any problems that may exist. To accomplish this, your agent must speak with promoters in the various cities along the tour and find out if there are any competing stations in one area for the present rights. Your agent can then contact your label, which can use this information to determine the most prudent and tactful approach. Whichever station gets the rights to present a show, you and your label must make sure that the other station is not offended. Otherwise, the station may quickly drop your single. As you can see, the world of radio is a beast in and of itself; a detailed discussion of its inner workings would fill the pages of this book. You might try checking out *This Business of Music Marketing and Promotion* published by Billboard Books, or *The Radio Power Book: Directory of Music, Radio and*

Record Promotion published by Billboard Books. Otherwise, keep your eyes peeled for articles in trade magazines like *Hits, The Gavin Report,* and *Records and Radio.*

Monitoring Show Publicity

Although talent agents are not responsible for the actual publicity for a show, they do question promoters to make sure that adequate promotion will be in place. Your agent might ask the promoter how much he or she intends to spend on advertising, what stations or newspapers he or she is going to advertise with, and what type of posters will be in place around town. Advertising must obviously correspond to when the promoter and agent determine it's best to put tickets on sale for a show.

Hall Fees

Hall fees are discussed in more detail in Chapter 14, but generally they deal with a commission (or fee) the venue (or hall) charges merchandisers for selling your T-shirts, hats, posters, and other goods. Percentages range from 30 to 40 percent of the gross sales. Note that the talent agent does not share in a percentage of your merchandising incomes, so it does no good for him or her to negotiate one way or another. Nevertheless, agents are usually pretty good at reducing merchandising charges. More on this later.

HIRING YOUR AGENT

So at what point should you think about hiring an agent? And if you are going to hire one, where should you look, and what qualities should you look for?

When to Hire an Agent

If you're in a new band that's playing around town, trying to build a local following, and looking for a record deal, you're a long way from needing an agent. At this stage of your career, you'll be better served by picking up the phone and doing exactly what you're already doing—*booking gigs yourself!* No matter what anyone tries to tell you, the simple truth is that until you've built up a decent following and can generate reasonable fees for your live performance, *you're simply not worth an agent's time!*

In any case, talent agents of any caliber usually only deal with promoters on a national level anyway. Surely talent agents can deal with the very same clubs that you're playing in your own hometown, but this usually only happens when he or she has an artist passing through on a national tour. Keeping you busy for months on end in a local setting is simply not what a professional agent does.

The best time to begin looking for a talent agent is when you're getting signed to a record deal and a tour seems imminent. "But on the other hand," says Ian Copeland, "some bands will specifically go out on the road for the very purpose of getting a record deal! Take the Police, for example. Although the band already had a deal with A&M records in England, there were no plans for the label to license the band's album in the United States. I purposely brought the Police over from England to get A&M's offices in the U.S. excited. Though my brother Miles [the band's manager] had

In major cities such as L.A., you will find some local agents for unsigned, original bands who can help you get gigs, but if you don't heavily promote your shows and get people to pay an admission at the door, they won't be interested in working with you. Check out Sean Healey presents at www.we bookbands.com.

to borrow money for airfare and start-up expenses, and the band had to travel with one crew member and sleep in a passenger van that hauled all of the equipment, it was all worth it in the end! A&M was blown away by the band's live performances and decided to release and promote the Police in the States. So as you can see, in some circumstances the talent agent can also get involved with a band before they have a record deal. But in the most typical scenario, I'll have to agree that the agent comes aboard right at the time, or around the time, a band gets a deal."

Finding an Agent

More often than not, once your band is signed to a record company, the label already has a pretty good idea of what agency they'd like to see representing you. They may even go as far as initiating the first meeting between the agency and your personal manager. Ultimately, the final decision is up to you, but the record company has a lot of influence over who will end up representing your career. Keep in mind that the record company usually pays for your first tour by advancing you start-up money in the form of something called tour support. Though you're responsible for paying this money back from royalties you earn from future record sales (I'll discuss this in more detail in Chapter 11), the label still wants to make sure that it's going to get the most out of its initial investment.

In some cases, the talent agency itself will be the first party to seek you out. As soon as a band with any amount of buzz gets signed, you can be sure that the agencies will start calling—especially the larger ones. This is what's called a lazy campaign. A more aggressive campaign consists of agents actually hanging out in clubs every night and keeping their eyes and ears peeled for new and promising bands. Some agents may even go as far as keeping in touch with what's going on in foreign territories. Ian Copeland often received phone calls from his connections in England to alert him of any band that appeared to be unstoppable. Copeland was into cutting-edge music and was particularly fond of the punk revolution in London, which had not yet caught on in the United States. When he'd get a call about a band, Copeland would get on a plane, check the group out, and sign them before any other agency could; Squeeze is an example of one such band Copeland signed.

Often a band's personal manager has to be the aggressor in finding an agent. Besides making the rounds at all of the major agencies, the manager can conduct a more thorough search by contacting other personal managers in the business and asking for recommendations. In some cases, the manager may even refer to one of the many source books available on the market today, such as the one published by Pollstar (www.pollstar.com) called *Agency Roster.* As one might expect, this resource lists practically every agency, its roster of artists, and the names of the agents who work for the agency. *Agency Roster* is published twice yearly. It's highly advisable for both you and your manager to get a copy of this resource and to spend some time reviewing it. From there, you can start contacting various agencies and setting up appointments. But with so many agencies to choose from, how do you really know who's going to be the best one to represent you? Read on.

> To find an agent, contact Pollstar at www.pollstar.com, or at the number (800) 344-7383. In California, you can call the number (209) 224-2631.

Qualities to Look for in an Agent

Your personal manager will spend the most time working with your agent; your relationship with your agent is usually limited to time spent hanging out after your shows. Nevertheless, it's your career we're talking about here, so you should be aware of some important things to evaluate in a potential agent.

◆ *Is the agent part of a specialized agency or a full-service agency?* Some agents specialize in only booking musical acts, or even more specifically, booking musical acts of one genre. A full-service agency, on the other hand, has a broader range of services, representing actors in television, motion pictures, and commercial work, as well as representing producers, directors, writers, and editors. This can be useful to artists who have multiple interests and talents. However, you should never choose one agency over another because they promise to make you a movie star. More often than not, this prospect is only used as a sales pitch to get you to sign with their company.

◆ *Does your agent represent a small agency?* A smaller agency might be exactly what you need in the early stages of your career. There won't be many bands to compete with on the agency's roster, and you'll probably get individualized treatment. A smaller agency, however, may be limited in the scope of services it provides, and in some cases, will not have the level of clout and power you need to get into certain venues or on certain tours. You always want to make sure the agency is experienced in negotiating venue expenses like rent, ticket commissions, and merchandising deals. If you're a headlining act, your agent must be experienced at handling these business issues to ensure that you get the best revenue per show. Smaller agencies may not have this experience.

◆ *Does your agent represent one of the larger agencies?* Larger agencies usually have a broad range of services, as well as the clout needed to get you the best gigs and tours. Concert promoters around the country know that larger agencies represent a number of money-making clients and therefore work harder at preserving their relationships with them. Promoters may even be more willing to "play" young and developing artists like you, knowing that once you're in demand and successful, it's likely they'll have an ongoing relationship with you. The downside of being with a larger agency, though, is that you run the risk of being overshadowed by other artists the agency represents who are more successful and established than you.

◆ *Does your agent represent other artists whose music is similar to yours?* If you're a rock band, it may not be in your best interest to be represented by an agency that only handles new age artists. But what happens when a new age agency, for instance, is planning to open up a rock department, and you're the first rock band it wants to sign? Though it may be easy to conclude that you're going to get specialized attention, Ian Copeland warns that you never want to be the guinea pig at any agency, no matter how hard it may try to sell you on the idea.

◆ *Is your agent excited about the style of music you perform?* Your agent's enthusiasm for your music will greatly affect how hard he or she will fight for you—both for better gigs and better money. No matter how reputable the agent is, or the agency he or she represents, you want someone who seems genuinely concerned about furthering your career. Ian Copeland feels that this is one of the most important points to consider when choosing an agent. "An agent who has real passion for an artist can make a huge difference," says Copeland. "It can sometimes mean the difference between an artist succeeding and failing. In an ideal situation, the agent should be just as enthusiastic, if not more enthusiastic, about your music than you are. Make sure your agent is someone that's willing to kill for you and not just some person blowing smoke up your ass so you'll sign with their agency."

✦ *Will the agent with whom you're meeting be your "responsible" agent?* It's extremely important that the person with whom you initially meet is the person who will be your responsible agent and not just the person who wines and dines you and gets you interested in signing with his or her firm. Your responsible agent is the key person who will serve as the liaison between you and the rest of the agency and who will do the bulk of the work. Your responsible agent must have the ability to keep everyone within the agency motivated and interested in developing your career.

✦ *Where does your agent stand in the hierarchy of the agency?* Is your agent the low-person on the totem poll or does he or she actually have a position of power and strength? Agencies usually assign specific geographical regions, styles of music, and size of venues in which each of its agents must be responsible. "It's great if the agent who's meeting with you has come out to 18 of your shows and thinks the world of you," says Ian Copeland, "but if the territories he or she handles is North and South Dakota, you'd better hope the agents handling the East and West Coast also think you're the shit! That said, keep in mind that when signing with a talent agent, you're also signing with an agency consisting of several other agents who will be working on your career. It's important that you're confident [about] everyone's enthusiasm and ability to represent you."

✦ *How long has your agent been a part of the agency he or she represents?* Is your agent known for jumping from one agency to the next? Does the agency itself have a high turnover rate? If so, you may want to be concerned with whether or not your agent's days are numbered with a particular agency. Once you establish a good working relationship with a certain person, the last thing you want is to lose continuity by having to re-establish what you've already worked hard to build, or in the worst case, get stuck with someone at the agency who's not as enthusiastic about working with you. This is one reason why it's important to get something called a "key-person" provision in your agreement with an agency. A key-person clause stipulates that if your agent leaves or is fired, you have the right to terminate your agreement with the agency, and follow along with him or her.

✦ *What ideas does your agent have about how you should be packaged with other artists?* As I've pointed out, this is an extremely important consideration. The band that you're opening for is a much more important factor in terms of getting your music to the right audience than, for instance, the size of the crowd for which you're playing. If you're a new rock band, and your agent wants to package you with a pop band from the '80s, you may have a problem.

✦ *Does your agent display an open-mindedness about how he or she will try to break your career?* In other words, does the agency's plan for you seem to be centered around getting you on tour with its major acts? If this is the case, you should be put off.

It only displays your agent's lack of creativity and enthusiasm in finding new ways to break your career. "And more times than not," adds Ian Copeland, "you're not going to get on the major support slots anyway. There's probably 20 other new bands signed to the agency who have all been promised the same thing. Some may even be selling more records than you. What's more, the agent isn't the only person responsible for making the decision regarding who will end up on an opening slot of a tour. The headlining act itself is very influential, and so are the record companies. Your agent must have the patience to help you work your way up through the marketplace, and rally everyone involved—from the other agents to your record company—to stick with you over the long haul."

♦ *Do you like the demeanor your agent projects?* Your agent is the person who sells you to potential buyers. You want to know that he or she is going to be aggressive enough to get you the best deals and tours. But while this is an important attribute to look for, Ian Copeland adds, "You want to know that your agent is going to have enough tact and salesmanship to handle business in a way that won't be damaging to your career. You don't want a bully handling your business. As the saying goes, you can get more bees with honey than you can with vinegar. Another important consideration to look for is, while you don't need an agent who's going to be your best buddy, you want someone who is going to be cool enough to hang out with you backstage after your shows. Bottom-line, you don't want an asshole representing your career."

♦ *Can you trust your agent?* Not only is it important to feel that your agent believes in you and will work hard for your career, it's also important that you trust that your agent will not participate in unethical behavior. For instance, an unscrupulous agent may promise you one rate for a live performance, and then sell you for a much higher rate and pocket the difference. This kind of thing can easily happen if you only see the contracts between you and the agent and not the contracts between the promoter and the agent. The bottom line is that it's in your best interest to keep both eyes open at all times.

TERMS OF THE AGREEMENT

As with any business relationship, there are specific terms of your talent agency agreement about which you need to be extremely clear. These are the agent's fee, exclusivity, the scope of the agreement, the territory, and duration and termination.

The Agent's Fee

Before discussing your agent's fee, it's important to note that most states regulate the licensing of anyone who promises, offers, or attempts to procure employment for an artist. In California, an agent must file detailed applications, post a bond, and have all contract forms between the agent and client approved by the state labor commissioner.

Licensed agents must also abide by the rules set forth by certain entertainment unions, such as the American Federation of Musicians (AFM) for musicians, the American Federation of Radio and Television Artists (AFTRA) for vocalists, and the Screen Actors Guild (SAG) for taped or live television actors or actresses. The unions' regulation of talent agents is called "franchising." Franchised agents can charge their clients no more than a 10 percent commission, although in certain personal appearance situations under the AFM's jurisdiction the commission can be as much as 20 percent.

Agents typically commission income from live performances, tour-sponsorships, and the work they may generate for you in television and motion pictures. *But watch out for the agent who will try to earn a commission from your record royalties and publishing.* It's also important to make sure that your agent is not charging you any hidden fees. For instance, some agents may try to charge you for making telephone calls and mailing out contracts. Make sure that your agent's 10 percent commission covers everything.

Exclusivity

When you take on a talent agent, he or she will typically want to have an exclusive agreement with you. This means that you cannot be booked by any other agent during the term of your agreement. You will also be required to inform your agent of all offers made to you personally. Note that the exclusivity clause is a standard in most agency agreements. It would be unfair to assume that your agent should put his or her time into booking you if another agent is doing the same thing. Note that there is an exception in cases where you're able to restrict your agent from booking certain territories, as you will see in a moment.

The Scope of the Agreement

As the beginning of this chapter mentioned, the bulk of your agent's job is to book you for live performances and tours. Nevertheless, most talent agencies will also want the rights to book you in a variety of other areas, such as film, television, commercials, or to represent you if you want to write a book. If you're just a rock star and not an actor or writer, you may be happy to have someone who at least promises you the possibility of work in other areas. But as you'll see in a minute, your decision to work with an agency should not be based on this promise. What's more, if you truly believe that you have a chance at a career separate from the music business, and you have talent in acting or writing, then you'll want another agency that will specifically deal with that side of your career.

When you're an artist being wooed by several agencies because you've got a record coming out and you're the new hot buzz on the streets, all of the larger agencies are going to tell you that they can get you into the movies as a way of getting you to sign with them. They're going to tell you that they represent the biggest directors and producers, and that you've got a really good chance at expanding your career horizons. But Ian Copeland says that all the different departments at an agency are so separate from each other that they may never come together on a plan of attack for your career; there's no coordination between one agent and the next. Unless you're talking about a major star, it's rarely the case that a musical artist gets the big acting role, commercial, or spokesmodel endorsement for a cosmetic line. And if it happens, it's usually self-generated. In other words, someone will call the agency specifically requesting you. "And I bet you can guess who will then turn around and take the credit for finding you the work," says Copeland. "The agency does!"

"An agency should be run the way doctors offices are run," Copeland continues. "A general doctor meets with his or her patients and then refers them to a specialist when needed. It would

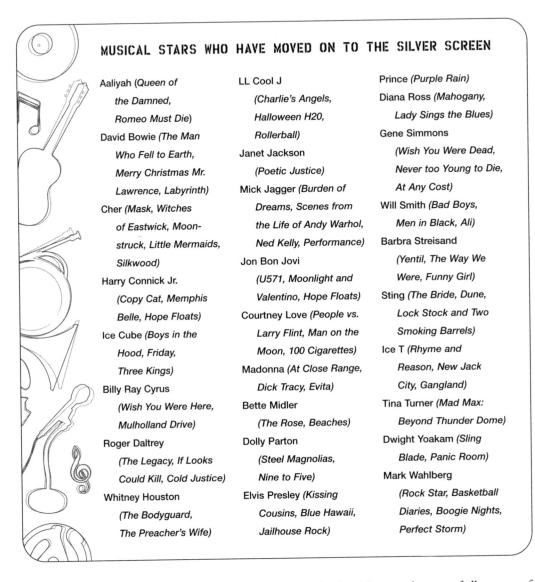

MUSICAL STARS WHO HAVE MOVED ON TO THE SILVER SCREEN

Aaliyah (*Queen of the Damned, Romeo Must Die*)

David Bowie (*The Man Who Fell to Earth, Merry Christmas Mr. Lawrence, Labyrinth*)

Cher (*Mask, Witches of Eastwick, Moonstruck, Little Mermaids, Silkwood*)

Harry Connick Jr. (*Copy Cat, Memphis Belle, Hope Floats*)

Ice Cube (*Boys in the Hood, Friday, Three Kings*)

Billy Ray Cyrus (*Wish You Were Here, Mulholland Drive*)

Roger Daltrey (*The Legacy, If Looks Could Kill, Cold Justice*)

Whitney Houston (*The Bodyguard, The Preacher's Wife*)

LL Cool J (*Charlie's Angels, Halloween H20, Rollerball*)

Janet Jackson (*Poetic Justice*)

Mick Jagger (*Burden of Dreams, Scenes from the Life of Andy Warhol, Ned Kelly, Performance*)

Jon Bon Jovi (*U571, Moonlight and Valentino, Hope Floats*)

Courtney Love (*People vs. Larry Flint, Man on the Moon, 100 Cigarettes*)

Madonna (*At Close Range, Dick Tracy, Evita*)

Bette Midler (*The Rose, Beaches*)

Dolly Parton (*Steel Magnolias, Nine to Five*)

Elvis Presley (*Kissing Cousins, Blue Hawaii, Jailhouse Rock*)

Prince (*Purple Rain*)

Diana Ross (*Mahogany, Lady Sings the Blues*)

Gene Simmons (*Wish You Were Dead, Never too Young to Die, At Any Cost*)

Will Smith (*Bad Boys, Men in Black, Ali*)

Barbra Streisand (*Yentil, The Way We Were, Funny Girl*)

Sting (*The Bride, Dune, Lock Stock and Two Smoking Barrels*)

Ice T (*Rhyme and Reason, New Jack City, Gangland*)

Tina Turner (*Mad Max: Beyond Thunder Dome*)

Dwight Yoakam (*Sling Blade, Panic Room*)

Mark Wahlberg (*Rock Star, Basketball Diaries, Boogie Nights, Perfect Storm*)

be ridiculous, to say the least, to have one doctor asking for the rights to take care of all aspects of your health.

"The best advice an honest agent can give a client is to separate [his or her] music career from other endeavors. It's my belief that an agent who's not honest enough to tell you this is simply greedy and only wants more control of your career."

The Territory

Your agent will want the worldwide rights to represent you as well. However, in some cases, you may be able to limit you agent's control over certain territories. For instance, you might be able to limit your agent's control to the U.S. only, and thus be able to contract with agents overseas who are more experienced with handling these areas. Ian Copeland advises that you should always try to hold on to your rights when it comes to booking outside of the states. Although your agency may have affiliations in foreign markets, they may not be the best people to represent you. If you can hold on to your rights, it's likely you'll begin touring the states anyway, and by the time you get to playing overseas, you'll have had the chance to see how your agent performs. Either you'll be confident in their connections abroad, or you can make the rounds of the various agencies yourself, and find someone you want to represent you there.

Duration and Termination

The typical term of an agreement between an agent and client is usually three to five years. However, it's not uncommon to negotiate for a shorter term such as one year. Note that under certain regulations set forth in your agreement with your agent, if he or she does not get you work (or an offer of work) within a specified period of time (90 days in the state of California), you may have the right to terminate your agreement.

It's also wise to have what's called a key person clause in your agreement with an agency. As previously mentioned, a key person clause gives you the right to terminate your agreement with an agency should your responsible agent be fired or leave the agency. This prevents the possibility of your being passed around the agency from one agent to the next or being stuck with an agent who is not enthusiastic about working with you.

In closing, Ian Copeland states his overall view on agency agreements this way: "Most agencies will tell you that you must sign a written agreement with them at the beginning of your relationship. But if you have any bargaining power at all, you may want to consider not signing anything at all. Think about it. There's no reason why an agency should ask you to sign a contract with them, because the truth is, the agency works for you. Tell them that you'll be loyal to them till the end of the earth as long as they're delivering "the goods," but if they're not delivering, you don't want some loophole in a contract that [prevents] you from moving on."

Copeland continues, "From the artist's perspective, I can't see one benefit of why they should sign an agreement with an agency. You already know that by law an agent can't take any more than a 10 percent commission. You also know that a key person clause is just a means to get out of your contract if your responsible agent leaves or is fired—but if you have no contract, you don't need a key person clause. If an agent adamantly insists you sign an agreement with them, could it suggest they're not confident you're going to stay with them? Assuming it does, then you better consider looking for an agent elsewhere."

CHAPTER 10

Your **Record** **Producer**

The most important thing to musicians is creating music. You spend years developing a distinctive sound and style before finally getting that big break when a record company is interested in investing thousands of dollars in recording and promoting your music or you find another way to record your music professionally. All the hard work you've put into developing a unique, original sound, however, may not be enough to create a successful album. Producing a great record is an art form in itself, and it requires the assistance of an experienced professional producer—a producer can actually make or break your career. The right collaboration can take you to creative places you never imagined, but the wrong one can be a nightmare whose implications are far-reaching. Understanding what producers do, and what they can do for you, can be vital to your future.

THE ROLE OF A RECORD PRODUCER IN YOUR CAREER

The record producer not only guides the artist through the entire recording process, including selecting and arranging songs, but also often co-writes and even composes complete compositions as well. The producer helps the artist get the most out of each studio performance, and works towards making that artist's work sound current in the marketplace even several years after its release. Stevie Wonder's record, *Songs In the Key of Life,* for instance, still sounds fresh and original 30 years later.

Steve Churchyard, producer for The Pretenders and INXS, discusses his role as a producer in Howard Massey's book *Behind*

> The key to a successful record is to first and foremost have quality songs and the best recorded vocal performance of those songs. The producer must do everything to ensure that you accomplish both of these goals.

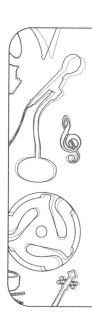

PULLING RABBITS OUT OF HATS. To illustrate one of the many roles a producer must play, in his book *Free At Last* (SAF Publishing) Steven Rosen spoke with legendary producer Eddie Kramer about his magical work with Bad Company. Kramer said: "We didn't have many recording effects in the studio at our disposal, so when the band wanted a swirling or tremolo effect for one of their recordings, I tied a couple of microphones together and spun them around in the air. It actually worked great! Sometimes you just have to try anything to get the right sound on tape." Another Kramer experience involved the late great Jimi Hendrix. For the intro to the song "Cross Town Traffic," the artist imagined a sound he couldn't quite explain. Musician and producer put their heads together and finally came up with something simple— Hendrix blowing through a comb covered in tissue paper (creating a kazoo sound). Hey, whatever works! To hear this effect, check out Hendrix's classic record *Electric Lady Land.*

The Glass: "As a producer, it's my job to make the artist's dream a reality and actually make it better than the dream."

Geoff Emerick, producer/engineer for the Beatles, Paul McCartney, and Elvis Costello adds, "The primary role of the producer is to pull the most talent out of the artist, to inspire the very best performance, even to the point of frustration if necessary."

When a Producer's Involvement Begins

A record producer's involvement in your career may begin with any number of situations. The most common are at the start of the development or demo deal, or the production deal, and the record label deal.

The Demo Deal In the early stages of your career, a producer may help you to record a demo and then shop the tapes to record companies using his or her connections. The producer may ask for a written agreement stipulating that if you get signed, he or she will receive a fee and a percentage of record sales in return for services rendered, and may even stipulate production responsibility for the final product.

> These days, up-and-coming artists are finding ways to fund the recording, production, and distribution of their own records and adopting a do-it-yourself approach to their careers. However, the record label deal is still the very thing that dreams are made of for most new artists.

The Production Deal The record producer may also be part of an actual production company. The production company will sign and develop you and record your demo, and then enter into a recording contract with a record company on your behalf. In this instance, you would then be asked to sign a "side letter" (an acknowledgement to the record company that you agree to perform exclusively for the production company, which is itself signed to the record company). In other words, the project is producer driven. The production company and the artist then both share in royalties from record sales.

The Record Deal

The last and most obvious scenario—and the main focus of this chapter—is when you enter into a recording agreement directly with a record company. In this case, the project is artist-driven. You are obligated by contract to hire an experienced record producer to help guide you through the recording process and to deliver a product that has the commercial sales potential to meet the company's expectations. The record company pays you an advance, typically known as the recording fund, from which all recording costs must be paid. For instance, if you have a recording fund of $300,000, a recording budget must be established within these limits. Whatever is left over you keep as an advance. And as you'll learn in detail in Chapter 11: "Record Royalties and Advances," the recording fund is considered a recoupable advance; meaning that you'll be required to pay the recording fund back from future record sales before you ever see one dime in royalties. You see, the recording fund is really your money up front, and you'll have to use it wisely to make the best record you can. That's really all you need to know about the financial aspects of record deals until later in this chapter. Let's move on to some of the record producer's other responsibilities.

Additional Responsibilities of the Record Producer

Besides his or her creative contribution to the recording of your material, the producer typically handles important business responsibilities. These include creating and maintaining your recording budget and handling administrative responsibilities such as union contracts, first-use mechanical licenses, and sample rights.

Creating and Maintaining a Recording Budget

As I've just mentioned, the record company allocates a recording fund from which a recording budget must be established. By contract, creating this budget is typically your responsibility, however it's usually the record producer and A&R man who first put it together. The producer gets you to agree to the budget and then submits it to the record company for final approval. Remember that the budget must stay within the limits of the available recording funds. If there are a number of producers on a given project, then your A&R representative is responsible for making sure that all of the producers submit individual budgets that, collectively, stay within the fund.

Here are some examples of what's typically covered in the recording budget and deducted from the recording fund, all of which are charged against future record sales:

+ The producer's fee
+ The engineer's fee
+ Studio rental costs (which may fluctuate greatly, depending on the rate you are charged, the advertised rate, or the discounted rate)
+ Tape costs
+ Editing costs
+ Mastering costs
+ Equipment rentals
+ Sticks, skins, strings, picks, and amplifier tubes
+ Union minimum-scale wages for musicians (or double or triple scale depending on what the band decides to pay themselves)
+ Union-scale wages for hired musicians (for over-dubs, guest appearances, etc.)

- ✦ Cartage (to transport your equipment to and from the studio)
- ✦ Lodging (depending on your needs and budget your accommodations could be either extravagant or conservative)
- ✦ Transportation costs

As you can see, expenses in the studio can add up quickly. And although it's the artist's responsibility to pay expenses back from future record sales, it's usually the artist who wants to spend more. There are a number of reasons for this. First, you may be new to the recording studio and you may feel you need more time to get the right tracks on tape. Second, you may want to be booked in the most expensive studios, record in Jamaica, and use the most expensive recording equipment simply for creative reasons. Third, you may want to fill up your budget with thousands of dollars in home recording equipment that you can keep for yourself after the sessions. Sometimes, as you'll see in the text box below, there is just no practical reason for eating up the recording budget.

Another important role of the producer is to make sure that the recording process runs smoothly and that the project stays within the intended limits. But this isn't always the way things turn out. Events in the recording studio aren't always predictable, mistakes are made, and projects go over budget when trying to get the right sounds and tracks. Although it's not uncommon for the record company to spring for the extra cash to complete a project, remember that the recording fund and any extra cash spent on your record are all charged against your future record sales. Essentially, it comes out of your pocket!

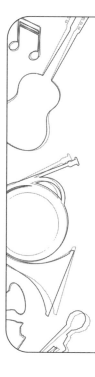

WHEN THE BUDGET GOES HAYWIRE. According to a former member of Billy Idol's band, the singer's days in the recording studio consisted of showing up three hours late, deciding what strip club they were going to visit, going there and getting loaded, and then showing up back in the studio past midnight—with Idol being billed for the studio time all the while. The band Korn reportedly spent $20,000 on Coors Light and Jack Daniels in the studio while working on their album *Follow The Leader.* Even in situations in which everyone is "behaving themselves" in the studio, a band and its producer can eat up thousands of dollars just trying to get the right sounds on tape. According to music journalist Steven Rosen, producer Ken Scott, when working on Supertramp's groundbreaking record *Crime of The Century,* took six months to get a snare drum sound. Producer Mutt Lange's work with Def Leppard consisted of recording hundreds of vocal tracks before finding one that he found acceptable. As he says, "Sometimes that's just what it takes." Obviously, once a band is successful, record labels are more tolerant of this type of behavior. Nonetheless, at the end of the day, the artist still pays for it. The truth is that if you're a hit and the money is rolling in, no one really cares.

HIDDEN AGENDAS. Though it's the record producer's role to oversee the recording budget, musicians may still have to be aware of how he or she handles recording expenses. As illustrated in Moses Avalon's book *Confessions of a Record Producer,* the producer may be able to arrange deals with side musicians, tape vendors, and recording studios, bill the expense at a higher cost, and then receive a payment in the form of a kickback. In other words, besides earning an advanced fee for his or her services, your record producer may be able to scam additional money from your recording budget under the table. If you don't think this type of activity takes place, here's another example. A colleague who wishes to remain unnamed recorded an album for a major label under the direction of two world-class producers. Unbeknownst to this young musician, he was entitled to earn a minimum-scale wage for his work as enforced in the union's collective bargaining agreements with the record labels (see Chapter 3, "Contract Employees and Self-Employment" for more on unions). Instead, the producers kept the musician's payment off the books and kept the money for themselves. Mikal Reid, who has produced records for artists such as Ben Harper, says, "Keep in mind that though there are definitely scammers in the business, most producers are also musicians and understand musicians—we're in it first and foremost for the art of making a serious record."

Administrative Responsibilities Besides putting together your recording budget, the producer assumes a number of administrative responsibilities when agreeing to work on a project. These include renting studios, hiring musicians, and sending out bills. Even more important to the success of your record, the producer fulfills important legal tasks such as filing first-use mechanical licenses, clearing samples, and filing union contracts (all of which will be discussed below). Since the producer's time is obviously better spent making records, the producer will typically pass these responsibilities over to someone called a "production coordinator" who specializes in administrative matters. The production coordinator is typically paid a flat fee or a percentage of the recording budget that ranges from 3 to 5 percent.

Here's a brief description of some of the more important responsibilities commonly handled by the production coordinator.

> *Food for thought.* Guess who owns the master recording tapes even after the record company recoups all of its expenses from your record sales? That's right, the record company does! But note that if the record company licenses these masters for motion picture soundtracks, compilations, or other mediums, you still benefit financially, as both a signed recording artist and author/owner of your compositions.

◆ *Filing first use mechanical licenses:* The production coordinator is responsible for filing a first-use mechanical license with the record company for all your songs that are going to be recorded and released for the first time. Under copyright law, the record company is then required to pay you a statutory licensing fee, called a mechanical royalty, for the use of your compositions on record. As of the year 2002, the statutory mechanical licensing fee is eight cents per composition for each record made and distributed. However, the record company, will want you to agree to take a 75 percent reduction of this rate (or six cents per composition per record sold) for all compositions you write or co-write with an outside writer (i.e., a writer not signed to the recording agreement). The licensing fees outside writers can charge for songs they have written entirely by themselves are unlimited on a first use. Therefore, it's especially important for the production coordinator to issue a first-use mechanical license *before* the song is recorded. In some cases, outside writers have asked for ridiculous amounts of money when they know that a particular artist is dead-set on using one of their songs. Though the record company is responsible for paying mechanical fees, the money ultimately comes out of your pocket. The record company usually pays new artists a mechanical royalty on a "cap" of usually ten songs per record. Therefore, for every outside song you use on your album, that's one less song for which you'll earn a royalty. (For more information on this, see Chapter 12, "Music Publishing.")

✦ *Filing compulsory mechanical licenses:* The production coordinator is also responsible for filing a "compulsory mechanical license" (or a license most typically used called a "mechanical license") when you cover an artist's song that's *already* been released commercially on record. For example, when the group Alien Ant Farm covered Michael Jackson's song "Smooth Criminal" in 2001, the group had to file a mechanical license. Limp Bizkit had to do the same when they recorded a cover of George Michael's song "Faith" on their debut record in 1997. Under what's called the "compulsory licensing provision" in the Copyright Act, anyone has the right to obtain a license from the owner of a composition as long as the character of the song is not changed (such as the lyrical content), and as long as a mechanical license is filed and a statutory mechanical fee is paid by the record company. But keep in mind that the production coordinator must be sure to file a compulsory license in a timely manner (before the record is released) to avoid copyright infringement charges from the owner. (The compulsory licensing provision is covered in more detail in Chapter 12, "Music Publishing.")

✦ *Clearing samples:* Samples are bits and pieces of other artists' songs (for example, a bass line from a David Bowie song, or a scream from a James Brown record) overdubbed or mixed into the recording of a new song to enhance its overall feel. Samples are used most commonly in rap, techno, trance, and R&B, though they're becoming more common in rock and pop music as well. Bands like the Beastie Boys have been using samples in their music for years. Moby's record *Play* featured numerous samples. In any case, the right to use any samples must be "cleared" in a timely manner with the original owners. This is extremely important! If your album is released before you've cleared the rights to use its samples, the owner could then insist you pay substantial sums for its use or otherwise won't grant you permission. Even worse, if you fail to clear samples altogether, the owner could sue you for copyright infringement; you don't want this to happen to you (see Chapter 12 for more on this). The owner is typically paid a negotiated fee for the use of a sample, called a "buy out," and in some cases, when a sample makes up for a significant portion of a composition, the original owner may even want to share in the ownership of your song.

✦ *Filing union contracts:* Major record labels and many smaller independent labels are signatories to agreements with the musician's unions, The American Federation of Musicians, and The American Federation of Television and Radio Artists. Under these agreements, labels are required to pay their artists, and all other musicians that are hired to perform on a recording, a union minimum scale wage. The label must also make contributions into pension and health and welfare funds on behalf of their artists. The production coordinator must be sure that all proper union forms are filed with the musicians' unions. If these forms are not filed properly, the unions may enforce penalties. Unions are covered in more detail in Chapter 2, "Band Membership" and in Chapter 3, "Contract Employment or Self-Employment."

✦ *Getting permission to use guest artists:* When an artist is making a guest appearance on your record, the production coordinator must first obtain permission from the guest artist's record label. The production coordinator must also make sure the proper credits are turned in to the record company so that they can be printed on the album artwork. For instance, on Carlos Santana's Grammy Award-winning record *Supernatural,* Everlast appears courtesy of Tommy Boy Records, Dave Matthews and Carter Beauford appear courtesy of RCA Records, and Eric Clapton appears courtesy of Reprise Records. However, getting permission to use guest artists on your record is not always as easy as it may sound. Korn waited for several weeks to get approval from Ruffhouse Records to use B-Real on their album release *Follow The Leader.* They were finally turned down. Instead, Korn was pleased to get approval from Flip/Interscope records to use Fred Durst of Limp Bizkit. Though there's no guarantee a record company will give the proper authorization, the earlier the production coordinator begins seeking approval for guest artists, the better chance you'll have to make the collaboration you desire a reality.

HIRING A RECORD PRODUCER

You already know how important a record producer is to your career, but who is ultimately responsible for selecting him or her? And once you select a producer, who actually negotiates the deal and does the hiring?

Responsibility for Selecting a Record Producer

When a record company signs a new artist to a recording agreement, it will initially insist on having the final say in choosing an experienced record producer. After all, the record company wants to ensure that they're getting the best possible product for its investment, which can run into the hundreds of thousands of dollars. However, since it makes no sense to have you locked up in the studio with a producer with whom you're unhappy, you can usually negotiate so that the selection of the record producer is mutual.

Most artists will typically give a great deal of thought to selecting a record producer. Your A&R representative may have a good sense of what type of record you want to make and also have

SELF PRODUCTION OR CO-PRODUCTION. What happens when you feel capable of producing your own record? Prince did and was successful at it. So was Paula Cole. But unless you have had some prior success, and the record company believes you're capable of delivering a worthy product, the label will not approve the request. If you feel capable of co-producing your record, the record company will want to be sure that the producer is experienced in making creative decisions, and not just someone who will be functioning as an engineer (i.e., the guys who are responsible for getting the right sounds on tape). Producer Humberto Gatica, who has worked with Michael Jackson and many other artists, clarifies the difference in Howard Massey's book *Behind the Glass:* "The whole idea of a great producer is to create a performance that's believable, and the engineer's job is to capitalize on that and put down on tape the best quality possible." Nevertheless, if the artist and A&R person feel strongly that the right record can be made with a particular person, it's possible the record company will approve co-production.

a few producers in mind. Will it be a slick, well-produced album with a lot of sequencers and samplings, or raw and in your face? These decisions, as well as the available recording budget, will obviously influence the list of producers you have in mind for the project.

Once your list of prospective record producers has been compiled and then approved by the record company, it's usually the artist (or artist's A&R person) who makes the first contact with the producers. The artist will send out demo recordings and/or meet with the producers to review songs. Keep in mind that if a record producer is in big demand, he or she can afford to pick and choose the projects and may simply be uninterested in working with you. It's also possible the producer will not be available for the project—or he or she may only be available to produce one or two tracks on the record. In the latter case, the artist, the A&R rep, and the record label must all decide if they want to use multiple producers. This is becoming increasingly common in many genres of music. (Multiple producers have long been typical in R&B and pop projects, but are now used

> Keep in mind that if a record company is unhappy with an artist's record, they'll approve additional funds in an effort to come up with a marketable product. But note that the more money the record company spends beyond its initial budget, the less committed they'll be to promoting the record if it's not immediately successful.

in rock and alternative music as well.) The record company may even suggest using a "staff producer" (one who is an employee of the record company). The benefit of using a staff producer is that the record company will absorb the cost of the producer's fee, which, as you already know, would otherwise be charged against your future record royalties.

Whomever the record producer is finally, it's important that everyone involved, especially your record label, is confident that the resulting product will be what they envisioned it would be. Sadly, if an album doesn't meet the expectations of the record label, it can mean the end of an artist's career with that label. Choosing the right producer is not just an important creative decision, it's also an important career decision.

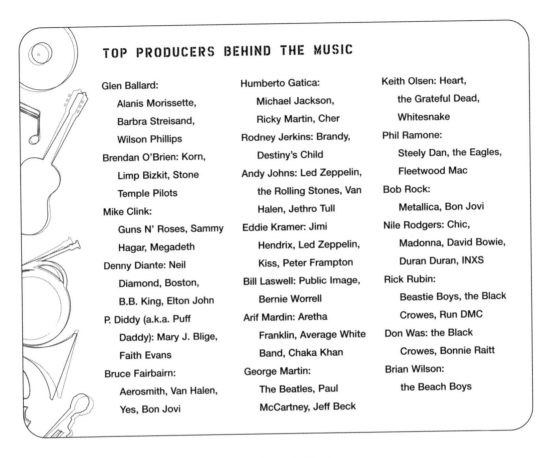

TOP PRODUCERS BEHIND THE MUSIC

Glen Ballard: Alanis Morissette, Barbra Streisand, Wilson Phillips

Brendan O'Brien: Korn, Limp Bizkit, Stone Temple Pilots

Mike Clink: Guns N' Roses, Sammy Hagar, Megadeth

Denny Diante: Neil Diamond, Boston, B.B. King, Elton John

P. Diddy (a.k.a. Puff Daddy): Mary J. Blige, Faith Evans

Bruce Fairbairn: Aerosmith, Van Halen, Yes, Bon Jovi

Humberto Gatica: Michael Jackson, Ricky Martin, Cher

Rodney Jerkins: Brandy, Destiny's Child

Andy Johns: Led Zeppelin, the Rolling Stones, Van Halen, Jethro Tull

Eddie Kramer: Jimi Hendrix, Led Zeppelin, Kiss, Peter Frampton

Bill Laswell: Public Image, Bernie Worrell

Arif Mardin: Aretha Franklin, Average White Band, Chaka Khan

George Martin: The Beatles, Paul McCartney, Jeff Beck

Keith Olsen: Heart, the Grateful Dead, Whitesnake

Phil Ramone: Steely Dan, the Eagles, Fleetwood Mac

Bob Rock: Metallica, Bon Jovi

Nile Rodgers: Chic, Madonna, David Bowie, Duran Duran, INXS

Rick Rubin: Beastie Boys, the Black Crowes, Run DMC

Don Was: the Black Crowes, Bonnie Raitt

Brian Wilson: the Beach Boys

Responsibility for Negotiating the Producer's Deal

Once the producer has agreed to work on a project, and his schedule is free and clear, your contract with the record company also holds you responsible for hiring the producer and negotiating the deal. What fee will the producer want? What record royalty is the producer going to receive? How will the credits be listed on the album cover? (You don't want the producer's name sprawled across the front saying, "John Doe presents.") Of course, this means that your attorney has to draw up contracts and negotiate the deal on your behalf, which means even more money out of your pocket at the end of the day. But if you don't want to incur the extra expense of hiring the attorney because you feel that the outcome of the deal won't make a difference one way or the other (the range of what a producer can charge is, for the most part, fairly standard), do you have another option?

In most cases, the record company will agree to negotiate the deal with the producer on your behalf. But understand that in such a situation you're relinquishing some control. Remember, you're responsible for paying back all recording expenses, including the producer's fee, so it's ultimately your money we're talking about here. Will the record company make a deal with which you're ultimately going to be unhappy? Will you feel more in control if you've negotiated the deal and hired the producer yourself?

Regardless of who actually negotiates the deal and hires the record producer, there may be some confusion regarding for whom the producer actually works—the record company or the artist? Consider the following basic points:

- First, no matter how you look at it, the record company is the entity that actually makes a recording project financially possible. Therefore, in the eyes of the producer, the record company is really the one putting the food on his or her plate.
- Second, the record company not only holds the right to approve the producer, it may even make persuasive suggestions regarding who they'd like to see working on your record. In fact, it's possible that your A&R representative and the record producer are friends who may have worked on projects together in the past. Record producers know on which side their bread is buttered. Consequently, when push comes to shove, the producer is going to work hard at maintaining his or her relationship with the record labels. Producers' know that bands come and go, but that the labels will be around much longer.
- Third, the record company's contract stipulates that you hire a producer to ensure that you deliver a commercially acceptable record. Therefore, you already have an indication that the producer is actually the eyes and ears of the record company. If the producer takes a stand on a particular arrangement or musical selection, believing "it's too out there" or not "commercial enough," there could be an ugly situation in the recording studio if the artist does not agree. Though this scenario may seem to be far-fetched, it's in fact quite typical. This doesn't diminish the integrity of the record producer, but rather presents a realistic view of the artist/producer/label relationship. Just keep one thing in mind: the producer's expertise is in the art of making records. As Moses Avalon eloquently states in his book *Confessions of A Record Producer*, "If you pay a doctor for his advice and you ignore him, who are you really hurting anyway?"

Ed Cherney, producer for the Rolling Stones and Bob Dylan, says in Howard Massey's book *Behind the Glass*, "You're going in to represent what the artist is doing, to be as honest as you can,

WHEN THE RECORDING PROCESS GOES SOUTH. The artist/producer relationship may not always go as smoothly as intended. Producer Glen Ballard (who has worked for Alanis Morissette and Michael Jackson, among others), admits that he's not really sure if he got fired or if he quit when working on a project with Aerosmith in Miami. In an article in *The Los Angeles Times* in August, 2001, Ballard simply said, "The recording process seemed endless due to complications in the studio." In another story, Korn's relationship with Steve Thompson (producer for Guns N' Roses, Rollins Band, and Blues Traveler) came to a screeching halt after four long months in the recording studio. The band was simply not happy with the direction in which Thompson was taking the mixes, and therefore opted to hand the producer reins over to Toby Wright. "Hearing the album now, it all seems worth it," says Korn vocalist Jonathan Davis in Leah Furman's book *Korn: Life In The Pit*. Although Korn's album cost $500,000 to complete, it ended up being a great success for all involved.

and hope for the best—hopefully making something where business and commerce and art meet, all at the same intersection."

And finally, Mikal Reid, producer for Ben Harper adds, "It's important that the artist gets a feeling of trust with a producer before ever choosing to work with him or her. Take the time to get to know your producer first so that there won't be any surprises or conflicting situations in the studio later. There [are] a lot of people claiming to be producers, but the truly talented guys are the ones concerned with making a record that everyone can be proud of. After all, it's both the artist's and the producer's career that depends on it."

THE RECORD PRODUCER'S FEE STRUCTURE

Now that you have a good sense of the role a record producer plays in your career, as well as who's responsible for selecting the producer and negotiating his or her deal, let's discuss your last contractual obligation to the record company: the producer's fee and the producer's royalty payment.

Advances

As mentioned briefly at the beginning of this chapter, most recording contracts today are structured as something called the recording fund. This means that out of the advances that you negotiate in your recording agreement, the producer's compensation must also be considered. For example, if you receive a recording fund of $300,000, $200,000 may be budgeted towards the recording cost budget, and the other $100,000 may be used as your advance. The fees typically paid to a mid-level record producer can be in the neighborhood of $50,000 for recording a full-length album, and up to $8,000 for a single master. (Superstar producers can get much more.) So if the budget for recording an album were $200,000, and the producer earned a fee of $50,000, you're now left with a recording budget of $150,000. That's pretty much it. Now lets move on to record royalties.

> In producer-driven projects, especially with star producers, advances can range from $200,000 to $500,000 and sometimes even higher.

Record Royalties

In addition to paying the producer a fee, you're also responsible for assigning the producer a record royalty for future sales. You see, most recording deals are structured as something called an all-in deal. This means that out of the royalty rate you negotiate with your record company, the producer's royalty must also be considered. For example, if the record company offers you a royalty rate of 16 percent of the suggested retail price of the record, and the desired producer for a project requires a royalty of four percent, you're now left with a net royalty rate of 12 percent (16–4=12). So before writing home to your friends and family about the whopping 16 point royalty you have, remember that you must consider the producer's share first. Hey, if this isn't quite settling with you, that's just the way it goes! And it gets even more interesting.

Guess who's responsible for paying the record producer for royalties that may become due to him or her? You guessed it, you are! Well, you don't actually have to take any money out of your own pockets to do this. The record company will typically agree to pay any royalties owed to the producer on your behalf, but they'll charge the expense against your royalty account. I know this sounds a little confusing, so I'll elaborate for a moment.

As mentioned at the beginning of this chapter (and as you'll learn more about in Chapter 11, "Record Royalties and Advances"), before you earn record royalties from sales, you're required to pay the record company back for *all recoupable expenses* incurred. Recoupable expenses include the recording fund, expenses for filming one of those cool promotional videos you see on MTV or VH1, and monies advanced to help subsidize your touring costs. Once all of these expenses are recouped, which, by the way, can add up to be well into the hundreds of thousands of dollars, you begin earning a royalty from sales from that point forward.

On the other hand, the record producer's royalty payments are structured far more favorably than the artist's. The producer typically begins to earn a royalty from sales after the recoupment of the recording fund only—and in some cases, only after the recoupment of his or her advanced fee. Here's the big punchline: *the producer starts making money from record sales long before you do*—and remember, as briefly mentioned above—*you're responsible for flipping the bill.* Again, the record company will typically agree to pay the producer's royalties on your behalf, but every dime is charged back to your royalty account.

Also note that the record company, for whatever historical reason, pays the producer retroactively *to the very first record ever*—a concept called "record-one royalties." In other words, if 500,000 records are sold, the producer gets paid a royalty on all 500,000 records (less of course, the monies he or she gets up front for a fee). And just in case you didn't catch it the first time around, the artist only earns a royalty from sales that occur *after* the recoupment of all costs. In other words, if 500,000 records are sold and the record company has recouped all of its expenses, you would start getting paid after 500,001 records.

That's pretty much all you need to know about the record producer's fee structure for now. (You'll learn more about record royalties and advances in Chapter 11.)

4

Sources of

REVENUE

> "Making music is an art.
> Making a living from it is a business."
> —BILLY MITCHELL, author of *The Gigging Musician*

Most musicians are quick to say that the reason for pursuing a career in music is for their love for music itself. While this should be your number one motivation, money is certainly integral to your livelihood, happiness, and future well-being. For this reason, it's extremely important that you understand the various revenue sources that can become available to you. These include record royalties and advances, music publishing, touring, and merchandising.

But before making plans to cash in and buy your new home, there's a lot more that you need to know about these sources of income. For instance, did you know that out of your initial recording advance, there may be very little that actually ends up in your own pocket? And although, the expression, "don't give up your publishing," is widely used among many musicians, do you understand what's really meant by this? Plus, while touring may seem like a lot of fun, did you know that it can be a very long time before it becomes a profitable endeavor? And finally, though we've all heard stories of bands getting substantial merchandising advances, are you aware that these monies are both recoupable and returnable; in other words, that you're obligated to pay them back?

As you can see, there's plenty of important information with which every artist should be familiar. In this section we will simplify these complex topics so that you can make your way safely through this legal minefield and put every dime you deserve into your pockets.

REVENUES AT A GLANCE: THE MONIES YOU MAY EARN

Record Advances	Publishing Incomes:	Touring Incomes and
Record Royalties	Mechanical Royalties,	Sponsorships
Publishing Advances	Performance Royalties,	Merchandising Advances
	Synchronization Fees,	and Royalties
	and Print Fees	

CHAPTER II

Record Royalties
and Advances

Once you're a signed recording artist, you can look forward to the substantial advance you're going to receive from the record company and all the record royalties that are going to begin rolling in. Right? Wrong!

Before you start thinking about how you're going to spend all that money, you should understand a few basic concepts about record royalties and advances. Of these concepts, the most important is that out of the initial recording advance, you're responsible for paying all recording expenses as well as all of the professionals you've hired to assist you with your career. One hundred percent of that advance, as well as any other advances offered to you by the record company, must be recouped from your future album sales before you ever receive a dime in record royalties—and that's if you *ever* receive a dime.

In this chapter, I'll explain the basic dynamics of recording advances and record royalties: I'll define "recoupable advances" and "cross-collateralization," and give a detailed analysis of royalties and computations. An interview with Fred Croshal, general manager at Maverick Records, gives some real-life examples of how these dynamics work and explains just what it takes for a record label and an artist to sell records.

TYPES OF RECORDING DEALS

Record deals with larger record companies are the focus of this chapter, and, for the most part, this book, since major-label recording deals are still what most artists dream about. However, it's necessary to discuss some of the other recording agreements

Many artists these days are taking a proactive approach to their careers, or what's called a do-it-yourself approach. Home recording gear, affordable CD manufacturing, and Internet sites that allow you to promote your band make doing so possible. If you want to go this route, just be prepared to put up the cash or you won't get very far.

that exist, such as the independent-label recording deal and the production deal. Although the royalty rates and advances offered by the independent label recording deal, the production deal, and the major label recording deal differ, the broad concepts each involves are basically the same.

The Independent Label Recording Deal

Independent record companies (also called indies) are typically more willing than major record companies to sign undeveloped talent and bands whose music is outside the mainstream. For instance, indies were essentially the breeding ground and lifeline for the punk rock and grunge revolutions in the music industry. Independent record companies are not usually owned or controlled by the major labels and are generally distributed by smaller regional distributors. (Distribution refers to the means by which stock is stored and shipped to suppliers; a company will warehouse all the manufactured CDs and albums and handle the fulfillment and delivery of orders from stores and online retailers.) Sometimes an independent record company may arrange a distribution deal or a pressing and distribution deal (P&D deal) with a major record company. This means that although you're signed to an indie record label, a major label may agree to handle getting your record into the stores and may also manufacture your album. Independent record companies may also rely on funding from major record companies (for the recorded masters, artwork, manufacturing, and distribution of an album) obtained through a "joint venture." The major would then receive a percentage from sales. In any case, the rate for record royalties that new artists can expect to receive ranges from 9 to 13 percent of the suggested retail list price (SRLP) of their record, or from 18 to 26 percent of the wholesale price of the record. Recording advances can range from as little as $10,000 to well up into the $100,000 range.

> Rather than signing with the major labels, there is a trend as of this writing for artists of a variety of styles, even pop, to sign with the indies with the notion that they'll get more personalized attention. Although you may indeed get more attention, keep in mind that indies usually don't have the marketing muscle or financial resources that the major labels have, and as a result, you *may* find them dipping into your publishing and merchandising monies by controlling these rights.

The Production Deal

Production companies typically consist of independent record producers who sign, develop, and record talent. Very much like independent record companies, production companies may be more willing initially to develop younger talent and less popular forms of music than major record labels. In a typical scenario, a production company signs an artist and then enters into an agreement with a record company on that artist's behalf. The record company then pays the production company a royalty for sales of the album, and the production company in turn pays the artist around 50 percent of the money it receives. For example, if the record company pays the production company a record royalty at 19 percent of the suggested retail list price of your record, the production company would pay you half of that rate, or 9.5 percent (19 x 50% = 9.5). The production company receives a recording advance that can range from $125,000 to $350,000, sometimes much more, depending on the stature of the record producer. If there are any monies left over after recording expenses, they will typically be split 50/50 between you and the production company. Shawna Hilleary, a Los Angeles-based attorney for Artist Law Group, adds, "It is not hard to figure out why production company deals are often referred to as 'selling your soul to the devil.' However, rather than a 50/50 split, it is not impossible to negotiate a more favorable percentage, or at the very least, have the percentage increase in favor of the artist for each album. 70/30 splits are not unheard of."

The Major-Label Recording Deal

Major labels, our focus in this chapter, seek artists who are commercially viable, thus giving the label greater potential for the quickest possible return on its investment. Major labels are responsible for the majority of commercial recordings that are sold in the United States. As of this writing, the five largest record companies are Sony, UMG, BMG, EMI, and WEA. Each major performs a variety of functions, such as A&R, promotion, advertising, sales, legal, finance, shipping, and merchandising. All the major record companies are also part of larger corporations that run a system of distribution channels, regional offices, international divisions, and other music businesses, such as music publishing and record clubs. The record royalty rates that new artists can expect for sales of their albums range from 11 to 16 percent of the suggested retail list price, or 22 to 30 percent of the wholesale price per unit sold (royalties based on the suggested retail price have been most common). Record advances can range from $125,000 to $350,000 (and often much more).

RECORDING FUNDS AND FORMULAS

Now that you have a general understanding of the different types of recording deals that exist, let's focus on the finer details of recording funds and formulas.

Recording Funds

Most record deals today are structured to provide all-inclusive recording funds. The recording fund covers all your recording costs (including the record producer, studio costs, and equipment rentals and purchases), and any money that remains serves as your advance. For example, suppose your band is advanced a recording fund of $300,000. Two hundred thousand of this sum may go to the budget for recording costs, and the remaining $100,000 may go toward your advance. Before you get excited about pocketing that hundred grand, you'd better read on.

READ IT IN THE PRESS. A press release announcing that a band has signed an eight-album deal with a total of $20 million in advances leads one to believe that recording deals are like striking it rich. On the contrary; you should know that recording deals are based on "option periods." In other words, the record company may guarantee payment of an advance for one album, and then will have the option to pay for another three records, one at a time. However, if your first record sells poorly, the record company may choose to exercise its right not to record another album and release you from your recording contract. You would then be free to sign with another record company, but that could be difficult because you have the stigma of having been dropped once already. Thus, you may have only one crack at hitting the big time!

Out of your $100,000 advance, $15,000 (or five percent of the total recording fund) may go to your attorney for negotiating your record deal. Another $20,000 (or 20 percent of your advance) may pay your personal manager's commission. An additional $5,000 (or 5 percent of your advance) may pay your business manager's commission. And, of course, out of the remaining $60,000, $18,000 (approximately 30 percent) will go to Uncle Sam for taxes. The remaining $42,000 may then be split between the four members of your band, which leaves each of you with a grand total of $10,500 for living expenses. Stacy Fass, a Los Angeles-based entertainment attorney, jokes, "The label expects a band to live for several months on what a label executive's expense account is [for] one month."

Although the above numbers are only estimates, they outline a pretty accurate picture of recording finances, so be realistic. Don't expect to get rich. And remember that a record deal is not the means to a certain end, but only a *chance* you're given to make your dreams come true. The following equation breaks down the distribution of the average recording deal.

> Although "recording funds" are typical in recording deals, anything and everything is negotiable. In some cases, your attorney may be able to get the record company to give you a "signing bonus," which are extra monies (usually not recoupable) that serve as an incentive for you to sign with their company. This usually happens when several different record companies negotiate to sign your band in what's generally known as a "bidding war." But bidding wars are rare, and just because a band finds itself in the middle of one of these tugs-of-war doesn't necessarily mean it will get the long-term label support it deserves after a deal has been inked.

$300,000 (The recording fund)
- $200,000 (The recording cost budget)
= $100,000
- $15,000 (The attorney's commission, 5% x $300,000)
- $20,000 (The manager's commission, 20% x $100,000)
- $5,000 (The business manager's commission, 5 % x $100,000)
= $60,000
- $18,000 (Uncle Sam's cut, approximately 30% x $60,000)
= $42,000 (The artist advance)
= $10,500 (The artist advance per each band member,
         if four people are in the band)

Formulas

The recording fund for your first album is typically a set amount. For instance, if your band signs to a major label, you may receive a fund of $300,000. However, your recording fund for subsequent albums are typically based on a percentage, or "formula," (usually 60 to 70 percent) of the royalties credited from prior records sales during a specified period of time—say the first ten months after your record is released. If your formula is 60 percent, and you were credited only $100,000 in royalties for your first record over a ten-month period, then your recording fund for your second record would be $60,000 (60% x $100,000 = $60,000). If, however, your record sells extremely well and you were credited $2,000,000 in royalties, your fund would be as much as $1,200,000 (60% x $2,000,000 = $1,200,000) for your second record. But as you'll see below, there are some variations to this formula, which are generally known as minimum (or floor) and maximum (or ceiling) formulas.

Floor/Minimum Formulas In the previous example, the recording fund for your second record was based on the royalties formula and was thus $60,000. How can you be expected to record an album for as little as $60,000 when the recording fund for your first record was $300,000? Doing so is difficult, and that's why you should have an attorney negotiate a floor (a minimum amount) for you. For example, no matter how poorly your first record sells, your contract can ensure that your recording fund for your second record be no less than $325,000. Note that if the recording fund for your first record was $300,000, a $25,000 fund increase between your first record and your second record suggests your attorney may also be able to negotiate a bigger recording fund for subsequent records.

Ceiling/Maximum Formulas To protect itself from paying ridiculous amounts of money should your first record sell substantially well, the record company will set a ceiling (maximum) in your contract for the amount of money you may receive for a recording fund. The ceiling is often two times as much as the amount of the floor but is negotiable by your attorney. For instance, if you have a floor of $325,000 on your second record, the ceiling for the recording fund may be $650,000. Keep in mind that these numbers are just examples.

ROYALTY RATES AND ESCALATIONS

Record royalties are percentages (also called points) that the record company pays to you for the sale of your record. As this chapter explained earlier, a typical royalty rate for a new band signed to a major label may range from 11 to 16 percent of the suggested retail list price (SRLP) per unit sold. Your attorney can help negotiate the best royalty rate possible, as with recording funds. But rather than giving you the highest royalty rate from the start, the record company will usually agree to adjust the rate based on the success of your record. So, if you have a royalty rate that begins at 14 percent of the suggested retail price of your record, the rate for domestic sales of your record may increase by one-half to one point after 500,000 units have been sold. For domestic sales of over 1,000,000 units, your royalty rate may increase by another one-half to one point. Take a look at the example below.

> Royalty Rate for Album One: 14% of the SRLP up to sales of 500,000 units
> 14.5% of the SRLP after sales of 500,000 units
> 15% of the SRLP after sales of 1,000,000 units

So, how are royalties structured on your second record? Well, if you had a royalty rate beginning at 14 percent for your first recording, your attorney may be able to negotiate for a royalty rate starting at 14.5 percent for your second album, with similar rate increases of one-half to one point when your record reaches predetermined sales figures.

> Royalty Rate for Album Two: 14.5% of the SRLP up to sales of 500,000 units
> 15% of the SRLP after sales of 500,000 units
> 15.5% of the SRLP after sales of 1,000,000 units

Of course, none of this may really matter anyway. If your record ends up being a huge hit, you'll have the leverage to go back to the record company and renegotiate your deal. As the saying goes, "He who has the gold makes the rules." On the other hand, if your record isn't successful—and unfortunately, the majority of records released aren't—the record company may not want to record another album with you, and you may end up getting dropped. This information is not meant to discourage you, it's just the plain and simple truth!

HOW RECORD ROYALTIES ARE CALCULATED

Now that you know the basics of royalty rates and rate escalations, it's important that you understand just what you can expect to earn for each record you sell. A detailed analysis of how the record company calculates your royalty follows, beginning with the suggested retail list and wholesale prices, to package cost deductions and free goods. Read carefully, because your royalty per CD may end up being far less than you ever imagined.

Suggested Retail Price and Wholesale Price

The standard royalty rate a record company will pay ranges from 11 to 16 percent of the suggested retail price of your record. However, the *suggested* retail price is not necessarily the price at which your record is *actually* sold in stores. If the suggested retail list price of your CD is $18.99, and you have a royalty rate of 16 percent, you're not necessarily going to earn $3.03 per CD ($18.99 x 16% = $3.03). The suggested retail price is merely part of a system that the record company uses to calculate royalties, and that price may be reduced dramatically by a series of deductions, which we'll get to next.

Package Cost Deductions

The suggested retail price for CDs averages around $18.99 as of this writing. The record company then deducts 20 percent for cassettes and 25 percent for CDs for what it calls a "package cost deduction." This theoretically covers the expenses for the plastic cases in which your record is sold and its accompanying artwork. However, the amount the record company deducts, approximately $4.94 per CD (25% x $18.99), is much more than the actual cost of packaging your record. In reality, it costs the record company around 70 cents to package each record. I know this doesn't sound fair, but package cost deduction is standard in the industry and it's usually not negotiable. Let's take a look at the computation below, assuming you're earning a royalty rate of 16 percent.

$18.99 (The suggested retail list price for CDs)
- 25%   (CD package cost deduction)
= $14.24
  x 16% (Your royalty rate)
= $2.27 (Your royalty paid per CD)

The All-in and Net Royalty Rate

Another cost that's deducted from your royalties is your record producer's royalty. The standard royalty rate a record company offers you is known as an "all-in rate" (both your royalty rate and your producer's rate combined), and the amount you actually get to keep is called a "net royalty rate" (your royalty rate after you deduct the producer's agreed-upon share). For example, if you have an all-in royalty rate of 16 percent, and your record producer negotiates a deal that gives him or her four percent, you now have a net royalty rate of 12 percent. As you can see, this is another factor that reduces your royalty per CD.

> You may be wondering whether you can hold onto those extra royalty points by producing your own record. The answer is no. Most new artists will typically be required by contract to hire an experienced studio producer to ensure the best possible product, and thus protecting the label's investment in you.

$14.24 (The SRLP minus packaging costs)

x 12% (16% your all-in rate minus 4% the producer's share)

= **$1.70** **(Your royalty per CD)**

Standard Free Goods

The next royalty deduction—for what are called standard free goods—involves the actual percentage of sales the record company agrees to pay you. Theoretically, for every 100 records distributed, the record company will only charge retailers for 85 records. The remaining 15 records are given away free as a so-called purchasing incentive, and since they were not actually sold, you're not paid a royalty on them. So, in effect, your royalty is based on 85 percent of all records sold (100 records - 15 percent standard free goods = 85). The truth is that standard free goods are just another means by which the record company lowers your royalty: in actuality, they rarely give away that amount of goods. The record company may offer retailers a discount in the range of five percent, but nowhere near 15 percent. Nonetheless, standard free goods is, well, a standard deduction in the industry and is not negotiable. If a company doesn't use standard free goods, it'll base your royalty on 85 percent of all sales—the end result is the same.

> Promotional records, such as those given to radio stations to encourage airplay, are always given away free and marked "not for sale," and you will not be paid record royalties for these records. But don't worry—airplay is probably one of the most significant means with which to promote the sale of your record. If one major station begins to play your music, sales of your record can take off like wildfire.

$14.24 (The SRLP minus packaging costs)

- 15%   (Standard free goods)

= $12.10

x 12% (your net royalty rate)

= **$1.45** **(Your royalty per CD)**

Breakage

To further reduce your royalty, the record company will sometimes negotiate your record royalty based on 90 percent of sales. The ten percent deduction historically covered breakage during shipping when 78's were commonly in production. 78's were manufactured from shellac and were much more susceptible to damage than cassettes and CDs are today. So if you're only getting paid on 90 percent of all the records sold, and you subtract an additional 15 percent for the standard free goods, then technically you're now only getting paid on 76.5 percent of all the records you sell. Nice!

$12.10 (The SRLP, minus packaging costs, and free goods)
x 90% (Breakage)
= $10.89
x 12% (Your net royalty rate)
= $1.30 **(Your royalty per CD)**

New Technologies

While we're on the topic of manufacturing, record labels still consider CDs a "new technology" that is expensive to assemble; therefore, your royalty rate can be reduced as much as 75 to 85 percent per unit. This is usually negotiable. (By the way, CDs make up over 80 percent of sales for most rock and pop groups. CD sales in urban markets fall close behind.) Therefore our examples are based on CD sales only. Let's take a look at the royalty computation below to see what your royalty rate finally yields per CD.

> Attorney Shawna Hilleary adds that at least one major label (UMG) is changing to a less confusing method of calculating royalties by paying a lower royalty rate; *but based on 100 percent of sales without packaging and free goods reductions. Though the royalty rate is lower, the dollar amount per CD should be the same. Other labels may change to this system as well.*

$10.89 (The SRLP minus packaging costs, free goods,
          and breakage)
x 85% (New technology reduction)
= $9.25
x 12% (Your net royalty rate)
= $1.11 **Per CD (Finally, your royalty per CD)**

EVEN MORE ROYALTY DEDUCTIONS

Okay, so the record company reduces your royalty with a number of different deductions, and if, as in the above examples, you started out with a royalty of $3.06 per CD, you finally wind up with $1.11. If there are four members of your band, each will get what works out to be about 27 cents per CD. But, believe it or not, there are still a few more deductions you should know about. These include mid-price records, record clubs, budget records, cut outs, foreign royalties, and reserves. A description of each follows.

Mid-Price Records

Albums that have been available to consumers for an extended period of time and are no longer considered a new release become catalogue items at the record company—these albums are offered to retailers at what is called a "mid price" (usually 60 to 80 percent below the top-line price). This not only means that the record company does not receive as much money per album as it did initially, but also that you receive a lower royalty as well. The reduction is typically 75 percent of your

PHYSICAL SALES VERSUS DIGITAL DOWNLOADS. If what you've read about royalty computations for physical product seems a little, let's just say, interesting, than what computational systems can we expect for music that's sold by digital downloading over the Internet? So far the royalty computation is the same! But are deductions for packaging costs, breakage, and free goods applicable for an electronic transmission? Perhaps not, but Don Passman, author of the book *All You Need To Know About The Music Business* has an interesting theory called "The Passman Theory of Technology Cycles." It goes something like this: Every time a new technology is discovered, it sends the record industry into a frenzy. Right now, downloadable music is still a new technology and the record companies don't know its economics. Despite the fact that digital sales may seem more profitable, there are huge costs for setting up download capability. This results in a royalty structure that is not particularly fair to the artist. Eventually, a reasonable system for computing digital downloads will be devised and an industry pattern will form. By then, the next technological advancement will be discovered and the cycle will begin all over again. (Note that according to a November 26, 2002 article in *Hits Daily Double,* Universal Music Group has also opted to eliminate packaging and free goods reductions on downloadable music.)

royalty rate. For example, if you have a royalty rate of 16 points, your royalty for mid-price records is 12 points (16 points x 75% = 12 points per unit sold). Contractually, the record company will agree to wait for a period of time after the record is released (typically nine months) before a record can be sold at a mid price. This is negotiable.

Record Clubs

Record companies will license your master recordings to record clubs (to manufacture, distribute, and sell) in order to reach consumers who theoretically cannot be reached at normal retail outlets. Since the record club's advertising costs are high and there are many past due debts from their customers, your record company pays you a lower royalty on sales—thus, for record club sales, you typically only get 50 percent of your normal royalty rate.

Because record clubs have massive sales drives to encourage membership purchases (e.g., "12 free CDs for the price of one"), the percentage of free goods that the record company gets away with deducting from your royalties for record clubs is typically much higher than for normal retail sales—it can be as much as 50 percent, compared to the standard 15 percent. This means that for every 100 records sold by the record club, you're not only receiving a royalty that is 50 percent less than your normal rate, you're only paid on 50 percent of the total number of records sold through record clubs. An artist's record can be sold to record clubs as soon as three months after its release, but this is negotiable.

Budget Records

Records that are selling poorly are sold to retailers at a budget price (e.g., 50 to 62 percent less than the top-line price). Therefore, the record royalty payable on budget records is typically reduced to

50 percent of your royalty rate. Contractually, the record company will agree to wait for a set period of time (say, 12 months after the record is released) before a record can be sold at a budget price. Again, this is negotiable.

Cut Outs

When your record ends up in the 99-cent record bin at record shops, it doesn't just mean that your record is selling poorly. To add insult to injury, it also means you're not being paid any royalty whatsoever on these records. The record company sells the records to retailers at cost, or below cost, as a way to get rid of them. These records are called "schlock" or "cut-outs." A notch is literally cut out of the packaging so retailers don't return them for full credit (more on returns later in this chapter). In some cases, the record company may even sell your records as scrap to be broken up and used for parts!

Foreign Royalties

Your royalty rate, based on the number of records sold in the United States, is also called the "U.S. basic rate." There is a reduced rate for American records sold in foreign major markets (Japan, the United Kingdom, Germany, Holland, France, and Italy), because their operating costs lead to smaller profit margins. The rate is typically 75 percent of your U.S. basic rate, but is negotiable. For example, if you have a U.S. basic royalty rate of 16 points, your foreign royalty is 75 percent of this rate (16 points x 75 percent = 12 points on each record sold). For other territories in the world, your royalty is 50 to 60 percent of the U.S. basic rate, or 8 to 9.6 points of each record sold.

It's interesting to note that 69 percent of worldwide sales occur outside the United States. Rap, jazz, and rock music are all big sellers in foreign territories. Yet it's also possible that your record will never be released abroad. Foreign labels have their own projects and priorities, and it takes a tremendous amount of work on the part of an American label to license a product outside its territory.

> You already know that record companies typically calculate royalties on the suggested retail price of your record. However, in foreign territories, royalties are usually based on something called the "price per dealer" (PPD). No need to get hung up on the details, but PPD is essentially the started price to be charged to wholesalers or distributors for the product they resell to consumers. Deductions are taken from this price to determine your royalty per unit.

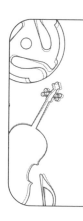

A PERFECT SCAM! In his book *Stiffed: A True Story of MCA, the Music Business, and the Mafia*, William Knoedelseder relates true stories of corruption and scams in the music business. When a major record company sold 10 million records to a vinyl reprocessing center to be destroyed and used for scraps, an independent operator stepped in and bought the records from the plant for next to nothing. Before the record company realized what had happened, twenty tractor-trailer loads of records were unloaded at the independent operator's warehouse and somehow sold for a profit of $900,000. The artists received no royalties from these records. It was a total rip-off, but it was perfectly legal!

Reserves

Record companies generally offer a 100-percent return policy to retailers as an incentive to stock new product. This means that although your album is ordered by retailers and shipped to their stores, it is not yet considered a bona fide sale as far as your royalties are concerned. If retailers can't sell your records, they can send them back to the record company for a refund. Therefore, to ensure that you're not paid a royalty on records that are later returned, the record company will withhold or "reserve" payments due to you (if any) of 10 to 50 percent of the payments it owes you. Royalty statements are sent out two times a year, 60 to 90 days after the close of each 6-month period (June 30th and December 31st). Reserves are liquidated throughout subsequent statements—typically over the two years following the statements in which the reserves are taken. In other words, the record company is intentionally behind in its payments to you so that they avoid paying you for records that are later returned by retailers.

Isn't there an easier way to run this whole reserve system than just waiting to see what records are returned? Absolutely! SoundScan, a service offered by *Billboard* magazine since 1991, tracks the retail sales of records by monitoring their bar codes, which are found on the packaging of records. This data is then utilized by record companies and often affects the percentage it withholds from the artists' payments. Though SoundScan is not 100 percent accurate, the record company has a pretty good idea which records are selling and how many. SoundScan is also a helpful marketing tool for record companies because it can monitor locations around the country where an album is selling or not selling. Record companies can use this data for pinpoint promotion, thereby focusing their marketing energies in specific regions.

> *The Art of Deception.* Before the advent of SoundScan, record companies sometimes offered small bribes to record retailers in return for reporting higher sales figures to *Billboard* (whose charts rank artists' recordings based on weekly sales statistics)—a higher chart position created the illusion and "hype" that artists' records were selling in larger volumes. This sometimes persuaded radio stations to give singles frequent radio play and convinced concert promoters to pay more money for live performances.

RECOUPABLE ADVANCES AND EXPENSES

Okay, now comes the really good stuff. Artists earn a record royalty for the sale of their albums, *but the monies that the record company advances toward recording your CD must first be recouped from your royalties before you ever receive a dime from sales.* In fact, recording agreements may state that "any monies spent on behalf of the artist are a recoupable advance, unless the company states in writing that it's not an advance." For this reason, you must be very clear at the time you sign your recording agreement about which monies will be deemed as advances and which will not. At least you'll know the ground rules, so you can cut expenses whenever possible. Take the R&B group T.L.C., for example, which found itself in deep debt after (among several other things) carelessly demanding the most expensive hotels and travel accommodations during promotional trips, all of which were initially charged to the record company. Unbeknownst to T.L.C., the costs were all recoupable. As a result, although it was selling millions of records, the group was nearly broke. Don't let this happen to you!

> Marketing expenses, such as retail campaigns (the promotion of your record in retail stores) and advertisements in consumer magazines, etc., are typically not recoupable by the record company.

What follows is a brief discussion of some of the advances and other expenses that are typically recouped from your future record royalties, namely, the recording fund, tour support, video expenses, and independent radio promotion. As you'll see, these expenses can add up quickly.

Recording Funds

The recording fund is considered a pre-paid record royalty that is 100 percent recoupable from your future record sales. If the record company advances you $300,000, and sales from your record total $100,000 in artist royalties, your unrecouped balance is now $200,000. In case it hasn't sunk in yet, until the recording fund is paid back, *you won't earn any monies in record royalties.* Worse, your debt to the record company keeps getting deeper because the recording fund is not the only advance recoupable from your future record royalties.

Tour Support

Tour support is exactly what it sounds like—additional monies advanced by the record company for the purpose of subsidizing a band's tours. It's usually impossible for a new artist to make any money on the road since expenses such as hotels, gas, crew, and tolls outweigh the fees you can expect to earn from performing. Although it's becoming less and less common, the record company may guarantee funds to help a group hit the road and promote the sale of its record. For instance, the record company may advance $50,000 in support of a tour; but this money is 100 percent recoupable from a group's future record royalties! Additionally, the record company may not be obliged to pay these funds unless a band meets certain performance requirements. For example, the record company may not advance tour support to you unless your band is scheduled to play in front of a specific number of people or you're already selling a certain number of records per week.

Video Expenses

The budget for promotional videos (such as the ones you see on MTV, VH1, local cable shows, clips before morning shows, and Internet sites) are also recoupable from your future record royalties. Typically, however, only 50 percent of these expenses can be charged against your future record royalties. So, if you have a video budget of $300,000, only $150,000 will be charged against your record royalty account. In some cases, a record company may structure its contracts so that costs in excess of a specific dollar amount (for example $200,000) will be 100 percent recoupable, while costs up to that amount will only be 50 percent recoupable. However, a good rule of thumb is to think of video expenses as 50 percent recoupable.

Independent Radio Promotion

Independent promotion refers to what it may cost to get your record played on the radio, specifically commercial radio (which includes national networks, regional networks, independent stations, and syndicators). Though independent radio promotion is not an advance that's directly paid to you, you can bet it's recoupable from your future record sales. A record company's regional salespeople can create hype for an artist's single, but independent promoters have connections with nationwide consultants who advise radio programmers what to add to their play lists. Commercial radio stations, and I stress "commercial," are businesses, and they're only interested in playing music that will attract the greatest number of listeners and advertising dollars. To ensure airplay, the record company may guarantee you $50,000 per single in radio promotion. Independent promotion is 100 percent recoupable from your future record royalties, but it can be negotiated down to 50 percent recoupable (and lower) in cases in which the record company chooses to spend excess sums of money on radio promotion. Of course, you want the record label to spend as much as possible, but you also want to avoid paying for it if you can.

ADVANCED ROYALTY COMPUTATIONS AND RECOUPMENT OF COSTS

Now that you have an idea of what you can expect to earn per CD as well as of the expenses you'll be responsible for repaying to the record company, let's start plugging in some numbers. Remember, you don't earn record royalties from sales until the record company receives all recoupable expenses! Let's say, for example, that your band has a recording fund of $300,000, a video fund of $300,000, $50,000 for tour support, and $100,000 was used for independent radio promotion. When you add all this up, the balance due to the record company is $600,000. Remember, only 50 percent of video expenses can be charged against record royalties, and 50 percent of the video fund equals $150,000.

> $300,000 (The recording fund)
> + $150,000 (50 percent of the $300,000 video fund)
> + $ 50,000 (Tour support)
> + $100,000 (Independent radio promotion)
> = $600,000 **(Balance due to the record company)**

In order for the record company to recoup these expenses, you must sell thousands of records. Remember that the record company recoups all expenses at your net royalty rate. Staying with the example from the royalty computation earlier in this chapter (see "How Record Royalties Are Calculated"), that's about $1.11 per CD. If your band sells 500,000 CDs, which by the way, earns you gold certification status by the Recording Industry Association of America (RIAA), you would still have an unrecouped balance to the record company of $45,000. It makes you think of that gold record you want hanging on your wall in a different way, doesn't it?

As Chapter 10, "Your Producer" explains, a producer's payment structure is more friendly than yours. Once the recording fund is recouped, the producer typically begins to earn his or her royalty from sales. That's right, the producer starts earning a royalty before you do! Though the record company is nice enough to pay the producer on your behalf, they charge that amount back to your royalty account. This means that the more records you sell, the more money gets tacked on to your debt. But don't despair. If your record is hugely successful, eventually everything can balance out and you'll get paid.

> 500,000 (CDs sold—certifying gold status)
> x $1.11 (The band's royalty per CD)
> = $555,000
> - $600,000 (Balance due to the record company)
> = $45,000 **(Balance still due to the record company)**

NON-RETURNABLE ADVANCES

Between the recording fund, tour support, the video budget, and independent radio promotion you have quite a debt to repay. As you can see in the above example, even after your record is certified gold, you still owe $45,000 to the record company.

But what happens if you never sell enough albums to pay back these expenses? Most advances by the record company are deemed non-returnable. This means that they are only recoupable from future record royalties. If you don't sell enough records to recoup expenses, you don't owe the record company anything out of your own pocket. However, if you're lucky enough NOT to get dropped by the record company, your debt will then extend to subsequent recordings and royalty earnings in something called "cross-collateralization."

CROSS-COLLATERALIZATION

Cross-collateralization refers to current earnings that pay for prior debts. This means that royalties credited from sales of your second record will go towards paying unrecouped expenses from your first *and* second records before you earn royalties from sales. It is possible, then, that the more albums you record, the deeper in debt you may become. For example, if you have an unrecouped balance of $300,000 from your first record and your recording fund for your second record is $325,000, you will now have a combined unrecouped balance you owe the record company of $625,000 before your second record ever hits the store shelves. Scary, isn't it! To make matters worse, the record company will charge interest on all unrecouped balances.

You may wonder, then, why some record companies often give a band a second and third chance to record an album. It's simple—the artist's royalty account bears no resemblance to the actual number of records the record company needs to sell to recoup all of its expenses. That's right! The record company begins to make a profit long before the artist does. While you may be credited $1.11 per CD, the record company may be earning as much as $4.00 for every record sold. The record company can thus realistically cover its expenses after about 200,000 albums are sold. If your band's record achieves these sales figures (which by the way, is also rare), you may not be considered a significant financial success to the record company, but, rather, in the words of an anonymous record executive, "The band who helps keep the lights on."

Attorney Stacy Fass adds, "The label heads have one- to three-year contracts that they want to see renewed. They want a quick hit so that they can collect their bonuses. They're not interested in building an eight-year career selling 200,000 records a year, because they probably won't even be at the label that long."

IS THERE ANY HOPE?

As estimated by the Recording Industry Association of America (R.I.A.A), the average number of records sold by a new band signed to a major label (as of the year 2001) is about 12,000 copies. It can take sales of 500,000 records or more to pay back all recoupable expenses and begin pocketing royalties from sales. *Less than five percent of all artists to do this!* Therefore, it's quite possible that you'll never receive any record royalties from sales.

So what does all this mean? Is there any hope? Of course there is! It begins with limiting your expenses. Expenses add up quickly, and most of them are recoupable from your future record sales. Do you really need to record your album in the Bahamas? Do you really need lobster catered after a long day of recording? Do you really need to call your girlfriend or boyfriend from the studio every night to talk for two hours? Do you really need to ring up $20,000 in alcohol expenses while recording? Do all four members of the band really have to fly to New York to be present for the

WHAT DREAMS ARE MADE OF. Let's end this chapter on a positive note by reporting what some superstars earned from their record sales in 2001, according to a July 2001 article in *Rolling Stone* magazine:

Aerosmith: $6.8 Million

Billy Joel: $12.7 Million

Blink 182: $15.7 Million

Bon Jovi: $5.3 Million

Christina Aguilera:
$13.2 Million

Creed: $14.1 Million

Dr. Dre: $43.1 Million

Eminem: $20 Million

Eric Clapton: $1.1 Million

Janet Jackson: $8.5 Million

Lenny Kravitz: $12.6 Million

Limp Bizkit: $13 Million

Metallica: $14.7 Million

*NSYNC: $13.8 Million

Neil Diamond: $1.2 Million

Sting: $20 Million

The Eagles: $4.6 Million

U2: $15 Million

As an up-and-coming artist, you want to watch your professional expenses—and not just because the record company deducts them from your royalties. Record companies hold weekly marketing meetings to discuss (among other things) the status of the artists they have under contract. If they see that the expenses are piling up and your career shows no sign of taking off any time soon, they're likely to cut you loose and turn their attention to another more promising band—abandoning you like a sheep without a shepherd.

mastering and sequencing of the record? Do you really need to spend a substantial amount of your tour-support funds to get the tour bus instead of a van? Do you really need four techs on your first tour? Did you really need to stay at the Sheraton instead of a Motel 6? Do you really need to record a video for $500,000 with rented mansions and exotic cars? These are all real-life examples of inflated expenses, and don't forget, *you pay for all of them!*

Q & A WITH FRED CROSHAL

Fred Croshal began his career in the music industry working in retail, where he saw hundreds of thousands of new titles going in and out of record stores. Some artists sold millions of records and became huge stars, while other artists flopped miserably. Unfortunately, the latter is the norm.

Fred Croshal now holds the prestigious position of general manager at Maverick Records. In this informative interview, he covers the general principles of music marketing and discusses just what goes into ensuring the sale of an artist's record, which is a team effort between both the record label and the band. Or as Fred Croshal simply puts it, "We're all in this together."

Q: What, specifically, are the responsibilities of the general manager at a record label?

F.C: The general manager's principal responsibilities are to bring everyone's efforts together as a team, including the new media, press, promotion, sales, and marketing departments. Each of these departments has a specific role:

✦ The new media department develops the websites for any given artist or band and continues to market them through various promotions.

✦ The press department writes the band's biography and sends out advance copies of their music to the various promotional outlets. It's all about getting exposure.

Whether it be through album reviews, features and interviews in magazines and newspapers, an appearance on *The Tonight Show,* or online exposure.

✦ The promotion department's focus is to get songs added at radio stations and to garner airplay. Whether that means getting a band to play at a special radio station event, or organizing contests such as ticket give-aways, fly-aways, and other promotions; whatever it takes! [Author's note: A fly-away is a contest that promises, for example, a free flight to Ireland to see U2 in concert.]

✦ The sales department's primary goal is to work with the distribution companies and retailers to get records in stores, on sale, and in the right positioning (or location) on the shelves. It's a matter of determining the number of records that should initially be shipped to retailers, the discount to retailers (10 percent, 5 percent, or 3 percent), and how the record is going to be priced—either at full price or the developing artist price. The developing artist price is intended to grow an artist's career without putting him in direct price competition with more established artists.

✦ The marketing department is comprised of a marketing head and a product manager whose responsibilities are all inclusive of the above. The marketing department works with all departments to develop the timeline and marketing plan for an assigned artist. The product manager also offers advice in the creation of marketing tools such as CD samplers, stickers, key chains, etc.

So again, I oversee the daily running of all these departments.

Q: Statistics show that in 1999 there were 31,000 records released, of which 143 went gold or better; that's less than one out of every 100 records. For those that sell well, is there anything in particular to which you would attribute their success?

F.C: Simply, the majority of artists' records that sold well had a hit song. I would like to say these artists had hit albums, but it seems as though our marketplace has turned from a great album that is selling the record to a great song. One hit song alone can generate sales of up to four million records. That equals about $40 million in gross revenue to a record company. That's a pretty substantial hit!

Q: Would you care to comment on what a hit song means to you?

F.C: If you're looking for a correlation between hit songs, I would have to say that it's a good hook, radio stations like it, and consumers respond to it. When a radio station plays a song, do 20 people instantaneously call the station and ask about it? Does Joe Consumer run out and buy it? Now, with that said, I have to also tell you that there is something in the industry we refer to as being a "turntable hit." A turntable hit is when radio stations love a song, listeners love it, but people are just not compelled to go out and spend $10 to $15 to purchase the record.

Q: I once heard someone compare a record company to an aircraft carrier. You have the guy waving the flags (the general manager) and all the airplanes (the bands) ready and waiting on the jetway. As soon as one plane is cleared for take-off, the next is immediately in line. With the number of records slated for release per year, what makes a record label get more excited about one artist over the next?

F.C: Yes, it can certainly seem as though we are an aircraft carrier. After all, we are a business. We basically run off of schedules. We try to time when a single should be released to radio stations, when an album is going to be released in stores, and when an artist is going to tour. A pop single may go to radio over a month before the record hits the shelves. A hard rock band's single may not go to radio until after they sold a several thousand CDs at retail. It's all timing.

You say, "What makes a record company get more excited about one artist's record over the next?" It's all about the quality. Really, truly, it's the quality! New music is constantly passed around. When one rises above the other, it's inspirational. You hear it coming out of everyone's office. It's infectious and it takes over the label. There is no doubt that people get more pumped up about certain records than others.

That said, when you talk about "waving flags," it's the product manager's job, as it is my job, [to] stay focused on all of our releases. There is a different kind of enthusiasm, however, depending on what kind of record we're trying to market. A rock band that requires a slower build on the streets through the utilization of street teams and touring is not going to get the immediate excitement or success that a pop record may get. The shipments won't be as high, and the response at radio slower. Again, it's my job to remind everyone that there's an artist out there and we need to step up certain avenues of promotion to see the band through. [Author's note: Street teams are a coalition of fans that pass out flyers and hand out CD samplers, etc., at concerts, at malls, and on the streets.]

Q: Record companies are in the risk-management business. They can spend well over a million dollars in marketing money to break one band alone. The odds are also against them, and they need to be careful. That said, are the days when record companies developed a band over the course of two or three albums over for good? Does a band essentially live or die on the strength of its first single?

F.C: I think for the larger record companies, the answer is yes. It's the conveyor belt; two weeks at radio and if it doesn't happen, it's on to the next one. Maverick Records, on the other hand, is a smaller record label and we do not have as many releases per year; we have about 10 to 15. This allows us more opportunities to determine how we're going to break a band. Can a campaign around an artist be press-driven? Can it be driven around street marketing and touring? Or can it be driven by the Internet? If we are stifled by any of these key areas, we have to find a solution.

Take the band the Deftones from Sacramento, California, for example. On the band's first two records (the first released in 1995 and the second in 1997), the group received little to no radio or MTV exposure. Therefore, we had to fall back on the utilization of street teams and touring. We built a vast and loyal fan base, and within a few years, the sales on both records grew into the half-million mark. Finally, by June 2000, the Deftones' third release debuted at number three on the *Billboard* charts and sold close to 200,000 records in just the first week alone. Additionally, the band is now receiving radio play and MTV exposure. It took a lot of money and also a lot of hard work from the band.

The Deftones are a classic example of how a label should take the time to build an artist. We often use this example for younger bands that are shopping at the various record companies. At Maverick, we feel it's really about finding the artist and believing in the long term. But again, I will agree that this is not typical of most record companies. [Author's note: Maverick Record's philosophy, as Fred agreed after this interview, may also have something to do with the fact that it was founded by an artist—Madonna.]

Q: "Product" is a buzzword in the industry that refers to an artist's record that has been turned over to the record company for release. Although most musicians don't like to think of their art as a product, they must understand that record companies are in the business of selling records, and that's an art form as well! Can you discuss the importance of an artist fitting into certain radio formats, retail categories, images, etc?

F.C: First of all, it's easy to misinterpret music with product, especially when you have titles at a record label like "product manager." But a product manager can just as well be called a marketing manager. I can't speak for other record companies, but at Maverick when someone refers to an artist's work as product, we correct them. We take this very seriously. I think of product as the physical packaging a CD comes in, but not the music that embodies that CD. That's called art!

Now to answer your question, great music should not have to be pigeon-holed into categories. Unfortunately though, there are gatekeepers, specifically at radio stations, who say, "This doesn't fit at Modern Rock radio, and this doesn't fit at Top 40 radio." Therefore, we have to act in the confines of these restrictions. After all, we're a business.

As far as the retailers are concerned, they'll generally take all kinds of music, but they do want a genre label when buying an artist's release. They want to know how the music should be categorized in their stores. Is it pop? Is it rock? Is it soul? Is it a soundtrack? These categories are usually very broad, though. Retailers are not as particular as radio stations.

When discussing imaging, it's important to an artist because it sends a message to consumers and identifies them with a specific brand. From how a group looks in pictures, the vibe they give off in the press, what their Internet site looks like, and the type of video a band makes, an image must all be consistent in everything the band does. The press and marketing departments at a record label will work with an artist to determine what it is they want to do. I find that it's usually the artists who have a very clear vision of their imaging that have the most successful careers. They can also be the most difficult at times.

Q: Music videos can cost anywhere from $100,000 to two million and more, yet only a very small percentage ever gets aired on MTV or VH1. What is the best time for a band to record their video? Is it wise for a band to initially make a less expensive video, say a live video, to be used in other outlets such as local morning shows, Internet video (MTV.com, SonicNet.com, etc.) and independent films? [Note: readers should keep in mind that video expenses are typically 50 percent recoupable against future record royalties.]

F.C: I think if you have a hit song, dare I say that even an adequate video will work just fine on MTV. It's really all about the strength of a song. A lot of people in the industry think just the reverse and try to make it all about the video. They believe that if they make a great video, they'll have a hit song. This is not realistic and it drives marketing costs sky high!

Here's how I like to approach videos for new and developing rock bands. I would make a $50,000 to $100,000 video and would service it to MTV II. As the single starts building at radio, the rotation at MTV II should also start to build. At this point, the video may possibly move to MTV and get into some rotation. If the song explodes at radio and there's a hit, then you haven't already spent too much marketing money to hurt yourself. You can go and film a more expensive video if needed.

One band that I'll keep anonymous opted to record a $75,000 video rather than spending what has typically become a $250,000 proposition. With the money that was initially saved at the label, major blocks of MTV ad spots were purchased. During a two-month period, the video looked like it was being played on MTV all the time and record sales exploded. It would have been more difficult to do this type of real marketing if the band had initially recorded an expensive video. There would have been more pressure on the label to look at the bottom line.

Yes, I agree that it's a great idea to initially record an inexpensive video in the $10,000 to $15,000 price range for use on Internet sites, clips before morning shows, and even EPKs (electronic press kits). Electronic press kits can tell writers a little bit more about an artist than just a bio and CD. Everything helps. We're trying to image an artist and tell a story.

Q: I was told that music mogul Donny Ienner (head of Columbia Records) once said, "No one cares about what you don't do, but what you do can ruin your career." Is there an anecdote you would like to share with us where an artist (or artist's personal manager, record company, etc.) made entirely the wrong decision that ended up negatively impacting their career? For instance, Extreme chose to release their single "More Than Words" in the early '90s; it was a great pop ballad, but not at all representative of their hard rock style. When people went out and bought the album thinking they were getting more pop rock, only to find a record full of metal tunes, the returns were substantial.

F.C: I don't really want to comment on the negative, but I think that what you're getting at is that you can't underestimate the strategic alliance of everyone being on the same page. When I say this, I am not speaking about the various departments I mentioned above; I'm referring to the band's personal manager and the band themselves. The manager must direct the artist so that when a label asks them to do something, we're not just pulling things out of our hats. We're experienced people, and we have reasons for everything we do. There needs to be an element of trust. That said, artists at times can generally tend to get a misconception of things; they get a little airplay, and suddenly they don't want to listen to anyone. Simply put, if an artist does not want to listen to experienced people, they are setting themselves up for failure!

Q: I've heard personal managers say on several occasions that they use the fact that their bands are about to be fully recouped to the record label as leverage in getting the record company to give them even more money for tour support, videos, or whatever. Thus, the band always stays unrecouped and never earns a record royalty. The focus for them is on making money from touring, publishing, etc. Can you comment?

F.C.: I really can't address this. It's really more a question for legal affairs. But your question is food for thought for your readers.

Q: Besides the recording fund, tour support, independent radio promotion, and video expenses, how much marketing money is a label willing to spend on a band that actually is not recoupable from record sales? Can you briefly touch on expenses such as point of purchase promotion, product placement and positioning, consumer advertising, etc.

F.C.: It's not about what's recoupable or not recoupable. It's about running a business. We look at all of these areas as overall marketing expenditures. As you mentioned earlier, a record company can spend over a million dollars total in marketing money to break one band alone. The advertising that's done in stores, the positioning of the record on the shelves (is it up front where everyone can see it?), the ads you see in magazines, these are all expenses. The way it's spent is really what's important. A band should tell me that they want to record an inexpensive video because they're on their first single, or that they want to go on the road in an RV rather than a tour bus. They have to realize that with everything there's a gamble. If you record a $500,000 video and it doesn't hit, there may not be a chance for that second single. You would be surprised at the number of $500,000 videos that are sitting on shelves and never played. I refer to them now as bookends.

When an artist shows a genuine hunger to make it and a willingness to go the extra mile, people rally around them at the record company. This can be shown by the band working closely with each department at the record company, so that there's a mutual camaraderie and feeling that *we're all in this together.*

Q: And finally, we can't forget to talk about the World Wide Web. Can you comment on how the Internet is changing or will change the way music is marketed and distributed?

F.C: From a purely basic level, the Internet provides an effective means to market music directly to the fans all around the world. Album release information, tour dates, and sample tracks of music can easily be made available via an artist's and/or label's Web site 24/7. It's a way to connect to the fans in the purest form.

Now, when we talk about digital downloads as an alternative means of distribution, one thing is certain: Napster, though it no longer exists, helped proved to the music industry that consumers want to get music conveniently over the Internet. The major problem at hand, however, is how to get the consumer to pay for music online. Despite this major hurdle, were going to start seeing more record labels making their catalogues available to a variety of high-destination sites such as rollingstone.com (www.rollingstone.com), and MTV.com (www.MTV.com) for a fee of, say, 99 cents per download. The truth is that while everyone is waiting around to uncover the ultimate solution

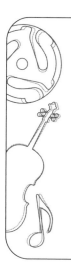

THE FUTURE. To rebuild consumer interest in purchasing CDs to turn fans' attention from the Internet and piracy, record labels have been introducing CD/DVD packages including video clips, live performances, and interviews—doing so gives consumers an added value and draws attention to an artist's new release. Labels are also experimenting with putting special codes in CD packaging that would allow the consumer to log onto a designated website and download free, authorized bonus tracks. Also a consideration, labels (with the approval of artists) are providing member cards in CD packaging that gives consumers special discounts on concert tickets as well as merchandising at live performances. As Jim Griffin, CEO of Cherrylane Digital says, "It's difficult to understand the future unless you participate in it." Stay informed about the latest news on the Internet's effect on how music is bought, sold, and enjoyed.

to the issue at hand, more and more people are still getting music for free all over the Internet. I think [there will] need to be an emphasis on customer satisfaction in order to make digital downloads successful. Consumers will want to visit legitimate websites to get music and won't mind paying for it because it will be accessible and easy to find, they'll know that what they're getting are authorized tracks and not duds, and if they have any problems whatsoever, they'll get some sort of tech support. Time can only tell how everything pans out for sure. Stay tuned!

CHAPTER 12

Music
Publishing

As Ed Pierson, Vice President of Business and Legal Affairs at Warner/Chappell Music aptly says: "Music publishing is the business of songs." It deals with everything from the ownership and control of your compositions to the incomes generated when your songs are used by record labels, motion picture and television companies, Internet sites, and print companies. Licenses for the use of your compositions can be issued by you or by a more experienced music publishing company representing you. If this all sounds complicated—guess what? It is. But you're not alone!

Music publishing is perhaps one of the most difficult areas of business for musicians to understand. It's based on complex and ever-changing laws, and as in any other legal setting, there are numerous exceptions to every rule. Covering each of these exceptions might make an interesting read for the sharp-eyed purist, but it would just confuse the hell out of the rest of us. So for the sake of simplicity, we'll take a straightforward approach to this chapter, discussing the "ifs," "ands," or "buts" only when necessary. Additionally, copyright laws differ in foreign territories, so we'll emphasize U.S. laws. Don't be frustrated if it takes a few re-readings before this information sinks in; most industry professionals will admit they had to deal with this stuff for years before getting a grip on it. (Well, at least some will admit it.) But make no mistake—music publishing is one of the most important aspects of your music-business education. It's an area in which fortunes have been both lost and found. So take everything you're about to read very seriously.

COPYRIGHT BASICS

The first step to understanding music publishing is to understand the basics of copyright and copyright protection. Why? Well, let's see if it becomes more clear when we break it down for you. The word "music" refers to the compositions you create. That's pretty obvious! The word "publishing" refers to the process of making your compositions available to the public by sale or other means. *Copyrights are the rights that constitute your legal protection against the unauthorized use of your original works.* Make sense? Great! Now you're ready to learn more about copyrights.

According to a myth that exists among musicians, in order to obtain a copyright for your compositions, you need to fill out a registration form and send it to the copyright office in Washington, D.C. Although copyright registration provides certain benefits under law and is highly recommended (more about this later), *a copyright exists as soon as an original idea is transformed into a tangible form.* In other words, as soon as one of your song ideas is recorded on a cassette tape or the lyrics to one of your compositions are written on a sheet of paper, you automatically have a copyright. It's that simple! So, in essence, a copyright basically exists when the song itself is transcribed in some form.

As the proud owner of a copyright, you get an exclusive bundle of rights that goes along with it. For instance, a copyright grants you the exclusive "first right" to reproduce, distribute, perform, and sell your compositions to the public. If so desired, you could sit around creating copyrights for days, only to lock them up in a drawer, never to be used. Although this would hardly be the most efficient way to spend your time, it's your right! A copyright also grants you the right to make any derivative work from your composition. A "derivative" work is a creation  based on another work, such as Weird Al Yankovich's version of Michael Jackson's song "Beat It," renamed "Eat It." (Weird Al needed permission from Jackson before recording that gem.) Comedian Cheech Marin did a version of Bruce Springsteen's "Born in the USA" called "Born in East LA." When Cheech was asked how easy it was to obtain approval from The Boss, he replied, "I would have an easier time giving birth." As you can see, without copyright law, there would really be no point in creating anything new at all, since anyone could conceivably use any of your works for any purpose for free—and that, needless to say, would suck! So rejoice! You get a lot of mileage out of owning a copyright, and all for simply being the creative person you are.

WORK FOR HIRE

Before you get comfortable, you need to know about a situation called a "work for hire." The term "work for hire" refers to a circumstance in which you create a work for an employer under the scope of employment, in which case *the employer then becomes the author and owner of the copyright.* For example, a work for hire arrangement will exist if you're employed by a jingle house to write songs for television or radio commercials under specific guidelines, or if you're commissioned to write songs for a film under a written agreement stipulating a work for hire relationship (the laws are actually a bit more defined here, but you get the idea). Aside from this one clear distinction under United States copyright law, our good friend Ed Pierson at Warner/Chappell Music says that the general principle underscoring copyright law is as follows: *if you write it, then you own it!* That said, make very sure to understand the conditions of any relationship in which you compose songs and, of course, make sure you never sign any agreement you don't fully understand.

JOINT WORKS

If what we've discussed about copyrights seems reasonably easy to understand so far, just wait—things get much more complicated when you get into discussing something called "joint works."

What's a joint work? It's exactly what it says. When two or more people come together with the intention of creating a song, and each person makes a musical or lyrical contribution, the resulting composition is considered a joint work. The copyright is jointly owned (see the diagram below). Take a look at the vast majority of records released today, and you'll find that there's more than one writer listed next to each song.

As previously mentioned, joint works falls in an area of copyright law in which things get a bit more tricky. Therefore, a few principles regarding joint works must be understood by all of the work's authors. The most important principles have to do with ownership and control.

Ownership of Joint Works

A primary concern regarding joint works is the division of ownership. Let's begin by taking a look at what copyright law says, then explore the exceptions to copyright law per written agreement, and finally consider its "all for one, one for one philosophy."

Division of Ownership Under Copyright Law. There's a presumption under copyright law that the authors of a joint work are automatically considered equal contributors. This simply means that if a band writes a song, *each writer automatically owns an equal share of the rights—no matter how big or small their musical or lyrical contribution actually was.*

Determining a *musical or lyrical* contribution is less simple. A "lyrical" contribution obviously constitutes the words written as part of a musical composition. What constitutes a "musical" contribution, however, is often the source of great confusion. Neil Gillis, Vice President of A&R and Advertising at Warner/Chappell Music, says that a musical contribution includes the melody, as well as any pre-existing riff or groove that becomes an integral hook to the song. Take the drum part of the song "Wipe Out," for example, or the bass riff of the song "Come Together." Would these songs be the same if either part were excluded? The answer is no! Nevertheless, Neil Gillis warns that he would never walk out of a writing session without first making it clear among all the writers what percentage of each composition he owned. A simple agreement will suffice. It's not a bad idea to record writing sessions on a small recorder, and to keep copies of original lyric sheets in case a dispute between writers ever materializes. Unfortunately, disputes between writers are not uncommon.

Exceptions To Copyright Law Per Written Agreement. Keeping in mind what copyright law says, if the split percentage in ownership of a composition is intended in any way to be something other than equal, there should be a written agreement setting forth what that split really is. For instance, if the other members of your band agree that the bass player's contribution in a song should only entitle him to a ten percent share in ownership rights, this must be put in writing!

You may be wondering whether any musician would carelessly agree to a smaller percentage share than he or she actually deserves. It's been known to happen! In fact, I've known several musicians who, throughout the course of performing with one extremely successful rock singer (who must remain anonymous), signed away 100 percent of their song shares in return for a small sum of money paid up front. Not realizing the potential value of their shares over the long term, the guys felt that it was what they needed to do at the time to keep their positions in the band. Needless to say, they're all kicking themselves now. This is one area in which you want foresight, not hindsight, to be 20/20.

The "All for One, One For All" Philosophy. With all this talk of what's copyrightable and who's entitled to what, you might ask what happened to the "all for one, one for all" philosophy that most young bands and writers swear to. After all, if a group of writers stuff themselves into a practice room to spend hours of their valuable time experimenting with song ideas and recording demos, is it really fair that the harmonica player gets zero interest in a song just because he wasn't feeling as lyrically or melodically creative as the others that day? And what happens when all the writers make relevant suggestions and have to determine whose chorus idea gets used? Can this potentially turn the writing process into a competitive game of who's getting credit rather than a group attempt to focus on writing the best song possible? I know this all sounds a bit immature, but it's a very real problem.

> Be clear that a joint work means each writer owns a piece of the *whole song*. For example, if one writer composes 100 percent of the lyrics and another writer composes 100 percent of the music, each writer owns 50 percent of the entire song. In his book *All You Need To Know about the Music Business*, Donald Passman uses a great metaphor to illustrate this point; he says, "It's like scrambling the white and the yolk of the egg together." The two parts are not easily separable afterwards.

Consequently, many bands have an initial agreement stating that all of its members will receive an equal split in the songs, regardless of who comes up with what.

The "all for one, one for all philosophy" makes perfect sense at first, and works for many years of a relationship. However, once a group becomes successful and everyone in the industry begins telling the vocalist or guitarist that he or she is the real star and genius of the band—trust me, the divisions in the new songs will quickly change in their favor. This is also when the Jimmy Pages and Robert Plants of the world begin wandering off on their own and creating demos of complete song ideas to bring back to the band. In other words, this is usually when other members get cut out all together! It may be a harsh reality, but one or two writers in a group dynamic are usually the principle creators, and it takes a great amount of maturity on the part of the other members to recognize this.

Control of Joint Works

The next issue of importance regarding joint works involves how the control of the rights to a song is shared. Let's take a look at your licensing rights under copyright law, then cover exceptions to copyright law per written agreement, and finally focus on the transfer and sale of copyright.

Rights Under Copyright Law. Under U.S. copyright law, each individual writer of a composition can issue as many "non-exclusive" licenses as he or she wants (to record companies, film companies, etc.), as long as he or she accounts to, and pays, all of the other writers their respective shares. For example, if four writers each own 25 percent of a composition, one writer can license (grant permission) the use of the complete song in a film for $4000, as long as he or she pays each of the other three writers $1000. But, as one can only imagine, too much freedom among the writers can eventually cause problems. One co-author might not want to see a composition licensed in a specific film, while the other co-authors may be thrilled by the idea.

To complicate matters, suppose the members of a band all collaborate on writing a large repertoire of songs, only to end up separating after a disagreement occurs. If any of the members form new groups, procure recording agreements, and then want to record the same song on their album, each author is technically entitled to the "first use" of the composition. It basically comes down to which writer beats the others to recording first.

Exceptions to Copyright Law per Written Agreement Clearly, when two or more writers get together to write a song, it's advisable for the co-authors to have a written agreement between them that not only confirms their individual shares in a song (as discussed above), but also defines *how a composition can and cannot be used, and who can use it first.* Some successful artists are known for going as far as having long-form agreements granting them primary control of a song whenever they collaborate with other writers. This means that if you ever write with such an artist, it's possible you can own a 25 percent share in a composition, and have absolutely no say in how the song will be used.

> Note that a license is only a partial and temporary grant of permission. A non-exclusive license means that other licenses (for films, etc.) can be issued simultaneously. When an exclusive license is issued—one with more restrictions, as in a national advertising campaign—no new licenses can be issued while the commercial is being aired. (See the "Points of Negotiation" section later in this chapter.)

Although written agreements are extremely important and are always the best remedy for avoiding potential misunderstandings or disputes, Ed Pierson at Warner/Chappell Music says you'd be surprised by the number of collaborating writers who *never* formulate an agreement. And despite what copyright law might say, the standard practice among most companies interested in using your music is to *first and foremost obtain permission from each author individually* anyway. This is in no way meant to undermine the importance of a written agreement. Again, a preliminary understanding between owners as to how a composition can and cannot be used is still the best precaution for all involved.

Restrictions to Transfer or Sale of Copyright Finally, one more brief point regarding joint works and the control each writer can or cannot exercise. This point deals with transferring or selling copyrights, as happens when you sign a publishing agreement with a publishing company. Remember, according to the principles you learned above, the joint owners of a composition can technically issue as many non-exclusive licenses as they want, as long as they account for them to the other owners. The exception to this rule is a case in which a written agreement between the writers exists that states otherwise. But note this one important distinction: There's a difference between licensing the rights and selling the rights, and *under no circumstances can the individual writers transfer or sell the rights in the entire composition unless all the writers jointly agree!*

Suppose you cowrote a song with a friend who was about to release an album with a major label. Since there was a lot of hype generated around the band, your friend decided to seek the assistance of an experienced music publishing company to help issue licenses for the use of his songs, place his songs in films and television, and as an added bonus, pay him a large advance against future royalty earnings. The price for all of this, however, is that he had to transfer copyright ownership in all of his songs on his forthcoming record (as is generally the case when signing most publishing agreements—more on this later). So here's the problem: your friend is permitted to transfer *his rights* in the song which you cowrote, but he cannot transfer the entire song unless *you*

FIRST-USE, NOT MIS-USE. In practically all situations, despite ego, pride, or any other hang up you can think of, most cowriters of a composition are simply happy to have their song released on phonorecord—regardless of which writer is using the song first! But as Leah Furman's book *Korn: Life in The Pit* illustrates, when the rock group Korn recorded its debut album in 1994, the group used a previously unrecorded song from vocalist Jonathan Davis's former band (SexArt) without notifying or giving proper credits to its co-writer. This, of course, shifted the issue from a matter of first-use to one of misuse. Ryan Schuck, also a former member of SexArt and co-author of "Blind," the song in question, promptly sued Korn for copyright infringement. The case was settled out of the court, and Schuck now receives both writer's credit and royalties from the song. And here's the storybook ending: Despite Schuck and Davis's dispute, the former band mates have buried the hatchet and are now friends. In fact, at the time of this writing, Schuck's new band, Orgy, is signed to Korn's new record label Elementree. But as you'll see later in this chapter, things don't always work out so amicably in infringement cases.

jointly agree. In essence, he can sign over his shares in the song to a publishing company, while you retain your rights and sign with a publisher of your choice. If that isn't clear, then compare it to two friends who jointly own real estate. If one owner wants to sell his share, it's his right; however, he cannot sell the entire property without your permission.

THE COMPULSORY LICENSING PROVISION

You've already learned that as soon as you transfer an original idea into a tangible form, you automatically get a copyright. But before you get too comfortable with all the exclusive rights you get with a copyright, you need to know about an exception to the rule that allows others to use your song under a provision of copyright law called "the compulsory licensing provision."

Understand that the word "compulsory" means "mandatory." Simply put, the compulsory licensing provision states that: (1) As soon as you record a composition for the first time on phonorecord, and (2) as soon as it's distributed for commercial sale to the public, (3) you *must* license it to any other artist who wants to release it on their record. That's right! As long as the above-noted conditions exist, and the lyric or melodic content is not changed or modified, *anyone who wants to record your song for commercial release on phonorecord has the right to obtain a license by law.* This rule grew out of a concern in Congress that the music business could become a monopoly, and, as a result, the members of Congress wanted to limit your rights as an author. But, don't worry, you'll get paid for the use. In fact, a committee called the Copyright Arbitration Royalty Panel (CARP) sets a fee called a statutory "mechanical royalty." Don't worry about the specifics of what a mechanical royalty is for now because we're going to go into that in detail later.

As of the year 2002, the statutory mechanical licensing rate for songs under five minutes was $.08 (8 cents) per composition per every record made and distributed. (In 2003, the rate became 8.5 cents.) It doesn't matter whether it's a Beatles song or a song by some guy no one ever heard of—the price is essentially the same! Any time someone wants to exercise their rights and obtain a license to cover one of your songs, rest assured you'll receive a payment. This can actually add up to a great deal of money if an artist or group makes your song successful and sells a lot of records. In fact, the artist covering your song may give it a whole new life and allow you to earn additional money for many years. But there's just one downside—the artist covering your song may make it more famous than you have, and the general public, which generally doesn't read album liner notes, will never know you were the author.

COPYRIGHT DURATION

Now that you understand what a copyright is and the bundle of rights you get when you create one of these valuable creatures,

When another artist covers your song, you'll also earn monies from performances of the composition on the radio (called performances royalties), and on television and in motion pictures (via a synchronization license). Both performance royalties and synchronization licenses are covered later in this chapter.

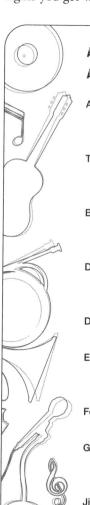

ARTISTS WHO COVERED SONGS FIRST WRITTEN AND RECORDED BY OTHER BANDS

Alien Ant Farm covered "Smooth Criminal" (Michael Jackson)

The Beatles covered "Twist and Shout" (The Isley Brothers)

Brooks and Dunn covered "Missing You" (John Waite)

David Lee Roth covered "California Girls" (Beach Boys)

Devo covered "Satisfaction" (the Rolling Stones)

Eric Clapton covered "I Shot the Sheriff" (Bob Marley)

Fear Factory covered "Cars" (Gary Numan)

Guns N' Roses covered "Live and Let Die" (Paul McCartney)

Jimi Hendrix covered "All Along the Watchtower" (Bob Dylan)

Lenny Kravitz covered "American Woman" (Guess Who)

Limp Bizkit covered "Faith" (George Michaels)

Mariah Carey covered "Open Arms" (Journey)

Marilyn Manson covered "Sweet Dreams" (Eurythmics)

Mötley Crüe covered "Smoking In The Boys Room" (Brownsville Station)

Natalie Imbruglia covered "Torn" (Edna Swap)

Phil Collins covered "True Colors" (Cyndi Lauper)

Poison covered "Your Mama Don't Dance" (Loggins & Messina)

Quiet Riot covered "Cum On Feel The Noize" (Slade)

Run DMC covered "Walk This Way" (Aerosmith)

Red Hot Chili Peppers covered "Higher Ground" (Stevie Wonder)

Sheryl Crow covered "Sweet Child of Mine" (Guns N' Roses)

Stevie Ray Vaughn covered "Little Wing" (Jimi Hendrix)

Sting covered "Little Wing" (Jimi Hendrix)

The Who covered "Summertime Blues" (Eddie Cochran)

Twisted Sister covered "Leader of the Pack" (the Shangri-las)

U2 covered "Helter Skelter" (the Beatles)

Van Halen covered "You Really Got Me" (the Kinks)

you may be wondering how long all this good stuff is going to last you. You may also be wondering whether, if you sell your copyrights, as in the case when you sign a deal with a music publishing company, you can ever get them back.

The Copyright Term

When discussing the term of a copyright (or copyright "duration") you should at least know that the law has undergone significant changes dating as far back as 1909. But all you really need to know for now is that according to the Copyright Act of 1976 (effective January 1, 1978), the copyright term in the U.S. lasted for the *life of the author plus fifty years*. Basically, that means that the copyright term lasts for the author's lifetime and then for fifty years after his or her death.

The license that can be obtained under the compulsory licensing provision is called a "compulsory license." However, it's so complicated that it's an absolute pain to use, and therefore, it rarely is (trust me on this one; you don't need to get bogged down on the reasons why). Instead, a less complex form of this license called a "mechanical license" is typically used, which encompasses the general principles of the compulsory license. Mechanical licenses are discussed in a separate section of this chapter.

However, the late great Sonny Bono, the musician who was married to Cher and who was part of the famous Sonny and Cher duo, successfully lobbied to extend the term of copyright for an additional 20 years. Therefore, as of the year 1998, *the current copyright term lasts for the life of the author plus 70 years*. So, you might ask, why didn't I say this in the first place? The answer is that at the time of this writing, the U.S. Supreme Court was hearing an appeal from a lower federal circuit court challenging the Sonny Bono extension, and it has just ruled in favor of retaining the Sonny Bono extension. I'm going to continue our discussion on the copyright term according to the law that stands as of this writing (that which recognizes the extension).

When two or more people get together to write a song, as is the case with a joint work, the copyright term currently lasts for *70 years after the death of the last surviving author*. After the term has ended, the composition falls into something called the "public domain," which essentially means anyone can use the composition free of licensing fees. But don't worry, by that time, you won't mind too much.

Reversion of Copyright

So what happens when you transfer or sell your copyrights, as is the case when you sign a publishing agreement? Are you permanently signing over your publishing rights to the song? The answer is yes! Well, sort of. You see, in most publishing contracts, especially when you have a little negotiating power, there's usually a clause incorporated into your agreement called "reversion of copyright." The reversion of copyright clause stipulates that your copyrights will revert back to you at a predetermined time in the future (say, about ten years after your contract expires). That's great news, right? Let me emphasize, however, that reversion of copyright is not part of actual copyright law; *it's a clause that must be negotiated into your publishing agreement*. Absent this clause, you do have another crack at getting back ownership. However, you may have to wait quite some time.

Thirty-Five Year Statutory Right of Termination

In the worst case scenario, if you don't have a reversion clause in your agreement with a music publisher, copyright law provides that *all original copyright owners (or their heirs) will have a chance to re-acquire ownership after 35 years of the date of copyright transfer.* This is called "right of termination," and it benefits the original owner should an unfavorable publishing deal be signed, or should you simply want your copyrights back! The procedure involved in getting your rights back becomes a little tricky though, and trust me, it's way too confusing to get into right now. But don't worry, you've got at least 20 years from the date of transfer before you have to start worrying about it anyway!

As always, there's an exception to the "right of termination" law that falls under a "work made for hire" relationship. If you've forgotten what a work for hire is, flip back to the beginning of this chapter to find out. Or, if you're too lazy for that, I'll briefly remind you that a work for hire is when you're hired to compose under the scope of very specific guidelines, or when you sign a written agreement that clearly states a work for hire relationship. And since the employer in that arrangement retains the rights of ownership in all of the compositions you create, *you can never get your copyrights back, despite the right of termination law!* Why? Because you never owned them in the first place. Again, it's vital that you're clear about the terms under which you compose for or with anyone.

COPYRIGHT REGISTRATION

As previously mentioned, as soon as you transform an original idea into a tangible form, such as recording your song idea on a cassette tape or a lyric on a sheet of paper, you automatically have a copyright. So, you might ask, what are the benefits of copyright registration? When and how is the best time to register?

The Benefits of Copyright Registration

Registering your compositions with the Copyright Office in Washington, D.C. provides you with three major benefits: (1) Provided that you register a work within five years of its first publication, you get the *"rebuttable presumption"* that you're the original author and owner of a composition. (Pay close attention to the word "presumption" here, because if you start randomly registering the next Michael Jackson, Madonna, and Prince singles, you won't get very far in a court of law when valuable evidence indicates you're lying.) (2) If someone intentionally uses one of your compositions without your permission, knowledge, and/or payment, you can file an infringement case in a court of law. (You cannot file an infringement case until you register your compositions.) (3) As long as your compositions have been registered prior to an infringement, or within three months after the date of the infringement, you may be entitled to receiving court fees as well as "statutory damages." (Statutory damages are a determined fee set by a judge when the "actual damages" of an infringement are difficult to prove—in other words, the infringer did not provide proper records in regards to profits, or otherwise, he or she hid the profits so well they were difficult to uncover).

Now that you understand the benefits of copyright registration, let's take a moment to discuss both how and when to register your prized creations. In the early stages of your career, you might use an unofficial method of registration called "the poor man's copyright," while for pre-publication you should use the Copyright Office in Washington, D.C.

The Poor Man's Copyright. If you've just completed your first week of guitar lessons and are still hacking away in the tool shed, it's probably not necessary to register every song you write—or, in fact, any song at all! But don't fret, "practice makes perfect," and, hopefully, in no time you'll have written a few number-one hits that you'll feel compelled to register. Does this mean you should begin shelling out your hard-earned money to the copyright office in Washington, D.C.? Probably not! In fact, as an alternative, you can save a couple bucks by mailing yourself a copy of your works by certified mail; have the post clerk stamp dates on the seals of the envelope, and *don't open the package when it arrives*. This procedure is a "poor man's copyright"; it establishes the date a composition was originally created, which is important. But note that this does not provide the same benefits as registering your composition with the Copyright Office in Washington, D.C. At this stage in your career, however, a poor man's copyright should suffice.

The Copyright Office When the big day comes for your songs to be commercially distributed to the public, such as when you decide to press your own CDs and sell them at your shows, I highly recommended that you officially register your compositions with the Copyright Office. You'll be required to file a performing arts form (PA) and send in a deposit copy of the published works (such as a CD or tape) along with a whopping $30 fee per song. As you can imagine, this can add up quickly.

To save money, you can register all of your compositions on one PA form under a "collection of works," as long as all the songs are written by the same author(s). For instance, you can register a batch of ten songs under the title "John and Jane Doe's Summer Songs of Love" (sappy, but you get the point). However, since all of the compositions will be listed under one title, this form of registration is simply not as effective, because individual songs will be more difficult to locate if someone is searching for them. But never fear, once you get signed to a record or publishing company and it looks like you're actually going to have a crack at a long-term career, you can also go back and register each song separately at a later date. In fact, upon signing a publishing deal with a publishing company, they'll customarily go back and re-register each song anyway. So you're covered!

> For registration forms, call the Copyright Office at (800) 688-9889, or go online to http://www.loc.gov/copyright.

THE COPYRIGHT NOTICE

When you create a copyright, is it really necessary to include a notice (for example, Copyright © 2003 John and Jane Doe music) on each and every finished work you create? Well, copyright law has always said that since it's impossible to put a notice on something you can't see, such as a song, it's not necessary. So why do you see the copyright notice on so many of your favorite albums? Well, sometimes the lyrics are printed on the inside booklet, which you can see. Or, in some cases, the creator of the artwork in which your music is packaged is indicating his or her copyright. Lastly, since the actual CD or cassette tape in which your music is embodied is a tangible form, the record company uses a different copyright symbol represented by the letter P in a circle to indicate its rights in the actual sound recording (which is an entirely separate copyright from your music, which the record company almost always owns). In any case, as of the new copyright law effective Jan. 1, 1978, a copyright notice is no longer necessary. However, it's still the most prudent approach, since it clearly shows others you're serious about protecting the work you so proudly create.

COPYRIGHT INFRINGEMENT

A "copyright infringement" occurs when someone uses the material you create without your permission, knowledge, or payment. But now that you've taken all the steps above to ensure the maximum protection of your songs, you shouldn't have anything to worry about—right? Wrong! *No matter what precautions you take, you can't stop anyone from attempting to infringe your copyrights.* With that said, worrying whether or not you're getting ripped off by every co-writer, band member, group you open for, or record company you send a package to is only going to drive you insane. And even if you discover that someone is infringing on your rights, you must first determine what the damage really is. Of course, in principle it's wrong (how dare someone steal your art), but in order for any attorney or judge to take an infringement case seriously, you need to have suffered a substantial loss. For instance, if you hear your song played on the radio or on MTV, or in a television commercial, or in a movie, you've probably suffered a loss of income as a result. Unfortunately, until a significant event like this occurs, someone using your song is essentially like a tree falling in the forest—it doesn't make a loud enough noise for anyone to really care. The best course of action is to simply understand as much as you can about your copyrights, handle your business in as prudent a manner as you know how at all times, and try to work with as many quality people in your career as possible. That's really all anyone can do! (See p. 208.)

PUBLISHING YOUR MUSIC

Congratulations! You've come a long way. And now that you understand a little bit about copyrights, we can begin discussing more about music publishing. In fact, after reading this chapter, you may even have to run out and get yourself some new business cards. Why? Because *by virtue of creating a copyright, you not only inherit the rights as the author and owner of a composition, but also the rights as the music publisher!* I bet you didn't know that.

By now, the word "samples" has probably crossed your mind since they are frequently examples of infringement. Samples are small (sometimes significant) snippets of music lifted from pre-recorded music for the purpose of enhancing a musical track. They can be found mostly in rap, rock, and dance genres. Samples are, of course, not free—they require compensation to both the copyright holder of the music, and the copyright holder of the actual sound recording that holds your music (which are two entirely separate copyrights). Although other musicians, producers, and DJs, etc., are supposed to get a clearance to use samples, they often get away with using them for free by disguising them deep in a musical track or even reversing them so that they are no longer distinguishable. It happens all the time.

In fact, when you publish your music by making it available to the public by sale or other means, the monies taken in are theoretically divided into two separate and equal categories: the writer's share and the publisher's share (see pie diagram, p.209). So, if one dollar is earned, 50 cents goes to the writer (which is you), and 50 cents goes to the publisher (which is also you). If this sounds absolutely crazy, it is, but it's just the way the publishing system works. Even crazier, it's the

The Song

Writer's Share

Publisher's Share

publisher who takes on most of the responsibilities, like ownership of the copyright, making sure the songs are being used and earning money, collecting all the generated incomes, and paying the writers their respective shares. It's like having dual personalities making good use of both sides of the brain; the left side or creative side is the writer, and the right side or analytical side is the music publisher—but there's still one brain! However, can't you contact a more experienced music publisher to take on the publishing side of the responsibilities for you so that you can

CRIME DOESN'T PAY, BUT INFRINGERS [EVENTUALLY] DO. In the early 1990s, a small, unsigned band sued a successful major-label recording artist for copyright infringement (sorry, the names must remain anonymous here). The band claimed that the artist's hit song contained a chorus that was an exact replica of one of their own. Not only did the band show that they were the first to register the song with the Copyright Office in Washington, D.C., they were able to prove a variety of other aspects necessary to resolving the case. First, the band was able to prove the likelihood that the artist could have stolen its composition. This is called "proving access"—the local band opened for the artist on several occasions. Second, the band was able to show that the artist's chorus was "substantially similar" to their own. Third, the band was able to show that their chorus was so unique in character, it undoubtedly was not copied unintentionally. In other words, the infringement was "willful." Fourth, the band brought in a witness whose life the lyrics documented. Finally, the band exhibited newspaper clippings showing performance dates of the song long before the artist's band even formed. Needless to say, there was mounting evidence in the band's favor. The case was settled out of the court, and the band received an undisclosed sum of money.

In another story, Led Zeppelin was repeatedly accused in the music press of stealing and recycling blues songs without acknowledging their sources. According to Stephen Davis' classic book *Hammer of the Gods,* the song "Dazed and Confused" was taken from folk singer Jake Holmes; the song "Traveling River Side Blues" was Robert Johnson's; the list goes on . . . Eventually, blues man Willie Dixon caught up with Zeppelin and sued their organization in 1991 over the song "Whole Lotta Love." Unquestionably, Led Zeppelin borrowed the lyrics from Dixon's song "You Need Love," first recorded by Muddy Waters in 1952. The band admitted to the infringement and settled with Dixon out of court for an undisclosed sum of money. Zeppelin was caught "blues"-handed.

Finally, in a well known case, Two Live Crew re-recorded both the guitar intro and first line of lyrics to Roy Orbison's song "Pretty Woman," and used it in one of their songs. Was using such a small part considered an infringement? Before addressing this question, perhaps it's a good time to clear up a common myth among musicians: The rule that you can borrow up to four bars of music without it being a copyright infringement is a fallacy. The issue is not of the amount used, but the "significance" to the original song. For example, a hooky guitar riff, even just two bars, would probably be considered a significant part of the original song, while perhaps a section of the bridge might not. It depends on the particulars of each individual case. But note, there is one exception to this rule that is worth mentioning, which brings us back to our friends Two Live Crew. Although the parts they used in their song were significant to Orbison's original, the judge ruled that it fell under something in copyright law called "fair use." Basically this says that small amounts of copyrighted material can be reproduced for the purposes of critical review, parody, news reporting, teaching, etc. Since Two Live Crew's version contained social criticism and parody of Orbison's original, they got off without owing Orbison a dime.

simply concentrate more on being the writer? Absolutely! In fact, in our discussion below, the word "publisher" can mean you or an outside publisher. But once again, before getting into detail about publishing deals, I'm going to leave you in suspense just a little bit longer while we take a minute to discuss some of the income you might earn when your songs are released to your adoring public.

SOURCES OF PUBLISHING INCOME

There are several types of income derived from music publishing: primary sources of income and secondary sources of income.

- ✦ Primary sources of income include mechanical royalties and performance royalties.
- ✦ Secondary sources of incomes include synchronization fees, print royalties, and foreign subpublishing incomes.

Each of these sources of income is discussed in detail below.

MECHANICAL ROYALTIES

Mechanical royalties are a major source of income that can be derived from music publishing. As defined by the United States Copyright Act and established by provisions set in law, mechanical royalties are licensing fees paid by the record company for the use of your songs on phonorecord. Don't confuse mechanical royalties with record royalties (discussed in Chapter 11). Record royalties are percentages of the suggested retail price of your record, subject to the recoupment of numerous recording and other expenses. *Mechanical royalties are mandatory by law and should not be subject to recoupment of recording costs by the record company.* In fact, mechanical royalties are one of the more immediate incomes you derive from sales of your record. For that matter, mechanicals may be the only income you get for a long while, since it will probably take quite some time before you begin earning monies from other revenue streams discussed in this book, such as touring (as you'll see in Chapter 13). So make sure to pay close attention to every detail below.

A Brief History

Mechanical royalties have quite a long and interesting history. The word "mechanical" refers back to the old days when music was mechanically fixed or copied to devices such as piano rolls—you know the ones you see in western movies when the piano plays by itself? Although piano rolls are long gone, the name has never been changed, but rest assured the mechanical rates surely have.

Dating back to 1902, the statutory mechanical rate was $.02 per composition. This rate existed until the new Copyright Act of 1976 (effective January 1, 1978), when it was finally changed to $.0275 per composition. There have been a number of increases since then, but as of the year 2002, the statutory mechanical rate is $.08 (8 cents) for compositions less than five minutes in length; this rate is sometimes referred to as the "minimum statutory rate." The rate for songs written above five minutes in length is 1.55 cents for every minute or a fraction of a minute thereof; this rate is sometimes referred to as the "maximum statutory rate." For example, if a composition is just 10 seconds over 5 minutes, the mechanical royalty payable by law is 9.3 cents per composition: (1.55 x 6 minutes = 9.3 cents). Nevertheless, the minimum statutory rate is the emphasis of our discussion. A committee called the Copyright Arbitration Royalty Panel (CARP) now adjusts the statutory rates regularly, so expect the next increase to occur in 2004, followed by a change in 2006.

IN A DIGITAL WORLD. Ed Pierson at Warner/Chappell Music notes that for decades the term "phonograph record" in copyright law specifically referred to the copying of music on 78s and CDs. However, as we enter the age of new technology, this term gets blurred a bit when we talk about DVDs, digital downloading, and streaming music. There are still a lot of legal issues that need to be resolved regarding how writers and publishers will be paid for their music that is transmitted over the Internet—so stay tuned! One thing is for certain though: When we talk about mechanical royalties, we're generally talking about the copying of a song and the fees paid to music publishers to make the use permissible.

One last thing: As defined by the United States Copyright Act, you're paid a statutory mechanical licensing fee for all records *made and distributed*. So according to law, even when records are manufactured and not sold, you still get paid. Sounds cool! Sure does, but there's one major exception that you'd better make sure you understand. If you're either a signed recording artist, or you're writing songs for or with a signed recording artist, a great deal of what we have just covered is all subject to change. Why? You'll see in a minute. But I'll give you a hint, it's called the "controlled composition clause." You won't want to miss this!

The Harry Fox Agency

When a record company wants to use your composition on a phonorecord, a license must first be issued by the music publisher. The license most commonly used, which I'm sure will come as no surprise to you, is called a mechanical license. The music publisher then monitors the record company to make sure the proper mechanical royalties are paid according to the number of records that are sold. In the United States, there's a major mechanical rights society called the Harry Fox Agency (HFA), which is more than happy to take care of these responsibilities on behalf of music publishers.

Founded in 1927, the Fox Agency (as it's sometimes called) represents well over 17,000 music publishers. In fact, Ed Pierce at Warner/Chappell Music notes that most publishers, both big and small, use Harry Fox's services. It's especially cost effective for the music publisher representing a huge repertoire of songs, since they would otherwise have to employ their own staff just to keep up with the work. Another advantage of Harry Fox's services is that the company periodically audits record companies, which can otherwise be extremely expensive for music publishers. Audits can cost as much as $30,000. Although you may think audits are unnecessary, you might find it very disturbing to know that most record-company audits by the Fox Agency show an underpayment of royalties to music publishers. The truth is that record companies are known to get sloppy.

Lastly, the best part of the Harry Fox Agency is that it will issue mechanical licenses and collect royalties for a relatively low fee of six percent of the gross mechanicals collected. This fee is known to change, both up and down, so keep your eyes and ears

> Contact The Harry Fox Agency at (212) 370-5330 or at www. harryfox.com. Also, see smaller independent companies such as the American Mechanical Rights Agency (AMRA) at (310) 440-8778 or www.amer-mechrights.com.

open for the latest news. By the way, Harry Fox will also negotiate synchronization licenses for television and film uses on behalf of publishers. The fee the Fox Agency charges is ten percent of the negotiated synch fee. Most major music publishers have their own synch departments; therefore, this function is typically reserved for the smaller music publishers.

The Controlled Composition Clause

Okay, as promised, now comes the really juicy stuff called the controlled composition clause, which we mentioned earlier. There are a few very important things you need to know about mechanical royalties and recording contracts. Remember, mechanical royalties are licensing fees defined by the United States Copyright Act and set by provisions of law. As of the year 2002, the minimum statutory rate is 8 cents per composition under 5 minutes, with the maximum statutory rate being 1.5 cents per minute or a fraction thereof for compositions over five minutes. (In 2004, the minimum rate will be 8.5 cents and the maximum will be 1.65 cents.) However, unlike the rest of the world, the United States has something called "the right to contract." This means that although the rate is set in law, it can be modified by contract. Therefore, in most recording agreements, *the record company will insist on taking a number of limitations and deductions, which will reduce your mechanical royalty dramatically.* These limitations are stipulated in your recording agreement under something called the "controlled composition clause." This clause applies to all "controlled compositions."

A controlled composition is any song written or co-written by the artist, or otherwise owned and controlled by the artist. To clarify, this means that no matter what copyright law says, the record company will want you to agree to a reduced mechanical fee or they may be unwilling to do business with you. Seriously! In fact, for all you composers out there who are co-writing songs with signed artists, or for those composers who write complete compositions for signed artists, the record company will want you to agree to this clause as well—even though you're not directly signed to them. Of course, it's your right to decline, but as a result, the song may simply not get cut. Let's take a look at some of those limitations and deductions:

✦ *The Controlled Rate.* For new or mid-level artists, the record company will typically negotiate a royalty that is 75 percent of the minimum statutory mechanical rate (e.g., 75% x $.08). The resulting rate (6 cents) per composition is known as something called "the controlled rate" or the "three-quarter rate."

✦ *The Cap.* The controlled rate usually applies to a maximum, or "cap," of only ten songs per record. In other words, it doesn't matter whether you have ten songs on the record or fourteen, the record company will only agree to pay you on the ten. Therefore, you will typically earn 60 cents per record (the controlled rate per song of 6.0 cents x the cap per record of 10 songs = 60 cents). If this sounds completely unfair, Los Angeles-based attorney Jeffrey Light offered the following encouragement in a lecture he delivered in 2002 at UCLA: "The best way to look at the cap is that you're getting 60 cents per record, period! Don't think you're not getting paid on the 11th or 12th songs. Make the record you need to make creatively; if that means recording 12 or 14 songs. Do it."

Now take a look at examples A and B below to see how your royalty has already been dramatically lowered by the record company—and we're just getting started! Assume that you have written fourteen songs for release on record.

A) By provision set in United States copyright law

$ .08   (The statutory mechanical rate per composition as of 2002)

x 14   (The number of songs written by the artist on the record)

= $1.12   (The mechanical rate payable per record made and distributed)

B) Under the Controlled Composition Clause:

$ .08   (The statutory mechanical rate per composition as of 2002)

x 75 % (Reduction under the controlled composition clause)

$ .06   (The rate per composition)

x 10   (The number of controlled compositions payable out of 14)

= $ 0.60 per record sold (The "cap" the record company pays)

Note: These deductions are standard and are usually difficult to negotiate for newer artists. However, in the words of Jeffrey Light, "Anything is possible." It's not unlikely that a savvy attorney may be able to negotiate the 8-cents rate per composition with a cap of as much as twelve songs. Note that although the 8-cents rate (or 5-minute-or-less rate) is technically called the minimum statutory rate, it's sometimes called the maximum or "full stat rate" because it's usually the most any record company is willing to pay.

- ◆ *Changing Rates.* As illustrated in the example above, the record company gets away with lowering your royalty by nearly 50 percent, and it'll want to make sure it stays that low, too! Since the statutory mechanical rate changes frequently (in the year 2004, the minimum statutory rate will increase to 8.5 cents per composition), the record company will usually lock the rate on the day your record is delivered or released. Therefore, if your record is released on December 31, 2002, and the statutory rate increased to 8.5 cents per composition on January 1, 2004, you would still be paid a percentage of your initial rate (i.e., 75% of 8 cents, or 6 cents per composition).
- ◆ *The Minimum Statutory Rate.* As you already know, the statutory mechanical rate also provides a higher royalty for songs over five minutes. As of the year 2002, the increase is to 1.55 cents for every minute or a fraction of a minute thereof. In 2004, it's 1.65 cents. Under the controlled composition clause, however, your royalty will always be based on the "minimum statutory rate" (i.e., the five minute or less rate). I wouldn't worry about this deduction, though. Unless you're doing something really wrong, most compositions should be less than four minutes, because that's just the way most radio-station formats like them!
- ◆ *Free Goods:* By statute, mechanical royalties are paid on all records made and distributed. But, for every 100 records distributed, the record company will contrac-

tually deem 15 percent as "standard free goods"—a so-called incentive to entice retailers to purchase your record. (This concept was also discussed in reference to record royalties in Chapter 11.) In other words, for every 100 records shipped, 15 are theoretically given away for free, and behold—you're not paid a royalty for them either. This may be indicated in your recording contract as payment on only 85 percent of all records sold. If you have negotiating power, the record company may agree to pay mechanicals on 50 percent of standard free goods (i.e., 92.5 percent of all records sold).

A) 50,000 (Records made and distributed)
   x 85 % (Free goods factor)

= 42,500 (Royalty bearing records payable)
   x $.60 (The cap per record sold: .08 x 75% = $.06 x 10 songs)

= $25,500 (Mechanical royalty payable)

Note: Do not confuse mechanical royalties with record royalties. Mechanical royalties are typically not used by the record company for recoupment of recording funds or other costs! Therefore, in the above example, even when the band sells a minimum of 50,000 records (which would be considered a flop by most commercial standards), the group is still credited $25,500 in mechanical royalties. "This is why mechanicals and making sure to negotiate the right controlled composition clause are so important to artists," says Los Angeles-based attorney Stacy Fass.

✦ *Reserves.* Remember that by statute, mechanical royalties are paid *on all records made and distributed.* However, the record company pays you on a reduced percentage of all records made and distributed and makes another little adjustment in their contracts to pay you only for *records that are sold.* And to make sure they make no mistakes, they'll take something called a "reserve." You see, the record company may send out royalty statements to music publishers every 45 days after each calendar quarter (March 31, June 30, September 30, and December 31), or otherwise semi-annually. In these statements, record companies typically withhold 50 to 75 percent of mechanicals as a reserve, which protects a company from over-paying in case records are returned by retailers. Monies held in reserves are liquidated throughout subsequent statements, usually within four quarters after the reserves were first taken.

Earlier in this chapter when I discussed the compulsory licensing provision, I explained that anyone can license your song after it's released for the first time on phonorecord. Well, you, too, can license songs. When you want to cover another artist's song (what's often referred to as an "outside song"), you must obtain a mechanical license and pay the publisher a mechanical licensing fee. Note that the publisher does not have to issue a license lower than the statutory rate—after all, he isn't signed to your recording agreement. Either way, just keep in mind that the fee paid to the publisher comes out of your cap per record, which ultimately reduces the mechanical paid to you.

♦ *Mid-Price Records, Record Clubs, and Budget Records.* Further deductions in your mechanical royalties are taken for "mid-price records," that is, records sold at a lower price after their run in current release, which amounts to 75 percent of the rate (e.g., 75% x 6.0 cents = 4.2 cents). For records sold in "record clubs," like the ones listed in magazines that offer ten CDs for one penny, and for "budget records," which are catalog items that are not selling well and are offered to retailers at big savings, mechanicals are paid at 50 percent of the rate (e.g., 50% x 6.0 cents = 3.0 cents).

♦ *Promotional Records.* You will not receive a mechanical royalty on records shipped to retailers during special promotions, and those free "promotional records" given to radio stations and disc jockeys that are marked "not for sale."

♦ *Video Limitations.* Also found in most controlled composition clauses, the record company will want to use your compositions free of licensing fees in promotional and home videos. This means that the record company doesn't pay you for the use of your songs in video. After all, videos are used primarily for promotional purposes on MTV and VH1, not to mention that they're also good for your ego.

> Mark Goldstein of Warner Bros. Records notes that the licensing fee the record company is referring under the video limitation clause is generally what's called a synchronization fee (as you'll learn later in this chapter). However, the language under the video limitation clause is often kept broad enough to cover *any other* kind of fee that might *possibly* come up.

So there you have it. If all of these limitations and deductions have depressed you, let's end on a positive note. You see, the record company may make allowances for rate escalations at predetermined sales levels. For instance, if sales of your record reach more than 500,000 units, the rate might increase to 85 percent of the minimum statutory rate (e.g., 85% x 8 cents = $0.068, or 6.8 cents per composition). It may not be what's referred to as the full-state rate (e.g., 8 cents per composition), but at least it gives you something to work towards.

PERFORMANCE ROYALTIES

If you've been paying attention throughout this chapter, you already know that under copyright law one of the many rights you get as author and owner of a composition is something called a performing right. This not only gives you the exclusive first right to perform your compositions to the public, but the right obligating anyone who wants to profit from the public performance of your music to ask permission and pay a licensing fee. This includes radio stations and television networks, cable stations (such as HBO, MTV, and VH1), Internet sites, restaurants, nightclubs, bars and grills, in-flight radio stations, hotels, colleges and universities, and virtually any other venue where music is played. But unlike a mechanical royalty, where there's an established fee for the use of your songs on phonorecord, the system in the performing rights area is much more intricate than simply saying you get x-amount of monies for the performance of one of your compositions. Additionally, if you think about the number of radio stations that exists in the United States alone (over 10,000), it would appear impossible for music publishers (even the larger companies) to individually issue licenses to each and every one, collect royalty payments, and police the world to make sure that all other music users are paying licensing fees. With the amount of music performed each day on one radio station, can you imagine the amount of paperwork that would be involved in seeking licenses from each and every music publisher? Surely, there had to be an easier system in place, and out of this concern, something called a "performing rights organization" (PRO) was born.

Performing Rights Organizations

The three performing rights organizations in the United States are The American Association of Authors and Composers (ASCAP), Broadcast Music Inc. (BMI), and SESAC (formerly known as The Society of European Stage Authors and Composers). Although each of these organizations conducts its business differently, they have similar functions and one general principle: *to protect the performing rights of songwriters and publishers.* Here's a very general overview of how they operate:

Blanket Licenses. The performing rights societies issue "blanket licenses" to music users (such as radio stations, television networks, nightclubs, restaurants, concert halls, airlines, shopping malls, and websites) for a negotiated fee that covers all of the compositions registered to a society by thousands of different writers and publishers. The fees paid by these music users are dependent on a number of variables. For instance, a radio station's broadcast range and/or yearly advertising revenue may be factors that influence determining its licensing fees. If you're really interested, each of the organizations provides schedules of available licensing fees. In any case, all of the monies are collected by the societies and then divided up and paid accordingly to writers and publishers based on the number of performances per quarter. Statements are generally sent out four times each year. But how do the societies keep track of the use of your compositions?

Monitoring Songs. The performing rights organizations (PROs) conduct research to give them a representation of the copyright titles aired during each royalty period. Although there is quite a variety of licenses issued by the PROs, royalty payments are based primarily on the number of radio and television performances each quarter, since these are the primary sources of license proceeds. Monies collected from general licenses, such as restaurants, nightclubs, hotels, etc., are thrown into the television and radio pool. Therefore, it makes sense to concentrate on the various monitoring methods used for radio and television.

> One hit song can easily generate a total (combined writer/publisher earnings) of anywhere from $500,000 to $1 million a year, at an approximate average of 7 cents per radio play. A theme song on a prime time network television show can generate an average of $150,000 a year, and about $1,600 per performance.

✦ *Radio.* There are generally two monitoring systems used for radio performances: "BDS" and random radio "logs." Broadcast Data Systems (BDS) is a service that monitors radio stations and updates a central data bank as songs are aired. Radio logs are schedule listings kept by radio stations listing all recordings played or programmed during broadcast hours, including titles, artists, and the respective performing rights society.

✦ *Television.* The monitoring of television stations, cable, etc., is generally accomplished by using "cue sheets." A cue sheet is a producer or editor's instruction detailing how, when, and where music is used. Information also includes whether the use was for a feature, background, or theme.

Since there are only so many hours of research performing rights organizations can conduct in a cost effective manner, it's more likely that only frequently played songs on the radio get picked up through monitoring. So does this mean that the system basically favors hit songs? Hate to say it, but in general, yes! In fact, it really dispels the myth among musicians that every time your song is played on the radio, it's an automatic "cha ching"—money in the bank. As far as television is concerned, monitoring by cue sheets is far more accurate than radio. Therefore, if your song is performed in this medium, it's likely you will receive payment.

Separate Writer Affiliation The payment of performance royalties is quite different than any other income derived from your songs. When the PROs collect licensing fees, divide them up, and send out the appropriate shares, they send the writer's share (50 percent) automatically to the writer, and the publisher's share (the other 50 percent) to the publisher. Supposedly this system was devised to protect writers from the big bad publishers who could potentially rip them off. In any case, regardless of whether you self-publish or enter into an agreement with an established music publisher, you must affiliate with a PRO as the writer. Of course, there's an individual publisher affiliation that's also necessary for publishers. But keep in mind, the writer and publisher have to affiliate with the same organization. In other words, both 100 percent of the writer's share of a song and 100 percent of the publisher's share must be affiliated with ASCAP. On the other hand, if two writers compose a song together, one writer and publisher can affiliate their shares with one organization, while the other writer and publisher can be affiliated with the other.

Neil Gillis of Warner/Chappell Music says that foreign collections for radio tend to be a little more accurate than those in the United States. The reason is primarily because it's not economically feasible for the societies to monitor every station. There are over 10,000 stations in the U.S. (both commercial and non-commercial combined). In foreign territories, such as Germany, there may be seven stations tops. England may have five. Therefore, it's more likely you'll be paid for more random performances in foreign territories than in the U.S. As for film uses, another benefit of foreign performances is that you're paid when your song is played in movie theaters, whereas in the U.S. you are not paid. More on foreign-performances royalties when we discuss foreign sub-publishing.

Which Performing Rights Organization Should You Join? There's an ongoing debate about which performing rights organization is better at doing its job. Within the industry it's said that the same song would be paid an equal amount in royalties, whether the writer and/or publisher was with ASCAP, BMI, or SESAC. Of course, a representative from any of these organizations would argue this point. It's best to look at the issue this way: *the performing rights organizations were set up to protect you, not screw you over!* They're, for the most part, non-profit organizations (except SESAC; more in a minute), which basically means that all of the money they collect gets allocated to their members after an operating charge is taken off the top to keep their lights on and pay employee salaries. And as mentioned earlier, until your songs are being played regularly on major radio stations (or aired on television), the bottom line is that you won't receive much, if any, in performance royalties anyway. In other words, perhaps you shouldn't be losing sleep on this matter right now.

The best suggestion is to speak with a representative from each office when you're about to have a song published. Base your decision on the information that seems the most reasonable to you, and on the organization that seems as though it will give you the most personalized treatment when you need it. This could mean that there's a representative at one of the organizations you really like, or simply that the vibe you got when you went into their offices was good. Keep in mind that if you ever want to switch organizations down the road, it's not all that difficult to do so. Be sure to ask each organization for membership details.

For more information, contact ASCAP at (800) 95-ASCAP, www. ascap.com; BMI at (212) 586-2000, (310) 659-9109, www.bmi. com; and SESAC at (212) 586-3450, (310) 393-9671, www. sesac.com.

PERFORMING RIGHTS ORGANIZATIONS AT A GLANCE

History:

✦ ASCAP is a non-profit organization established in 1914 that is run by writers and publishers.

✦ BMI has been operated as a non-profit organization since 1940. BMI was founded by broadcasters, but its "day-to-day" decisions are made by management.

✦ SESAC is a "for profit" organization founded in 1930. SESAC is a much smaller organization than ASCAP and BMI, representing only 5 percent of all the licenses issued. As a private organization—unlike ASCAP and BMI, which are non-profit organizations—SESAC is not monitored by the Justice Department and it can conduct its business as it wishes.

Joining:

✦ ASCAP members must have a song that's about to be published. Writers pay a yearly fee of $10, and publishers pay $50.

✦ BMI members must also have a song about to be published. It's free for writers to join, and publishers pay a one-time fee of $150 (for an independently owned company) or $250 (for a partnership or corporation).

✦ SESAC members must be selected by a referral process. Since SESAC is a much smaller organization, it has precious resources that must be utilized carefully. It prides itself in giving the best individual attention.

NOTE: Rates are subject to change.

SYNCHRONIZATION FEES

Like mechanical and performance royalties,, synchronization fees are yet another source of income derived from music publishing. Synchronization refers to the art of synching your music with visual images in motion pictures, television, CD-ROMs, DVDs, the Internet, and other media. Unlike mechanical royalties, there are no statutory fees for the use of your compositions in synchronization. Synch fees are completely negotiable, and are based on a number of factors that will be discussed in detail in a moment. But first, you should know that generally, there are two types of income derived from the use of your compositions:

◆ The actual "synch fee" (or up-front fee) which, again, is negotiable.

◆ The performance royalty income generated by the use of your songs on the back end (i.e., as a result of the initial synch use). Remember that performance royalties are paid to you by your registered performing rights society (ASCAP, BMI, or SESAC).

NOTE: In addition to the incomes mentioned above, anyone requesting a license for your music will technically have to negotiate a second fee to the owner of the actual master recordings (see "The Copyright Notice" earlier in this chapter). This is called a "master use" fee. Typically, independent musicians and bands will own both the rights to their compositions and the master tapes, entitling them to two separate fees (or an "all-in" fee). On the other hand, artists who are part of a signed recording act will typically not own the master rights. Therefore, it's the record label that earns the master-use fee for the actual sound recording, while the artist earns the synch fee for the music embodied on the masters. For practical purposes, the following discussion emphasizes the scenario in which an artist does not own the master tapes and is a signed recording entity, since that is the main emphasis of this book.

Points of Negotiation

As previously mentioned, there are no statutory fees for the use of your music in audio/visual projects. Synch fees are 100 percent negotiable. In the words of Michael Eames, President of Penn Music Group, "Synch fees are the Wild Wild West."

Below are a few questions that publishers typically ask when negotiating up-front synch fees:

◆ *Type of use.* Is your song being utilized as a featured use or a background use? In either case, the more prominent your song is, the more money you can charge.

◆ *Context.* What is happening in the scene of the movie or television program while your song is being used? More specifically, is your music being used over the beginning or end title credits of a movie or a television program? If so, you will generally be compensated more favorably than if your music is used in the main body of a work. This is obviously because there's more emphasis being placed on your composition during the beginning or end titles. Certainly, you've seen the art cards at the ends of some TV shows (usually on the WB Network) where they say, "Tonight's episode features music by . . . " These spots are hard to come by, but they can be wonderfully effective in increasing sales.

◆ *Timing.* For how many minutes and/or seconds is your music being used? The longer the use, the more you can charge.

◆ *Term.* How long will your music be licensed? For instance, your song may be requested for as short a period as one year and as long as perpetuity. The longer you license your rights, the higher the fee you will receive. It's important to understand that most synch uses are non-exclusive; you will still be able to license your music in other projects. If someone wants exclusivity to your music (which often occurs in the case of TV commercials), there's a premium that must be paid. Since you will not be able to use your

If your composition is being used with negative implications, such as during some unfavorable dialogue or in an unpleasant scene of a movie (e.g., a murder scene, etc.), you may not even want it used in the first place.

composition anywhere else, you are potentially losing income and must be compensated well.

◆ *Territory.* Where will your music be used? In the U.S. or the entire world? In the latter case, the use of your compositions will command a higher fee.

◆ *Media.* In what media will your music be used? TV? Theaters? Home video? The Internet? All of the above? The more types of media used, the higher the price you can ask.

◆ *Stature of the song.* How successful is the song? The more popular the song is, the more you can charge. You can be sure Bob Seger is receiving hundreds of thousands of dollars for the use of his hit song "Like A Rock" in the Chevrolet commercials that have been airing for the last ten years.

◆ *Credit.* Will you receive credit for the use of your song over the beginning or end titles of a movie? If so, you must consider that the exposure in a prominent film can lead to other uses of your compositions. This holds true for credits you receive over television programs as well. The exposure in these two instances alone can make up for a situation where you are not receiving adequate income, due, for example, to poor negotiations.

More Than You Bargained for

The initial synch fees negotiated for the use of your compositions are not the only monies that can be generated. In fact, the use of your song in a film can snowball into a number of potential revenue streams. For example, if the record label that holds the rights to release the soundtrack albums wants to use your song, you earn a mechanical licensing royalty per each record sold. If your song then gets played on the radio to promote the film or soundtrack, you earn a performance royalty as well. Last but not least, if the film ever makes it into theaters outside of the United States—you guessed it—you also earn a performance royalty for the public performance of your composition (note that theater performances in the U.S. for some reason are not payable). As you can see, the use of your song in just one film can often generate monies that are more than you ever bargained for. Not bad at all for a day of songwriting!

> Soundtrack albums are a great way for a record label to get a band's name out to the masses. If a record company out-bids other labels for the rights to release a soundtrack, it'll use this opportunity to feature its newly signed artists.

PRINT ROYALTIES

Another source of income you can earn from music publishing are print royalties. These are the monies you make when your compositions are sold in sheet music and music books. If this doesn't ring a bell, just take a look in your grandma's piano bench the next time you're over for Thanksgiving dinner. Print today represents only an extremely small percentage of the overall income derived from your songs. In fact, unless you have a hit song or album, or at least some sales success, it's not likely your songs will ever make it to print. Nevertheless, print is worth mentioning, so here's a brief—and I mean brief—overview.

EXAMPLES OF FEES FOR ACTUAL SYNCH USES

For songs that are either well-known or current hits:

◆ Television. $5000 to $9000 per use per song. For use over the beginning or end title credits, or as the theme of a television program, fees can be as much as $80,000 and more per use per song.

◆ Film. $10,000 to $40,000 per use per song. For use of your compositions over the beginning or end title credits of a film, fees can be as much as $100,000 and more per use per song. Can you believe the techno band Prodigy was offered $500,000 for the use of just one of their songs in a film? If a director really wants your music, the money here is big.

For songs that are unknown or non charting:

◆ Television. $325 to $1500 per use per song.

◆ Film. $500 to $5000 per use per song.

Print Uses

There are four primary uses of your songs in print music form: single sheet, folios, matching folios, and mixed folios.

◆ *Single Sheet.* Single sheet music, often called piano sheet music, is just what it sounds like: individual sheets sold in music stores. Sheet music can be a big seller for currently popular or classic songs. Examples include: "Wind Beneath My Wings" by Larry Healey and Jeff Silbar, "What a Wonderful World" by George David Weiss and Bob Thiele, and "At Last" by Mark Gordon and Harry Warren.

◆ *Folios.* Folios are music books that contain a complete library of music by one artist. Examples include *Led Zeppelin Complete* (Warner Bros. Publications), *The Best of The Police* (Hal Leonard), *The Best of Kiss* (Hal Leonard).

◆ *Matching Folios.* Matching folios are music books that match a particular record by an artist. The actual album cover is also the cover of the folio, and there are usually pictures of the artist inside. Examples include *The Jimi Hendrix Experience* (Cherry Lane Music), *Master of Puppets* by Metallica (Hal Leonard), *The Wall* by Pink Floyd (Pink Floyd Music Publishing, LTD).

◆ *Mixed Folios.* Mixed folios are music books that contain works by a variety of different artists. Examples include *The Gigantic Guitar Songbook* (Hal Leonard) featuring songs like "Come Together" by the Beatles, "Hey Joe" by Jimi Hendrix, and "Radar Love" by Golden Earring. Another example is *The Motown Anthology* (Hal Leonard), featuring songs like "My Girl" by the Temptations, "I'll Be There" by the Jackson 5, and "Let's Get It On" by Marvin Gaye. Mixed folios are probably the most popular of the three folios because they contain so much variety.

PRINT—FROM PAST TO DIGITAL FUTURE. In what was coined the Tin Pan Alley era (1911 through the 1940s), print represented a much more significant income to publishers and songwriters since it was essentially the predominate form of distributing and selling music. Tin Pan Alley referred to a concentrated area in New York City and London where music publishers' offices were located—the name Tin Pan Alley was derived from the noise created by the sound of pianos playing while all the writers worked on their next big hits.

Attorney Peter M. Thall, author of the book *What They'll Never Tell You About The Music Business* (Billboard Books, 2002), theorizes that in the digital world, print is bound to become a more significant source of income to music publishers and songwriters. Thall estimates that today less than one percent of the world's printed music is available through retail outlets, but with digital distributors of printed music, consumers can find more variety 24/7 to download immediately with relative ease. Some of the more notable sites in business today are musicnotes.com (www.musicnotes.com), Sheet Music Direct (www.sheetmusicdirect.com), and Sheet Music Plus (www.sheetmusicplus.com).

Division Of Income

Things get a little weird when discussing the payment structure for print music. Unlike other sources of income, such as mechanicals, performances, and synchronization, whereby the publisher receives a sum of money and essentially splits it with the writer 50/50 (i.e., the writer's share and the publisher's share), *print music is the only source of income derived from a royalty system based on the suggested retail price or wholesale price.* Remember when reading the following information that the word "publisher" can mean you or an outside publisher. Here's a quick breakdown:

- ✦ *Sheet Music.* The music printer (the company that transcribes the music and makes the books) pays the music publisher a royalty of 20 percent of the retail price. The current retail price is approximately $3.50 for a single sheet of music, so the publisher receives around 70 cents ($3.50 x 20% = 70 cents). Of that 70 cents, the publisher then pays the writer a flat rate of around 5 to 7 cents. Why is this so low? Because that's just the way it's always been and no one has thought to change it. If you publish your own music, you don't have anything to worry about because you're both the writer and the publisher. However, if you enter into a deal with an established music publisher, don't expect much from single sheet music sales.
- ✦ *Folios.* The printer pays the publisher a royalty of 10 to 12.5 percent of the retail selling price. The current retail price ranges from $15.95 to $18.95, so if the publisher has a 10 percent royalty, and the price of a folio is $15.95, the publisher receives around $1.60 per folio sold. Of the $1.60, the publisher also pays the writer a royalty of about 10 percent, but it's only based on the wholesale price—the price for which the printer apparently sells the book to retailers (which is basically half of

the retail price of $15.95, which rounds out to $7.95). If the writer has a 10 percent royalty, he or she receives about 79 cents per folio sold ($7.95 x 10% = 79 cents—which is basically half of what the publisher gets).

- ✦ *Matching Folios.* Royalties for matching folios are the same as we discussed for folios. (God forbid we should have to repeat this.)
- ✦ *Mixed Folios.* Royalties for mixed folios are the same as for folios as well, but different. Confused? It'll make sense in a minute. The printer pays the publisher a royalty of around 10 to 12.5 percent of the retail selling price (which is the same as the other folios), but the royalty for mixed folios is *pro-rated based on the number of works in the book.* Remember, a mixed folio contains the compositions of a number of artists, not just you. For example, if there are 20 compositions in a folio, and you've written half of them, the publisher collects the pro-rated amount of 10/20ths (one half) of the standard 10 to 12.5 percent royalty rate. So, to plug in some real numbers, say the retail selling price of a mixed folio is $15.95, and the publisher has a 10 percent royalty rate, the publisher then collects about 80 cents per mixed folio sold [$15.95 x 5% (10/20ths or one half of the publisher's royalty rate) = 80 cents, rounded off]. Now, of the 80 cents, the publisher typically pays the writer a royalty in the range of 10 percent (also pro-rated based on the number of works in the book), but only if it's based on the wholesale price of the mixed folio, which is about half of the retail selling price quoted above. Therefore, the writer receives about 40 cents per mixed folio sold ($7.95 x 5% = 40 cents, rounded off).

FAKE BOOK/REAL CRIME. Although print doesn't really generate a substantial income for the authors and owners of songs, infringers certainly don't help matters any. Stephanie Rinaldo of Hollywood Sheet Music in Hollywood, California reminds us that, although the focus of infringement over the Internet has been recorded music, there are still hundreds of unauthorized sites that infringe on print rights by allowing people to download transcriptions of music and lyrics. But even more obvious rip-offs are the music books that have become very popularly known as "fake books." Fake books contain hundreds of transcribed classic songs that are sold illegally in front of music schools all over the country. They can even be found in many popular bookstores. You've seen them—you know, those books about three inches thick with plastic binding and handwritten music inside (it's not always correct either). Although everyone knows fake books are illegal, publishers have not really made an effort to stop them, so they've almost become accepted. But make no mistake, for every fake book that's sold, the writer and publisher don't make a dime.

FOREIGN SUBPUBLISHING INCOMES

Foreign subpublishing incomes are the monies earned when your music is published overseas. It's not a type of income itself, but rather it encompasses the various incomes previously discussed. Why is it necessary for a separate categorization? Because the monies in foreign territories are handled much differently than they are in the United States. In fact, U.S. publishers need to seek the assistance of "subpublishers" (publishers in foreign territories) to help with the collection of monies. Let's first take a close look at how the two primary sources of income (mechanical and performance royalties) are handled, then discuss something called "black box monies," and finally talk briefly about subpublishers.

Foreign Mechanicals

Remember when we discussed mechanical royalties earlier in this chapter and how you get so many pennies per composition per record? This system only applies to the United States and Canada. *In foreign territories, mechanical royalties are calculated differently.* Foreign mechanicals are payable on a percentage of either the retail selling price (RSP) of the record, or the price per dealer (PPD)—which is basically an equivalent of the wholesale prices. Percentages differ from territory to territory but are generally in the range of 6 to 10 percent, covering all the compositions on a record. For instance, at the time of this writing, mechanicals in Japan are based on 6 percent (RSP); in Germany 9.03 percent (PPD); and in the United Kingdom 8.5 percent (PPD). These rates are unaffected by either the length of the compositions or the number of songs per album. In other words, unlike in the U.S. and Canada, *writers and publishers cannot be asked to waive their rights to mechanical payments under a system similar to the controlled composition clause. I bet that makes you happy!*

Also much different than in the United States and Canada is the method by which foreign mechanical royalties are collected and paid to publishers. In the U.S. and Canada, publishers can choose to have the record companies send mechanical royalties directly to them, or they can have an agency such as Harry Fox collect on their behalf. However, in foreign territories, mechanical royalties are collected by "mandatory mechanical rights collection societies." For instance, in Japan, mechanical royalties are collected by a society called JASRAC, in Germany it's GEMA, and in Great Britain it's MCPS.

So, with all this talk of mandatory stuff, one might ask, "How the heck do I get my money?" That's a very good question. Essentially, the Harry Fox Agency in the U.S. can collect foreign mechanicals by making agreements with foreign societies, but this is usually not the most effective means of getting your royalties. I'm told the Fox Agency is not very good at dealing with foreign monies. Instead, U.S. publishers typically seek the help of what are known as local subpublishers, which are, as mentioned earlier in the "Foreign Subpublishing Incomes" section of this chapter, publishers in foreign territories who will collect mechanicals on your behalf. *If you don't have a subpublisher representing you, then your monies may go uncollected and often end up in what's known as "the black box."* Sounds ominous, doesn't it? Hold that thought. We'll discuss subpublishers and the black box in detail in a minute.

Foreign Performance Royalties

Foreign performance royalties aren't as complex as mechanical royalties, but there are a few things you need to know. Your performing rights organization in the U.S. (ASCAP, BMI, or SESAC) has reciprocal agreements with all of the performing rights societies around the world for licensing and royalty collections, and all of the performing rights societies have agreements with them as well. The performing rights society in Japan is JASRAC, in Germany it's GEMA, and in Great Britain it's PRS. (JASRAC and GEMA collect both mechanicals and performance royalties.) In any case, the foreign performing rights societies send the writer's share of performance royalties to the U.S. organizations (remember the "writer's share" of performances always gets paid to the writer, even for foreign performances), and then the U.S. society pays the writer directly. That's pretty straightforward, right?

However, the "publisher's share" of performance royalties is handled a bit differently. So again, the U.S. publisher will want to seek the assistance of a subpublisher to collect the publisher's share of performance monies. If you don't get a foreign subpublisher to represent you, the publisher's share of performance royalties will theoretically make its way back to you via your U.S. performing rights society. This method takes much longer than contracting a subpublisher, though, and is not an effective means of ensuring that all your performance income is collected. Like mechanicals, these monies are also subject to falling into the "black box."

Black Box Monies

When the foreign rights societies collect royalties earned by a song, they hold onto them and identify to whom the monies belong by checking registrations made by local subpublishers. *If the societies are unable to identify where the money should be sent, they forward them to an escrow account known as the black box.* Every society has one of these infamous black boxes holding unclaimed monies. After a certain period of time (usually about three to six years), if no claimant has come forth, the monies are deemed unclaimed or unidentified and are then divided among all of the subpublishers of the territory pro-rata based on their income. Successful writers who are contracted with a subpublisher, and who also have negotiating power, sometimes share in a percentage of the black box fund. This means that if you do not have a subpublisher in a foreign territory representing you, *other artists will gladly take your hard earned money instead.* But this can be prevented.

Sindee Levin, entertainment attorney and president of the American Mechanical Rights Agency (AMRA), notes that one should be realistic about when one can expect to receive foreign monies. It can often take up to two years before monies are collected and you are then actually paid.

Foreign Subpublishers

So who are these heroes of your foreign monies? As briefly mentioned before, a subpublisher is essentially a publisher in a foreign territory who's more than happy to collect monies for U.S. publishers (they can actually take care of other matters, too, but we'll get to that in a moment). Subpublishers first make sure that all of the U.S. publisher's works are properly registered with the foreign collection agencies mentioned above. When the foreign agencies collect royalties earned from your songs, they acknowledge the subpublisher's registration and forward the monies onward to it. The subpublisher then takes its share, ranging from 15 to 25 percent, and remits the net receipts to the U.S. publisher, which then divides the monies with the writers accordingly. Other functions of subpublishers include seeking uses of your songs in synchronization, printed music, and covers. Covers are when other artists literally cover your compositions, and sometimes adapt the lyrics into their own language as well. The subpublisher makes sure these sources of income are collected properly and sends them back to the U.S. publisher.

At Source Royalty Collections

There's one more thing that you should know about subpublishers; this concerns something called "at source royalty collections." As you already know, when the subpublisher collects monies earned from your songs, it takes a share and sends the net receipts to the U.S. publisher, which then divides it with the writers. If you're both the publisher and the writer, what I'm about to say may not matter. However, if you enter into a publishing deal with a U.S. publisher to represent your works worldwide, and that publisher then enters into a subpublishing deal, you may be able to get your writer's share of income based in the territory where the original dollar was earned, before the subpublisher takes its cut, and sends the net receipts to the U.S. publisher to be divided with you.

Let me try to clarify this for you. When you enter into a publishing deal with a U.S. publisher, the monies are theoretically divided equally between the writer and the publisher 50/50 (the writer's share and the publisher's share). But if $1.00 is earned in Germany, and the U.S. publisher enters into a deal with a subpublisher who takes its share of say 15 percent (remember, the subpublisher's fee ranges from 15 to 25 percent), then the subpublisher sends the U.S. publisher the net receipts of 85 cents. From this 85 cents, the publisher keeps 50 percent or 42.5 cents (85 x 50%), and sends the other 42.5 cents to you, the writer. But on an "at source" deal, your writer's share is based on the original dollar earned. So, if $1.00 is collected in Germany, you will earn 50 cents rather than 42.5 cents. Got it? I'm aware we're only talking about a small difference in change, and there are no "dollars" in Germany, but *the point is that when your foreign royalties are collected at source, you'll make more money as the writer!* Note: At source agreements are negotiable and not standard.

WHAT ESTABLISHED MUSIC PUBLISHERS CAN DO FOR YOUR CAREER

You already know that by virtue of creating a copyright, you inherit the rights as music publisher. You also know that there are several sources of income derived from music publishing, including mechanical royalties, performance royalties, print royalties, and synch fees. You might ask, "Why should I sign over my copyright ownership and a percentage of future earnings to an experienced music publisher?" First of all, don't be misled that publishing deals are being handed out on every corner. They aren't. The information that follows will give you a better sense of what publishers look for, as well as of what they can do for your career. The five major services usually provided by a music publisher include song plugging, securing recording agreements, paying advances, distributing marketing funds, and handling administrative duties.

> If you're looking for a publishing deal, check out the Music Publisher Registry (www.music-registry.com), published by the Music Business Registry, which lists all the major and independent publishers in California, New York, Nashville, Atlanta, Miami, and London.

Song Plugging

For many years, one of the primary roles of a music publisher was to "plug," or place, songs with other artists for commercial release on phonorecord. Most writers didn't perform their own music, and most performers didn't write. Someone needed to bring these two parties together, and music publishers were just the people to do it. But today, song plugging in the traditional sense has changed dramatically. Most artists both write and perform their own music, and are therefore self-contained and less reliant on the music publisher. So the conventional role of the publisher as song plugger has shifted its focus into what is now an emerging growth-area called synchronization.

MUSIC PUBLISHING IS BIG BUSINESS. According to a July 2001 article in *Rolling Stone* magazine, here's how much money some of today's superstars earned from their songs in 2001. (All quantities refer to U.S. dollars.)

AC/DC: 3.8 million

Backstreet Boys:
   3.5 million

Bon Jovi: 5.9 million

Blink 182: 2.6 million

Christina Aguilera:
   4.8 million

Creed: 6.6 million

Dave Matthews Band:
   9.7 million

Elton John: 6.2 million

Eminem: 5.8 million

Jay-Z: 2.9 million

Jennifer Lopez: 1.9 million

Korn: 3.4 million

Lenny Kravitz: 6.1 million

Limp Bizkit: 6.5 million

Madonna: 6.5 million

Matchbox Twenty:
   6.7 million

Metallica: 6.6 million

Ozzy Osbourne: 1.5 million

Sade: 1.2 million

U2: 11.3 million

Whitney Houston: 3 million

We've already discussed this source of income, but to refresh your memory, it refers to synching your music with visual images. Synchronization is not a new concept; it's been around for a long time, but the thought of merging music with commercial products, television shows, and even movies, was once considered selling out by most artists, until recently. Today you can hear Sting advertising for Jaguar cars with his song "Desert Rose," Led Zeppelin promoting GM with their classic song "Rock and Roll," and Aerosmith endorsing Dodge with its song "Just Push Play."

It's not just the successful artists who are in synch (pardon the pun); you can also hear newly signed artists on network television shows, and even in movies. When you think of how difficult it is for newly signed artists to get airplay on radio stations, you understand that the right exposure on, say, a television show can be an alternative method to breaking new artists into the main stream. The group Sixpence None The Richer broke due to a substantial amount of film and TV exposure for their song "Kiss Me." Singer Lisa Loeb can credit her success to the initial exposure she received from the movie *Reality Bites,* both from the movie itself, and from the soundtrack album. Publishing companies also try getting artists in foreign territories to cover your songs, and will also find uses for your songs in printed music, such as sheet music and music folios. Print is a less significant source of income and exposure by far than film and TV exposure, but it all adds up!

Securing Recording Agreements

Publishing companies are also known to help unsigned writer/performers procure recording agreements with record companies. The publisher may team you up with seasoned writers to help you compose a collection of well crafted songs, and will then strive to place your songs in television shows and other mediums to create as much excitement about your career as possible. Basically, an artist's affiliation with a reputable publishing company can be an attractive feature in and of itself to a record company. It sends a message throughout the music industry that a credible establishment stands behind your career. Unfortunately, A&R representatives aren't always able to determine the worthiness of an artist. The more players you can get in your court, the better chance you have at getting a label interested in you.

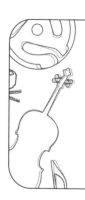

A LITTLE HELP FROM HER FRIENDS. Singer/songwriter Alanis Morrisette was signed to MCA Music Publishing when a company representative introduced her to producer/writer Glen Ballard. Together, Morrisette and Ballard crafted songs that not only helped land Morrisette a major recording deal, but also constituted an album called *Jagged Little Pill,* which sold over 30 million copies worldwide. And as if that weren't enough, *Jagged Little Pill* landed Morrisette a Grammy for Best Album of the Year. With a little help from her friends at MCA, Morrisette was able to put all the right pieces of her career together.

Paying Advances

Music publishing companies are often willing to advance money against your *projected* future earnings. Note the word "projected" here. The truth is that no one really knows whether your songs are ever going to make money (including you), but as long as you're willing to enter into a publishing deal with an interested publishing company, publishers are willing to take the gamble and give you an advance. Essentially, the advance is another source of income. The question then is: *how much money can you get the music publisher to give you up front in return for entering into a deal?* If you get a large advance and your record ends up failing, you'll have made out like a bandit on the publishing deal itself. On the other hand, if your record is extremely successful, then you gave up your copyright ownership and a very hefty piece of your earnings in exchange for the advance. It really comes down to how badly you need money up front, and how convinced you are that your publisher is going to be responsible for your future stardom. This is the gamble, and essentially you're gambling against yourself to a degree. Remember, your advance is really your money paid up front—it's recoupable against your share of future earnings (as we'll discuss in the section of this chapter called "Types of Publishing Deals").

Since advances can range anywhere from $20,000 to $400,000, and in some cases can be as much as one million dollars, publishers must be extremely cautious about whom they sign and what they decide to pay. The publisher looks at a few variables:

+ Is there hit song potential?
+ Do you have an energetic live performance, and does the audience seem to respond well to your music?
+ Are you a writer/producer with resources to place your songs with top artists?
+ Are you a writer/performer who has already signed a recording agreement?
+ If you're already a signed artist, then which record company holds your contract?
+ What's your A&R representative's success rate at the label?
+ How enthusiastic and supportive is the record company about your future?
+ If the record company already released your first single, is it getting played on the radio?
+ Is your record selling well in stores?
+ Are you booked on any upcoming major tours?

WHEN THE ADVANCE REALLY COUNTS. In the early 1990s, the band D.O.D (an abbreviation for Disneyland After Dark) entered into a publishing agreement with Warner/Chappell Music and received an advance for a million dollars. The "buzz" in the industry was that D.O.D. was sure to be the next big band. Warner/Chappell Music took a big gamble by offering such a large advance, but as it turned out, D.O.D.'s album was "dead on delivery." According to one source at Warner/Chappel Music who wishes to remain anonymous, sales figures reached a whopping 606 units—perhaps an exaggeration, but you get the point. You might say that D.O.D. made out like bandits on the initial publishing deal and advance, but that depends on how you look at it. Their record failed and they were never to be heard from again, but imagine how much worse off they would have been if their record failed and they hadn't had the publishing agreement at all.

Simply put, the more value the publisher sees in your compositions, the more money they may be willing to pay you up front. So in fact, the longer you can hold on to your publishing rights before signing a deal, the more money a publishing company may advance you. Again, it all depends on how badly you need the advance, and what you plan on doing with it. Even the smallest advance can be exactly what you need to keep you or your band up and running in the early stages of your career. In any case, it's nice to know that the publishing advance is essentially another source of income available for the taking—if and when you need it.

Distributing Marketing Funds

Publishing companies are also known to specifically earmark advance dollars that go towards a "marketing fund," which is a wise move. When a publisher signs a writer/artist who's also signed to a record label, they'll want to have a "plan B" just in case your record company all of a sudden loses interest in your band—which, by the way, is likely to happen in this day and age. According to the terms of your contract, the marketing monies may go towards hiring an independent radio promoter in hopes of getting airplay, or might otherwise go towards buying a van or perhaps musical equipment so that you can hit the road and build a fan base. *This money can be what saves your failing career if the record company decides to fade out on you.*

It doesn't stop there. Some publishers have even been known to continue supporting a band above and beyond the allotted marketing fund. For instance, Warner/Chappell Music continued to offer the band Remey Zero small advances even after they were dropped from Capitol Records. The band literally used the advance money to cover living expenses while they looked for a new record deal. Eventually, the band signed to UMG, made a great record, but it was dropped once again. Nevertheless, Warner Chappell Music stuck by the band and continued offering support and the occasional small advance. Finally, Remey Zero signed with Elektra and enjoyed moderate success with their single "Save Me" in 2002, which is used regularly on the television show *Dawson's Creek*. The moral of the story here is clear: The record business is based on a one-shot, do-or-die philosophy. Since enormous odds are stacked against you, *the question then becomes whether or not you want the major muscle of an established music publisher helping to promote your band. Remember, the more people you can get in your court, the better off you'll probably be!*

Handling Administrative Duties

Last but definitely not least, the core function of a music publisher beyond the creative and financial components mentioned above is administrative business, whose importance cannot be underestimated. Administrative duties include registering your compositions with the Copyright Office in Washington, D.C., making sure your songs are properly registered with one of the three performing rights organizations (ASCAP, BMI, or SESAC), issuing all types of licenses for the use of your songs (including mechanical, synch, and print licenses), negotiating the proper compensation for synch and sample uses (publishers understand proper rates), making sure all generated incomes are collected worldwide (including establishing foreign subpublishers on your behalf), keeping a watchful eye out for unauthorized uses of your songs, filing infringement claims, and, filing the occasional audit to be sure you're getting every last dime from the use of your songs. As you can see, administrative duties would be a handful for anyone to handle by him or herself. Because established publishers don't have to be artists like you, they can concentrate on tasks like this all day long! It also just so happens that established music publishers are pretty good at it.

TYPES OF PUBLISHING DEALS

Now let's take a close look at the various types of publishing deals that exist. We'll concentrate specifically on how these deals have evolved throughout the years in regard to transfer of copyright ownership and sharing of income. Remember that until you enter into a deal with a publisher, you own 100 percent of all income that is divided into two separate and equal categories; the writer's share and the publisher's share (see pie diagram). Let's take a look at the single song and exclusive song-

writer's agreements, co-publishing agreements, administration agreements, subpublishing deals, and finally self-publishing.

Single Song and Exclusive Songwriter's Agreements

For years, music publishers served as the mighty middleman between writers who needed their songs placed and artists who needed songs to record. Even as more artists began writing their own material, music publishers retained a tremendous amount of leverage in the industry. Publishing was simply a mysterious concept to everyone, and you can bet that music publishers liked it that way. In traditional publishing deals, such as "single song" and "exclusive songwriter agreements," publishing companies acquired 100 percent of the copyrights in a composition for the duration of the copyright term. This means they received 100 percent of the publisher's share of income, which essentially amounted to 50 percent of the gross song income (see pie diagram). Needless to say, this was a big piece of the pie, and arguably a bigger piece than publishers really deserved. So, for essentially every $100,000 the publishing company collected in earnings, the songwriters earned $50,000, and the publishing company earned the other $50,000. Keep in mind that with the exception of your writer's share of performance royalties, which is always paid to you directly by your performing rights society (ASCAP, BMI, or SESAC), your share of earnings is always charged against the initial advance. It's like your credit card company receiving a payment of $1.00 and only crediting 50 cents of that payment to your account. If the advance sounds more like a high-interest loan, it is, but this is basically how all publishing deals work. Once the advance is recouped, you start collecting your allotted share for subsequent earnings. The Beatles and Bob Dylan are examples of artists who signed exclusive publishing agreements. For all the money they made, they gave half of it away. In the words of Ed Pierson at Warner/Chappell Music, "These types of one-sided deals made publishing companies huge cash cows."

Co-publishing Agreements

> In some cases, the publishing company further reduces the writer's share of income by taking an additional fee of up to 10 percent for administration charges.

Rumor has it that after Brian Lane (the manager of Yes), balked at the idea of relinquishing 100 percent of the band's copyright to its songs and 50 percent of its earnings (by about 1975), publishing deals finally began to change for the better. Enter the concept of "co-publishing." Co-publishing deals (also called "co-pub deals") have become the most common arrangements today for the writer/performer, especially for those who have already procured a recording deal. In fact, the co-pub deal has become the norm for many individual writers as well.

In co-publishing agreements, the publishing company still administers the entire copyright for the full term; however, the writer now gets some benefit by transferring only 50 percent of copyright ownership. Therefore, the sharing of income in co-publishing deals is essentially 75 percent to the writer, 25 percent to the publisher. The writer receives not only the 100 percent of the writer's share, which is 50 percent of the whole, but 50 percent of the publisher's share, which is 25 percent of the whole (see pie diagram). This essentially means that for every $100,000 in monies collected by the publishing company, the writer is now credited $75,000, and the publishing company takes in the remaining $25,000 (as opposed to the 50/50 income split I discussed in single-song and exclusive agreements above). This is by far more advantageous for the writer than the single song and exclusive songwriter agreements.

CO-PUBLISHING AREEMENTS

The Song

Writer's Share

Publisher's Share

Administration Agreements

There are alternatives to the aforementioned agreements. Rather than receiving a substantial advance for the transfer of copyrights, as with the above agreements, the writer can retain 100 percent ownership (acting as a self-publisher) and pay a fee to a publishing company to specifically handle administrative duties (see pie diagram). These types of arrangements, known as "administration agreements" (also called "admin deals") have become increasingly popular these days for the artist who writes and performs his or her own music or otherwise has a means to place songs. The term of most administration agreements ranges from only 3 to 7 years. Fees range from 10 to 20 percent of the gross income collected, but are more commonly 15 percent. If an artist ends up being successful, his or her willingness to receive either a small advance or no advance in exchange for retaining ownership and a greater share of the profits really pays off. Hey, it worked for both R.E.M. and

ADMINISTRATION AGREEMENTS

The Song

Writer's Share

Publisher's Share

15 to 20 percent fee

Prince, artists who signed administration deals early in their careers. They bet on themselves and hit the jackpot.

Subpublishing Agreements

Subpublishing agreements (also called "sub pub" deals) are very similar to administration deals, except that they relate specifically to foreign territories. In fact, subpublishing deals are often described as "limited territory administration agreements." Keep in mind that most of the agreements mentioned above cover both the territories of the United States and those overseas (contractually known as "the world"). Therefore, it's not necessary to enter into a subpublishing agreement yourself unless you choose to handle business by self-publishing (which I'll discuss in a moment).

SUBPUBLISHING AGREEMENT

The Song

Writer's Share

Publisher's Share

15 to 25 percent fee

In sub-pub deals, the writer/self-publisher retains 100 percent of the copyrights and assigns the rights to the foreign subpublisher to handle all administrative duties. Subpublisher's fees range from 15 to 25 percent of the monies collected (see pie diagram, p. 232). Advances against your future earnings are not uncommon. The term of most subpublishing agreements ranges from three to seven years. Remember that the collection of income in foreign territories is far more complex than it is in the United States, so the services of a subpublisher are absolutely necessary when your music is going to be released in foreign territories (that is, if you don't want your money to go uncollected and ultimately be lost—but who in their right mind would want that to happen?).

Self-Publishing

To take the concept of retaining 100 percent ownership and control of copyrights to its farthest extreme, the writer can act as a self-publisher by directly becoming a member of the various collec-

DECISIONS. DECISIONS. Initially, if an artist can settle for what is usually a smaller advance (or none at all), an admin deal appears to be more appealing than the co-pub deal, since the writer gives up a lesser percentage share of earnings with no transfer of copyright ownership. But one must consider whether the gamble of taking a lesser advance or no advance at all with an admin deal is really worth it. After all, the odds are unfortunately against you being a success. Attorney Jeffrey Light looks at it this way: "The difference in income between a co-pub and an admin deal is usually just ten percent. Is ten percent worth the gamble of not taking a larger advance or no advance at all? In the one in a million chance you become as successful as, say Metallica , and you make a lot of money, will ten percent really matter anyway?"

tion organizations in the United States, such as ASCAP, BMI, or SESAC (to collect performance royalties), and the Harry Fox Agency (to collect mechanical royalties and issue synch licenses). A subpublisher can then be established to handle foreign administration. Fees run from 6 to 10 percent for Harry Fox and from 15 to 25 percent for a foreign subpublisher. In this scenario, the writer/self-publisher now maintains a greater level of control and a larger share of the profits than he or she does in the various publishing options discussed in this chapter, but *does not receive an advance or the various services provided by an experienced music publisher.*(See the following pie diagram.)

SELF-PUBLISHING

The Song

Writer's Share

Publisher's Share

4 to 10 percent fee (US)
15 to 25 percent fee
(Foreign)

Writers may choose to become self-publishers for a number of reasons:

+ They were not offered a publishing deal (very common).
+ They were not offered a large enough advance to entice them to make the deals mentioned above (also extremely common).
+ They write and perform their own songs, or otherwise have resources to place songs, and choose to hold on to their publishing rights and gamble on the big
"pay off" down the road (also very common).

Ed Pierson at Warner/Chappell Music reminds us that, "If you hold onto your rights, then you'd better be prepared to do the work. Assuming you already have a means to publish your works, it's absolutely essential that you make sure your monies are properly collected, especially in foreign territories, or otherwise you will lose money. Many artists start off as subpublishers, but with the good fortune of even moderate success, they eventually see the advantages in entering into an admin or co-pub deal."

Michael Eames of Penn Music Group adds:

"Deciding on what to do with your publishing rights is always a matter of doing the math and weighing the pros and cons. If you were to be hugely successful, it [would be] quite lucrative to hold onto your publishing. Paul Simon, Bruce Springsteen, and Diane Warren are all successful writers who own their own publishing. But a publishing deal can also bring opportunities to the table that wouldn't otherwise exist. The decision at hand is whether you feel it is worth giving up partial or complete ownership in your songs in order to get access to these contacts and opportunities. Also, if an advance is being offered, does it make sense to accept? Any advance is just your own money that you will have to pay back, and sometimes at a high cost compared to a typical bank loan. If the success you achieve is due to the publisher's efforts, then it makes sense to have done the deal. If you're responsible for the success and the publisher has done nothing, you've given up ownership and control in your creations to someone you wish you hadn't. Just find people who believe in you and [who] will work with you over the long term. That is invaluable."

SELF-PUBLISHING: STARTING YOUR OWN PUBLISHING COMPANY

Self publishing becomes an option for writers who weren't offered a publishing deal, who weren't offered the "right" publishing deal, or who chose to hold onto their publishing rights in order to gamble on the big "pay-off" with a greater share of the earnings. In any case, here's a very brief overview of the bare minimum you have to accomplish to get started.

Affiliate with ASCAP or BMI

The first step in starting your own publishing company is to contact one of the two performing rights organizations (ASCAP or BMI), affiliate yourself as a writer and a publisher, and fill out the necessary clearance forms. Yes, I'm aware I'm leaving SESAC out of this discussion, but that's only because you need to be asked by SESAC to join. SESAC is by far a smaller organization and is therefore selective in choosing its members. Unless you're a fairly established writer, or you feel you're going to be the next Diane Warren (who, for those of you that don't know, is an extremely successful songwriter), it's not likely you're going to start with this organization.

Publisher Affiliation. As a self-publisher, you're required to affiliate with one of the performing rights organizations, and to pick a name for your music publishing company—for instance, "John Doe Song Works." You're also asked to include two more alternate titles (three names total) in case your first choice is already being used by another music publisher. The less common the name you choose is, the better chance you'll have of no one else using it. As of this writing, the fee for affiliating with ASCAP as a publisher is $50 per year. BMI charges a one-time fee of $150 if you're an individually owned company, and $250 if you're a partnership or corporation.

Writer Affiliation. Writers are required to have a separate writer affiliation with the performing rights organizations. Remember that the performing rights organizations always send the "writer's share" of earnings directly to the writer, regardless of who the music publisher is—even if it's you. So again, whether you self-publish or not, you must always register as a composition's writer. Oh, and in case you're wondering, you cannot affiliate with two performing rights organizations at the same time. However, should you be the joint writer of a song, your partner can affiliate with one organization while you affiliate with the other, as long as song percentages are cross-registered to match. In other words, an ASCAP writer can register as 50 percent writer of one song, while a BMI writer can register as 50 percent writer of the same song. The fee for affiliating with ASCAP is currently $10 a year. BMI charges nothing.

Clearance Forms. As both the writer and publisher of your songs, it's absolutely essential that you provide your performing rights society with detailed information for every composition so that you can be entered into their system and paid. More importantly, because a song is divided into two separate and equal categories—the "writer's share" and the "publisher's share"—you must indicate the percentages in the compositions you own. If you're the sole writer of a composition, you own 100 percent of the writer's share, and 100 percent of the publisher's share. However, if you write a composition with your band and you're dividing the credit equally, then each member owns both 25 percent of the writer's share (4 x 25 = 100), as well as 25 percent of the publisher's share (4 x 25 = 100). It's not uncommon for bands to form one publishing company under a partnership agreement or corporation. Under these circumstances, all of the songs are registered to that company as the sole publisher. Incomes are then divided under the terms of the partnership.

Filing a DBA or FNS

The next thing you have to do to become a self-publisher is to file for a DBA statement with your county clerk's office (see your local yellow pages). A DBA, or "doing business as" statement, sometimes called a "fictitious business name," or FBN, statement. The reason why you need one of these lovely pieces of paper is to enable you to cash checks made out to that clever publishing company name you've come up with. Can you imagine the headaches you'd have in the bank when you try to cash a check made out to John Doe Song Works without one piece of identification proving the connection? That's what a DBA is for.

Getting a DBA is easy. After filling out specific forms furnished by your county clerk, paying a fee ranging from around $45 to $60 dollars (fees vary from place to place), and printing the contents of the form in a local newspaper (a procedure for which your county clerk will provide assistance), you'll receive your certificate soon after.

One more thing: since your bank won't allow you to deposit money into an account with a different name (such as one under your personal name), you also need to set up a bank account under the name of your publishing company. When opening a bank account, you may need to provide a social security number or a federal tax identification number (which, for a business, is basically the equivalent of an individual social security number). A tax identification number can be obtained through applications filed with the IRS. (Contact the Internal Revenue Service at 1-800-829-1040.)

Filing Copyright Forms

Remember when we discussed filing copyright registration forms earlier in this chapter? Well, should you have already filled out forms in your own name, you have to refile them using your publishing company's name as the copyright claimant. Again, if you have any questions regarding how to fill out a copyright form, the copyright office will be more than happy to assist you. (Contact the U.S. Copyright Office at 1-800-688-9889.)

Other Administrative Duties

Okay, you've finally got your publishing company set up. You've registered with ASCAP and BMI, so you know you can start receiving performance statements, but how do you ensure the proper collection of other incomes derived from your songs, such as mechanical royalties, synchronization fees, print royalties, and subpublishing monies?

Mechanical Royalties. As previously discussed in the "Mechanical Royalties" section of this chapter, when a record company wants to use one of your songs, they'll ask you to sign a mechanical license. The license is fairly straightforward, asking you to indicate your shares in the song, and at what rate you agree to license the composition to them. Remember that when you're a signed recording artist or a cowriter with a signed artist, the mechanical licensing rate for your songs may be less than the statutory rate, in accordance with the controlled composition clause found in most recording agreements. In any case, record companies can then send you your mechanical royalty statements directly, or if you choose, you can have a major mechanical rights collection society such as the Harry Fox Agency both issue mechanical licenses and collect royalties for you. Again, the benefit of using the Fox Agency is that they periodically audit record companies—and disturbingly, almost all audits show an underpayment of royalties to publishers. The Harry Fox Agency charges a percentage of your gross earning which is currently 6 percent, but is subject to change.

Synchronization Fees. When someone wants to use one of your songs in a film, television commercial, television show, etc., they'll contact you and ask you to agree to a synch license. But unless you're banging on advertising agencies' doors, schmoozing with directors at parties, and generally being a salesman, it's not likely your phone is going to be ringing off the hook whether you're a signed artist or not—unless, of course, you have a hit song and your label's film and TV department is on the hunt for you. Hey, remember what Ed Pierson at Warner/Chappell Music said: "If you want to keep your rights, then you have to do the work." And unless you have some experience negotiating licenses, it's not easy to know what you should charge for synch fees—there are a lot of factors involved (see our discussion of synchronization fees earlier in this chapter). Therefore, you might want to ask your good friends at the Harry Fox Agency to help. The Fox Agency has a synch department that will issue licenses and collect fees. The Fox Agency charges a fee based on gross earnings ranging around 10 percent. But make no mistake— the Fox Agency is not going to run around plugging your songs. As a self-publisher, that's your job.

> Check out *The Film and Television Music Guide* (published by the Music Business Registry) for a list of contacts that include music supervisors, film composers and their agents, music editors, music libraries, and may others who can help you get your music in film and television. See www. musicregistry.com.

Print Royalties. What we've discussed for synchronization above applies for print. Unless you have a hit song, it's not likely print companies are going to be tracking you down. There are really only a few print companies in the U.S. anyway; the most important are Cherry Lane, Hal Leonard, Warner Bros. Publications, and Mel Bay. If you're aggressive enough, you might have a chance at striking a deal. Anything's possible.

Subpublishing Incomes. Remember that in order to collect subpublishing incomes, you must find a subpublisher in the territory in which your music is to be published. You can ask the record or film company releasing your music overseas to recommend a subpublisher. You can also contact one of the performing rights or mechanical rights agencies (such as GEMA in Germany or JAS-RAC in Japan) and ask them for a list of their registered local publishers. (If you have a song being released in a foreign territory, most subpublishers will at least be happy to collect money on your behalf.) And last but not least, a far easier approach to the subpublishing game is to seek one U.S. publishing company that has worldwide conglomerates (e.g., Warner/Chappell Music, EMI Music Publishing, BMG Music Publishing, Universal Music Publishing Group, Sony/ATV Publishing, etc.), rather than setting up individual subpublishing deals in several foreign territories. If they think representing you is worth their time from an economic standpoint, a deal can be established to cover "the world," except for the United States and Canada. Considering the time differences and language barrier of doing business abroad, this approach to administering foreign territories makes doing business much easier.

Q & A WITH NEIL GILLIS

Neil Gillis is the Vice President of A&R and Advertising at Warner/Chappell Music, Inc. In the following interview, he provides an overview of this chapter and music publishing in general.

Q: Musicians often feel that if they sign a recording deal with, say Warner Bros. Records, then they automatically have to sign a deal with Warner/Chappell Music. This, however, is not the case. Please elaborate.

N.G: Most multinational companies today work in a synergistic way in terms of trying to at least have a writer/artist [who is] signed to a record label consider their sister publishing company, or otherwise to have a writer/artist signed to a publishing company consider some record labels within the publisher's family. However, most writer/artists have a team of personal advisors making them aware of how they can benefit in a larger sense by shopping their publishing rights. What a writer decides to do with his or her publishing is essentially up to that writer.

There is one caveat, however, [that is] worth mentioning. There are instances where artists signing with certain smaller independent record companies are asked to sign over their publishing rights as part of the recording agreement or the deal's off! This can be disadvantageous for two reasons: (1) The record company may not be an experienced music publisher, or have an affiliation to one, and (2) publishing earnings may be cross-collateralized with recording expenses. In other words, you won't earn one dime in mechanical royalties, for instance, until all recording and recoupable expenses are recouped. If one does sign a deal with a label who wants the publishing as well, I'd simply caution that writer/artist to be careful with the deal points so that they benefit as much as possible from keeping the rights distinct.

Q: When we discuss entering into most publishing agreements, we talk about the transfer or selling of copyright ownership. This often implies feelings of great loss and anxiety for many musicians, causing them to dwell on what they're giving up rather than on what they're getting. Please comment.

N.G: First, while there are many horror stories out there regarding people who gave up their publishing rights, this is the exception rather than the rule in today's legitimate world. Let's use a current co-publishing deal as one example of how the rights are split. If you're the sole writer and publisher of a composition, and you enter into a traditional co-publishing deal, you normally wind up with 75 percent of the song's earnings (50 percent as the writer, and 25 percent as the co-publisher). The publishing company you entered into the deal with only receives 25 percent and administers 100 percent of the rights. When one looks at it this way, and when you consider what you get both economically and in services, it's a much healthier picture.

Second, most deals today contain approval language. By this I mean language that sets out what a publisher can or cannot do with your songs. If a writer is very sensitive to how his or her work will be exploited, this can be a very important clause in the publishing agreement.

Third, one must remember the value of all the behind-the-scenes services you're receiving from that publisher. Whether it's helping you secure a record deal, getting one of your songs cut with a major artist, placing one of your compositions in a national advertising campaign, or assisting you in solving a royalty/licensing issue in a foreign territory, the list of these services can be quite extensive and valuable.

Overall, I think it's safe to say that writer/artists are in a much better position today to enter into publishing deals than they were in prior years. As long as you're represented by legitimate people and you're dealing with a reputable publisher, the process and end result should be healthy for all concerned.

Q.: Okay, let's get into the actual negotiation of deals now. When entering into publishing agreements where copyright transfer occurs, artists typically receive a reasonable publishing advance against future earnings. However, the whole game of holding out for the largest publishing advance often takes a back seat to other important contract matters. Please comment.

N.G: Though money is important, there are other deal points that can be equally, if not more, important. The two that come to mind are "reversion of copyright," and "prior approvals." While there are many more, these are two quality examples.

First, reversion of copyright is commonplace in deals today. Simply put, it's a point in time after the termination of the deal when your rights return to you. That can be very important in terms of how your career moves forward. Upon getting your copyrights back, assuming you had any success, you can renegotiate for a larger advance or benefit by earning a greater share of monies by virtue of owning 100 percent of the songs.

Second, prior approvals are vital in that they are your control factor in terms of how a publisher can and cannot utilize your works.

On a side note, one must consider the objective of managers and attorneys advising their clients to hold out for the larger advance. Though most artists' managers and attorneys in the business are straightforward and have the best interest[s] of their clients in mind, there are some folks out there who may simply wish to bring in a large front-loaded advance amount because it could have ramification[s] [for] how they're paid for their services (i.e., the greater the advance, the greater their commission). If your representative is capable of negotiating quality deal points on a majority of the important issues mentioned above, and they get you a large up-front advance, then you have the best of both worlds. Just be sure to understand that one does not always accompany the other, and it is in your best interest to have both issues met.

Q.: Can you please discuss how "agreement terms" are structured in publishing contracts, including a mention of option periods, delivery commitments, and any other information you feel relevant to our discussion? Additionally, please clarify the difference between the "agreement term" and "copyright duration," a topic which is often a great source of confusion for musicians.

N.G: The best course here might be to simply define each of the terms you mention.

"Agreement term" is language found in publishing agreements that specifically relates to how long the publishing deal will last. (It has nothing to do with copyright duration as you'll see in a moment.) Agreement terms are usually based on a certain number of years, or in many cases, a certain number of LP's.

"Copyright duration" is different than the agreement term. It deals with language found in publishing agreements that specifically relates to the amount of time the publisher will continue to own your song [that were created during the term] after your agreement term has expired. For instance, the publisher may continue to hold on to your songs after the agreement term for the full life of copyright (L.o.C), or in the case you've negotiated a reversion of copyright clause into your agreement, the publisher may have to revert the rights back to you at a specified period of time (say, ten years after the agreement term expires). It all depends on the finer points of your agreement and what you're able to negotiate.

"Option periods" is language in publishing agreements that deals with the publisher's choice or "option" to extend the term of your deal upon it expiring. For instance, if your publishing agreement is time based, your publisher may exercise its option (or multiple options) to continue the agreement for another year(s). If your agreement is LP-delivery based, your publisher may exercise its option (or multiple options) to continue your agreement for another LP(s).

"Delivery commitments" is language in publishing agreements that defines what you're responsible for delivering to your publisher during the term for your agreement. For instance, your agreement may require you to write a certain number of "commercially acceptable" songs, or it may require you to write a certain number of songs that get recorded and released by you, or by other artists who desire to use your songs. This language is extremely important for artists to consider when negotiating their deals since they can end up getting stuck in a deal that theoretically never ends.

Q: I once heard you mention that the "four food groups" of music publishing income are mechanical royalties, performance royalties, synchronization fees, and print royalties—with mechanicals and performances being the primary source of income. Where does sampling fit into this total picture?

N.G: Sampling truly fits into the picture as an additional source of income. When another artist uses a sample of your song to enhance an individual track, they must clear it with the music publisher and pay a sample fee. In the case that the sample usage is so significant that it essentially becomes the hook to the song, the user may even be required to give up a portion if not all of the copyright or [they will] otherwise not be granted the license. Sampling was once particular to the folks in the hip-hop and rap worlds, but has really become mainstream in its usage. Rather than outright covering an artist's song (as was commonly done in the past), artists today use sampling and [create] a new version so to speak. Sampling actually became a sort of "covers of the 90s" [thing] in that one popular song might be utilized by many different artists. Therefore, it became a lucrative business for those songs and catalogs that were popular to sample.

Q: Can you touch on publishing rights in the digital millennium in terms of what types of payment artists will receive for a digital download, or for streaming music on the Internet? Needless to say, it seems to be the source of much confusion at the moment and probably will continue to be so for many years to come.

N.G: This is a tough question to answer. As you can see by reading any of the trades as of late, we're still in the initial stages of discovering how to create a payment structure that works for all concerned. All I can say is that from a publishing perspective, a download constitutes both a mechanical and a performance royalty. Streaming music with no ability to download appears to be more of a performance right. None of these issues has been clearly defined, and everyone appears to have a difference of opinion. Stay tuned. It'll be pretty exciting to see how everything pans out.

Q: I held this off till the very end, but I'd like you to comment on an historical event that's still known to freak musicians out about publishing deals: the highly publicized sale of Paul McCartney's catalogue. While attempting to repossess his songs from a U.K. publishing company with which he made an unfavorable deal, McCartney lost out when the publishing company sold the rights to the songs to the highest (or richest) bidder,

Michael Jackson. It's stories like this that make musicians want to hold onto their publishing rights and never enter into a deal with a publishing company. Please elaborate.

N.G: I was not involved in the transaction you mentioned. However, I do understand that it was typical of the way copyrights are "bought" and "sold," which I will explain here.

If a publishing company is able to "buy" your songs at the inception of a deal for the full life of copyright (as was most likely the case in the deal between a U.K publisher and the Beatles), that company would also typically insist that they have the right to assign those copyrights to whomever they please, as long as the original agreement terms made with the artist are honored.

As mentioned, it was a U.K. publisher that purchased certain rights from the Beatles, and later in the history of these copyrights, that publisher therefore decided to "sell." The new owner, Michael Jackson, after having paid a handsome price, obtained all rights including the need to continue to honor the terms of the original songwriter's agreement with McCartney. (These terms may have included paying McCartney a certain percentage of the song earnings, giving him the right of prior approvals, etc.). I don't know the specific terms of the agreement. In any case, this should serve as yet another reminder to musicians that music is not just an art form, it's also a very serious business, and it needs to be treated as such. They don't call it the music "business" for nothing.

CHAPTER 13

Live Performances
and Touring

At one time or another, almost every musician has seen a shiny tour bus driving down the road and imagined how great it would be to be on tour in a band. To travel from city to city, performing night after night: what an exciting experience that would be! But as you're about to learn in this chapter, touring is not just about fun and adventure; there's a lot more involved than what may initially meet the eye.

THE LONG ROAD TO SUCCESS

Touring is one of the most basic ways for artists to introduce their music to the marketplace. By hitting the road and performing live before audiences around the country, interviewing with radio stations and the press, visiting record stores, and connecting with the fans, a new group can build a grassroots following of music lovers that will loyally support them for years to come. A classic example of this is Guns N' Roses, which was out on the road for almost nine months before its record *Appetite For Destruction* started to take off. With a great live show and unique brand of raw "in your face" rock, the band slowly but surely won over more and more fans, which subsequently led to increased record sales, to radio stations and MTV playing their single, to concert audiences growing into the thousands. The rest, as they say, is history.

What few people understand is that *touring is a very serious and expensive business*. Every year we read stories in magazines and newspapers about artists who sell thousands of tickets to their live performances at costs above $50 a pop (and more). It's no wonder most people think there are millions of dollars to be made from hitting the road. Though major artists have earned substantial sums of money through touring, DO NOT BE DECEIVED! The truth is that it usually takes a long time before a group can expect to turn a profit from performing live—if it ever happens at all!

THE VENUES YOU CAN PLAY:

◆ Coffeehouses and bars: approximate capacity 20 to 100 people

◆ Clubs: approximate capacity 100 to 2000 people

◆ Amphitheaters: approximate capacity 3500 to 20,000 people

◆ Sheds (or outdoor theaters): approximate capacity 3500 to 20,000 people

◆ Arenas: approximate capacity 10,000 to 35,000 people

◆ Stadiums: approximate capacity 35,000 to 300,000 people

Whether you're in a band that's playing local clubs, you're part of a new group that's just been signed to a record contract, or you dream of one day making it all the way to the big leagues of touring, what you're about to read may intrigue you.

Your Local Club Scene

"A journey of a thousand miles begins with a single step."—Lao-tzu

Before discussing touring, it's important to take a moment to briefly discuss performances at the local club level, since this is where almost all bands begin. In the beginning, most groups will strictly perform for the love of music and in the hope of one day getting a recording deal. You start out booking your own gigs and playing coffeehouses, bars, and small clubs in the early part of the week for free, and you may even have to buy your own tickets and sell them to your friends and family just to make your money back (a concept known as "paying to play" in Los Angeles). As your following of fans begins to build, you will move up to playing weekend gigs and you may even get a guaranteed fee for your performance. Fees may range anywhere from $50 to $250. In some cases, you may even earn a straight percentage of the door charges from the people that pay to come see you. For instance, a club owner may pay you 100 percent of the door admissions and expect to make his profit from selling alcohol. At this level of live performing, though, practically any arrangement can exist. And until you have a record pressed and a record company (or other backer) that is willing to promote you, you're *probably* going to be playing your local market and surrounding areas for a long time before it ever makes sense to hit the road. Why? You'll find out in a minute. Just remember one thing: playing your local clubs is a necessary part of developing your career, from finding your target demographic audience, to establishing your identity or "brand," to building a buzz around your group. In fact, the more your band can develop before getting that coveted record deal, and the greater a fan base you can build, the bigger and better a deal you're going to get. You'll simply be less of a financial risk to record companies. So hang in there.

The Early Stages of Touring

"A record release is the flagship on which a tour is launched."

—Richard Bishop, Henry Rollins' manager

The first time many bands hit the road is after they've pressed a record and have a record cpany (or some other backer) willing to promote them. With a record in hand, a band can simultaneously

TAKING CHARGE. As the old saying goes, "You can't save souls in an empty church," and the band Hootie & the Blowfish was definitely not playing empty clubs before getting signed. Hootie & the Blowfish was a hugely successful club and college band in its hometown before it was discovered by a low level A&R man at Atlantic Records. The band had even recorded its own album to sell in "mom-and-pop" record stores in surrounding regions. The albums actually sold well, too! The band created such a buzz in the industry on its own that one representative at Atlantic Records was paraphrased as saying, "I don't care if these blowfish guys suck, just find them and give them a deal." When its record was finally released by Atlantic, sales figures in the first week were quite impressive, thanks to the loyal grassroots fans the band established in their small region. That was enough to get Atlantic excited about the group and to put some full-court marketing muscle behind them to break them throughout the world.

establish its name in the press, on the radio and on the Internet, and in retail stores across the country, which will lead to more and more fans attending its live shows. But this is not as easy as it sounds, and without the marketing expertise as well as the financial support of someone like a record label to set up such promotional events, hitting the road *may* otherwise make no sense. Why? Momentum is everything; everything has to hit at once if you expect to make an impact on a national level. A new band will only last on the road for so long before it simply can't afford to tour any longer. New groups with a record deal can only command fees in the range of $250 to $1200 per club performance. This may sound like a lot compared to what you're used to getting paid for performing locally, but after budgeting in tour expenses, this equation simply does not add up to a profit. Tour expenses may include the following:

+ Transportation such as a passenger van and a trailer to haul your musical gear
+ Fuel to get your vehicle from point A to point B
+ Tolls for the state highways on which you travel
+ Hotels to provide you with a decent night's rest and a hot shower
+ Food for nourishment and to relieve hangovers
+ Insurance for theft or damage to your instruments and vehicle
+ Crew members (respectfully known as roadies) to help set up the gear and drive your band and equipment from gig to gig

Minimizing tour expenses will help. Traveling in a van with one crew member, sleeping five to a hotel room, and allowing for salaries that are just enough for everyone to eat at fast food restaurants are all sacrifices your band can make to save money (and to go insane). But even then, a new group signed to a major label can easily return home from a tour owing money. Expenses may initially be paid by the record company in the form of some-

> Merchandising (i.e., the sale of T-shirts, hats, stickers, etc.) is a common means by which a band can help finance a tour. For major artists, merchandising can even generate substantial profits. Merchandising will be discussed in detail in Chapter 14.

thing called tour support (an additional advance to help subsidize a tour), but these monies must eventually be paid back. As I've explained in Chapter 11, tour support is 100 percent recoupable from the band's future record sales. That's right! Tour support is basically a loan in exchange for the opportunity to go out and promote your band and record. So, your time on the road must be spent wisely. In the words of manager Tom Atensio, who has worked with artists such as No Doubt and Perry Farrell, "It's not enough for artists to play and look cool. They also have to work their asses off. If a band is not signing autographs and collecting names for its website [email list], they're not working."

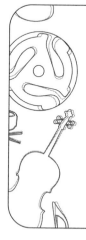

ROAD DOGS. One group that made every sacrifice possible in order to tour and promote the sale of its record was Everclear. After the group finished recording its first album for a small independent record label, its members borrowed money from their bosses at work and hit the road in a van to play surrounding cities. The band returned home a week later, worked at their day jobs for another month to pay back their bosses, and hit the road again. All the while, their fan base grew larger and larger. After a year-and-a-half of repeating this touring/work cycle, they caught the attention of Capitol Records, which signed Everclear and re-released their record in 1994. Thanks to the band's fan base and Capitol's "priority" marketing support, the band's CD quickly sold millions, establishing them as a very viable touring entity. Needless to say, Everclear's hard work on the road finally paid off.

Mid-Level Touring

"Watch the pennies and the dollars take care of themselves."—Danny Goldberg, music industry executive

Once a group reaches the level where its record is starting to sell well, its single is getting played on the radio, and the number of fans attending its concerts is increasing, the fees it can receive for a live performance will be much higher. Let's call this stage in your career "mid-level touring." Mid-level bands may receive guaranteed fees in the range of $5000 to $15,000 for headlining larger clubs or small theaters. In some cases, a group may even earn a percentage of income based on the total number of tickets sold (which will be discussed in detail under "How You're Paid for Live Performance Deals"). Yet despite these increases in fees, a band might only break even by the end of a tour or, if they are careful with handling finances, earn a small profit at best. This is due to the inevitable increase in expenses at this level of touring. Additional tour costs may include the following:

+ A tour bus (complete with a bus driver) for a more comfortable and sane means of travel
+ A trailer to haul the band's equipment
+ A larger crew to set up and break down the band's equipment
+ A live-sound engineer to help replicate the nuances of the band's studio recording
+ A tour manager to ensure that day-to-day business matters are run smoothly, to collect the money at the end of the night, to make sure the artists get on and off stage on time, and to coordinate press interviews

- Additional hotel accommodations for the bus driver, crew, and tour manager
- A business manager to help put together the tour budget and insure that all finances are in order and that everyone is paid
- A talent agent to coordinate tour dates, determine the pricing of tickets, negotiate performance fees, and collect deposits from the concert promoter in advance of the show (typically 50 percent)
- A personal manager (whom you've already had for a long time at this stage of your career) to hire touring personnel, inform the record company of the tour dates so that they can set up press interviews for the band, help the talent agent coordinate tour dates, and negotiate performance dates

The more a band tours, the more efficient it should become at minimizing expenses and profiting from the road.

As you can see, though the band may begin earning more money per performance, it can also incur many more expenses. You may have already been subjected to some of these expenses at lower levels of touring. Nevertheless, in case it hasn't sunk in already, keep one thing in mind: *you pay for it all!*

The Big Leagues of Touring

"It's hard to make money by touring. Managers make money, the people in the service organizations make money, the crews make money, but there are so many times when a band spends six or seven months on the road and ends up with very little to show for it, even when a tour is grossing millions of dollars."

—*Bud Prager, manager for Foreigner*

If a group can work hard, overcome incredible odds, and make it to the level at which it's headlining larger venues, the guarantees it can earn are much greater. Bands whose records are selling

WHAT YOU BREAK, YOU PAY FOR. Unaware of (or blatantly disregarding) the financial responsibilities involved with touring, many bands will still perceive it strictly as fun, even to the point of destruction! The legendary stories about television sets flying across hotel rooms are actually true. But all damages ranging from smashed television sets to cigarette burns on tour bus seats to golf balls slammed into hotel walls are deducted from the band's touring income. This is not the worst of it. Sometimes the entire group can be banned from certain hotels or hotel chains, from using certain tour bus companies, from being re-booked by certain promoters, and even from playing in certain states. The Who was banned from staying in Holiday Inns after drummer Keith Moon smeared a custard pie in the hotel manager's face. Although this episode was by far the least of Keith's antics, it still cost the band a great inconvenience. Bassist Nikki Sixx of Mötley Crüe, whose road stories go head to head with those of the most destructive bands, reflects on their past in the book, *Dirt:* "Words like consequences, responsibility, morality, and self-control didn't apply to us. Or so we thought."

upwards into the hundreds of thousands of units may earn guarantees in the range of $50,000 or more for playing amphitheaters, and often as much as $250,000 or more when progressing to playing large stadiums. (The Backstreet Boys were reported to have earned guarantees of $1 million for stadium dates in 2001.) An additional percentage of ticket sales is also typically offered to the band at this level of touring. For example, the group may receive a guaranteed fee *plus* a percentage of ticket sales (which I will discuss later in "How You're Paid for Live Performance Deals"). Nevertheless, while it may appear as though a group can now earn substantial profits on the road, it must still be very careful with its expenses. Additional expenses may include the following:

The challenge for any artist putting on a live performance is to make it exciting, to deliver a statement, and return home from a tour with a profit. In 2002, *Rolling Stone* magazine reported that Britney Spears grossed over $23.7 million on her concert tour. But due to inflated costs, sources say she netted less than 8 percent. Still not bad, but this gives one an idea of the tremendous expenses. Custom stages and risers, a climatic rainstorm, costume changes, dancers, and 18 tractor-trailor trucks sure added up for the diva.

+ Massive stage set designs, such as the huge television screens U2 set up behind them on the Zooropa tour, or the gigantic wall Pink Floyd had erected on stage on the The Wall tour
+ Special effects, such as the mechanical contraption Tommy Lee had hooked up to his drum set that extended him over the audience and spun him around 360 degrees, or the climatic rainstorm Britney Spears used assimilating a real rainstorm on stage
+ Pyrotechnic explosions to add a bang to the band's presentation
+ Sound and lighting systems, which groups must rent at this level of touring
+ Trucks (complete with drivers) to haul the sound, lights, and staging
+ Loaders, who unload and load the trucks
+ Lighting crews, who operate the lights during a performance
+ Lighting directors, who ensure the artistic quality of the light show
+ Riggers, who climb above the stage and hang the sound and light gear
+ Monitor engineers to ensure the best quality sound on stage and to assist the sound engineer
+ Elaborate stage costumes in order to look outrageous or glamorous for the fans, such as the many costumes Britney Spears wears during her performances
+ Dancers to enhance the presentation of the live performances
+ Wardrobe personnel to take care of the elaborate costumes

As if those expenses weren't enough, when factoring in five-star hotel accommodations, rented limousines, and perhaps even Leer jets as an extravagant means of transportation for the band, tour costs can reach into the millions of dollars. Some bands may even get into "hubbing," when they centralize themselves in one major city, settle into one hotel, and fly back and forth between performances. Although hubbing is more comfortable for the band because they don't have to unpack and pack their suitcases every day, it gets expensive since they incur round-trip costs for each gig. When all is said and done, though the guarantees for playing larger venues are high, costs can quickly eat up profits and leave you with nothing but red ink when the tour is over.

AN INTERESTING FACT. At the end of a concert performance, when the lead singer screams, "To hell with the establishment, we're gonna' play all night for you guys," it may seem really cool, but it can also cost the band thousands of dollars. If the hall in which the group is performing is regulated by the union, the group can be charged for playing even one minute over curfew time. In addition, keep in mind that there are also staffs of people waiting to load the trucks with all of the stage equipment. Every single one of them must be paid overtime fees! So the next time your favorite band begins its concert 90 minutes late (Axl Rose of Guns N' Roses was notorious for doing this), you better believe it's costing them. And when the sound system cuts out and the lights are suddenly turned on, you may have a good idea why it happened. In efforts to avoid major fines and overtime for everyone who helps put on a show, the band got *cut off.*

As one way to minimize expenses, some major artists choose to play smaller venues (such as theaters) for two or three consecutive performances in one city rather than performing in a larger venue such as a stadium for a single night. Not only does this create excitement, since tickets are more likely to sell out quickly, but a band can save money by keeping the equipment set up. The costs for tearing down equipment, traveling to the next city, and setting it up again can be very expensive. Playing consecutive nights in one venue also spreads out the band's exposure in a particular market and increases its availability for press and promotion. Rather than booking Sting into the Staples Center (a large venue in Los Angeles) for one night, agent Ian Copeland booked the artist at a smaller venue called The Greek Theater for three consecutive nights. The shows were an incredible success.

> A band needs to understand that it is a product. It has a responsibility to present itself in the best possible way to the people that pay for them to be there. If a group can establish itself as a reputable touring act, it can continue to work for years to come—even after record sales have dried up, radio stations are no longer playing its singles, and it's no longer in the "what's-happening-now category." Touring can therefore become a band's only livelihood for the long haul.

Corporate Sponsored Touring

"With public opinion on its side, nothing can fail."—Abraham Lincoln

If a group is able to reach the level at which corporate sponsors are willing to exclusively underwrite world tours, its profit potential is considerably greater. In fact, the potential is huge. Corporations have paid fees as high as $15 million for the rights to advertise their products in conjunction with an artist's tour. For example, Pepsi Cola worked exclusively with Michael Jackson, Sears Corporation sponsored Phil Collins, Jovan worked with the Rolling Stones, and Trojan worked with Ozzy Osbourne. Corporations can increase their sales base and profit margins by targeting audiences in the concert industry. Keep in mind, though, that an artist must decide whether he or she wants to be branded with a specific product. What will the effects be in the long run? It may be, for instance, damaging to a band's career to be sponsored by cigarette or alcohol companies, regardless of the amount of money they may offered.

Full Circle: Back to Where We Started

"The distance isn't important; it is only the first step that is difficult."   —*Marquise Du Deffand*

Before getting too excited about headlining stadiums, receiving guarantees into the hundreds of thousands of dollars, and attracting corporate sponsorships worth millions, you should also know that only a few groups ever make it to this level of touring. In fact, to zap you back to reality, if the record company with whom you're signed refuses to contribute funds in the form of tour support (which they often do), new bands may not get the chance to tour at all. The band may not be deemed a priority, which inevitably leads to it getting dropped. It happens all the time!

So the next time you see that shiny tour bus cruising down the road, you'll understand some very important facts: Touring requires hard work, a lot of sacrifices, and a great deal of tenacity. Although it may appear that you're making substantial profits, remember that every expense on the road comes out of your pocket. If you're conservative with your finances, and if you can use your valuable time on the road to promote your band and help sell records, the rest, as they say, is gravy.

HOW BANDS END UP ON THE RIGHT TOURS

Record labels are in business for one specific reason: to sell records. That is accomplished mostly through their expertise in retail distribution and radio promotion. Touring, though just as important to selling records, is generally the responsibility of an artist's personal manager. In fact, the record company will often evaluate the manager's strength based on whether or not he or she can deliver the right tours for their artist. The "right" tour doesn't necessarily refer to how large an audience a band plays for, but, rather, to what band it opens for. A new band just starting to tour will often need to rely on exposure from playing with more successful artists before it grows to the level at which it's headlining larger venues itself.

A couple of approaches that personal managers often take to ensure that their bands end up on the "right" tours are securing licensed talent agents, pulling favors from people in the business (such as other managers), using connections at the record label and publishing company, and something called "ticket buys," all of which I'll explain. Personal managers rely heavily on the marketing power and tour support dollars from the record company to help launch a band's career. In the words of personal manager Jeffrey Jampol, who has worked with artists such as Tal Bachman, "We want to utilize the record label in any way possible to help us build a brand name for our band."

Securing Talent Agents

First and foremost, managers will try to secure a licensed talent agent to find and procure employment for their artists and negotiate live perfomance deals. Agents' fees are typically ten percent of the gross, but can be as much as 20 percent under certain circumstances. Since new artists are usually not able to generate live performance fees high enough to make it worth an agent's efforts, it may be difficult to get a good talent agent involved at first. Says manager Jeffrey Jampol, "A new band may make a few hundred dollars a day if they're lucky, and it can cost them at least four to six thousand a week to tour. For this reason, over 50 percent of all new bands do not have a talent agent when first contracting their record deal." Therefore, the following steps may be more appropriate.

Pulling Favors

Concert promoters (the people who organize live events) are in the "putting-asses-in the-seats business." They hire and pay attractions that will make them money, whether it's a rodeo or a tractor pull. Again, as a new band, you're not all that attractive to promoters, and you'll need to attach yourself to a more successful band. Therefore, managers may network with other managers in the business and pull favors in order to get their band on a tour. Andy Gould of AGM Management commented that his smash young band Linkin Park could not understand why they initially could not take their friends' bands out on the road with them. Jokes Andy, "For every 100,000 records they sell, the band needs my opinion less and less. They couldn't take their friends because I have favors to repay to others that have helped me throughout the years. It's the way the music business works."

Using Connections at the Record Company

Managers may use the connections of a band's A&R representative at its record label to get the group on tour. The A&R rep is a band's best ally at the label, and it's the manager's responsibility to nurture this relationship. A&R reps will usually have numerous connections with bands and managers.

Utilizing Relationships at the Publishing Company

Assuming an artist has signed a music publishing deal, managers may also utilize relationships at the publishing company as a means to getting their artists on tour. Like A&R reps at the record label, publishers naturally have many relationships with bands and managers.

Ticket Buys

Managers may utilize marketing money from the publishing company or record label for "ticket buys" in order to get an artist on a tour. That is, a manager can promise another act that a certain number of tickets per market in a certain number of major markets will be bought. Since headlining acts want opening acts that can help sell tickets, ticket buys guarantee sales. Managers can also use ticket buys for ticket give-aways and contests promoted on the radio to further promote a show.

Offering Headlining Acts Point of Purchase Promotion

Managers may promise a headlining band "point of purchase" promotion in conjunction with their own artists in order to get on the right tour. Point of purchase is a term that refers to a retail promotion at the "point" the record is sold. For example, an advertisement in a record store may read: "On Sale—Alien Ant Farm, on tour this summer with Papa Roach." The manager will try to push the record company to support this type of promotional campaign.

Promising Exposure in Sniping Campaigns

To get their artists on the right tour, managers may promise another act exposure in "sniping" campaigns throughout major cities. Sniping refers to the illegal plastering of posters on telephone poles, city walls, and anything else on which you can stick a poster. Though sniping is illegal, just look around—it happens all the time! Of course, no one will admit to supporting this activity.

Including Other Artists in Co-Op Advertising

Managers may also promise to advertise a band in conjunction with their artist in trade publications. This is called "co-op advertising." Trade adverts are typically very expensive and are often used as a bargaining chip to help get bands on certain tours. Remember, managers will rely on the marketing dollars of the record company to support this type of campaign.

Creating a Buzz First

Managers will take the initiative and get their bands out in front of audiences on their own in order to create a buzz. A group may start playing in front of small crowds, but good old-fashioned hard work will eventually build a fan-base and create a buzz in the industry. Prominent entertainment attorney Jeffrey Light suggests, "Get the band touring a month or two before its record comes out. Kids might see a poster or hear the name, and when they hear the single on the radio, they'll have something to connect with. If they go out and buy the record—boom!—there's a fire. Other bands will then track you down and ask you to go out on the road with them because they know you can draw an audience. A group must be willing to work hard to build [its] own career."

Relying on Personal Friendships

Lastly, to take some heat off of the manager as the individual solely responsible for getting his or her band on the right tours, a band itself can sometimes get on tours by simply being friends with other artists. The band Papa Roach took a friend's band, Alien Ant Farm, on tour in the winter of 2001. Alien Ant Farm, being a rather new band, got a golden opportunity for exposure in front of a great band like Papa Roach and its large audience. And don't forget that Alien Ant Farm appealed to the same demographic audience as Papa Roach. This is important! Touring with the "wrong" act can potentially damage a band by branding (or associating) them with the wrong market. For example, a modern rock band that opens for an '80s metal act will help no one—that is, no one except the critics, who will have a field day giving the show bad press.

HOW YOU'RE PAID FOR LIVE PERFORMANCE DEALS

There are a number of methods used to compute how you're paid for a live performance. The most common are:

+ A straight percentage of ticket sales
+ A flat guaranteed fee
+ A guaranteed fee versus a percentage of ticket sales
+ A guaranteed fee plus a percentage of ticket sales

A number of factors determines which of these payment methods is used, including the stature of the artist, the size of the production, the size of the venue, whether the band is an opening act or a headliner, and the reputation of the talent agency (if there is one) negotiating on the band's behalf. The concert promoter wants to pay as little as possible, and the band wants to make as much as it can. This makes the deals as well as the sums of money negotiated difficult to nail down. The truth is that anything goes.

Straight Percentage

In a straight percentage deal, a concert promoter pays you a percentage of the total money it takes in at the door. Percentages can range from 100 percent of the door money down to 65 percent.

Straight percentage deals are more typically handled at the club level of touring when a band has not yet proven its ability to draw a crowd. If a band expects a sold-out house, a straight percentage may work out fine. If ticket sales are minimal, however, the band could find itself in a jam since it won't be able to meet its expenses on the road. For this reason, more experienced bands with a proven track record will usually not take the gamble of a straight percentage deal. They will want at least to be assured that their expenses are met by agreeing to a more secure form of payment, such as a flat guarantee as discussed below. Tour professional Chris Arnstein, who has worked with the Eagles, Madonna, and Julio Iglesias, offers this additional piece of advice, "In percentage deals, a band should have their own people counting the door sales. This will help prevent the promoter from letting in an excessive number of people for free. A promoter may otherwise let people in for free at the door and profit from alcohol sales, but you'll lose money at the door in the process."

Flat Guarantee

A flat guarantee is one of the most common deals between an artist and a promoter. A guaranteed fee allows you to rely on a set amount of money, regardless of the number of people who show up on the day of the performance. For a new band touring in unfamiliar territory where its fan base is questionable, a guarantee ensures that you'll at least be able to cover your estimated costs. A flat guarantee can also be advantageous to more established artists if it is negotiated so that it's reasonably high. The amount, however, usually depends on the risks the concert promoter is willing to take. If the promoter pays a high fee and ticket sales are low, he could potentially lose his investment. Therefore, in order to split the risks between the promoter and the artist, the two parties usually agree upon deals like the "versus" or "plus percentage" arrangements discussed below.

Guarantee versus Percentage

In the "guarantee versus percentage" deal, a concert promoter will pay you a guaranteed fee *or* a split of the gross receipts, *whichever is higher.* Gross receipts are the sum of all tickets sold, minus ticket agency charges (such as Ticketron), facility fees, box office charges, and taxes. Some promoters may also try to include a 15 percent profit in this equation, which must first be clarified in your contract to avoid any surprises at the end of the show. So if a mid-level band is guaranteed $50,000 for playing an amphitheater, it will either take home that amount, or up to 50 percent of the adjusted gross receipts—whichever ends up being the greater sum of the two. This way, the band is rewarded if the concert is a success and is also ensured a guaranteed fee to meet all of its traveling expenses if it is not.

Guarantee Plus Percentage

In a "guarantee plus percentage" deal, mid-level or superstar artists can receive a guaranteed fee plus a split of the net profits. Net profits are basically the gross receipts *minus all of the promoter's expenses,* which may include the following:

- ✦ The band's negotiated guarantee
- ✦ The promoter's agreed upon profit (typically 15 percent of the gross ticket sales)
- ✦ Hall rentals for the venue in which you perform
- ✦ Opening act fees for the bands that play before you
- ✦ Insurance for theft and damage to your equipment and for personal injury

- Police to make sure fans behave, to control traffic outside the venue, etc.
- Security guards to keep fans from climbing on stage or getting too out of control, and to watch the buses and trucks parked around the venue
- Barricades to keep fans from climbing on stage and entering unauthorized areas within the venue
- Medical personnel and supplies in case of injuries at the venue
- Advertising (including radio, TV, and print) to ensure that people show up for the event
- Telephone usage backstage for the road manager and production crew
- Power, sound, and lights to ensure the sound and look of the show is top quality
- Electricians to make sure the wiring for the lights and sound is functioning properly
- Stage hands to set up and break down equipment
- Box office personnel to sell tickets and take tickets from fans as they pass through the venue gates
- Clean-up crews to make sure all the plastic cups and garbage from the night's performance is removed
- Dressing room facilities (which include everything from the furniture to the phone lines to the towels that you use to dry off after the show)
- Catering (which includes everything from the beer and pizza backstage to the M&M candies to the cooked meals)
- Runners (the people on-call to literally run around taking care of last-minute business matters like making sure all of the band's catering requests are met)

After the promoter deducts all of his or her expenses, the net profits are typically divided 85/15 between the artist and promoter respectively, although it can be as much as 95/5. So if the adjusted gross receipts from sales of a superstar's concert were $500,000, the promoter's total expenses were $300,000, and the band's guarantee was $125,000, the remaining balance of $75,000 ($500,000 -$300,000—$125,000 = $75,000) would be split between the band and the promoter. Seventy-five thousand dollars multiplied by the band's percentage split of 90 percent equals an additional $67,500 payable to the band on the night of the show. When you add the $67,500 to the

SETTLEMENT IS A BLOOD SPORT. Promoters will try to lie about the expenses of putting on a show in order to reduce the amount to be split with the artist at the end of the night. For example, since promoters advertise their events regularly with the local radio stations, they may receive a discounted price, but bill you for the top advertising rates. Promoters may even try to bill you at the top dollar for the food provided backstage, when in reality, they're providing you with leftovers from the band the night before. They may also intentionally underestimate the number of people who actually paid to attend a concert to reduce the gross calculations when "closing out" or "settling" a show. In the words of Chris Arnstein, "Settlement is a blood sport."

band's guarantee of $125,000, that's a total of $192,000 for the night. If this seems like a lot of money, remember that the group still has thousands of dollars of its own expenses.

Here's a breakdown of the band's pay for the night:

$500,000 (Gross ticket sales)

- $300,000 (Promoters total expenses, including promoter's 15% share
of the gross ticket sales: $500,000 x 15% = $75,000)

= $200,000

- $125,000 (The band's negotiated guarantee)

= $75,000 (The amount to be split between band and promoter)

x 90 % (The band's percentage split)

= $ 67,500 (Additional payable to the band on the night of the show)

+ $125,000 (Band's guarantee)

= **$192,000 (Band's total pay for the night)**

Now here's a breakdown of the promoter's pay for the night:

$75,000 (The amount left over after expenses
to be split between band and promoter)

x 10 % (The promoter's percentage split)

= $7,500 (Additional payable to promoter)

+ $75,000 (Promoter's negotiated 15% share of the gross ticket sales of $500,000)

= **$82,000 (Promoter's total pay for the night)**

In percentage deals, promoters are known to drum up false receipts, exaggerate expenses, and lie by underestimating the number of people who actually paid to attend a concert, all in order to reduce the monies that are split with the band at the end of the night. For these reasons, a tour manager must be scrupulous in reviewing all expenses when "closing out" a show with a promoter. Mark Goldstein, vice president of business affairs at Warner Bros. Music, puts it strongly, but fairly: "It's not that promoters are lying, cheating scumbags, but there's a good chance that they are, and you have to assume the worst."

Chris Arnstein adds these final words of wisdom: "In general, settlement is a game of hide and seek. The promoter's job is to hide from you anything they can and to deny any expenses they feel they are not contractually obligated to pay. The job of the person settling the show for the act is to play seek and grab. Figure out how the promoter will try to work the system. Find the hidden or amortized expenses. Demand the contractually agreed upon expenditures. Destroy any inflated or created expenses on behalf of the promoter. Seasoned settlers know the tricks of the trade, and recognize the game. They enter into the negotiations with some level of respect between them, like poker players, so that compromises can be reached in a business-like manner, and [are] not based on ego."

HOW LIVE PERFORMANCE DEALS ARE NEGOTIATED

As mentioned earlier in this chapter (also see Chapter 9, "Your Talent Agent"), it's the job of the talent agent to negotiate performance agreements on behalf of the artist. One way they do this is to first determine the type of venue the artist can reasonably pack as well as the ticket price that is most acceptable to charge. There will also be different prices within the venue itself depending on the location of the seats (are the tickets in the first front rows or all the way in the back?). These ticket prices are then multiplied by the capacity of the venue in which the artist will be performing. The resulting figure is called the "gross potential." For simplicity, say the average price of a ticket is $20, and the seating capacity of a venue is 25,000. Twenty dollars multiplied by 25,000 seats equals $500,000. Negotiations are then worked downward from $500,000 to a point at which both sides believe it is a reasonable risk to put on a show. If the promoter is also the owner of the venue, he will count on the money taken in from food, alcohol sales, parking, etc., for a reasonable profit. But, if a promoter is simply renting the venue and does not share in these ancillary revenues, he could potentially lose money if the show is not at its fullest capacity.

When booking U.S. tours, talent agents individually negotiate performance deals with a variety of promoters across the country. However, there are also mega-promoters (such as Clear Channel Entertainment, Beaver Entertainment, Concerts West, and House of Blues) that own a variety of large venues across the country. In essence, the talent agent negotiating on behalf of the band is offered one lump sum for an entire tour. Chris Arnstein explains:

"Bands that are contracted by mega-promoters are routed to play venues across the country that are owned by the mega-promoters. Thus, the talent agent negotiating on behalf of the band is guaranteed an entire tour's worth of income rather than individual spot dates. The good part is that it's easier to do business this way, but on the other hand, deals negotiated by an agent on an individual basis with a variety of individual promoters may yield more monies at the end of the day. There is another drawback, though.

"Mega-promoters[specifically Clear Channel Entertainment] own radio stations across the country, and though it may go unsaid, if an act decides against playing for the mega-promoters, they will have less chance of getting their new CD on one of the mega-promoter's radio stations. Mega-promoters are also owned by stockholders who are expecting immediate returns on their investment. This means that the mega-promoters are less able to give developing artists a chance. Since mega-promoters control a great deal of venues, it may be harder for many up-and-coming artists to develop their skills to the point where they ever become a viable touring entity."

LIVE PERFORMANCE CONTRACTS AND RIDERS

The first few pages of a contract between an artist and concert promoter include basic terms such as payment, percentage splits, dates, and times. Attached to this contract, however, is a separate form called a "rider"; that is where things can get really interesting. A rider provides the specifics of what a band needs for a performance. Depending upon a group's stature, negotiating power, and individual needs, the rider can be many pages in length. A rider may include personal requirements for sound and lighting, dressing rooms, security, complimentary tickets, catering, and legal issues such as cancellation policies and anti-bootlegging provisions. Remember that in percentage deals in which the artist earns a split of the net profits (i.e., the total ticket sales minus all the promoter's expenses), every expense listed on the band's rider reduces the money the group will take in at the end of the night. Therefore, to ensure maximum profits per performance, close attention must be taken by the group's attorney, talent agent, and personal manager when establishing an agree-

YOU CAN'T ALWAYS GET WHAT YOU WANT (OR CAN YOU?)

To satisfy his very large ego, legend has it that rock star David Lee Roth of the group Van Halen requested on their rider that the M&M candies supplied backstage must not include the brown-colored variety. This meant that all the brown M&Ms had to be separated out of the five or six other colors of the candy included in a package. Needless to stay, all the candies taste exactly the same. If Roth and the band didn't get their demand fulfilled, they would allegedly wreck their dressing rooms, and, of course, have to pay for the damage.

Although most artists are mistreated in the early stages of their careers, they should request the conditions and items on their riders that they actually need, and not just frivolous things to prove they can now make people jump through hoops.

ment with the promoter. Below is a brief discussion of just a few of the items that may be listed on a group's rider, including dressing room accommodations, catering requests, free tickets, security, internal transportation, cancellation provisions, and video and audio taping restrictions.

Dressing Room Accommodations

Besides the basic requests for a clean room, ample chairs, a mirror, a toilet, and a sink with running water, some groups may have more elaborate dressing room needs. A group may want a specific room or even multiple rooms. The Black Crowes were known to request specific carpeting, black lights, lava lamps, incense, and throw pillows in their dressing room.

Catering

Most bands have specific needs for the food and drink they need back stage. In addition, there are requirements for breakfast, lunch, dinner, and tour bus supplies. Some groups may have simple requests, while other artists require lavish spreads. All kinds of food including pretzels, candies, gum, pizza, soda, bottled water, beer, hard alcohol, potato chips, cheese and crackers, deli meats, roast beef dinners, vegetarian pasta, baked or broiled fish, and even lobster can be found on a group's catering rider. Most bands leave a lot of the food uneaten backstage, which is then usually devoured by the guests, so a group can actually limit its expenses by making prudent catering requests.

Free Tickets

The rider also stipulates the number of free tickets a band can give away to family and friends. Again, when a group is working for a split of either the gross or the net profits, each ticket given away potentially reduces the income that band can earn at the end of the night. Elvis Presley is said to have given away no free tickets to his performances.

The number of free tickets the promoter is permitted to give away to radio and television stations in an effort to promote a show must also be indicated on the group's rider. In fact, the promoter is also required to provide the group with a statement that details to whom each ticket was given. This is to prevent the promoter from engaging in unscrupulous activity. At a concert featuring the band Hootie & the Blowfish, for example, the show's promoter sold his share of free tickets to scalpers for a large profit rather than using them as he should have for promotion. According to agent Ian Copeland, this kind of thing happens all the time.

If ticket sales for an event are low and the promoter is unable to meet all of his or her expenses (the band's guarantee being one of those expenses), that promoter may ask the group for the rights to "paper the house." This means that the promoter will give a vast amount of tickets away in the hopes of packing the venue with thirsty bodies. If a promoter owns the building, at least he or she will take in money from alcohol sales and parking fees. Papering the house also benefits the artist by creating the illusion for the fans and press that the artist has sold a substantial amount of tickets. That way the band at least takes home its guarantee, and is also spared the embarrassment of playing to empty seats.

Security

Specifications for security are also included on a band's rider. Though we've all heard the lead singer of a band cuss out security guards for not letting the fans start a mosh pit or get closer to the stage, it's the band that essentially hires and pays security to be there. Security ensures the safety of the band and the band's staff and also protects the equipment and touring vehicles. Security costs are yet another expense deducted from the gross receipts before the artist receives a split of the profits.

> Security's job is to make people feel "secure" at the venue, not to behave like prison guards containing an unruly bunch of thugs. Security should be obvious, visible, and professional. Its purpose is to prevent problems in an emergency—not create them.

Internal Transportation

A group may request that a passenger van and a responsible driver are available on the day of the performance. Some groups may even request that multiple vehicles or limousines are available to them at all times of the day.

Sound and Lights

The specific needs for a band's sound and lighting are also listed on the rider, along with the requirements for power. In the event that the venue cannot meet the power requirements, a generator may be supplied.

Insurance

The rider must include provisions that require a venue to have general liability insurance. This will protect the band in case of personal injury or damage to the group's equipment. On several occasions, The Doors had their equipment trampled and destroyed after fans rushed the stage, although Jim Morrison himself usually incited this behavior.

Cancellation Provisions

Upon cancellation of a performance by the promoter, a group may ask for 100 percent of the agreed payment with two weeks notice, or 50 percent with one month's notice.

The agreement with the promoter is subject to the artist's unavailability due to health, sickness, death, or an act of God (i.e., a hurricane or earthquake). In other words, you cannot be held responsible for loss or damages the promoter may incur as the result of a cancellation under such circumstances. This clause in a performance agreement is called "force majeure."

HIGHLIGHTS FROM VARIOUS CONTRACT RIDERS

Cher requested one "wig" room to store her wigs back stage

Prince requested one physician to administer B-12 vitamin shots before each performance

Elton John requested one large arrangement of colored flowers (no chrysanthemums, lilies, or daisies)

Mariah Carey requested Cristal champagne, champagne glasses, and bendable straws

Tina Turner requested five menus from upscale restaurants (open past 10:00 P.M.) for take-away food on the bus

The Red Hot Chili Peppers requested one meditation room

Busta Rhymes requested one box of ribbed condoms

The Foo Fighters requested one large dressing room with all lewd artwork on the walls covered up or modified

Moby requested ten pairs of white cotton crew socks and ten pairs of cotton boxer shorts

Bush requested that no less than 10 percent of all security be female

P. Diddy (a.k.a. Puff Daddy) requested that all food and ice be inspected for hair and that catering personnel must wear nets on their heads

Matchbox Twenty requested two boxes of Kleenex (unscented)

The Goo Goo Dolls requested vanilla-scented candles

Britney Spears requested one dressing room phone (outgoing calls only) with a $5000 fine payable by promoter for any incoming calls she received

The Backstreet Boys requested peanut butter and jelly sandwiches and milk

Christina Aguilera requested police escorts with the authority to route the vehicles in which she was traveling through any potential traffic delays to and from the venues

Limp Bizkit requested a dressing room with an "apartment vibe" and dimmable lighting

Live requested toilet paper; no colored or scented rolls

Bad English requested one oxygen tank with "mask 1800 lb." capacity

Devo requested ten green drinks (8 oz. drinks that contain some combination of the following: spirulina, blue green algae, chlorella, green tea, barley grass, echinacea, or spinach)

Tricky requested two pints of fresh goat's milk

Wasp requested 14 pounds of fruit salad

Korn requested one jumbo bag of beef or turkey jerky (pepper or teriyaki) loose, not vacuum-packed or thinned

James requested tea-making facilities and Yannoh & Bamboo cereal beverages

For more wacky rider demands, check out www.thesmokinggun.com.

Video and Audio Taping

Most groups prohibit the recording or filming of their live performances in order to prevent the unauthorized reproduction and sale of their music. The rock group the Grateful Dead, however, allowed its fans to both tape and film their live performances. The venues in which the group performed often looked like a sea of telephone poles, with thousands of microphones affixed to boom stands pointing towards the stage.

Q & A WITH CHRIS ARNSTEIN

Chris Arnstein is a personal manager, international tour manager, and booking agent who has provided services for the Eagles, Madonna, John Waite, Michael McDonald, Natalie Cole, Bad English, Helen Reddy, Brett Michaels, Styx, Sam Kinison, Journey, Stevie Nicks, Joe Walsh, Boz Scaggs, ELO, Julio Iglesias, Earth, Wind & Fire, John Secada, and Flip Wilson. Mr. Arnstein has also worked with the Beijing Olympic Bid Committee for Summer 2008, the Nanning International Folk Festival, the cruiseline "Festival at Sea Cruises," as well as a number of major hotels and corporations.

In this informative interview, Mr. Arnstein speaks candidly and offers practical advice about the realities of hitting the road, and talks about the financial, moral, and ethical responsibilities involved in pursuing one's dreams. You won't want to miss this.

Q: Can you describe what live performances and touring mean to you from a business perspective?

C.A.: A band or artist is best served by recognizing that they are selling a product. The product is the creative output of that artist or band. The unique sound, the certain type of songs, the live show that makes the public want to turn off [its] TVs, get in [its] cars, drive to a venue, find a place to park, and pay to see the product. In business terms, this is called branding, and is defined as that certain something that delineates the brand from every other brand. While every band claims that they are unique and not like any other band, all bands fall into some defining category. If you do not fall into a definable category, a record label and radio station will claim that they do not know what to do with your music. Whether it's Coca Cola, Lexus, or Sting, the buying public needs to have a realm of expectancy. They want to pretty much know what they're going to get for their loyalty and their money.

The business of live performances and touring is the band's product development. You find out what works and what doesn't. You determine what you want to represent and what you don't. If you're smart and lucky and develop a substantial customer base, you will create a brand that becomes so successful that the labels will feel they have to sign you. And after a few successful albums, when the label has fired everyone you know, and gotten over the excitement of your success, and you find your album sales waning, you can go back to touring as a way to support your new expensive way of life. Remember, no one can take your live show from you. It's yours, and it's your career.

Q: Can you briefly discuss how bands or individual musicians get the opportunity to go out on the road?

C.A: Individuals and bands get the opportunity to tour because someone feels that their presence is worth more than the cost of having them perform. Whether it's an act being considered for a booking or an employee being hired by the artist, each expense must be justified as a business decision. Touring with record label support (which is usually recoupable), must be of immediate value to the label in terms of selling the artist's CDs or it is not worth the investment.

A band is hired because they . . . put butts into seats, are willing to work cheap for the exposure, bring some sort of cachet to the headline act (hipness, musical credibility, etc.), receive a favor from a business associate, or because someone in the band has the hots for someone in the other band.

A musician or crew member is hired for his or her musical flavor, personal style, audience drawing ability, because he or she is a friend of the artist, or once again because someone in the band has the hots for him or her. Often, these employees mistake their friendly relationship with the artist for job security. It is not wise to start thinking of oneself as [being] on equal footing with your employer, whether you are a better musician, smarter, prettier, more experienced, or whatever.

In any case, always remember that whether you are an opening band or an employee, regardless of what you think of your benefactor, you must always remember that ultimately you work for yourself. The time you are spending doing this is time you are not spending on doing something else. Thus, you must demand of yourself an honest answer to the question of [whether] what you are doing now is the best utilization of your time given the options. Always conduct yourself in a manner that is most beneficial to you and your career.

Q: What is the biggest misconception young artists have about hitting the road?

C.A: First and foremost, there has to be a reason to go on the road. It's not summer camp. There needs to be a valid business reason for a band to accept the mental, physical, and financial strains of going on the road. One must try to determine the return on [the] investment of time, money, and resources before hopping in the van. Unless there is a well-thought-out marketing plan, the road is the road to nowhere. It is just a vacation from reality.

Many people think "famous" is "rich." It's not. Quite a few very well-known bands who toured for years never really made any money. Often young bands think in the short term. They delude themselves that just because their band's income has gone from $1000 to $1500 to $2500 per night that they will be bringing home more money per person. They forget that in addition to their road expenses, their basic expenses at home for rent, car payments, and credit card bills continue. The cocoon of traveling with a group of people that are going through the same dream as you is an easy escape.

Q: What are some of the biggest problems that musicians experience while touring?

C.A: The first realization everyone should have is, "This is really what you are doing with your life." Your actions are your responsibility. Thus, one should be aware of the following things to look out for.

Many artists like to pretend that being an artist absolves them of personal responsibility for their behavior. They rationalize that they are unique because they are "artists," and as such cannot be held responsible for things like business commitments, monetary obligations, and personal responsibility for the way they treat other human beings.

Unfortunately, in our society, "money rules." The ability to sing, rap, act, play a piece of wood with six strings, shoot a three-point jumper, etc., often absolves perpetrators of immediate consequences for their actions. But it does not alleviate the effects of negative behavior against others.

Rapper Tupac Shakur, a convicted sex offender, was also caught on a surveillance tape at a major casino jumping a confirmed gang rival after a heavyweight championship boxing match. The footage was shown on the news nationwide. Later that night Tupac was assassinated. Yet, he is remembered as a mythical figure and respected by many because he was charismatic, handsome, and sold [sells] a lot of records. One can only wonder how this behavior is forgiven.

While this case is somewhat extreme, it is not that unusual. Always remember that no one is a success in a vacuum. In the entertainment business, it is the job of many men and women to create an image for the artist that makes them look as appealing as possible to their target market-demographic. This may not necessarily be complimentary or in the artist's best interest. More careers are lost because musicians have angered their professional supporters (radio programmers, promotion people, record label presidents, label publicity departments, fans, etc.) with more arrogance, ignorance, or flakiness than one can ever imagine. These professionals see acts come and go every day. They are going to put their professional energies into the acts that will give them the best return on their investment.

People will put up with almost anything when you're delivering huge dollars to the bottom line. But the minute you are not creating enormous profits for the company, you're more trouble than you're worth. You are no longer a good return on [an] investment. You'll be dropped like a bad habit. Professionals may smile at you and tell you that you are great, but their efforts are going to go towards furthering their own careers, which means positioning themselves next to success. If you have been a jerk, they won't act on your behalf. Failure exists in a vacuum, a vacuum of interest.

The second most common problem that musicians incur while touring is that they fail to remember that while everything costs on the road, expenses continue at home. Many bands don't always think about personal and professional cash flow, which causes them to face hard realities when they are broke and have no established credit in their personal life.

Lastly, when you are on the road with a group of people, a "group dynamic" develops. Unfortunately, the people outside of that dynamic (such as wives, friends, and family) do not necessarily fit in. Though they are important to you, they are not necessarily important to the others on the tour. This can create problems inside and outside the band. Therefore, it is in one's best interest to treat the band as a job and the family as private life. While the two occasionally intermix socially or at special events, on the whole they should be kept separate.

Q: What advice do you have for musicians or bands that are about to embark on a tour for the first time?

C.A: One should determine early in a band's life what the intention of the project is. Realistically speaking, is this a party band just looking to pick up a few bucks, exercise one's creative muscles, and get laid, or is this a business?

If it is the first option, understand and accept that it is a time-consuming and expensive hobby and you're lucky if it's profitable.

If the band is meant to be a business, then it's time to get serious! Keep in mind, however, that the time that you spend trying to develop a musical voice, learn the business, and become a viable commercial act is time away from building a more sensible and stable career. I don't say this to sound negative. I say this so the reader can get the view from one who has spent decades on the road learning about the importance of using one's time and resources consciously. It is wise to consider a band or artist's career like that of a professional athlete. First, a career can be cut short for any and no reason—marketplace demand (currently popular music), age, drugs, needs of the team (label needs a radio friendly artist), politics (who's in and who's out at the label), an incompetent or angry label employee who does not attend to their responsibilities and causes interest in your project to be placed elsewhere (a cheap-shot injury). Very few make it into the professional ranks (get a label deal and actively tour). Fewer still actually make it into a starting lineup (get an album released and promoted as well as being able to tour at a level that makes a profit worth the investment.) Finally, fewer still have lasting careers; most professional careers are in the realm of three years.

Q: What is the primary reason bands go out on the road?

C.A: There are different stages in a band's career that go a long way towards dictating what they are trying to accomplish. I'll explain these different stages one at a time.

Starting Out. Early in a band's career, the band is trying to earn enough to stay alive, create a sound (or identifiable "brand") with which to build an audience, and get a record deal.

Becoming a Real Band. After a band starts to draw enough of an audience to justify club owners paying them some real money, they begin to believe that they can actually do this for a living. (Please note that "living" means that one can live like a human being, eat decent food, choose the type of mammals with whom they live.)

As the band gives the signs of being a viable economic entity, a manager, attorney, and possibly an agent start to get involved. During this period the band should either have, or be considered for, some type of record deal (indie or major label). Band members have now reached the stage where they are going to have to sign legally binding agreements with other band members. They begin to recognize that they have to take the business, their band mates, and professional advisors seriously. This is often a time when a few band mate changes occur.

At this point, the band will need to start making business decisions that will seriously affect their future. The band may have to balance accepting less money per gig as an opening act in [the] hopes of gaining a larger audience. One never knows where their big break will come. Radio stations, award shows, and TV programs flat out won't play your single/video unless you play their live radio show, award show, or TV program. If you're lucky, they'll cover expenses, but usually these events are at a cost to the band, even if it's their record label that advances it. Thus, the band has to reinvest their limited resources back into the business. This is where you can become famous and broke.

The Band Starts to Fly (Literally and Figuratively). If the band progresses beyond the former stage (which most don't), it usually means that they can go on the road, travel in a bus or occasionally a plane, and at the end of the tour, end up with something above a secretary's salary in their pockets if they don't succumb to self indulgence.

The Band Ignores Sage Advice. Somewhere along the road the band meets an older, grizzled veteran who was great when they were kids, but is now looking a bit, shall we say, worn. He will try to take them under his wing and say, "Make every dime you can and save it. Try not to piss off the people you are going to need, such as radio station disc jockeys, when the roller coaster starts its thrill ride to the bottom. Whatever you do, do not marry the [man or] woman who suddenly finds you at the peak of your fame and earning potential. It's also wise to tell your relatives that your business manager has invested all your money in non-liquid assets and won't allow you to loan them money. Enjoy your success while you can, because even a great career rarely lasts ten years, and you've got a lot more than ten years of living (and spending) to do." The band smiles, thanks the grizzled veteran, and the minute they are out his sight declare him creepy and vow never to become like that old pitiful geezer.

A Wave of Recognition Lifts the Band. When this occurs, most bands get out and play everywhere that will have them and can afford them. Hope reigns supreme—hope that somehow the band will get a hit record, soundtrack cut, TV show theme, live appearance, or other break that will build their base of paying fans, while not alienating their old fans (which success will). Then, just as the band is burnt out creatively and spiritually, and at the end of their rope, if the fates decree, the big break comes!

Get It While the Gettin's Good. The band has some hits. You are able to tour all year and make great money (for a very short couple of years). The people at the label take your calls. [Members of the opposite sex] think you are really interesting. Your presence is commanded for radio interviews by morning disc jockeys.

The Band Is About to Break up! The lead singer starts thinking about going solo. The lead guitar player resents the attention the lead singer gets. The keyboard player wants to start doing soundtracks. The bass player just wants to get one of his songs on the next album. And the drummer hates everybody because he starts realizing that the only money he is getting comes from the live gigs while the singer, guitar player, and keyboard player are living large off their publishing revenue.

The Band Breaks up. Eventually the lead singer does his or her first solo album. Everybody else in the band is suddenly slapped with the reality that the singer was the voice of the band. Regardless of the fact that the singer may not have written one tune or played the great solos, no one cares about anyone but the lead singer. The other band members may try other projects and even have some success, but ultimately, after the bitterness, people start realizing that the winning combination that results in a successful band is a rare gift from God.

Time and Trends Pass and the Lead Singer Falls off the Charts. Over the next decade everyone watches their income fall. The band members begin to understand the consequences of their career choices. Friends and business associates have established real lives and careers for themselves, while you (the band) traveled around the world being a band. It's tough to be a nobody at the bottom of the food chain once you have tasted fame, money, and [attractive members of the opposite sex]. Fans and various management types try to get the band back together. Pride, and in some, an inherently nasty inner self, prevent the reunion from happening.

I Love You, Man. Eventually, the drummer is broke. The bass player is producing demos. The keyboard player has a home studio and is doing soundtracks. The lead guitar player is finally, really getting out of rehab. The lead singer has to face the fact that he can either play to a smaller audiences as a solo artist or to larger audiences if the band reunites. Everyone realizes that carrying the burden of past anger is costly and unproductive.

Finally, the pettiness gives way to the better memories. Maturity and money rear their older and wiser heads to remind the band that while everyone else was going to law school or medical school or slaving for "the man" to move up the corporate ladder, they were building a successful business, and hopefully for a few more years, opportunity is knocking at their door. Otherwise they are S.O.L.[Sorry Old Losers]

The Band Reunites. Touring is now really a business of making every dime you can, because this is the money you will be living off for the rest of your life. The lead singer suddenly doesn't feel that meeting fans is beneath him. The rehabbed lead guitarist and his new best friend, the lead singer, are now happy to get up at an ungodly hour to interview with radio DJs. Walking out of the radio station, the two meet a young up-and-coming band. The lead guitarists and singer try to take the young band under their wing and say, "Make every dime you can and save it. Try not to piss off the people you are going to need when the roller coaster starts it's thrill ride to the bottom. Whatever you do, do not marry the [men or] women who suddenly find you at the peak of your fame and earning potential. Accept that many morning shock jocks have a perfect face for radio, and laugh at everything they say. Tell your relatives your business manager has invested all your money in non-liquid assets and won't allow you to loan them money. Enjoy your success while you can, because even a great career rarely lasts ten years and you've got a lot more than ten years of living (and spending) to do." The up-and-coming band smiles, thanks the grizzled veterans, and later declare them as creepy pitiful geezers; vowing never to become like them. And the cycle continues.

Q: Wow! That deserves a moment of silence! I hope people will understand and use that lesson wisely. What other words of wisdom do you have, particularly for musicians or bands that have problems readjusting to life off the road once a long tour has ended?

C.A: One must always remember that you are more than what you do for a living. In the future, this year's big tour is last year's big tomato, a fond and distant memory. Once again, you would be well advised to consider if what you are doing [i.e., pursuing a career in music] is the best use of your time at this period in your life. Reality dictates that a band's chances of "making it" in a real career sense are similar to the chances of a high school athlete making it in the pros. If a band is lucky enough to make it, they should acknowledge that, at best, the duration of their career parallels that of a professional athlete. After 35, both one's own record label and the public's perception of older musicians start working against you. Most "civilians" have no idea what a musician, tour manager, keyboard programmer, or roadie really does. They think it's all party time out there. Thus, it is in your best interest to establish personal credibility and recognizable skills in an arena outside the touring world as well.

Q: What else would you like to add that might be helpful for new artists?

C.A.: Each of us has soul-searching tests that are placed in our path during the course of our lives. Whether it's drugs and alcohol, an unreasonable sense of greed that causes you to step on others in order to get what you want, an inherent self-destructiveness that undermines success every time it comes close, or an unwillingness to make difficult decisions because one does not want to be disliked; these tests are not easy. There are often unpleasant consequences for choosing the right path.

These challenges are karmic lessons that periodically rear their heads throughout our careers. Overcoming these tests is not about being noble or self-righteous. They remind us that we are all human and imperfect. The test is in how we will choose to react. The answer is found in maintaining our ability to honestly look oneself in the mirror while respecting who you see; regardless of the cost. I will simply say that one must be willing to pay the price for setting personal behavioral boundaries. To fail oneself in meeting these challenges is to expose oneself to great peril—spiritually, legally, and professionally!

The sun rose the day before you were born and it will rise after the day you die. The only things in life that are important are the people you care about and who care about you and the work that gives your life purpose. Use you talent to connect to others. True art lasts past politics, war, and even civilizations, whether [the artist is] Aristotle, Beethoven or the Beatles, and there is no greater gift than to have been able to positively touch people generations away.

CHAPTER 14

Merchandising

Merchandising refers to the process of selling merchandise—T-shirts, hats, stickers, programs, posters, and other goods—that bears an artist's name and often his or her likeness. When these products are sold in conjunction with a concert tour, they can generate substantial sums of money. Merchandising monies are especially useful in helping new artists subsidize touring costs when the money they're earning for a live performance is minimal. Merchandising is also helpful to artists when their record companies fail to provide adequate tour support funds. In any case, it's important to have a basic knowledge of how merchandising works, and to have a broad understanding of everything from your merchandising rights, to making merchandising deals, to handling your own merchandising independently.

MERCHANDISING RIGHTS

The first step to understanding how the merchandising business works is to understand a simple law called "the right of publicity." This refers to an individual's rights to grant or not grant the use of his or her name and/or likeness for commercial purposes. In other words, you have the right to decide who, if anyone, can use your name and likeness on T-shirts, hats, posters, or other products for commercial sales. When considering your legal rights to a fictitious name, such as your stage or band name, you should register the trademark or service mark with the federal government. This is especially important when you reach the point in your career at which you will be exposed on a national level. Federal trademark and service mark registration makes it easier for you to successfully sue anyone who attempts to use your band name or logo without your permission. To avoid lawsuits, choose a distinctive name that is not confusingly similar to that of other bands or entertainment-related companies, and then conduct a trademark search to make sure no one else has already claimed the name.

When your name is going to be exploited at the international level, foreign registration may also be necessary. (For more information on trademark registration, see the interview with Attorney Jeff Cohen in Chapter 2.)

Now that you know something about your merchandising rights, let's discuss a few options for using them.

GRANTS OF RIGHTS

There are three typical scenarios that apply to using your merchandising rights. They are as follows: the grant of rights to your record company, the grant of rights directly to a merchandiser, and handling your merchandising independently.

> The term service mark and the word trademark are sometimes used interchangeably; however, the two have different meanings. A service mark identifies a service, such as your live performances. A trademark identifies products that are bought and sold, such as your records and merchandise.

Grant of Rights to Your Record Company

When signing a recording agreement, your record label typically wants to secure your exclusive merchandising rights. This is especially true when you are a new artist signing with a small independent record label or when you have little or no negotiating power when dealing with a major label. Your record company then licenses these rights to a third-party merchandising company to manufacture product and oversee sales. The merchandiser pays the record company a merchandising royalty, and the label in turn splits it with the artist 50/50.

This arrangement puts you at a disadvantage for two reasons. First, yu make less money than you would if you were able hold on to your own merchandising rights and make a deal directly with a merchandiser. Second, your record company will typically want to cross-collateralize your merchandising royalties with your record royalties. In other words, *any monies that would otherwise be payable to you from merchandising sales go towards paying back all the outstanding expenses for which you still owe your record label.* Therefore, it can be a long time before you ever see any money from merchandising sales. Needless to say, it's best try to avoid giving up your merchandising rights if at all possible. However, if you're in a "take it or leave it" position in your negotiations, weigh the pros and cons before making any decision. (See Chapter 11 for more on record royalties, recoupable expenses, and cross-collateralization.)

Grant of Rights to a Merchandiser

If you're able to secure the rights upon signing a record deal, you can enter into a merchandising deal directly with a merchandising company. The merchandiser agrees to manufacture products and oversee sales and then pay you a royalty and an advance against projected earnings.

As this chapter has already mentioned, merchandising monies, especially in the form of a merchandising advance, are often a much needed source of income for bands and can help them cover start-up expenses before they hit the road. The costs of rehearsals, air fares, tour buses, trucks, and production can add up. An advance is especially helpful if your record company is no longer providing you with tour support funds to cover expenses

> Don't confuse exclusive merchandising rights with promotional rights. A record company always has the promotional rights to manufacture products using your name and likeness in connection with records, videos, and biographical information. A label may also give away T-shirts, stickers, and posters via record stores, web sites, or radio stations to promote record sales.

and/or if the fees you're receiving for live performances are small. In any case, securing merchandising rights and entering into an agreement directly with a merchandiser is more advantageous for you than is our first scenario because you not only keep a bigger percentage of royalties since there is no middleman, but you have more control to negotiate the deal you want, or not make a deal at all and handle your merchandising independently.

Retaining Rights and Handling Merchandising Independently

The last option for merchandising is retaining your merchandising rights and handling your merchandising independently. In other words, rather than licensing your rights to a merchandising company, you simply hire a printer who is experienced in handling merchandising for touring performances to supply you with the product, and you then handle the merchandising sales yourself. This way you will make more profit per T-shirt or item, although you'll forgo a merchandising advance.

This scenario is usually applicable to the beginning of an artist's career when a merchandising deal has not yet been offered, when the artist is playing small venues in which handling the merchandising is still manageable, or when the artist fails to negotiate the type of deal he or she wants (such as a higher royalty or larger advance) and chooses not to make a deal. However, once an artist progresses to a point in his or her career where he or she is playing larger venues, the burden of ordering product, shipping, accounting, and sales may not be practical. Hence, the merchandising deal with a merchandiser becomes necessary.

Since it's possible for you to successfully negotiate to maintain your merchandising rights at the time of signing a recording deal, and since this is what you ultimately want to shoot for anyway, the next part of our discussion deals with entering directly into an agreement with a merchandising company. Following this discussion, Bob Fierro, president of Zebra Marketing discusses his views in a Q & A on independent merchandising.

MERCHANDISING COMPANIES

As of this writing, a few major merchandising companies control most of the merchandising business. They are Giant Merchandising, Sony Signatures, and Bervado Merchandising Services. Winterland Merchandising has been a major player in the business for many years as well but is now in chapter 11 bankruptcy. All of these companies are divisions of larger corporations, and, with some discretion, can afford to pay their artists substantial merchandising advances.

The current trend has been for these companies to deal mostly with teen bands, such as the Backstreet Boys and *NSYNC, since they generate substantial sums of money from sales. But, as in any other business, merchandising goes through trends, and it has already shifted to dealing with more rock-oriented bands, such as Creed and Korn. It's also important to note that in addition to the major companies mentioned above, there are a handful of smaller companies that are perfectly capable of taking care of your business. In fact, Bob Fierro says that you shouldn't choose a company primarily because of the size of the advance it can offer, but on the basis of whether it shares your ideas about what you want to do with the merchandising. "It's also about relationships," says Fierro. "How excited the company is about signing your band, the types of designs and products they're interested in manufacturing for you, and the quality of services they provide, are equally important factors to consider before entering into a merchandising agreement with a merchandiser."

TYPES OF MERCHANDISING DEALS

Merchandising deals typically fall into two different categories: tour merchandising and retail merchandising.

Tour Merchandising

Tour merchandising refers to the sale of merchandise at your live performances. Since most concertgoers are usually pumped up for months before a show and are ready to take home a souvenir of the event, the money generated from tour merchandising can be substantially more than that from retail sales. Fans already know to bring enough money to cover the costs of a T-shirt, hat, or tour program, plus a little extra cash for food and drink (but that's another story). In fact, have you ever noticed how the merchandising booths are strategically placed at the venue's entrance? That's not coincidental. It's done to ensure that fans make a purchase just as they're coming through the main door. The merchandising company hires its own personnel to follow your band on the road, check in product with the venue, set it up in the booths, count the number of items sold at the end of the night, check out the merchandising with the venue, and then move on to the next city to do it all over again. If this seems like a great deal of effort just for the sake of selling a few measly T-shirts and buttons, note that major stars like Garth Brooks and Madonna can gross well over $100,000 in merchandising sales alone in just a single night. Needless to say, *that's not small potatoes!*

Retail Merchandising

Retail merchandising refers to selling products through department stores, T-shirt shops, record stores, Internet sites, mail-order operations, and sublicensing agreements. Sublicensing occurs when your merchandiser grants the rights to a specialty company to manufacture items such as dolls, trash cans, telephones, napkins, lunch boxes, and stationery products—anything beyond the manufacturing capabilities of your primary merchandiser. Note that marketing items at the retail level requires a slightly different approach than marketing them on concert tours. For instance, merchandisers know that it's more likely for fans to purchase more obscure items (such as a KISS lunch box) at retail outlets than at live concerts, so merchandisers push novelty items at retail. Merchandisers also know that fans will want to buy T-shirts unique to the live performances they see, so they may also work at designing shirts exclusively for sale at retail outlets. (You may be able to get a KISS T-shirt at a retail store that's unavailable at one of the band's shows.) But in any case, even though artists such as Michael Jackson, the Rolling Stones, Guns N' Roses, and KISS have all earned substantial sums of money through retail sales, tour merchandising is still, by far, more lucrative. The excitement generated by a live concert performance is nearly impossible to duplicate at a retail venue. Unless, of course, you decide to tour the malls across America.

KEY TERMS IN MERCHANDISING CONTRACTS

When signing a merchandising deal, it's possible to separate your rights and sign with two different merchandisers—one to handle tour merchandising and one to handle retail and sublicenses. However, this is typically not what happens. Your merchandiser generally uses one contract form to acquire all your rights. Our discussion will emphasize touring since the legal and business issues of merchandising agreements deal primarily with that. Important issues in a merchandising deal include the agreement term, royalties, advances, performance guarantees, creative issues, territory, exclusivity, and the sell-off period.

Royalty Rates: Tour Merchandising

Merchandising royalties are far easier to calculate than record royalties. Several deductions are taken before arriving at your royalty per CD (see Chapter 11 for more on record royalties), but merchandising royalties are usually based on your gross merchandising sales less taxes and credit card fees. That's generally it! The royalty rate that merchandisers pay their artists for concert sales in the United States ranges anywhere from 25 percent to 35 percent, with 30 percent being the norm for new artists. So a T-shirt selling at $25.00 multiplied by a royalty rate of 30 percent equals $7.50 (I left out sales taxes and credit card fees for the sake of simplicity, but you get the idea). In some cases, merchandisers pay a higher royalty of up to 50 percent, but only after deducting an additional expense, known as a "hall fee," which we will discuss in a moment.

The merchandising royalty rate for sales in foreign territories is usually less than the U.S. rate—generally, it's around 80 percent of your domestic rate. For example, if your U.S. royalty rate is 30 percent for merchandising sold at live performances, your royalty for sales in foreign territories is 24 percent (30 x 80% = 24). Your foreign royalty is lower because the profit margin to the merchandiser is reduced by higher taxes, customs duties, and other costs of doing business abroad.

Royalties for products sold on tour, such as T-shirts, sweatshirts, and baseball caps are paid at one negotiated rate and computed on the gross merchandising sales (as we already discussed above). However, products such as tour programs and designer tour jackets are usually based on the "net" profits received by the merchandiser. This is because the costs of manufacturing these products are much higher, and merchandisers figured out they weren't making much of a profit. Therefore, the royalty rate paid to you for tour programs and higher quality items is typically 70 to 75 percent of the net profits (that's after the merchandiser deducts all of its manufacturing costs).

Hall Fees

You already know that your merchandiser pays you a royalty based on the gross sales less taxes and credit card fees. You also know that a common royalty rate for a new band is around 30 percent. However, sometimes your merchandiser will agree to pay you a higher royalty of 50 percent (sometimes more), but only after deducting an additional expense known as a hall fee. So, you might ask, what the heck are hall fees?

Each of the venues where you perform hires its own personnel (or an outside concession company) to handle all of the merchandising sales within the building. In return, the venue takes a percentage of your merchandising sales, ranging anywhere from 30 to 40 percent. This is standard procedure. Your merchandiser sends out his or her own personnel to show up at every gig, check in the right amount of merchandising, make sure all the displays are set up properly, and then check out the merchandising at the end of the night and pay the hall a percentage.

Again, since your merchandiser typically pays you a royalty on the gross sales (*before* deducting hall fees), artists were historically not affected by the percentage the merchandiser paid the hall each night. But, as more and more artists began beating up merchandisers over the years for higher royalty rates, merchandisers started to compute royalties for some artists *after* deducting the hall's fees first. So now, a T-shirt selling for $25.00, less a 35 percent hall fee, multiplied by a 50 percent royalty rate, yields a royalty of approximately $8.00 per shirt (again, for simplicity, note that I left out the sales tax, and credit card fees). The resulting figure usually works out to be the same as it would have been if you had a lower royalty computed before the hall fees. However, the lower you're able to keep the hall fees, the more money you'll make from merchandising sales. And since it's your talent agent's responsibility to call promoters across the country and negotiate your live performance fees and other expenses (see Chapter 9 for more on talent agents), you might go as far as telling your agent to include a clause in a section of your contract (called a rider) that says you'll agree to pay only a certain amount for the hall fees. Again, the standard hall fee is about 35 percent, but it can range anywhere from 30 percent to 40 percent. Whether you can get the venue to budge on its percentage is based on your band's success and negotiating power, as well as on your agent's incentive to fight for you. But remember that your agent only gets paid a percentage of your live performance fees, and not a percentage of your merchandising sales revenue. In other words, the hall fee doesn't matter to your agent one way or another. As Donald Passman notes in his book *All You Need To Know About The Music Business,* "Your agent's incentive goes way up when you stare daggers at him or her." In fact, agents have gotten quite good in the past few years at muscling down hall's fees. Apparently, Passman's advice is working.

Advances

To quote Donald Passman once again, "Where there are royalties there are advances." In fact, the merchandising advance is usually the key reason why most young bands first enter into a merchandising agreement with a merchandiser. Nevertheless, one of the biggest misconceptions musicians have about merchandising advances is that they're based on some arbitrary figure. On the contrary, merchandising companies make careful calculations about what they can advance their artists based on something called a per head or per cap (per capita) figure. *The per cap figure is the average amount spent on merchandising by each fan who sees you perform.* This is determined by dividing the total amount you gross in merchandising sales by the total number of people who pay to see your live performance. If this sounds confusing, let me try to clarify it for you.

Suppose you're in a hard rock band touring clubs and you play in front of 1000 paid attendees every night for 30 shows (1000 x 30 = 30,000 total paid attendees). Your merchandising sales for each of the 30 performances total $4,000 ($4,000 x 30 = $120,000 in gross merchandising sales). This means that you have a per cap figure of $4.00 per person over the course of the tour ($120,000 in gross merchandising sales divided by 30,000 paid attendees equals $4.00 per cap).

Now let's say that you're playing a second and third leg of a tour in which you're expected to play a total of 60 more club dates. You're also expected to play before the same average number of paid attendees each night as you did on your first leg (1000 x 60 = 60,000 total paid attendees). With this information in mind, it's safe to assume that you are going to gross another $240,000 in merchandising sales by the end of the tour (60,000 total paid attendees multiplied by the average dollar amount spent by each fan or per cap figure of $4.00 equals $240,000).

Now, if you add your total merchandising sales from the first leg of your tour ($120,000) to the sales from the second and third leg of your tour ($240,000), your total gross sales in merchandising over the course of the tour is $360,000 ($120,000 + $240,000 = $360,000). Here comes the fun part. If you're a new band with a royalty rate of 30 percent, then you can expect to earn an advance in the area of $108,000 ($360,000 in total sales, multiplied by your royalty rate of 30 percent, equals $108,000). Of course, this is an oversimplification of how your advance is really determined, but it at least gives you a ballpark figure to consider.

Okay, I can hear the questions flying. How is it possible for your merchandiser to figure out what your per cap figure is going to be if you're a new band that's never toured before? And if the merchandiser doesn't know what your per cap figure is, then how can they figure out your advance? These are good questions. The first thing that the merchandiser does is look at the per cap figures of other bands with a style similar to yours. The merchandiser, of course, must also look at the total number of tour dates you're expected to perform, the types of venues in which you may be playing, the capacity of the venues in which you're performing, whether or not you're playing festivals with a number of other bands on the bill, the management and record label you're signed with, the talent agency booking you, the "coolness" factor of your band name and logo, the sex of your group (whether you're male or female), the demographic audience you appeal to, and so much more. Merchandisers have actually gotten really good over the years at "guess-timating" a per cap figure based on this information. Bands can do anywhere from 50 cents to $12.00 (and higher) per cap. On average, metal bands tend to do $7.00 to $10.00 per cap since their audiences tend to be more fanatic. The English pop band Depeche Mode actually hit an all-time high of $25.00 a head at one time. With a per cap like that, when you're playing in front of thousands of people every night for several nights on a tour, your total gross in merchandising is huge!

Performance Guarantees

Since merchandising advances are based on an estimate of the total number of paid attendees in front of whom you're going to be playing, plus the average amount of money each paid attendee is expected to spend on T-shirts and other items, it's easy to understand why your merchandiser will want you to agree to something called a "performance guarantee." This means that, when accepting a merchandising advance, you're also agreeing to play a specific number of live performances in front of a specific number of people *or, otherwise, as your guarantee stipulates, you must automatically repay the total unrecovered balance of your advance.* Before you freak out, you should know that this usually happens only in the unfortunate circumstance that your band breaks up in the middle of a tour or if someone suffers an untimely injury or death and the merchandiser is afraid it will never be able to recoup its advance from sales. If you've already spent the advance, merchandisers have been known to sue if necessary to get it back. (See the text box "Bankrupt" in Chapter 2.)

You may be wondering how your merchandiser estimates a per head count when you're playing festivals with other bands. How can you tell which band the fans actually paid to see? The answer is: you can't. Therefore, the merchandiser makes an adjustment by reducing the number of paid attendees, for example, by half.

If you fall short of meeting your performance guarantee, the merchandiser will—usually—let the advance repayment ride and wait to recoup the advance on your next tour, or on the tours that band members may book as solo artists or as members of other bands. And as you'll see in a moment, the merchandiser will not be required to pay you another advance until he or she makes back every last dime *with interest!*

The Agreement Term

The term of most merchandising agreements is based on one or two "album tour-cycles" (the period of time between one album release and the next, including all touring done in connection with the first recording). One reason why the agreement term is structured this way is that all of the images, designs, and logos used in promoting an album may be used when creating merchandising products. For instance, your album title, cover artwork, or special logo may all be replicated in T-shirt designs, baseball caps, and/or bumper stickers. Since each album release projects a new vibe and image, an album tour-cycle is a logical milestone at which to evaluate your relationship with your merchandiser. In addition, merchandising deals are structured in cycles because it would obviously be awkward to change merchandisers midway through a tour.

The term of merchandising agreements may seem like a simple concept, but it can actually get quite complicated. The agreement term is also structured to continue until the the merchandiser recoups all advances it has paid to you. Clearly, if your advance is recouped at the end of your album tour-cycle, then you're free to renegotiate your contract for better terms and another advance. However, if your advance is unrecovered at the end of your cycle, *your merchandiser automatically gets the rights to your next tour without having to renegotiate anything at all.* Even if you recouped all but $10,000 of a $100,000 advance, you could still be locked into your original agreement. This is obviously not the ideal situation to be in since the terms you negotiated at the beginning of your career may become less favorable as you become a more established artist. You may need another advance as well in order to survive while writing and recording your next album or to help cover the start-up cost for your next tour. Plus, it's possible that you may have been unhappy with the service your merchandiser provided and you may simply want out of your agreement—something an agreement term may not allow.

For all of the above reasons, your attorney may be able to negotiate for something called "buy-out rights." In this scenario, you can get a competing merchandising company to actually pay your unrecovered balance and buy you out of your existing contract. You can be sure, however, that your attorney is going to have to fight for this clause. Why would your merchandiser take a chance on investing in your career when you're just getting started, only to give you the opportunity to change allegiances to a competing company later? The company will at least want to have the opportunity to reap the benefits of the relationship as you develop into a more successful artist.

If your merchandiser agrees to a buy-out clause, you can count on a number of stipulations being attached to it. For instance, you may be required to pay back the unrecovered balance with added interest. Or, you may even have to pay back an amount greater than 100 percent of the unrecovered balance, e.g., 110 percent of the unrecovered advance. And finally, the merchandiser may insist on the "rights of last refusal," which means that if a competing company makes you an offer, your merchandiser has the right to either match the offer or let you out of your deal.

> A large advance isn't always desirable. If your merchandiser doesn't earn it back, it could mean that the term of your agreement never ends; worse yet, you may be asked to repay the advance immediately. Therefore, it may be better to take a smaller advance to ensure that you'll be a free agent at the end of your agreed-upon number of album tour-cycles. You may then be in a position in your career to renegotiate for a deal with better terms.

Creative Issues

Most artists are given creative control over and the right to approve all merchandising designs on products to be sold. In fact, the merchandiser sometimes asks the artist to supply them with a series of photographs and designs. Your name and likeness, your album artwork, and the dates and cities of your upcoming tour are typical designs included on products such as T-shirts, hats, and posters. But Bob Fierro, president of Zebra Marketing, notes that artists are often unsure of what they want, and end up holding up production as a result. That said, "The artist has to trust the people with whom they get into bed so to speak," says Bob. "Keep in mind that as merchandisers, we have years of experience in the business and know what sells and doesn't sell. You'd be surprised at the number of artists who purposely go out of their way to design a really bad shirt. And these artists are very serious. I once heard of one artist who wanted his name printed upside down, and another who didn't want his name and logo on the shirt at all. I understand that these guys were trying to make an anti-capitalistic statement to their fans, but isn't this a bit hypercritical after they just pocketed a large advance? Remember, merchandising is a very calculated business where hundreds of thousands of dollars can be made. There's a science behind designing that catch phrase, logo, and design, and then putting all together in just the right way [so] that a product sells like hot cakes."

The Rolling Stones' tongue logo is a great example of a hugely successful merchandising design.

Moving on to the legal aspects of creative issues, you should know that all artists are responsible for getting permission from, and paying fees to, the owners of any outside designs used in connection with the merchandising. While you may be set on using a special design or a unique photograph from a book, to get the rights to use it, you may either be asked to pay a fee or a royalty from the sale of any merchandise that features that artwork—*that cost will come out of your pocket*. In cases where the artwork from your forthcoming album is used in connection with the merchandising, your record label usually owns the rights to it and may ask for compensation for the costs of producing the applicable artwork. But in most cases, notes Bob Fierro, the record company is usually willing to let this one slide.

Territory

The designated territory for most merchandising deals is *the world*. However, once you're an established artist and have some negotiating power, you may be able to limit your agreement to certain territories, such as North America. This way you can negotiate with companies in foreign territories for an additional merchandising advance. Promoters in Japan are especially eager to acquire merchandising rights when you venture into their country on tour, and in some cases they're willing to pay large advances to get them. Therefore, even if you're a new artist, you might try limiting the territory with your U.S. merchandiser to "the world except Japan." Whether or not they agree to this, of course, is subject to the individual situation.

Exclusivity

When you're a new group entering into an agreement with a merchandiser, remember that you're signing over the *exclusive* rights to utilize your name, likeness, and logo in connection with the manufacture, advertisement, distribution, and sale of products. In plain English, this means that you cannot enter into another agreement with another merchandiser during your contract term. It's also important to note that merchandising companies want to secure not only the rights to your band as a unit, but also the rights to each individual band member. So, as pointed out earlier in the section "Performance Guarantees," if you leave the group and start your own solo project, you may still be obligated to the pre-existing terms of the contract.

The exclusivity clause may also restrict radio stations and sponsors from giving away promotional materials (such as T-shirts, stickers, and hats) within a 20-mile radius of your live performance, and within a 48 hour-period before the event. However, nothing should preclude the record label or its distributors from standard record promotion in connection with the sale of your album.

Sell-Off Period

After the term of your agreement with your merchandiser has ended, you will be free to license your rights to manufacture, advertise, distribute, and sell product to a new company; these products can be similar or even identical to previously licensed items. In other words, if you had a particular style of product that sold well, such as a long sleeve, black shirt with your name in white lettering down the sleeves, you have the right to authorize your new merchandiser to manufacture this very same item. Your former merchandiser can no longer continue to manufacture products, but will have the rights to sell off any leftover stock they may have. Your attorney, however, can attempt to negotiate a few restrictions with the merchandiser:

+ The merchandiser's sell-off period will only last for a limited period of time, such as 90 to 120 days after the agreement term.
+ The merchandiser will only have non-exclusive rights during the sell-off period. In this way, you can enter into a new deal with another merchandiser and negotiate for a new advance.
+ The merchandiser will only sell-off product at wholesale prices through department stores, T-shirt shops, and mail order companies, and will pay you a royalty set forth in your agreement for retail sales (which will be discussed in a moment). Your merchandiser, however, cannot sell product at drastically reduced (or distressed) prices in order to get rid of them; this would obviously put your new merchandiser in direct competition with your former merchandiser for sales.
+ The merchandiser will be unable to mass manufacture product (known as stockpiling) for a period of 120 days before the end of your agreement term. The merchandiser does, however, have the right to manufacture product to meet any reasonable demands during the remainder of the term.
+ The merchandiser will notify you of the quantity of unsold product after the sell-off period. At this time, you or your new merchandiser have the right to buy the existing product at cost.

MORE KEY TERMS IN MERCHANDISING CONTRACTS

Okay, as previously stated, the key terms in merchandising agreements deal with touring, but it's a good idea to understand a few things about how you'll be paid for retail merchandising sales as well.

Royalty Rates: Retail Merchandising

Merchandising royalties for retail sales (i.e, sales in department stores, T-shirt shops, and record stores) are computed differently than they are for live performance sales. Rather than being computed on the total gross income less taxes and fees, royalties for retail sales are based on *the wholesale price*, which is the price at which your merchandiser sells products in bulk to distributors and retailers. So, you might ask, what's a typical wholesale price for a T-shirt sold to retailers? Although this is impossible to nail down, let's use $10.00 as a guesstimate. The retailer then marks up this price as much as 150 percent (even 200 percent at times), which means the $10.00 shirt sells to consumers for $25.00 (the wholesale price of $10.00, marked up 150%, which equals $25.00). Your merchandiser then pays you a royalty rate ranging from 12 to 18 percent of the wholesale price of the item in the U.S., with 15 percent being the norm for new artists. Therefore, your royalty for a T-shirt selling at $25.00 in a department store is approximately $1.50 (the wholesale price of $10.00, multiplied by your royalty rate of 15 percent, equals $1.50). This is a far cry from what you can make for a similarly-priced T-shirt selling at one of your live performances; if you remember our example above, you can make an average of $7.50 per shirt in sales at one of your concerts. This isn't to say that substantial sums of money can't be made via retail sales. Artists such as Guns N' Roses and Michael Jackson have made millions. But those examples are definitely not the norm.

Retail sales include sublicensing agreements your merchandiser enters into with third-party companies to manufacture specialty products such as lunch boxes, trash cans, bumper stickers, trading cards, dolls, condoms, stationery products, and any other product that's beyond the manufacturing capabilities of your primary merchandiser. (Your merchandiser should always be willing to give you the final approval on the sublicenses into which it enters.) The sublicenser then ships these products into retail stores, monitors sales, and pays your primary merchandiser a royalty. Your merchandiser keeps a 20 to 30 percent share of these monies, and remits the balance of 70 to 80 percent to you. Essentially, your merchandiser does nothing more than act as the middleman. And until you're in a megastar band like KISS and choose to negotiate a variety of licenses and handle the accounting yourself, you might as well get used to having a middleman. In fact, if it's any consolation, I'm told the merchandiser is actually well worth the fees it takes for acting as a middleman. The profit margin from sublicenses is only minimal in the early stages of your career, and trying to deal with a number of companies all at once can be a royal pain in the butt!

According to *Rolling Stone* Magazine, Kiss made over $2 million in 2001 from more than 130 merchandising licenses. Among the most notable were a KISS coffin and a Sterling Marlin collectable car.

Your royalties for products sold through mail-order and Internet sites are much higher than the royalties for items sold through the other retail avenues discussed above. The reason for this is that your merchandiser essentially acts as the retailer (in most cases), and there are no middleman distributors to take a cut. The royalty rate that merchandisers pay their artists is therefore around 25 percent of the *price charged* (and is not based on the wholesale price).

Just as with touring, merchandising royalties for retail sales in foreign territories are usually 80 percent of your U.S. royalty rates.

Cross-Collateralization

Finally, it's important to note that your royalties from both retail-merchandising sales and tour-merchandising sales are cross-collateralized. In other words, if the same merchandising company has the rights to both your tour merchandising and retail merchandising (which is usually the case), all royalties go toward paying back any advance monies paid to you by the merchandiser. Thus, if you are paid a large advance by your merchandiser before one of your concert tours, the royalties from both your tour merchandising and your retail merchandising go towards paying back that advance. (For more information on cross-collateralization, see Chapter 11.)

BREAK A [BOOT] LEG. In an infamous scene in Led Zeppelin's legendary film *The Song Remains The Same,* manager Peter Grant accuses a concert promoter of allowing bootleggers to sell unauthorized merchandise within the venue and taking a cut of the profits. Grant, who was formerly a wrestler and was often described as "two hundred and fifty pounds of East London bulk," was terribly upset—and rightfully so! Bootleggers not only sell products of inferior quality, but also substantially cut into both the bands' and the merchandising companies' profits. Bootleggers have seemed to slow down in the last few years, but you can still catch them out in front of venues before a show. Merchandising companies have been known to actively pursue anyone they suspect of infringing upon their merchandising rights and will often ask their artists to share in the costs of putting these pirates out of business. The costs are usually fronted by the merchandising company, and a share is then deducted from the artist's future royalties.

Q & A WITH BOB FIERRO

Zebra Marketing is an entertainment tour-merchandising company that handles custom screen-printing and production, licensing, concessions, and wholesale distribution. Its clients past and present include Henry Rollins, the Red Hot Chili Peppers, Adam Ant, Siouxsie & the Banshees, Crystal Method, Mötorhead, Prodigy, and Boy George & Culture Club (to name a few). Zebra Marketing has been in business over 20 years.

In the following Q & A, Zebra's President Bob Fierro discusses the process of independent merchandising, from artwork and printing to selling merchandise on the road.

Q: Merchandising deals and substantial advances have become less and less common than in the past and are usually reserved these days for the most successful artists. Where there were once several major merchandising companies, now Giant Merchandising and Winterland Merchandising (which is in chapter 11 bankruptcy at the time of this writing), are two of the last standing. Can you offer some insight as to why? And what is the current trend in the merchandising business today?

B.F: For the moment, there's only a small number of merchandising companies that are backed by larger corporations. These companies have to report a profit, and despite their substantial cash flow, the net profit margin from merchandising sales can often be too small for them to stay in business. Therefore, they must focus on artists who are sure to gross substantial amounts of cash. The trend in the merchandising business today is to deal with "teen" bands such as the Backstreet Boys. Though it is slowly shifting to rock and alternative acts, those bands have taken the back seat for the time being. Bands of these genres must therefore look towards smaller companies to sign merchandising deals, or they might handle the merchandise independently and sell it themselves. The last scenario, of course, is the focus of our discussion.

Q: Can you briefly describe the process of independent merchandising, from the band selecting the printing company, submitting the artwork, and selecting the T-shirts, to the actual silk-screening and shipping of the final product to the band on the road?

B.F: First and foremost, bands that handle their own merchandise must consider the start-up costs. These include art, design and separation, screens, and sample fees. Though almost any screen printer is capable of printing shirts, it's best to work with a company that has actual tour experience. A company must understand the necessity of getting merchandise to the band on time and into the specific city where they need it. This requires much more planning and experience on the part of the company than you may expect. If the merchandise arrives one day late, the band will have already moved on to the next city.

Q: What are the average costs per printed shirt for the artist, taking into account the many variables, such as quantity breaks, artwork costs, etc?

B.F: On the average, colored shirts printed on both the front and back usually run between $4.00 and $4.50. The cost depends on how elaborate the artwork is, the number of colors used, and the quantity of shirts to be printed. Quantity breaks begin after 12 dozen, with increased savings per shirt at 24 dozen. Despite these savings, it's usually better to order a smaller line of items at a smaller quantity first. Once you've determined what products are selling the best, you can have a larger quantity printed and sent to you while out on the road.

Q: Many bands will use money from the sale of merchandise to help subsidize their tour. Despite this fact, what is the average potential profit margin for the artist per shirt? And what do shirts typically sell for on the road? Finally, what are some of the expenses that must be considered?

B.F: First, I've always stressed that bands should try to keep their merchandising money separate from other expenses on the tour if possible. This way, no matter what happens, they'll go home with some profit. You'd be surprised at the number of established artists that return home from a tour with nothing more than the per diems they've saved or their small road salaries they were allocated. This may be due to bad ticket sales, production costs going over budget, or the record company or sponsor backing out of their commitment to support a tour. The bottom line is that anything could happen on the road.

On average, T-shirts sell for about $25, though superstars such as Madonna are known to have charged up to $40. The venue where the artist is performing will typically require around a 35 percent cut or $8.75 [$25 x 35% = $8.75]. Tax must also be factored in at about four percent or $1.00 [$25 x 4% = $1.00]. The cost of goods is about 20 percent or $5 [$25 x 5% =$5.00]. Miscellaneous expenses for freight and shipping charges and for the staff you pay for selling the shirts must also be considered at 4 percent or $1 [$25 x 4% =$1.00]. Once you deduct all these expenses, the average profit margin per shirt for the artist who is handling their own merchandising is around $9.60. Remember that this figure can vary, though, depending on what the artist charges per shirt. Now, let's take a look at the equation.

$25.00 (Cost of Shirt To Consumer)
- $ 1.00 (4% Taxes)

= $24.00
- $ 8.40 (35% Hall Fee))

= $15.60
- $ 5.00 (20% Cost of Goods)

= $10.60
- $ 1.00 (4% Miscellaneous)

= $ 9.60 (Profit To The Artist)

Q: How does a band handle sales tax issues with merchandising when traveling from state to state?

B.F: Larger venues usually have inside concession companies that take out the local state sales tax and pay it for you. Before the venue takes its hall percentage, the state sales tax gets taken off the top. It is important to make sure that you leave with a signed receipt and a copy of the hall's contract stating that they are responsible for the tax. If the club or ballroom only takes a hall commission and has no inside concession company, the club will often ask you to fill out a receipt saying that you will pay the state and local taxes yourself.

Q: Who is responsible for selling the shirts for the artist while out on the road?

B.F: To answer your question, I'd like to ask your readers to bear with me while I sidetrack for a minute. You see, when a band signs a deal with a merchandising company, the company will send out an experienced road merchandiser (known as a "merch guy" or "merch girl") to handle product. On smaller tours, the road merchandiser will usually travel with the band or crew. And on larger tours, when there's more stock to carry, the merchandising company rents a truck and hires an additional person to help drive and assist with other responsibilities. The merchandising company usually pays the salaries for road merchandisers, as well as the costs of renting a truck.

Now, on an independent level, a band can always find an experienced merch guy or gal that's between gigs and willing to work for you. Sometimes your road manager may even be willing to do the merchandising in addition to his regular duties, or he'll phone ahead to each of the venues making sure that a local experienced merchandiser will sell for you. Many bands often make the mistake of hiring a friend of the band with little or no experience. This is a good way to lose both your friends and your money. You will usually find that an excess number of free shirts are given away and that the person you hire is more interested in hanging out backstage and partying. The accounting will always be off. Remember, you get what you pay for. It's not a matter of friendships or trust, but simply accounting!

An experienced merch guy or girl is worth his/her weight in gold. They are responsible for making sure that the artist's merchandising gross per night is as high as possible. If the artist is playing larger venues, it is the road merchandiser's responsibility to check in the right amount of merchandise. If he doesn't check in enough merchandise, sales may be lost if he runs out. If he checks in too much merchandise, they may hold up the band's departure at the end of the night by extending the hall's check-out. The tour merchandiser must make sure that proper displays are set up and the top selling items are in the most strategic spots on the display. He must also make sure that the opening band (considering that there is one) is not given too much display space. There must, however, be enough space to give the opening act a fair chance to sell product.

The pay for a road merchandiser is hard to pinpoint. It depends on a number of factors, such as the experience of the merchandiser and the length of the tour. Small tours last from about three to six weeks. Larger tours may last from three to six months, and often much longer.

Q: What are some of the other ways an artist can sell his or her own merchandise independently (e.g., over the Internet, through fan clubs, etc)? Can you discuss sites that help sell merchandise, such as ARTISTDirect, etc? How are the deals usually structured?

B.F: Internet sites are a great way for an artist to expose their products to the public. Sites such as ARTISTdirect (www.ubl.com) are generally a facilitator for mail-order sales. It actually takes a great deal of management to handle sales orders, and most bands don't have the time to do it themselves. Internet sites generally buy product directly from the artist at a wholesale price and then sell it to the public. These sites also make substantial profits from advertising. For example, many record companies buy banner ads on the Artist Direct site because it's a frequently visited site. Another example of an Internet site that sells merchandising is www.dotmusic.com. I'm sure there are many others. Just get online and surf away.

The deals that are structured with Internet sites are usually non-exclusive. This means that a band can continue to sell merchandise through their own site as well or while out on the road. A band can use its website to sell limited items such as shot glasses or mugs that may not be the best selling items at a concert venue. If anything, it's a good way to test the market to see what you should manufacture in volume and take out with you on the road.

Q: Besides T-shirts, what are some of the other merchandising products typically sold on the road? Are these products also included in the venue's percentage share of sales?

B.F: T-shirts and tour programs are the number-one sellers. These days, laminated lanyards (the tour passes that artists wear around their necks) are also becoming popular sales items. Bumper stickers used to be popular but have tapered off. Everything that's sold independently by the artist at concerts is subject to the 35 percent average hall fee.

Q: Is there anything else you feel is important to know about merchandising?

B.F: I'd like to re-emphasize that not all bands are offered million-dollar advances from major merchandising companies. This, of course, also has to do a lot with the fact that you're probably not the Backstreet Boys, Madonna, or Korn. Therefore, you have to look towards smaller companies and be willing to accept smaller advances. A merchandising advance of any amount may be a godsend to a band in the beginning of its career. However, if you really don't need the money up front and it's still practical to handle tour merchandising independently, the pay-off could end up being greater. Bottom line, it's important to [know that] you always have to weigh the pros and cons of every business decision you make, and always seek out the advice of your professional team before signing anything!

INDEX